A ZEST FOR LIFE
Biography of economist David B. Jones
told in letters

A ZEST FOR LIFE
Biography of economist David B. Jones
told in letters

Compiled and Edited by
Sheila Wright

KISUMU
BOOKS

ISBN 978-0-9555417-2-8

Published November 2008

British Library Cataloguing in Publication Data.
A catalogue reference for this book is
available from the British Library.

Published by
Kisumu Books
Kisumu, The Street,
Wickham Skeith, Eye,
Suffolk IP23 8LP
Great Britain

Telephone 01449 766392
E-mail – sheronkis@hotmail.co.uk

Cover by Paul Chilvers
Printed and bound by Antony Rowe

CONTENTS

Photos on back cover

Top right: Dug-out canoe on Motloutse river, Botswana

Top row (left to right):
Grandsons Logan and Alistair Jones, Ascent of Mount Kenya, Patio of the house in Gaborone, Botswana

Centre:
Bernard, David, Dominic and Nicole, Kenya

Bottom row (left to right):
House in the sunflowers, Bordepaille, France, Snorkelling in Guadeloupe, On Safari in Khutse Game Park, Botswana

FOREWORD

This is the story of a life full of adventure, a life enjoyed to the full, by a man with endless curiosity about this extraordinary world we find ourselves in. Although cut tragically short by death through accident at the age of fifty-four, David Jones had packed more into those years than countless folk who live to a ripe old age.

I, Sheila Wright, compiler and editor of this book, am his sister, older by three years. Although I saw him rarely during his adult years because he so often worked abroad, we maintained a strong bond of love and friendship that began the first moment I realised I had a baby brother. He was always on my side, and I loved him. So it has been a labour of love to collect, and select from, the hundreds of letters he wrote to the family.

The vast majority of these letters were addressed to our parents, Herbert and Marjorie Jones, and latterly to our mother Marjorie during her long widowhood. She followed all David's activities in her heart and was justly proud of him. She entreated me to create a book out of the letters, but for many years the loss of David was too raw for me to attempt the task. Sadly, by the time this book was achieved, Marjorie had also passed away.

I hope this book will be a source of comfort and pride to Nicole, David's widow, to his sons Bernard and Dominic, his grandchildren, and our extended family (huge!). Also, that for his many friends and colleagues (David was a great amasser of friends) the book will revive pleasant memories.

I would like to think that all who read these excerpts from David's letters will in some measure find themselves sharing his amazing zest for life.

Sheila Wright, Summer 2008

has just brought me a bundle of large terrestrial orchids from the Comoro Islands — badly hacked around, but I think most of them will recover.

We gave a West Indian party last night. I think Nicole was the only West Indian there, but that did not hold us back. We therefore got up very late today, & have done rather little other than clear up — put the furniture back in place.

On Friday we went out to dinner with my old friend from Botswana & ODA, Peter Agar, who has now left the civil service & is working as a consultant with Coopers & Lybrand. With him was another (young) old colleague who has become a tax expert & is working for a year with a government commission in Zimbabwe. As you can imagine, we were not particularly hungry today after all this rich food.

Thank you for having Bernard & Dominic over

CHAPTER ONE
THE EARLY YEARS

The best person to begin this chapter is Marjorie, David's mother. She began an account of his life, after his death on 30th March, 1997, but was not able to get very far. These are Marjorie's words –

"David was the first son, and third child, to be born to Marjorie and Bert Jones, then living in Leicester. He was a delightful little boy, very friendly and always cheerful, though he did have quite a gift for getting into mischief. His ally in youthful escapades was his sister Sheila, three years his senior.

His first few years at school were not very promising – he found the look-and-say method of learning to read extremely dull and frustrating and after studying a card with the words *"he put in his thumb and pulled out a plum"* day after day for many weeks he simply gave up – it was not worth the effort! Later in life he was a terrific reader who liked to tussle with difficult books, which had to be well written and with something worth saying.

He made good progress at school, without putting too much effort into it, and never did learn to write very legibly. His early written work was full of smudges and alterations and not good to look at, but the thought behind it was always worthwhile. At one parents' day at his secondary school, City of Leicester Boys' School, one master's comment was *"David is the most brilliant boy in the school, but oh dear! His work!"*

He had many interests. He was a Cub Scout for several years, reaching the exalted rank of Sixer, and went on to the Scout Troop, where he found scout camps and trekking weekends very enjoyable. His nickname among the scouts was "Smiler" and he was certainly a cheerful lad. He joined the school orchestra as the only cellist, far from brilliant and a sore trial for the music master, who was no good at keeping the boys under control. He was very keen on acting and took part in several of the school Shakespearean productions, most memorably playing the part of Juliet in *"Romeo and Juliet"*. This was a sore trial to him, playing the girl's part, but he did cope extremely well and gave word-perfect performances. Dressed in pink satin, to his great disgust, his pink cheeks and golden hair were natural and quite effective, but the effect was somewhat spoiled for those whose eyes strayed to his footwear – black boys' lace-ups! It says something for his character that he managed to cope with Juliet without getting a lot of teasing from the other boys.

Although no favourite with the Headmaster, owing to his outspoken views on various school rules, particularly the wearing of absurd little school caps, the rest of the staff insisted that he should be made a prefect and this he did well, becoming known to the small boys as "Uncle" (later, younger brother Michael became Head Boy).

David managed four adequate passes in his A-Level exams and to the surprise of all, came through his first university interview without any trouble and was accepted at Hertford College, Oxford. Here he had a wonderful time reading Politics, Philosophy and Economics (known as P.P.E.) and thoroughly enjoying the independence of university life. He had a really dreadful little room, with no mod. cons. and only cold running water from a tap in the passage outside his room, and a bath available on the other side of the quad, but he was truly happy there."

Our mother's account ends here. I think she missed David and his frequent letters dreadfully, and found the situation hard to bear. But I will add some of my own memories, and more detail from school records, to fill in the picture.

Left
David aged four years

Right
Marjorie and Bert Jones
with their children

1943

1945

In my early childhood, David was known as "Sonny Day" (or "Sunny Day", as a child I was never sure which was intended!) He was a dear little boy. He joined me and older sister Margaret at Portland House School, Stoneygate, Leicester, in the summer of 1947, aged four and a half. This school, run in a small mansion set in leafy grounds, had a Montessori kindergarten where Margaret and I had thrived. David didn't take to school quite so easily, being rather absent-minded and dreamy and spilling a large pot of red paint on his very first morning! However his first School Report was mildly encouraging, with remarks such as *"Improving"*, *"Tries hard"*, *"Enjoys games"*. He was *"an appreciative listener"* at story time, *"very enthusiastic"* in music; altogether *"a pleasant member of the kindergarten"*.

However, he did not remain many terms at Portland House. Keeping us at Portland House was expensive, and our parents decided to move all three of us into State schooling, where conditions were not quite so lush but results were better. My first class at "St. John's", Clarendon Park Road, was held in a church hall, no less than four classes with no partitions, at least forty noisy children per class and only scrap paper to write on (this was post-war Britain). Somehow we all survived – Mr. Bowden, the headmaster, was a charming, kind man – and as the years went by all four of us, down to youngest brother Michael, passed the 11-Plus.

I remember David's first attempt at writing a story was quite telling. It told of a boy who ran away from home to see the world. *"He paced his trunc"* and left, just like that! David himself packed his trunk one morning, and set off secretly for adventure. Unfortunately for him, we had a front door with a porch, opening into a large entrance hall. David stepped down from the hall – a high step – and somehow managed to pull the door to behind him. But he couldn't open the outer door, and nor could he reach the handle of the inner door to re-enter the house. Since we mostly used the side or back doors for our comings and goings, it was several hours before a disgruntled little boy was rediscovered and reunited with his family!

Another fond memory is of a church concert which took place when David was around seven years old. We belonged to a large Baptist Church at Stoneygate, Leicester. Everyone had been invited to perform a party piece and the hall was full. Centre stage stood my little brother, primed to recite *"The Land of Counterpane"* by Robert Louis Stevenson. All went well until he reached the last verse, which runs –

"I was the giant great and still that sits upon the pillow-hill,
And sees before him, dale and plain, the pleasant land of counterpane."

Alas! Loud and clear, David declaimed-

"I was the giant great and still, that sits upon the hillow-pill ..."

Realising his mistake, he dissolved into helpless giggles, and gradually all that rather unbending middle-class audience joined in. As everyone wiped the tears from their eyes, David was given the most rapturous applause heard that afternoon.

School group, David (centre) aged nine

Sheila, Margaret, Michael, David

He was an inventive boy. In our chilly Edwardian house, David's bedroom was the only room at the end of a long corridor. I remember he rigged up a system of wires, batteries and bells, hidden under the lino (no warm carpets in those days!), so that long before any intruder reached his bedroom sanctuary, a bell would ring in warning.

He was resourceful and imaginative. He and I each owned tortoises; mine was the larger, name of Oswald. I sewed "pyjamas" for Oswald out of soft stripey flannel, and cosily wrapped, Oswald survived several winters in his straw box. But one springtime, my tortoise failed to wake and was buried with full honours.

David's little tortoise succumbed some years later. This too was buried – but six months later, David dug it up; as he foresaw, the soft body was decomposed, the shell, upper and lower, still joined and perfect. David washed, dried and polished this shell. It now reposes in a bowl of rocks, fossils and shells in my living room.

We seem to have been slightly obsessed by death. In the Derbyshire Peak District, we searched for the skeletons of sheep on the high hills. Then finding a bare flat site on some hilltop (preferably a flat rock) we carefully arranged these bones to suggest a human skeleton. The idea was to surprise passing pilots of aircraft!

Our home was somewhat unconventional. Visitors were surprised, on entering the hall, to find a trapeze hanging from the beamed ceiling. Whenever we had occasion to pass through the hall, we children would leap up to this trapeze to hang by our knees or feet for a few moments – or, leap from the stairs to catch the bar in mid air. It certainly gave us strong muscles!

David had a wonderful sense of humour. One day I brought home a school friend, Susan, who placed her belongings on a chair in the hall. There sat her navy velour hat, her leather satchel, and her tennis racquet. When it was time for Susan to leave, she remembered her things, and found – an old badminton racquet, a small shabby cloth shoulder bag and a bright red hat!

Left
Country walk 1952, David second from left

Right
Scouts and Sea Rangers, David on the right

Always independent, David set off on solo hitch-hiking journeys around Europe at a young age – well before he left school. I envied him his sporting prowess, his confidence on stage, and the freedom that in those days was not accorded to girls – although I did my share of shinnying down drain pipes, exploring roof-tops, trespassing in the large gardens of houses in the neighbourhood, and illicit hitch-hiking in lorries (with friends, never alone), I would not have dared to venture abroad alone as David did. This was a foretaste of his adult life.

David's progress through Grammar School is amply illustrated through termly Reports, old Programmes, certificates and a few press cuttings. Teachers enjoyed his presence in their classes – *"excellent conduct and disposition"*, observed one master. David was always somewhat erratic and unpredictable, as the mood took him, but beneath some of the *"could-do-better"* remarks lay an awareness of high ability. For example –

"---inclined to day-dream during lessons… he can do well when he puts his mind to it…untidy…..rather talkative in class….very good at original thought, but he must learn to express those thoughts logically and neatly on paper…rather exuberant in class….careless….I am sure the ability is there, but he must direct it…"

Our mother tried to direct his homework, and this was spotted by one French teacher who wrote *"I find it difficult to make a true estimate of his progress owing to the help he gets at home with his written work"*!

Yet the spark of intelligence showed through, gaining him comments such as *"has a discriminating and perceptive mind….has shown considerable promise"*. In his last year, his teacher of Constitutional History said *"He writes well and has shown a mature grasp of the subject"*. His class teacher wrote *" This has been a most successful year and I am very pleased to proffer my best wishes for his future career at Hertford College, Oxford. His help as Prefect, as Instructor in Life Saving, his performances in the school plays and in the orchestra and debating society have been warmly appreciated"*.

"A Midsummer Night's Dream", 1959, Krefeld, Germany David as "Lysander", kneeling, front left

"Romeo and Juliet" 1958 – David as Juliet!

Even the Headmaster, overlooking those minor battles when, for instance, David appeared at school on a summer day wearing open sandals rather than lace-ups, wrote *"He has given much to the School and he leaves with our very best wishes."*

Certainly a pile of yellowing certificates and programmes survives to back up this view. Between 1951–1961 David was awarded school prizes for Art, English, All-Round Merit, Progress, Metalwork, and both Junior and Senior Public Speaking. He sang in the Choir, and played solo cello in concerts. His stage career was impressive! Graduating from "Soldier and Messenger" in *"King Lear"* and Harry Hotspur's widow in *"King Henry IV Part II"*, he played Fleance in *"Macbeth"*, the Duke of Norfolk in *"Richard II"*, Lysander in *"A Midsummer Night's Dream"*, and rose to (unwished for!) prominence as a most desirable Juliet in *"Romeo and Juliet"*. Fortunately he was not required to grow his own light gold hair to shoulder length for this part, being provided with a wig.

He also appeared on stage in James Bridie's *"Tobias and the Angel"* and George Bernard Shaw's *"St. Joan"*. Some of these productions took place in the School, others in the Little Theatre, Dover Street, Leicester. Several times the troupe went on tour to German colleges and schools.

The School entered its pupils into the City of Leicester Education Committee's Competitions, where David received awards for Verse Speaking and cello playing.

He was a true all-rounder, winning awards on Sports Days in running the mile, and High Jump. A certificate from the Royal Life-Saving Society was awarded for *"Practical knowledge of rescue, releasing oneself from the clutch of the drowning and ability to render aid in resuscitating the apparently drowned"*. A useful man in a crisis!

Far more important than all these worthy achievements are the personal characteristics that endeared David to those around him, throughout his life. For he was pleasant, agreeable, tolerant - just generally rewarding company. This does not mean he was a yes-man, far from it; he spoke his mind, he did not suffer fools lightly; he expected others to do any job well, just as he did himself. He could sometimes seem patronising, a bit of a know-all. Although he worked for a fairer world and to improve the lot of the underprivileged, he was never a self-sacrificing saint; he always enjoyed the comforts and pleasures of life, and he enjoyed the prestige (and the servants!) which various posts brought him.

David was fundamentally honest, hard working, adventurous and endlessly interested in the world. Throughout his life, and wherever he travelled, people liked him and enjoyed his company. This is borne out by a letter, written in 1959 to my father by David's cello teacher, Haydn Hopkins. David was no musical genius, nor did he overdo his practice sessions, but the letter speaks volumes –

"Dear Mr. Jones,

Over the past twelve months, I have noticed that David's lessons have been somewhat haphazard and I am wondering if he would care to come whenever he feels like having a lesson, and if you would care for him to pay for an odd lesson when he comes. I think it would be better for him to do this; although at the present fee scale, it would amount to 10/6d per lesson.

I know only too well the difficulties he is encountering; to pull in a little practice with all his homework is asking too much of him. Albeit, when he gets to University I have not the slightest doubt that he will enter into the musical life of his College and help in the orchestra from which he will derive a tremendous amount of pleasure.

I need hardly say what a pleasure it has been knowing David and your good selves, and seeing him develop into the fine lad he is. It will always be a pleasure to my wife and myself to see him, whenever he feels like coming, and even if he calls just to see us to let us know how he is getting on, we shall be happy. One never likes to see the last of old pupils, especially those of David's calibre.

With kindest wishes to Mrs. Jones and your good self,

Yours very sincerely, Haydn Hopkins

Mr. Hopkins' faith in David's love of the cello was not unfounded, as he continued playing over many years, even taking it with him to Africa on some postings. He was for years a valued member of amateur orchestras in Gaborone and Nairobi .

As my mother has implied, David's success in being accepted by an Oxford College was somewhat unexpected. But it was well deserved. There is a letter from Richard Malpas, Secretary for Admissions at Hertford College, Oxford, which reads –

"Dear Jones,

Congratulatons on your distinction in prelims. I am sure it was very well deserved, and hope that it will encourage you for further triumphs."

I was myself busy producing a family at the time of David's studying, so seldom visited him. I do remember getting a distinctly different impression from that of my mother when I did first see his rooms at Hertford; I marvelled at his panelled corner turret room overlooking the serene lawned quadrangle. There was an "oak", that solid heavy door giving him privacy, and a "scout" to do odd jobs for the students. Around the angled window walls of the room (built in either hexagonal or octagonal form) were oaken window seats, hinged to provide storage. By this time, David had met and fallen in love with Nicole, a stunningly beautiful girl from Guadeloupe in the French West Indies, who was to become his wife. I will never forget my father's joking remark as I lifted one of these heavy cushioned seats to look inside – "That's where David hides Nicole!" It was all the more comical because, my father having learnt his French at a London Grammar School without ever entering France or speaking with any French person, he persisted for at least a year in pronouncing Nicole's name as "Nickle".

I remember receiving a twelve-page letter once from David during his first college year, describing the all-night Midsummer celebrations on the river, the revelry, and the fantastic sunrise seen from a boat moored under the willows. This letter, like many, is lost. But enough survive to show how gifted a communicator he was. He had an irresistible desire to write down his experiences and feelings. Not for him the shorthand of today's texting young folk. He actually enjoyed writing, surely quite unusual for a young male. I still enjoy his description of mixing dough, in a letter written shortly before his nineteenth birthday, when our mother was staying with me in Hertfordshire as I awaited the birth of my second son.

In 1964 when studying for his Finals, David had serious misgivings about the quality of his work. Everyone who has ever sat an examination must surely have some sympathy with the torment and doubt that assail the hapless student. He obviously was trying to prepare our parents for his possible failure when he wrote this letter in June 1964 –

"I fluctuate between despair and flippancy; I do not know how I could write so many bad answers. They tend to be vague, off the point, and ill-planned. The worst of it is that I really know what I ought to be writing, but I never quite manage to put it down. I have only been really happy about scattered questions, for instance I know I wrote one good answer in economic principles; several good answers in general philosophy; two good answers in moral philosophy; one good answer in political theory; and one good answer in constitutional history. My second paper, economic organisation, was rather a tragedy, and the history paper was extraordinary – it was simply obscure. I wrote about two of Derby's minor governments (knowing nothing about either), party organisation in 1867 (with almost equal ignorance), and I compared King William IV with Edward VII, making some rather enlightened guesses.

Tomorrow I have "Economics of Under-developed Countries", and on Wednesday "Currency and Credit", then I am finished, unless they want me for a viva voce on July 24th.

Please banish all hopes. I am told that it is difficult to fail, but even so my performance has been, at best, mediocre.

As you can imagine, there is no other news. Denys is coming to Oxford on Wednesday, and no doubt we shall all be coming home in the near future.
Love, David and Nicole

(NOTE – Denys is Nicole's brother, coming to England in preparation for the wedding of David and Nicole that summer).

David did not fail his exams, but went on to a very varied career. The letters tell the story.

Because David's interests were so wide, I have taken the liberty of giving a title to each extract as a clue to content. Hopefully readers will be able to pick and choose according to personal preference. David's interests included world religions and lifestyles, sea food, gardening, building, animal husbandry, music, antiques, old tools, Greek tragedy, orchids, safaris, linguistics, geology, archaeology, climate, land management, and more....

Given the nature of his work, it is no surprise that David's letters contain much political and economic comment. Much of this is included; much has since been proved prophetic.

David and Nicole were devoted parents and valued all relationships. Omitting all passages concerning family and friends would not give a true picture, therefore some are included. The letters also illustrate the deep unwavering commitment to family of our parents Bert and Marjorie, even in their old age.

I have tried to bed excerpts into context by brief explanations. Excerpts are presented in date order. I apologise for any mis-spellings of places or names; no doubt I could spend years checking, but since it is now over eleven years since David died, I want to get this story out into the world while those who knew him are still alive to read it.

While this memoir of David's life is told mainly through letters he himself wrote, I have also included excerpts from Nicole's letters, because they fill out the picture of their life together. Nicole was a wife of rare calibre, loyal and courageous in what were often difficult circumstances that she would not herself have chosen.

There are a few extracts written by our mother, by David's sons Bernard and Dominic, and others. Unless otherwise stated, the letters that follow were written by David himself. I hope readers will find them informative, amusing, inspiring - and above all, a celebration of life in all its fullness.

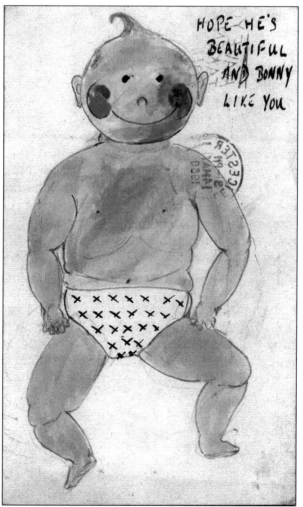

Home-made congratulations card sent to sister Sheila on the birth of her first child, May 1960

CHAPTER TWO
LETTERS 1961–1973

Letter written by David to mother and
Sheila, who were awaiting the arrival in
Hertfordshire of Sheila's and Ron's second son   Leicester, 18/07/1961

Home Alone!

One soon gets used to sleeping in an unmade bed, and cooking eggs whenever a meal fails to be present. Our cooking is interesting. On Sunday we made one and a half pounds of bread; I found some instructions, which told me to knead the dough until it ceased to stick to the bowl or my fingers. I managed to separate it from the bowl, but it had a sort of affinity for my fingers. It was like trying to remove a piece of sellotape. I wandered around the house for about half an hour winding the sticky rubbery mass from one hand to the other, wearing it first on one hand, then the other as a sort of boxing glove. In the end despite the obvious mutual attachment I had to effect a cruel separation with a kitchen knife, so that I could go unaccompanied to 20th Century Club (a church youth group). I left it in Daddy's hands (not literally) and it was very good when it had been scraped.

Meringues, Gingerbread and Doughnuts

Daddy must have been very enterprising when we were out, for he made some very hot, very brown, gingerbread (only slightly charred round the edges) and some meringues which Margaret found today (in the oven). I decided to do some more yeast cooking today. I have always wanted to make doughnuts, and the estimated time was 75 minutes in the recipe. I started before tea at about 6.30pm. The dough was like pastry but a lot stickier, and every surface touched by it had to be thickly protected with flour, which in the end covered almost every flat surface in the scullery, including the floor.

When I finished the deep frying (which was not very deep, because there was not enough fat to cover the things) some of the objects really were nuts, with jam oozing out of little holes. Others were like volcanoes with big holes in the top, where the jam had burst its bounds. At 10.30 when I finished clearing up I had made twenty-one, and they look all right covered in sugar; there was a peculiar layer of thick black sludge in the saucepan, and the dough was like putty in the mixing bowl.

Garden News

The garden is very wet and sort of soggy. The sweet peas flower slowly and gently, but the bees just cannot get out to fertilise them, so they wither and drop off. The lettuces will be pick-able in about a week's time, and the onions and shallots are beginning to die down healthily. My tomato plants are within 10 inches of my window, and I am planning to divert two so that I can keep on leaning out of my window. The second gloxinia is very healthy, with three vigorous shoots.

A Last School Prize

They have found an excuse for giving me a prize – the Gater Memorial prize for Merit; I have chosen a good anthology of modern verse (Twentieth Century Verse).

I wish Sheila would hurry up. I get questioned every time I go into the secretary's office.
Love, David

Student Life

I really feel as if I am stealing time from work when I write. Don't think that this means I am working all the time; I constantly steal time from work, but all the same, the exams are getting oppressively close (17 days) and there is still a lot of new work to do, and a colossal amount of revision.

I work with my oak up for most of the time, but I get so bored that the moment I hear footsteps stop outside my door, I run to open it.

On Friday night I was steadfastly preparing for an essay on the exciting question: *"What is it to Say of a Thing that it Exists?"* which had to be read out at 9am on Saturday. At about ten, Marius arrived and banged on my oak. He finished all my food except one slice of cake, and stayed for about one and a half hours, so that I was still writing about "existence" at two o'clock on Saturday morning. This always seems to happen on Saturday; I have about five and a half hours' sleep, then a logic tutorial at 9 and a maths tutorial at 10.30. After this I have a bath till 1 o'clock, and do no work for the rest of the day. Sometimes I go to sleep in the afternoon; usually I go out in the evening.

Messing About in Boats

I was rather sorry not to be in Torpids this week. There was a very good, mainly second-year, first boat, and a very bad second boat. The first boat made two bumps, but very little notice was taken of this, because the second boat was so exciting. On the first day it was pointing into the bank when the gun went off, and half the crew had their sweaters over their heads. The Captain of Boats had been relegated to the second Torpid, and he broke an oar trying to get the boat away from the bank. In the meantime the boat behind quietly rowed up and bumped them.

This was nothing to the second day: Brazenose bumped our boat, after the captain had lost his seat, and the strongest oarsman had caught a crab. Hertford immediately downed tools and sat back, but Brazenose continued to row vigorously, over the back of the Hertford boat, so that it drove into the bank at an angle; the bow went up the bank; the stern went underwater, and it sank. The cox, who was all dolled up in white flannels and a blazer with a red carnation in the buttonhole, stepped out of the boat, and went underwater. Marius, who was nearer the bank, dived headlong out of the boat, and almost hit the bottom with his stomach, because the water there was only two feet deep.

After this a lot of people went to watch the last two days, but to our disappointment Hertford II only succeeded in getting bumped ignominiously both times.

A Hitch-hiking Holiday

You may be wondering about my reference to Spain last week. I can't remember how much I told you, but John S and two friends of his are renting a villa in Palmas for £5 for four weeks. Marius and I will probably hitch-hike across France and spend about two weeks there. I am afraid this will mean that I shall not have much time at home, as Professor Tryparvis wants us to stay up here rehearsing for at least one week.

The Trials of Studying

By the way, don't be too surprised if I fail Prelims. this term. A lot of people do, and the work is very intensive. We have another try at the end of next term, although apparently this ruins the summer term.

John S was told by the doctor that he was working too hard, and had to rest and sleep a lot for about a week, as he was suffering from a slight nervous breakdown. He seems to be all right again now.

Love to all, David

P.S. – I have just paid a termly bill of £62, but I am still solvent.

Letter to all the family

Villa Sollange, Le Trayas, near
Cannes, Var, France. 14/04/1962

Exploring France

We have gone about as far as we can in the time we have left. We were told that the Italian Riviera was not nearly as good as the French, and that it was no good going to Italy unless we went quite a long way south, so we will not make very strenuous efforts to reach Italy; anyway, the hitch-hiking round here is very chancy. It was bad enough getting to Avignon, but further south it is almost impossible. At the moment we are at Le Trayas, which is between St. Raphael and Cannes. Perhaps we will go to Nice and Monte Carlo, but we are pretty comfortable where we are.

The warden *"Père Aub"* is a student from the Sorbonne who picked us up in his car on the way to Frejus Youth Hostel (Frejus is the place where a big dam burst last year or the year before). The hostel is an old children's home and is enormous. Marius and I have a dormitory of our own, we don't have to do any work, and nobody cares what time we go to bed or get up, or when we are in the hostel. Today it is cloudy, which is most unusual, but yesterday five of us went to Cannes in Claude's (the *Père Aub*) car, and sunbathed and bathed in the Mediterranean.

I have seen the snow on the Alps, and the bridge at Avignon, and Marseilles and Cannes. Altogether it's been a very successful holiday so far. There are palm trees growing all over the place, and in the gardens there are enormous cacti up to about five feet high with "leaves" bigger than my outspread hand. People grow oranges and lemons in their back gardens, but they don't seem to grow them commercially. There are mountains all around, covered in fir trees where there is enough soil, but usually they are very rocky and are covered with little prickly evergreen oak bushes and wild lavender.

A few days ago we stayed at Cassis Youth Hostel which is about five km. Out of the village. It's a big bungalow sitting in the middle of the bleakest countryside I have ever seen; just miles of grey rock with a few bushes and fewer trees. The French students have just started their holidays and one of them sang French songs to us all evening accompanying himself on his guitar. The room was lit only by an enormous wood fire. It sounds rather lame when I describe it, but it was a wonderful evening.

When we were travelling South my belt went in three inches, but since Avignon I have been expanding again on a diet of eggs, risotto, bread, cheese, and spaghetti. Today we pooled almost all of our food for dinner, and seven of us shared a great big bowl of spaghetti, a tin of peas, half a loaf of bread and three sausages; I don't know what we shall eat till Monday. Love, David

Letter to Sheila and family

Oxford, 03/06/1962

"Oedipus"

… Our play (Greek Tragedy) was received very well, although the Chorus came in for some gentle knocks. We treated these with contempt, saying what a pity it is that nobody in England understands the Greek chorus. All the same, some of the criticisms seemed to be very true. *The Times Educational Supplement* ended its report with –

"When the Chorus does the conga across the quad. it's frankly funny".

We had a professional actress for the one female part, and she kept on forgetting her lines. On the last night she remembered some for the first time, and threw Oedipus right out of his stride. On that night, the Chorus were all saying *"darkness fills my eyes"* when all the lights failed, and stayed out for *"I dare not see"* and *"dark sights for the eyes of man"* – then they suddenly went on again. The aftermath of this play will chase me to the end of term.

End of Term Jollity

We had a party on the last night in College, and an all-night party at our choreographer's house on Wednesday night, since when I have been falling asleep all over the place. It was a fine party, and it lasted till sunrise. We all went out onto a hill nearby to do a druidical dance, and watch the sun rising.

If I have ever watched it before, I have never seen how it was that morning.

On Tuesday we have a dinner which is going to cost a guinea, and probably bore me stiff.

Working as Barman

Over Whitsun I am going to Bognor Regis to work as a barman. A friend of mine (Oedipus) is in charge of an enormous ballroom bar at a caravan camp, and we are travelling up on Saturday morning and staying eight days. I shall get very comfortable board and lodging in the proprietor's house, and be paid as well. Apart from anything else, I need the money, but it should be good fun.

How are the chickens and the garden doing? At odd spots round the College garden there are odd little rows of turnips, radishes and lettuces, planted illicitly at night....

Top
Jones family 1963
(from left) – Michael, Sheila, Bert, Marjorie, Margaret, David

Left
Family holiday on Anglesey 1960. David centre back

There is a charming letter dated July 1963, written in French, from Nicole's parents Roger and Suzette Fortuné. M. Fortuné was Director of Guadeloupe's Office de Tourisme. His letter is in response to a letter from David, requesting the hand of their daughter Nicole in marriage. This was warmly welcomed and arrangements went ahead.

Top
Wedding of David and Nicole, August 1964

Left (from left) Marjorie, David, Nicole, Madame Suzette Fortuné, Denys Fortuné, Bert

David and Nicole were married in August 1964. Nicole's parents had flown over for the wedding, bringing with them dozens of exotic anthuriums in all shades of white, pink and red which made a dramatic display in both house and garden. The marriage took place at Leicester Registry Office and the reception was held in our parents' garden. David and Nicole set up home together in Oxford.

During their first years together, David studied for his Doctorate while also working for the "Oxford Institute of Economics and Statistics". He enjoyed tutoring individual students, including a Lord of the Realm and a Benedictine monk. He also edited an updated version of "The Oxford Economic Atlas".

Enjoying the Good Things of Life

Last week we went to the theatre to see *"The Cherry Orchard"* by Chekov, and enjoyed it very much.

On Thursday I spent a very pleasant evening being dined at the Benedictine House from which my priest comes. I was a little apprehensive, but there was no question of bread and water. We started off with sherry, and finished on port and cigars, with a very good meal in between, cooked by an ex-Cunard chef.

Trial by Exams

The Master seems to be under the impression that I am treating my priest extremely well, even though he only just passed his preliminary exam. I was amused, however, to find that out of nine P.P.E. freshmen at St. Catharine's, five failed in Economics, and one in Logic (in my first year at Hertford, the only failure was John S, who only took half of one of the papers). Francoise's present boy-friend was one of the economics failures, so I asked him who his tutors were, and was surprised to find that they were two of the best-known in the University, including one of the examiners.

Roman Catholic Headmasters

The Master at St. Benet's Hall was formerly assistant headmaster at Ampleforth, and a visiting Father was the retired headmaster; this one was extremely amusing, and made us roar with laughter when he described the state visit of the Paramount "Chieftainess" Regent of Basutoland to Ampleforth (where the Paramount Chief was a student). She brought a present for the Abbot – a ceremonial grass hat – but left it in York Railway Hotel.

I am sorry my writing is getting so bad. I type all my notes now, and am not used to using a pen. Lots of love, David and Nicole

On November 10th 1965 Nicole gave birth to a son, Bernard. Now being proud parents, David and Nicole started looking for a home of their own rather than continuing to rent. They eventually purchased an attractive stone cottage in Woodstock, five miles from Oxford.

The Trials of Tutoring

Although term has ended, this week was similar to the preceding ones, with several tutorials. I finished a term of revision with two boys I had taught once before, and who appear to have enjoyed a rather informal approach to work – I hope it was good for them as well. I gave the Lord rather a bad report, but on reflection he deserved even worse – I don't think he did any work, and I think I succeeded in making him feel rather silly during his last tutorial. I had set him two questions, which presumably he did not even attempt until one hour before his tutorial, when he borrowed a biro from Ashar, my next door neighbour, whom he knows. From that time he appears to have searched relevant chapters in the most elementary text-book for something remotely resembling the question I had asked, and chancing upon something with an apparent resemblance to the question, jotted it down in garbled note-form. I was a bit irritated, and made him explain (without criticism) the rubbish he had written, sentence by sentence, and in the end he had to refer back to the book, because he had no idea of the meaning of some of the pieces he had copied, and was totally incapable of explaining them, except by insisting that *"it's in Samuelson"*. Perhaps I should have been brutal earlier, but at first I believed that he was just plain stupid. Anyway, it isn't my job to teach, but to set reading and criticize essays.

Farewell to the Priest

With some reluctance I have refused to teach the priest again this term, on the grounds that I have already taught him for three terms, and will almost certainly teach him for at least one more term, so that it is in his own interest to get a bit of a change. I have seen him since then, but at the end of Michaelmas term last year I had to rush out of his last tutorial because Nicole was having the miscarriage. He was very interested to hear that we now have a baby son.

Mainly because Arthur Hazelwood is in Africa for four months, I have had more demand for teaching than hours available this term, but it should be quite interesting. Altogether I shall teach six undergraduates from Pembroke, plus an African headmaster (said to be hard-working but slow), an undergraduate from Mansfield College (Congregational) and five girls. This vacation I am doing an extra job teaching an English/ Polish/ Pakistani girl.

Improving Language Skills

I have started to read *"La Guerre et La Paix"*, and found I can go quite fast. Of course there is no reason why a translation from Russian should be read in French rather than in English – I probably lose a lot – but I found it much easier going than Proust. Nicole has volumes II and III of *"Une Recherche du Temps Perdu"*, but volume I has been borrowed and not returned. I suppose starting at the second volume doesn't make it easier to understand – but the principal difficulty is that all the sentences are half a page long, and contain so many clauses and sub-clauses, and so few commas, that it is difficult to fathom.

Doctorate Awards Day, Oxford 1969, with Marjorie, David, Nicole, and sons Bernard and Dominic

Bernard has given me the draft of a poem written by David. I think it was probably composed when Bernard was a toddler, one day when the proud young father was walking along the Cherwell with his little son. Despite being unfinished, I think it's worth including –

> Bernard and I went walking by the riverside one day.
> And we were gravely talking, but we were happy and gay.
> We crossed the clanking Bailey Bridge,
> Watched geese go paddling by,
> A tractor ploughing the far-off ridge,
> And seagulls skimming the sky.
>
> Up and over the Rainbow Bridge into the Medley Reach.
> Opposite on the other side is the summer bathers' beach.
> But the water today is cold and grey
> Like lead on an old church font.
> I wouldn't swim over if I were a lover
> And it were the Hellespont.
>
> A perch is here for a spot of cheer,
> Lemonade and a glass of beer…..
> ….and a beady look as we pass,
> From the white-tail, fantail, put-him-in-the-pan-tail
> Pigeon strutting the grass.

In March 1969 a second son, Dominic Hugh, was born.

In August 1969 David took up an advisory post with the UN in Geneva, for "United Nations Trade and Development" (UNTAD), now become "World Trade". He was somewhat frustrated in this post since however well-founded and fair-minded the advice given by economics advisors, politicians seldom implemented new ideas unless they were advantageous to their own nation and government. But the family, including Bernard, all enjoyed skiing throughout that winter.

In March 1970 they returned to England, and David began preparations for a job in Dar es Salaam, Tanzania. (Tanzania had been created by the (not universally welcomed) union of Tanganyika and the island of Zanzibar). He was to work for the Ministry of Economic Affairs and Development Planning. They hoped to find a tenant for the house at Woodstock. Initially David went out to Tanzania alone, staying in a hotel. The family would join him as soon as possible.

Letter to parents   New Africa Hotel, Dar es Salaam,
                                                                                 Tanzania, 08/05/1970

First Experience of Tanzania

I expect Nicole will have given you some of my news already, so you will know that I am comfortably installed here. Dar es Salaam is quite a civilised place, but I gather that civilisation ends within 25 miles from here, if not earlier.

The other day, in a final display of rainy season, we had 4cm of rain in 24 hours (well over an inch), but now it is dry, and it's getting hotter. Incidentally, I do hope my friend's house (which I am moving to soon) has air conditioning in the bedrooms – it makes life so much more comfortable. I still have no news about a house for us here, although there is really no reason why Nicole and the children should not come and stay at the hotel (except for heavy food bills – if I eat in the hotel it costs me about £1 a time for lunch and dinner, and it's not much cheaper eating out in reliably clean places).

I was delighted to find in the Tanzania *"Standard"* an article on a production of *"A Man for All Seasons"* at Tahera (only 500 miles from here!) with an ex-student of mine – a Belgian white father – as the producer.

I seem to be getting down to some work, although we still don't know (or haven't decided) what I shall do in the long term. I'm afraid I can't write any more tonight, as I want to get some background reading done before meeting someone tomorrow, quite apart from going to bed reasonably early. I find I get very sleepy getting up at 6.30am and working right through from 7.30am to 2.30pm.
Love, David

Letter to parents   Dar es Salaam, 17/05/1970

Luxury Surroundings

I have now moved out of the hotel to stay in a friend's house. My host is Stewart MacFarlane, chief veterinary research officer here. He himself only has a house on a temporary basis, during someone else's long leave (known as "housewarming") but for the two of us we have an enormous colonial house with two bathrooms, six or seven bedrooms, and a Malawi houseboy called James, who despite his name speaks next to no English.

Housing Problems

I do have a bungalow of my own now, with living room, two bedrooms, kitchen, bathroom, and two lots of servants' quarters in an enormous overgrown garden. When I first saw the house there was a good mango tree just behind it, but someone must have noticed my arrival, climbed the tree, and broken in through the roof – which has made rather a mess – and in so doing so weakened the tree that it has since collapsed. There are various things to be done to the house, like repairing the roof, so I shall not move in quite yet. In any case Stewart is going on safari next week, and wants someone in his house, which actually contains things that might be burgled (all I lost was a bunch of keys, but that may cause trouble in the future). Another difficulty in moving is that my bungalow is about five miles from Dar, so that I need a car, and until Nicole comes I shan't have the wherewithal to buy one.

Plans for Work

Work seems slowly to be developing some structure. I find something to do, although I expect I shall drift into a more definite niche eventually. I would like to work with the *parastatals* (government-controlled industries) which are dynamic but awkward customers, but I don't know if I shall manage that.

Exploring the Coast

Dar is a delightful city. Even the harbour is attractive, with the sort of beaches from which you could swim if you felt inclined, although the best beaches are further out – including one five minutes walk from my bungalow. Apart from the big ships, there are all varieties of yachts, dug-out canoes with outriggers, and even a few Arab *dhows* trading up to the Persian Gulf and India.

Today Stewart and I drove to Bagamoyo, which was once the principal port on the Tanzanian coast, and was the starting point of at least one of Livingstone's great expeditions. It's forty miles down the coast from Dar – mostly dirt track through fishing villages and palm plantations. Nowadays it is a very run-down place, although there are still some attractive buildings left over from the earlier days. The beach – like so many here – was marvellous. It stretched for about eight miles, with Bagamoyo in the centre of the bay. The beach was all sand, with palm trees behind, and no company except for a half-mile stretch where the town faced out to sea. We went up the coast a bit to have a look at some 15th century Arab ruins.

It's time I got off to bed. I don't like starting work at 7.30am or going to bed early enough to make up for this.
Love, David

Letter to parents   Dar es Salaam, 20/05/1970

Preparing for the Family

Nicole tells me she is coming on 27th and that you are driving her to the airport. Thanks for doing this. I had told her that she would have to take a taxi, because it's no fun going by coach or trains, but she will certainly like to be seen off by you.

I'm afraid life will be a bit Spartan at first. We have used up most of our available cash on the house in Oxford, and now we shall have to start buying things here. I have more or less made up my mind to buy a second-hand (1967) Volkswagen "beetle", but that's going to cost about £770 including insurance. I shall have to borrow money here at 12% interest to buy the car. Maybe I should hire the same tax accountant as a friend of mine did when he was here for four years. He succeeded in paying no taxes for four years – not because the accountant was a financial wizard (by all accounts, he was a complete idiot when it came to legal tax-avoidance) – but because he was so dilatory at replying to the Inland Revenue. Of course this tax will all have to be paid, but in view of the difficulty in getting money out, this must have been a great help.

Holes in the Roof, Puddles on the Floor!

Nicole may have told you about our house – living room, two bedrooms, kitchen, bathroom, two lots of servants' quarters and an enormous garden. As you know, burglars broke in through the roof the day after I took the keys, and since the rains have unexpectedly started again, there is a big puddle on the floor. Luckily it's concrete, so there is no real damage. I made a start at cutting the long grass yesterday – otherwise it's very tempting to snakes – but I found it very hard work. Someone else at work is going to lend me his *"shamba boy"* who is under-employed at the moment. I have plans for cultivation and/ or chickens. I toyed with the idea of having a goat, but it's already bad enough getting up at 6.30am to get to work, without adding the milking as a prior chore.

Swimming with Sharks

I haven't been swimming for the last few days, but I was talking to a fisheries expert two days ago who was of the opinion that shark accidents might start to happen when there were more people using the beaches. Apparently potentially man-eating sharks are caught inside the reef, but I am not worried, because a lot of people have been using the beach near our house for years and years, and there are still no recorded "accidents".

Finding Servants

I have started looking round for an *"ayah"*. There is no shortage of potential houseboys, but I want a woman servant because of the children, and I want references I can trust, not dirty scraps of paper covered in bad and faded writing. Everyone seems to have one of these. I must have turned away about a dozen uninvited applicants the other day while I was making a start on the garden – with *panga* and hoe – I turned away about ten people who wanted jobs for themselves and their "brother". Apparently word travels fast, but the flow dries up eventually.

I have decided that I also need a large dog although I don't want a ferocious one.

Finding Useful Work

At work I have enough to do, but I still haven't found or made a permanent niche. All the same, I have some ideas that I want to push – for the last week I have been writing about *njamaa* villages (self-reliant socialist communities) for the annual "plan" – although I'm afraid it's more like a progress report than a plan.

Now I really do need to go to bed.

Love, David.

Our parents collected together the following extracts from letters David sent during May 1970, to circulate among friends and family.

My first impression of Africa was a rather surprised one of empty green pasture, with a few muddy rivers. There is no jungle of any sort round here. I think the greenness will disappear later on in the year, when the rainy season officially comes to an end, and even now there is relatively little rain.

Fellow Travellers

Most of my fellow passengers were Asians going either to East Africa or Mauritius, and a rather bad-tempered French (or French speaking) musical group. They got off at Dar es Salaam and were most put out to find one of their battered suitcases had been damaged. They also had a sort of flat packing case, which looked as though it might contain a harp, but actually had something electrical in it. It was unloaded the wrong side up, and in the course of turning it over the porters let it flop down on the concrete – very funny reactions.

The New Africa Hotel

The Ministry apparently sent someone to meet me and booked me into an hotel, but for some reason I cannot fathom they failed to identify me, so I took the first taxi I found to the

New Africa Hotel (which is almost the only hotel whose name I knew) and paid 25s instead of the normal 15s for the fare, plus a 10% commission for changing my money. I am extremely comfortable here at the New Africa, for 85s bed and breakfast. I have a new air-conditioned room with its own shower and lavatory, and the service is excellent and most efficient.

Exploring Dar es Salaam

I have spent a lot of my time since I arrived walking round Dar. At the moment the weather is just right – if anything a bit cooler than Marseilles last year in summer. On Thursday I made no attempt to go to work. I arrived half-way through the working day (10.30 a.m.) and slept until about lunch time. Yesterday was Labour Day, which is a public holiday. I could have gone to listen to *"Mwatimu"* (teacher) Nyerere give his May Day speech, but felt my Swahili wasn't up to it. I am reading *"Swahili"* by D. V. Perrott in the English University Press "teach yourself" series. It seems to be well written and I am finding that some Swahili is almost essential. Most Africans speak no English, even in Dar …

Mixed ethnicity

…It is surprising how very few Europeans one meets in the street. Of course most of them drive everywhere, and I am always being accosted by taxi drivers who assume I want a cab. I have just realised that they normally blow their horns as they pass in the hope that I will hail them. I spent most of the afternoon walking in Dar and I doubt if I saw more than half a dozen Europeans. In the African township Europeans were so rare that I was an object of great curiosity. Generally speaking however, people are very friendly and I am always having to say *"Jambo"* or shaking hands. It's funny to think that Dar has an African township. The structure of the town is roughly that the old centre is Asian, and about a third of the population of Dar is made up of Asians – Arabs, Persians, Erlchi, Hindus and Moslem Indians. They run most of the shops and businesses, including those that have been taken into the State sector. They are very much more Europeanised than, say, Indians in England. The girls work, often dress in European clothes, and are very beautiful. To the south of this area there is the African town, laid out in a grid pattern, consisting mainly of mud and wattle houses, of quite decent size, with corrugated iron roofs. The streets are wide but unpaved. The houses have electricity, but water comes from communal taps, and is sold from house to house to those who want to avoid queuing and carting the stuff around.

Inventive Local Industry

A lot of the houses double as small shops and so on. One of the most interesting things I saw this afternoon was a section of small "lock up" workshops owned by the National Development Corporation, each consisting of a room about 12 ft square with a concrete floor, let to small craftsmen. I was amazed to see ironsmiths making perfect galvanised buckets out of sheet metal, or old corned beef tins. Charcoal barbecues (we must buy one) were being made out of old oil drums and all sorts of scrap metal. Packing cases were being turned into quite presentable upholstered furniture, and the noise was fantastic. I was impressed by the skill and ingenuity with which primitive methods and materials are used to produce quite presentable products. Even jacks to lift heavy lorries are apparently home-made – mostly out of wood.

Local Markets

There is also a magnificent market in the African town. I don't know if it functions every day, but I am sure that Saturday must be the biggest day. I happened to be there on Friday evening, and people were already arriving in buses and lorries from the country. Today I went after work, and found all sorts of vegetables, sugar cane, fruit, oranges (carefully arranged in little handfuls), meat, live chickens and fish. There is a great variety of fresh, dried and smoked fish. I would have my doubts about eating the dried fish, but not the fresh or smoked. There are also magnificent prawns, I could hardly resist them, but of course they were not cooked. Again I was the only European anywhere in sight. People kept offering me pineapples (huge!), cabbages, chickens etc, but no-one was too persistent, and there was nothing embarrassing on refusing.

Oyster Bay
Finally, to the north of the town, there is the Oyster Bay area. I went there yesterday afternoon for a swim, and found a very spacious upper-class suburb, with bungalows (often Government owned) in large gardens, asphalted country lanes – a bit like the Blackthorn Lane area of Leicester and infinitely better lighted at night. It obviously was a European suburb in the Colonial period, and is still about 50% European. Its social standing certainly hasn't declined, and I find it a bit shocking after the African town. As someone pointed out however, it would be difficult to do anything about it now, short of digging up roads and pulling down street lamps.

I went to Oyster Bay by bus, which isn't nearly as bad a way of travelling as everyone seems to make out. I'm sure the service compares favourably with that from Oxford to Woodstock (distance about five miles). Buses seem to run about every half hour. The seats are hard, and buses are sometimes rather crowded, but the fare is only 50c *(senti hamsini)* and the buses go fast. I didn't see any other Europeans travelling by bus, which probably explains why they think it is an impossible way of travelling.

Oyster Bay itself is a beautiful beach, with enough other bathers to give one confidence, but still plenty of room for all. The water isn't nearly as clear as the Mediterranean, and I could not see much underwater. At each end of the beach there are coral rocks (grey and unbeautiful) and there are actually some oysters embedded in these, although it would be quite impossible to dislodge them.

Hermit Crabs
I was fascinated by the crabs living in holes in the rocks. If you pushed a stick in they made a grab for it with a claw that looked so big and powerful that one imagined that the crab itself must be enormous. However I managed to dig two of them up out of their holes by tempting them with a stick, and getting my fingers round the main claw. In fact they turned out to be less than 2″ across the body, but one main claw was enormously developed to reach out of the hole, while the other was just a feeding claw. All the same I am sure they would have tasted good, and I was sorry to let them go.

Local Food
I am eating a variety of food. Everyone seems to survive, so why shouldn't I? Today I had lunch at an Asian restaurant, where most of the custom was African. For 5s. I had an enormous and excellent chicken *biryanik*, plus red beans. It was much better than a chicken curry I had on Thursday at the "Cosy Café" which is a rather higher-class Asian/African restaurant (for 10s 50c) and I really enjoyed it more than my evening meal at the New Africa, which cost about 28s (lobster thermidor – I can't see anything special about lobster eaten hot). I reckon I am safe enough with bananas bought in the street, and when I buy an orange I get the boy to peel one (done very quickly with a knife) from the unpeeled pile, rather than give me one which has been standing around peeled for an unknown time. A peeled orange costs about 10c (about three halfpence). Probably my biggest food risk is milk shakes from Indian cafés, although these are really delicious.

Meeting the Locals
Yesterday, coming back from Oyster Bay, I went too far, and got off the bus at the market place. It was already dark, and rather fascinating with all the country buses. Here and there were little pavement stalls, selling hot maize, kebabs, beans and flour meal; and boys with Arab coffee machines (can't think of a better word than machines, but they are very traditional brass affairs about 20″ high), chinking the little china cups to attract attention. I was wandering along, *jambo*-ing all and sundry, and I was wondering whether to try a meal in a very native restaurant, when two boys started to talk to me. I was a bit cautious, because in my

experience (in England) anyone who starts talking to a foreigner in the street is (a) a pimp (b) a homosexual (c) trying to sell something legitimate at an unreasonable price (d) trying to get your money out of you some other way or (e) trying to get a laugh at your expense. Anyway, this just doesn't seem to be true in Tanzania. They insisted on taking me somewhere cleaner, and took me into a NUTA café (NUTA is the only trade union, and is more or less part of the state). There I had a meal which probably would have done for three Africans – rice, beans, a two-egg omelette, and a fried fish. My friends refused food, and I wasn't at all sure if I managed to pay for their cups of tea. It only cost me about 3s 50c, but I was really rather taken aback by the lack of variety. I had just about everything the restaurant had to offer, and I began to understand why all the restaurants were Indian.

At Home in the Township

I then went to their house, which was in the African township. I didn't try and sort out how many people lived in how many rooms, because they were obviously self-conscious about Tanzania's poverty; but there was another friend who spoke no English, a small brother, and somewhere in another room was at least one woman who must have belonged to another family or been someone's mother. I had a meal with them, although I ate very little because I had already eaten lots of rice, but the staple was maize flour in a sort of cake – a very stiff sort of porridge without any flavouring, that you took (with your right hand) and kneaded into a sort of ball. To go with this there was a plate of boiled fish – one fish about the size of a small mackerel for three people. This too was eaten with the fingers.

The house had electricity, but the electric light wasn't functioning. There was a really excellent radio taking stations from all over the world – they gave me the BBC news for Africa, beamed from London according to them, and they could also get Moscow, Peking, India, Bonn and Radio South Africa. There was no ceiling – just rafters and corrugated iron – but there were comfortable chairs, probably the sort that I had seen being made from packing cases.

A Student Dance

They then took me to see a students' dance for medical and pharmacy students. One of the two was a dispenser for a NUTA clinic, and had been a student there. The other one was an accounts clerk at the state brewery. I had to go back to the hotel to change from rubber sandals to shoes (their suggestion). On the way they pointed out an African bar, and when they saw I was interested, they took me in, but I am afraid they were rather embarrassed. There was nothing really to be embarrassed about. It was noisy, but quite orderly. There were one or two men drunk, but they were sleeping peacefully. The beer is brewed quite officially at the state brewery, but I found it rather unpalatable. It comes in big plastic pots, holding about a quart, with a plastic plate on top to keep out the flies, and a spoon to stir it up. It's thick with yeast, which must be rather healthy, and a sediment of flour from which it is made, and you keep stirring to keep this from settling.

The students' dance was very orderly. There were about twice as many men as girls, but many of the men danced on their own, or together in a small group. I didn't dance. My friend the dispenser went to fetch his girl friend, but didn't come back, much to the other chap's annoyance. He suggested that she was probably on duty at the hospital, but I shouldn't be surprised if he was in trouble with her, because they must have made themselves very late looking after me. I left about midnight, because I was dead tired and had to go to work this morning. I was really rather embarrassed by their hospitality. They really were not trying to get anything out of me except possibly some English conversation.

Settling in at Work

At work I have been put into an office with another English economist from Cambridge, Zambia, and Ministry of Overseas Development. We are air-conditioned, which is rather a relief. No-one has yet decided what I should do.

Come here as soon as you like, but warn me so that I can try to arrange for rooms. We can reckon to get a house about the end of the month, although there is no certainty about the date. Today I was offered a flat during someone's four-month leave, but turned it down....

Letter to parents-in-law from Nicole   Dar es Salaam, 01/06/1970

Nicole Settles In

Bernard and David have been working hard in the garden. It is an enormous garden and one could have three more houses built on the land with enough garden for each house. The house is quite cool. There is wire netting at the windows so that the various insects cannot come in and the wind blows through. The furniture is quite attractive and there is plenty of storage space.

Thank you very much for lending us the sheets. They are most useful as we have not received our luggage yet. We have borrowed some plates, cups, one pair of sheets and one saucepan from friends for a few weeks. We went to the African town yesterday and bought several household items. The African market was most interesting; one has to bargain a lot. We bought three lobsters for 6s – the real price was 10s but we managed to get away with them for 6s.

Jobseekers

Every five minutes people come and ask for jobs; they are really desperate. After seeing several applicants we have engaged a couple. The wife will look after the children and the husband will help his wife do the housework and will mainly work in the garden. He will also make breakfast. It is a pity none of them can cook, but I hope the man will learn. Anyway if the man had been a cook he would not have volunteered to work as a *shamba* boy (gardener).

The children seem to have acclimatised themselves quite well. They soon will learn Swahili as the *ayah* (the woman who will look after them) hardly speaks any English. One has to learn some Swahili in order to communicate with the servants.

We have a car (a Volkswagen) and a fridge. Both things are a necessity here. I want to learn to drive again as soon as possible.

Thank you very much for everything you have done for us.

Love, Nicole

P.S. from David
Theft on the Beach

Since Nicole wrote the above letter, we have been to the beach and had a bag with my camera and Nicole's watch stolen almost under Nicole's nose (Bernard and I were exploring another part of the beach at the time). To my immense relief, the keys to the car and the house were not in the bag. But I am rather upset about the camera; I got on well with it.

I have been promised a dog (named Zog), and a banana tree by departing neighbours.

Love, David

Letter to parents   Dar es Salaam, 07/06/1970

Memories of Switzerland

Hope you are enjoying Switzerland. We were there years and years ago – or at least that's what it feels like now. It must be very different now to what it was like in February. I hope that despite your car-lessness you manage to get about satisfactorily.

New Acquisitions

I think Nicole told you we now have a 1966 Volkswagen, guaranteed for 3,000 miles or three months. As for the house, it is liveable, but we are still waiting for new cushion covers and a new cooker (we have a cooker, but it is too small and too slow). Yesterday I bought myself a rather superior model of local charcoal stove for 8s. The standard size, made out of old oil drums, costs 3s, but mine is made out of new sheet steel. It works OK and will be just the thing for barbecues.

Did I describe our house and garden to you? We have two bedrooms, living room, kitchen, bathroom and verandah, and in the garden an outdoor kitchen, store rooms, garage and servants' quarters. Other expatriates have rather more; but so far as I am concerned, the garden makes up for this. There's a wonderful frangipani tree. I can't work out the precise shape of the garden. I measured out the Mkwawa Road side at more than 60 paces, and the Zambia Street side at 78 paces.

Welcome Help in the Garden

Our garden/ house boy (*shamba*, named Isaac) and *ayah* are in residence now. They both seem to be good workers. Most of our long grass has been cut, and a small start has been made on the vegetable garden (by Isaac, not me). I had to buy him a pick-axe before he could make much progress at all. We have planted five banana trees and five pineapple plants, but we shall be lucky if we get much out of them before we return to the U.K.

Bernard and Dominic are happy enough, after a few slightly fractious days getting used to the heat. At the moment (9pm) it is a cool 80 degrees in the house. We actually had some rain, and went for a run in the car this afternoon instead of going on the beach.
No room for any more – love, David and Nicole

Letter to Sheila and family   Dar es Salaam, 19/07/1970

Too Much Sun!

Today, being Sunday, is a nice lazy day. We got up later than usual – about 7.30am – and I spent much of the morning putting a little grass roof over my rows of carrots to keep the sun off. I have left this rather late. Most of my first seeds either failed to come up, or died rather quickly. I am also making a larger "shade house" over my two sickly rows of peas. There will be room for more plants in there when it's finished. I found some dry palm leaves that would have been ideal for roofing it over when we were out this afternoon, but I couldn't fit them in the car with the family there.

Gardening Under Difficulties

My other job this morning was digging a small garden for Bernard. This was more difficult than it sounds, since he wanted it near the house where the "soil" is mostly coral rock. I dug with a pickaxe and a crowbar. Fortunately it is a very weak rock, but it was still very hard work making a hole about 3ft x 4ft and 1ft deep. Since I had to take all the big stones out, there wasn't much left but a hole when I had finished, so I emptied the dustbin into it, and filled up with leaf sweepings, buckets of soil from other places, and seaweed. The result should be a very fertile little patch, but it's largely a waste of effort, since we have much more receptive soil down the garden.

With the aid of insecticides and fungicides, my vegetable patch is looking business-like, although all we have had from it so far is French beans (this lunch time). I plan to have a lot more done by the time the rains come. Fortunately I shall not have to do much of the digging. Isaac always comes and insists on doing it when I start, except on Sundays which is his day off. Even on our best soil, all initial digging has to be done with the pickaxe, followed by a 3lb hoe which is used in much the same way. I can keep it up for a morning, but it is very exhausting work.

Fun on the Beach

This afternoon we went out to the sea, but it was such high tide that there was no beach at all at the first place we went to. I managed to get a swim later on at another beach, but it was already getting cooler by then. I was sorry not to get any interesting goggling. The best places for underwater swimming are over rocks. On sand there are few fish, and the water is generally too murky to see much anyway.

Last week I had a very good swim. In only about 4ft of water I found a lot of very colourful little fishes (up to about 8 inches). The problem is that that there are spiny sea urchins all over the rocks, and these can give a powerful sting. However they have some use. I found that if I smashed them up, fish quickly appeared to eat up the pieces. I also found two (smallish) giant clams. The larger one is about 8 inches long by 5 inches wide. We ate the clams and kept the shells. The shells are better than the meat!

How is your house-buying progressing? I hope everything is settled and that there are no last-minute slips. My house in Woodstock, to my disgust, is not yet let – very frustrating. Love to all, David, Nicole and family

Letter to parents Dar es Salaam, 02/08/1970

A Week at Dodoma

I had a pleasant week at Dodoma. The Conference was rather a waste of time, but I got an opportunity to see the place. We stayed (myself and a Tanzanian civil servant) at the Christian Conference Centre, although ours was not specifically a Christian conference, being on land management.

Dodoma is one of Tanzania's largest towns but that doesn't make it very large – I would guess about 20,000 inhabitants. There are perhaps a dozen European-type shops, a fair number of small *"dukas"* owned by Asians, two markets, a cattle market, a newly opened wine factory, a collecting centre for sunflower seeds, a grain milling establishment, a railway station, an airport, an almost open-air magistrates' court, and the Regional Administration, housed in an obviously defensive building, built by the Germans. That's about the lot. The area around is fairly highly populated, heavily over-grazed, very very dry for most of the year, and suffers from soil erosion.

It is much colder than Dar because it is at 4,000 feet. I suppose you could say it is a pleasant climate – so long as you are not a cow, or a blade of grass, and so long as you don't have to grow your own food.

We travelled there in twenty-seater propeller-driven planes, safe, but alarmingly small.

Entertainments

Yesterday we went to see *"Till death us do part"* at the Drive-in Cinema – amusing, but not really a very satisfactory film. I was interested in the cinema; it is quite a good way of seeing a film, and certainly the laziest way I have ever come across.

Today we went to a *Ngoma* (dance) in which Isaac was involved. It was an all-Malawian affair, and was very much more restrained and respectable than what we have seen so far of Tanzanian *Ngomas*. All the dancers were men, and they wore pill-box paper hats, white shirts with dark neck-ties, white shorts, white stockings with black ribbons at the knee, and white plimsolls. The dancing was mostly slow, accompanied by singing and drums, or drums and various odd pipes, mostly made out of garden hoses. Tanzanian dancing is very lively and much noisier, with lots of hip-shaking. Afterwards we found another entertainment: a masked man on high stilts, dancing to two drums – pleasant to have all this free entertainment around.

I am amazed and pleased to hear that Ron and Sheila have moved into their Suffolk farmhouse. Hope everything goes smoothly.
Love, David

Letter to parents Dar es Salaam, 09/08/1970

Family in England

I'm glad to hear Sheila and family are so pleased with their new house. I look forward to visiting. I suppose Sheila's baby may be here by now. I hope that goes smoothly.

Flood Plains and Irrigation

My visit to Dodoma was interesting. You're right to say that most of Dodoma is suitable for irrigation. The only trouble is that there is not much water around with which to irrigate it, and the soil structure is so poor, as a result of drought and overgrazing plus over-cultivation, that quite a lot of Dodoma disappears down the rivers in the rainy season. One thing that does grow well is tomatoes. These were "pushed" as a political initiative, and now there are people with cans full of tomatoes all over the place, but nothing much to do with them.

Their other new crop is grapes – pioneered by Italian monks, then taken on by the prisons and now being "pushed" for *njamaa* (vaguely socialist) villages. There is a wine factory, but there is a real risk of over-saturating the very limited local market.

Cosmopolitan Neighbours

You asked about neighbours. We seem to get on very well. The Norwegians are opposite us; and diagonally opposite us (we are on a crossroads) there is a fairly senior Tanzanian economist from "Development Planning" with whom we get on well, although his wife has little English. Next door on the other side we have the Secretary General of TANU Youth League (the government party). We never see him, because he is away up-country most of the time, but his wife is very friendly. Just down the road there are two new Indian families, here on contracts, who have boys around Bernard's age. Bernard often eats there and we get on well with them.

Late Luggage

We are expecting our luggage any day now. The ship is in port. Hope we don't have to pay duty. By the way, if you ever send us clothes, wash them, remove the labels, describe them as used, and understate the value if your consciences allow you to do such things. I was amazed to have to pay about 70% sales tax and duty on a trouser-suit for Nicole..
Love, David and Nicole

Letter to parents   Ifakara, Tanzania, 19/11/1970

On Safari

I am writing this in a sort of dormitory at the Roman Catholic Mission here. The safari has really been very interesting so far. We went up to Morogoro on Sunday, spent two nights there, and had some meetings on Monday. Then we took a Land Rover (with driver) down to the Kilombero valley, mostly on dirt or gravel roads. We went through Mikume National Park and saw a fair number of zebra, elephant and buffalo, although these were mostly some way from the road. At the moment we are quite near to Selous game reserve. We went round one sugar estate which runs right up to the reserve, and where one of the hazards is elephant and buffalo from the reserve trampling or eating cane.

Ifakara itself is a town of around 5-6,000 people. There are no tarmac roads, nor electricity, although the mission has a supply. The town is on the edge of the Kilombero valley, which is a very wide flood plain, joining up with other flood plains. At some point higher up the valley the flood plain is 40-50 miles wide. Here it is relatively narrow, only about ten miles, which is completely flooded for about three months a year. Everyone who sees it thinks it an area with wonderful potential, but in fact flood control is very expensive, and generally irrigation is needed as well, after the end of the rains. Yesterday we went across the Kilombero by man-powered ferry. Out of interest, we went by dug-out canoe and left the Land Rover to follow, which took about 45 minutes because the ferry is so slow. We sat and drank coca-cola in the "hotel" on the other side – a mud and bamboo building which is rebuilt every year when the floods go down.

Health Hazards

I left Nicole with rather a lot to look after. Bernard had just started to feel chirpier after a nasty bout of malaria. He had a temperature of 104' on the day he was expecting to have his birthday party. It reduces my faith in the little pills we take against malaria. I think I have had a small dose myself, but much milder than Bernard's. I hope he is himself again when I get back. Love, David

Letter to parents
Morogoro, Tanzania,
26/11/1970

Morogoro
   We have almost finished with Morogoro now. In fact we would have been back in Dar es Salaam had it not been for a hold-up in getting money to pay my colleague's hotel bill. I like the region very much. It obviously has enormous agricultural potential in its wide flat river valleys. The main problem is initiative and know-how, and of course money for flood control, irrigation etc. The climate is hot, but I don't find it nearly as oppressive as Dar es Salaam because as well as being a few degrees cooler, it is far less humid. No doubt this will change during the rains, which are due soon. These turn much of the region into malarial swamp and cut off about half the area from the outside world.
   The town of Morogoro is pleasant enough – much better than Dodoma. There are tarmac roads, a cinema, a big market, a decent Italian restaurant, barely tolerable food in two hotels, and quite reasonable meals in bars. The bar industry is very healthy of course. There were no African bars until 1959 (apart from *pombe* markets) because there were laws against sale of liquor to "natives", but now there are lots of decent bars, all owned by Africans. In fact they are either owned by political organisations – the official trade union or the Tanzania Women's Union – or by enterprising capitalists from a couple of tribes. They all have great numbers of "bar girls" some of whom have another profession as well.
   Behind the town there is a large area of mountains going up to 7,000 feet in parts, and more densely populated than any other part of the region. I went for a long walk there on Sunday. It is a surprising experience to walk up little footpaths like those in the Peak District, and find houses all over the place. In fact there are more houses the higher one goes, because the lower slopes are now badly eroded. It's a very pleasant healthy place to live, and the people can grow temperate fruit and vegetables, but there is no erosion control. I saw a gang of women clearing a 45-degree slope for planting. This will be useless in one or two years, and of course causes big siltage and flood problems in the lowlands.
   An unusually educative letter for me. I must be careful not to become a missionary.
Love, David

Letter to parents
Tanzania, early 1971
(The first page, with address and date, are missing. The letter opens with details of a successful coup in some other African country)

Home Truths from abroad
.......the government here was also somewhat put out by the U.K.'s indecent haste in recognising the new government. This was much faster than is usual in similar cases and could only be interpreted as a mark of approval for the coup. All in all, Britain is in very bad odour here, with this coming on top of the sale of arms to South Africa. Heath's policy of "making Britain count in world affairs" seems to consist largely of behaving arrogantly to small countries he doesn't like. The U.K. economy seems to be in such a terrible mess that there is not much scope for being arrogant towards anyone else.

Shortages
   The other things that have made life interesting are the shortages of this and that – first and foremost, water. We are told that there is still enough water in the river that supplies Dar es Salaam but there have certainly been shortages. We are patriotically refraining from watering the garden or washing the car. Over the last few days the pressure seems to have gone up again so either it has rained somewhere in the headwaters of the Ravu, or the pumping station has been patched up. We just seem to have weathered a ten-day shortage of sugar which, in

my estimation, should never have occurred. Usually we produce enough sugar for domestic requirements, but there has been an insect infestation at one of the estates which has cut production. However there should have been ample time to arrange imports. Before that we had a period when there was no meat. We have some of the lowest meat prices in the world and the government can't steel itself to raise them. This, combined with a take-over of cattle purchases by District Councils, is playing havoc with supplies. Now, we cannot find any liquid milk (I don't say "fresh", because it's normally 50% reconstituted Kenya dried milk). I don't yet know the reason for this. There is also a shortage of Tampax! Many of these shortages can be blamed on the State Trading Corporation, which is trying to take over the whole import-export trade. I expect they will get things straight in a year or two.

Exotic sea shells

I brought back two big cowrie shells from my swim today. I shall have to leave them outside until the animals inside have decomposed, otherwise they stink. I have made up my mind not to collect any more, in the interests of nature. In fact I left a couple that I spotted today. I also have clam shells about ten inches across. These are so difficult to get off the bottom that I usually don't try. Some people get shells over a foot across.

Bernard's progress

Bernard is getting much braver in the sea. As soon as I can find a small face-mask I shall buy him one (they're out of stock of course). He puts my diving mask on and this lets him lie face down in the water with his eyes open without being stung by the very salty water. However my mask is too big, and anyway I want it myself. Today Bernard let me throw him up in the air so that he came down with a splash in the water and went under for a few minutes. A few weeks ago this would have caused a real scene. There is still no real swimming, but a lot of movement.

Love, David and Nicole

Letter to sister Sheila   Dar es Salaam, 22/01/1972

Farming home and abroad

Your "farm" sounds flourishing. It sounds as if the cow is in good health again if you are getting two and three-quarter gallons a day, and are trying to get her in calf. Cows here mostly give two pints or less a day (no joking) and are even smaller than Jerseys. There are more cows than people, but a ridiculously low off-take – about 5% per year. Meat is cheaper than in just about any other country, the only trouble being that since the town and district councils have taken over the cattle purchases and most butcheries (all, in Dar) it's got rather difficult to find good meat – sometimes it's difficult to find any meat at all.

Looking ahead

We only have another six months here, and I still have to find myself another job in England, or elsewhere, which may not be easy at the moment. I feel that I have become rather un-academic over the past three years. Still, I've enjoyed it very much here. I shall probably bore people by talking about Tanzania for the next thirty years. We have generally kept very well too. None of us has had a serious case of malaria, although any fever, diarrhoea, headache or stiffness is liable to be diagnosed as malaria. I have not had a day's absence from work, and the children have only had the normal sorts of temperature, and very occasional upsets (dangerous to talk like this!). Bernard thinks nostalgically of England but I expect he will find it unpleasantly chilly when he gets there. Dominic obviously has no recollection of anywhere else.

I would have liked more travelling up-country, but Dar is not to be sneezed at, with warm swimming all year round.

Beach fun

Yesterday I went sailing (but capsized, lost the rudder, and had to retire) and today we went to the beach nearest the house to swim and try and keep out of the sun. Only tourists sunbathe – the rest of us get burnt enough without trying. Yesterday at the Yacht Club there was a pair of Canadian tourists who insisted on sitting in the sun to drink their beer. Over and over again people sympathetically offered them a place in the shade.

Love, David and Nicole

Letter to parents   Dar es Salaam, 09/04/1972

Assassination of Vice-President Karume

We have had a little excitement here: the President of Zanzibar, who is also the First Vice-President of Tanzania, was assassinated two days ago. There were lots of rumours, as undefined trouble in Zanzibar was reported on the BBC about twelve hours before Tanzanian Radio made any announcement. At first people supposed that there might be an attempted coup, but now it appears that there was nothing further than the assassination. Tomorrow is a day of official mourning, but I doubt if there will be many genuine tears shed by the mainland government. The Union of Tanganyika and Zanzibar has always been more theory than practice. Karume kept control of his own army and foreign exchange reserves (to the extent of transferring large amounts of the country's reserves to his own bank account, and causing an acute food shortage by banning imports, despite plentiful foreign exchange earnings). He governed the country in a way that was arbitrary, bizarre, and sometimes brutal. Zanzibaris could be sentenced to death for minor infringements, although on the other hand he recently closed all the prisons, and sent the prisoners to do farm work (with death as the punishment for any further offence).

I think that, privately, the Government here would have been delighted if there had been a pro-Tanzanian coup which allowed the island to be truly integrated with the mainland.

Garden battles

I am hard at work battling with the slugs, snails etc. for the life of my plants. We are getting plenty of rain now, but even one day of continual sun (like today) really dries out the soil. I sowed lots of onions and similar things two days ago, and am waiting to see if the seed is any good. Last week I sowed a whole packet of French beans, and four came up, one of which has now been eaten. You do have an easy time gardening in England.

Children's progress

Bernard is on holiday from school now, and within ten days has apparently forgotten all he ever learnt. However, I know this used to happen to me (probably still does for anything that is not very firmly embedded in my head) so I am not unduly worried. Dominic remains as devilish as ever. He goes on being naughty until we just have to smack him, but this never has any curative effect. He plagues the life out of poor Bernard, who is a reasonable and fairly peaceable child – climbing on top of him or pinching him while he is sitting quietly looking at a book. However, if we are cross with Dominic, Bernard sticks up for him and gets very upset.

Love, David and Nicole

Letter to parents   Dar es Salaam, 28/4/1972

Career Moves

I am now fairly certain of my next job – another rather short-term one. I shall do an 18-month research project assessing U.K. aid to Botswana, Lesotho and Swaziland for the Overseas Development Institute in London. This will involve two visits to Africa, for a total of about six months. I expect I shall get a room in London for myself and commute from Woodstock. When my work is finished, it will be published. Pay is moderate – probably

£3,500 p.a.. I am interested because I think it's high time I did some more solid research work to keep myself saleable as an economist rather than just a Tanzanian Civil Servant. Still, I am giving up the possibility of a second Tanzanian contract which would probably have been much more lucrative if UN money had been available. My Principal Secretary was trying to get me to stay.

Troubles in Ireland

It's funny to hear you talk about the "Irish problem"; somehow it seems so out of date – appropriate to the 1880's or 1920's. I had another letter from Chris Woods who is very happy in the other half of Ireland doing his historical research.

News of the boys

The children are well but as un-angelic as usual. Dominic remains devilish and intractable – much rougher and tougher than Bernard ever was, and naughty for the sake of being naughty. Bernard is a dreamer. I'm afraid he just isn't interested in school work and even when he means to work he goes off into a day-dreaming haze straight away. Still, he is a very sociable and well-meaning boy.

We got a letter from Sheila the other day – rather damp and sticky from two months' sea voyage with bubble-blowing liquid from a present for the children leaking over it. It will be very nice to see them again and, of course, to have a look at "Kisumu".

Garden news

. The rains are raining, but my garden is not (yet) a tremendous success this year. The beans I bought are a total failure – I plant the seeds and wait, and two weeks later I dig them up again, rotten and smelly. Curse the seed merchants here! Your broccoli has also proved rather less robust than the variety I had last year. It has to be constantly nursed, and yet doesn't seem to grow. Still, some of the cabbages are making good progress, and we have green peppers, aubergines, and tomatoes from the garden today. I bought some beans in the market and planted them. I shall be interested to see what comes up. I have a good supply of a local green spinach called *mchicha* and a reasonable row of Swiss Chard too. Yesterday we planted a long row of sunflowers in the front garden.

Love, David and Nicole

Letter from Nicole to parents-in-law

Dar es Salaam, 16/5/1972

Thoughts of Holland

We were pleased to hear about your trip to Holland and to know that you went to Kerkenhof. My boss, who is Dutch, recommends that town. Did you go and see the Floriada in Amsterdam? Apparently it is a beautiful 18-acre exhibition of flowers and shrubs from all over the world. I find the Dutch people very pleasant and I have heard so much about Holland for the last two years that I really want to visit the country.

Pressures of Work

I do not think David will write at all this week. He is very busy with the preparation of the budget and the annual plan. I hardly see him at all as he works until the small hours of the morning and comes home for a meal between 4–7pm. Even on Sunday he had a meeting at 8pm and came back home at 2am. He is worn out and will deserve his two months' leave before he takes up his new appointment.

Looking forward to England

I am pleased to come back to England and live there for the next two years. Of course I will miss the servants, but shopping will be easier and there will be no shortages of food. I shall live on cheese, milk and lamb when I come back; we do not see much of them here. The milk is not very good and tastes too much of dried milk.

The children are very excited at the idea of going to England, but they will miss their friends and the free life they have here. Bernard will not be allowed to go out on his own on his bike, as he does here.

Fear of Burglars

We had some excitement last night. At about midnight (David had just come back from work) our Norwegian neighbours' *ayah* who was baby-sitting while the parents were out, came to call us to come to her rescue. She said she had heard somebody shaking the windows in the children's bedroom. David took the dog and the *panga* and went round to see, but found everything quiet. The poor woman was very frightened, but David was dead tired and could not stay to keep her company. I heard our neighbours coming back half an hour later. They were burgled three weeks ago while they were on holiday. When they came back they were surprised to find they had no clothes left.

Love, Nicole

Letter to parents   **Dar es Salaam, 12/6/1972**

Political Terrorists

I was going to go to work this evening, but an explosion as we were sitting down to high tea changed my mind. We were woken up last night at about 2.15am by a loud explosion, followed by another fifteen minutes later, and a more subdued one after another forty-five minutes. There was a plane in the air, and I wondered whether we were being bombed, but in fact someone was trying to blow up a bridge on the main road to work. They bungled the job – they cracked two pillars and put the traffic lights out of order, and the police have apparently arrested a few people. However it seems that there was another explosion in a car in the main street this afternoon, and, of course, the one we heard this evening. Rumour has it that the aeroplane was hostile too, but I doubt if it did the bombing. In the past, there have been aeroplanes dropping hostile leaflets.

The press and radio are very reticent – there wasn't a word about it on the evening news – so naturally there are plenty of interesting rumours. The normal way of finding out is to ask a cook or messenger or houseboy. I already feel rather blasé about it. The only unpleasant bit is that if the terrorists are planting bombs, they might choose a crowded street – or a ministry – next time. Probably the trouble comes from supporters of the former vice-president Kambona, who is in England financed by the Portuguese. At least there is no apparent anti-European feeling as a result. There is probably a link-up with discontented areas in Tanzania, where people resent being socialised. I expect that most of the army is loyal. An effort is being made to start a People's Militia – ostensibly as an anti-imperialist force, but probably equally motivated by a desire to generate enthusiasm and, if it has a military arm, to act as a counterweight to the army. This afternoon there were little squads training all round the Ministry (civil servants and messengers) stripping down their rifles and putting them together again. Tonight there are planes in the sky, and it sounds as if there is a lot of traffic on the road – all very exciting.

I hope I don't alarm you unduly – I'm sure this is still a much safer place than Belfast. For a start, there are hardly any private firearms.

Sailing

Yesterday I had an excellent day's sailing – the opening regatta of the season – which left me rather sunburned. My normal helm is away, but he lets other people use his boat, so I crew for them.

Love, David and Nicole

Letter to parents   **Dar es Salaam, 13/7/1972**

Safari Excitements

We went on a parting safari last week in my little Volkswagen – 1,600 miles in eight days to Dodoma in the middle of a dry overgrazed overcropped overpopulated plain, then to a green hilly place called Babati where we almost got stranded, because the battery fell through the floor of the car – a combined result of battery acid from a previous invalid battery, rust, corrugated gravel and earth roads, and continual beating from the stony ridges between the wheel tracks. There is no repair garage at Babati but fortunately we were able to locate a man who had some knowledge of the workings of cars (we had other troubles as well as the battery), and we bought a clapped-out battery and limped to Arusha for a welding job (50s) and a brand new 6v. battery (178s here – amazing contrast between cost of work and cost of materials!)

From Arusha we travelled on more earth roads through some beautiful temperate farmland to the Ngorongoro crater (10,000 feet) where we camped for the first time in a borrowed tent and almost froze. We decided not to shell out £16 for a Land Rover trip to see the game in the crater for 2-3 hours, it seemed ridiculously expensive. After looking in vain for a cheap way of getting into the crater we went on to the Serengeti National Park where we saw thousands and thousands of animals, standing around or standing in the road – wildebeeste, zebra, Thompson's gazelle, topi etc. We camped uneventfully in a deserted spot half a mile from the only other tent in sight and listened to gnus all round us all night. The next day we paid a ranger 10s to drive around with us and show us lions, hyenas, a leopard up a tree eating a gnu, warthogs and a cheetah, then drove on via Moshi (near Kilimanjaro) to a "little" game reserve we had never heard of before (little, i.e. only about 200 square miles) where we slept in a government rest house (15s per night per person) surrounded by elephants. Then back to Dar es Salaam.

Return to England
We intend to leave in two weeks, but still have a lot of things to do. We shall probably stop off with friends of Nicole in Tunis for a few days. I hope you can find someone to meet us at the airport when we arrive – (I shall tell you when I have the exact time and date) – it makes travelling with children so much easier. We would like to stay with you for a few days too while we settle down.
Love, David and Nicole

P.S. from Nicole
Thanks for the comics for the children. Bernard is thrilled to receive them and always shares one with Dominic.

Letter to Sheila and family   Hilton Hotel, Cairo, 18/08/1972

A Letter En Route
…I'm not sure of your address, but I shall risk a guess. I have just time to write one letter while I'm waiting here for the airlines office to open (don't imagine for one moment that I'm staying at the Hilton – however, it's a very comfortable place to go to write a letter, with its soft chairs and air conditioning). All being well I shall soon be back in England, but first I shall go to Luxor to have a look at some temples. Yesterday I saw the pyramids and the Sphinx, and refused pressing invitations to ride on a camel just like Sir Alex Douglas Home! I'm staying at a cheap hotel in the middle of Cairo, sharing a room with a German from Dar es Salaam who was on the same plane as me.

First Impressions of Nairobi…
Before Cairo, I spent two days in Nairobi, which is a great modern "western" city, not like Africa at all. In fact it's probably more like Cape Town (which I haven't visited) than any other independent African capital, with the poor living a long way from the prosperous town centre.

…and Addis Ababa….
I next spent a day in Addis Ababa, where contrary to popular belief, they rob the tourist and bother the tourist much worse than in Cairo. Addis is a most peculiar town with lots of traffic

and big modern buildings and wide streets, BUT if you step a few yards behind all this you find the most revolting smelly slums I have ever seen – mud houses, goats in the street, and watch where you tread!

…..and Cairo

Cairo is a much bigger and more modern city than I had imagined – six million people. It's really much less squalid than I had expected – certainly no worse than many towns in France or Spain from the point of view of dirt, smells and housing. In fact it is very like Southern France or Spain. If it were not for the fact that I cannot understand a word of Arabic I should feel quite at home. In fact I can understand a few Arabic words because the language has a lot in common with Ki Swahili, but if I try and make up a sentence in Swahili I get very blank looks.

I hope we can visit you when I get back – I want to see you and your house.
Love, David

David and family moved back into their Woodstock home on returning to England. It was good to have them within visiting distance for a brief while.

In November 1972, our maternal grandmother Margaret Childs passed away at age ninety-four. She had been an important figure throughout our lives. We had enjoyed summer holidays at our Grandparents' home in Herne Bay. Like David, she was a cellist, also an avid gardener, and I remember that in her mid-eighties she constructed a summer house in her garden at Northwood, using as foundations railway sleepers embedded in concrete that she laid herself!

After the funeral, David and I were driven to the Hampstead home of our mother's distant cousin Daphne Tracy, since we both had time before catching our respective trains. Daphne particularly wanted to show David her home as she would have liked him to lodge with her when his work required overnight stays in London. We were entranced by Daphne's intrepid driving through busy London streets – she had never married and stayed home to care for ageing parents so was on home ground. We were equally fascinated by her lovely home, set in a large garden best described as "natural"! I remember a spacious beamed entrance hall with grand piano, and upstairs, a large billiard room with low-hung lighting. Entering her home was like stepping back in time, maybe to the years between the World Wars.

We enjoyed our visit too much, so that I missed my train home. David declined Daphne's invitation to lodge with her, as this could not have been on a purely business footing so he would have felt obliged to spend much free time with Daphne (who was charming company, but lonely) rather than going straight home to his family.

I remember the day with pleasure (despite the funeral of a much loved grandmother) because throughout our adult years I spent so little time with this brother who had been my close childhood companion.

David's role and work during the 18 months beginning September 1972 is fairly well documented; he was a Research Officer at the Overseas Development Institute in London, and was preparing a book entitled "Europe's Chosen Few" outlining the Policy and Practice of the EEC Aid Programme.

Britain had joined the Common Market, and twenty developing Commonwealth countries were offered the option of "association". Chapter Two of David's book is headed "The Wider Issues of Association" and the text begins thus:-

"The issues involved in the association of Commonwealth countries with the EEC go far beyond those of most bilateral or trade negotiations between rich and poor countries. The main feature of the EEC policy is that a specific group of developing countries is being picked out and offered a special relationship with the EEC, including trade and aid advantages that are denied to other developing countries….. this selective approach to developing countries must inevitably raise the questions: what is the EEC hoping to get in return, and why concentrate on these specific regions?"

The elusive cause of equity and justice between rich and poor nations was always close to David's heart and I am sure he put every effort into exploring and explaining the issues and decisions made at that time. An article published in The Guardian on 22nd August 1973 (author unknown), headed "Undivided Third Division?" and dealing with the same topic, includes these words –

"The Commonwealth associables are still working out what their policy towards the Common Market should be. They would do well to read, before negotiations press too far, the study by David Jones just published by the Overseas Development Institute, and called 'Europe's Chosen Few'."

The end page of David's book outlines the ODI's raison d'etre, as follows –
"The Overseas Development Institute is an independent, non-government body aiming to promote wise action in the field of overseas development. It was set up in 1960 and is financed by donations from British business and by grants from British and American foundations and other sources. Its policies are determined by its Council."

There follows a set of "Functions", of which I personally find Number 3 the most vital, which is "to keep the urgency of development issues and problems before the public and the responsible authorities."

For David, the concern was always that decisions and resulting actions were wise in ethical terms, rather than in western-interest business terms.

I have a very clear memory of Whitsun week 1973. I had finally succeeded in passing my driving test. I resolved to take my family of six children down to Brixham in Devon, to visit our sister Margaret and her family, who had recently returned from the Belgian Congo (now Zaire), where she and her husband had been medical missionaries. This would be my first long journey, and I was at the time six months pregnant (as was my sister!) So into our small car went six children aged 2-13 years, a fat mother and as much luggage as we could pack in. We waved goodbye to my husband, who would remain in Suffolk to care for our livestock, and set off – first stop Woodstock, where we would stay with David, Nicole, and their sons. Bernard and Dominic were enchanting children, each having a winning smile and a shock of curly fair hair. It was good for all the cousins to spend time together.

The next day I packed eight children into our small car (well before the seat-belt era!) and set off for a picnic in the parkland of Blenheim. Reaching the Palace, the man on gate-duty looked at me and my entourage, refused to let us pay a penny for entrance, and waved us through with "In you all go, dear!" and a sympathetic shake of the head.

David must have been finalising material for his book at this time. I had only the haziest understanding of his work; but thanks to the constant flow of letters and post cards, I and all the family knew he was seldom in one location for long. There is an Itinerary for the months of September – December 1973, carefully stored away by our father, which provides the following mind-boggling information –
12th – 13th September - 72, Oxford Street, Woodstock.
14th September - call at ODI for mail in morning. Fly Heathrow to Nairobi.
Contact: Susan Fisher, Ford Foundation, Silopark House, Nairobi. Hotel: Norfolk.
18th September - Fly Nairobi to Dar es Salaam.
Contact: Stewart MacFarlane, Central Veterinary Laboratory, Dar es Salaam, Tanzania.
Hotel: probably Sea-View.
22nd September – Fly Dar es Salaam to Blantyre, Malawi.
Contact: Antony Polatajko, Ministry of Tourism, Trade and Industry, Blantyre, Malawi.
Hotel: probably Ryalls.
(From this point on the journey was to continue by hired car)
25th-27th September - leave Blantyre for Johannesburg/ Maseru.
Contact: Kevin Sparkhall, Assistant Secretary, Ministry of Finance, Maseru, Lesotho.
Hotel: probably Holiday Inn.

2nd-4th October – leave Maseru for Gaborone.
Contact: Mike Stevens, Ministry of Finance and Development Planning, Gaborone, Botswana.
30th October-1st November – leave Gaborone for Mbabane.
Contact: Tim Simkins, Economic Planning Office (Education), Department of Economic Planning and Statistics, Mbabane, Swaziland.
26th-28th November – leave Mbabane for Maseru.
Contact: Jeremy Lester, Ministry of Finance, Maseru, Lesotho.
10th-12th December – leave Maseru for Blantyre
14th-16th December – leave Blantyre for Woodstock, England.
(Phew! Home in time for Christmas!)

Letter written to parents   Blantyre, Malawi
                                                                   23/09/1973

Return to East Africa

So far I have had a most pleasant trip. I spent four days in Nairobi – mostly in my hotel room going through papers on Botswana. Then I went to Dar es Salaam for four days. There I spent much of my working day in the hotel where the Commonwealth Finance Ministers were meeting. Each time I had to talk my way past a police guard, but they never turned me back. I think I managed to justify my presence by meeting people and finalising contacts. Apart from that, it was simply good to have an excuse to visit Dar, meet old friends, and do a bit of swimming in the Indian Ocean.

I went to have a look at "my" garden, and found it neat but unproductive, apart from the banana plants which I had put in, which appeared in good heart. The *shamba* boy told me that he had heard there used to be "too many tomatoes there before"!

Impressions of Blantyre

I got here yesterday afternoon. Blantyre is.a very pleasant little town… I've admired even such flowers as phlox, roses and honeysuckle. The blue jacaranda trees are flowering now before the leaves grow (in the rainy season). The leafless trees, covered with little flowers, give a strange effect of hazy purple light, and the fallen flowers on the pavements look like a reflection of this.

I spent this afternoon (Sunday) with a chap I had met in Dar, whom I have to see here. He drove me around the town, and into the hills, with his wife and three children who evidently only get taken on this jaunt when they have visitors. And – of course – I swam in their swimming pool.

I hope you are well and – if this is consistent – that Daddy is still not waiting for a date for his operation. My next contact address, in Gaborone (for about one month) is on the back of the letter.
Much love, David

Letter to parents   Maseru, Lesotho, 26/10/1973

Arrival in Lesotho

Next country please! I took two days to drive the 500 miles here from Botswana, although I managed half a day's work on the day I left, and arrived early enough on Tuesday to get myself set up at a hotel without any difficulty, and see a few people. The High Commission had been told I was coming and was flapping around a bit, wondering where I was in a very solicitous way. In fact, before I left they sent an enormous telegram to the High Commission in Botswana, asking what plane I was arriving on; did I know the local airport was closed and I would have to land at Bloemfontein; had I booked into the Holiday Inn, and did I realise it was normally overbooked; had I arranged to be collected at Bloemfontein, and if not, they would arrange with the Holiday Inn bus, and if they couldn't fetch me …? It's just as well I decided to pay a fairly early call on the High Commissioner the day after I arrived. He assumed I had just come, and invited me to lunch and dinner and to stay the night at the

High Commission, which I did, rather to the confusion of the hotel. I think they must be used to rather helpless British Civil Servants being sprung on them at short notice, and are really rather surprised that I seem to be able to look after myself.

Maseru is a much slower place than Gaborone. This country is over-populated and poor, with no resources except for beautiful and frighteningly eroded land, and income from migrant labour in South Africa.

Child beggars

Yesterday afternoon I drove out and up through a pass and onto an upland plateau, but I wouldn't like to get out of my car because of the aggressive begging by lots of little children. One disappointed boy even picked up a stone and threw it at the car, but fortunately missed. This simply doesn't happen in Botswana or even Malawi, and in Tanzania the situation is different because out of town there are so few Europeans anyway.

A Favourable Climate

The climate is excellent. I suppose we must be 4,500 feet up, and far enough south to have a very distinct summer and winter (with snow). All sorts of temperate fruit trees grow here, and the favourite trees are poplar, Mediterranean pine, and eucalyptus, with occasional oaks, and weeping willows along the river banks.

I hope that you are keeping well, and that Daddy is beginning to feel benefit from his operation.
Love, David
(NOTE - Our father's successful operation was a hip implant)

Letter to parents

Mbabane, Swaziland,
1/11/1973

First Day in Swaziland

I should really be working, but as this is my first day in Swaziland, and I am still feeling rather worn out after driving 500 miles yesterday, I feel justified in writing a few letters.

Lesotho Experiences

I was sorry to leave Lesotho; it's a miserably poor country, but still rather charming. The people I met were really rather pleasant – apart from begging children, who probably are poor and hungry, but who are an awful nuisance. Usually they just ask for sweets. When I first arrived, I had a big bag of oranges with me, so I handed some of those out, but as you give out the first two oranges, the next five children arrive, and more are still rushing towards you as you drive away. It's a very substantial disincentive to going by foot.

Swaziland – But Who is in Charge?

Swaziland is hotter and richer, although about half the land is owned by foreigners (mainly South Africans), and a lot of Africans are involved in poor subsistence farming and are very much under the thumb of traditional chiefs.

I have managed to get myself cooking space – in fact a whole office – in the Department of Planning. Here Europeans seem to be even more in control than in Gaborone or Maseru – which I confess I don't really like. You are never sure whether what you get told is true/ the official/ or the expatriate line. There is an African Permanent Secretary (whose name begins with a tongue click which I find I can manage, though most Europeans can't). The local advisor doesn't seem to know his place (which is in the background, rather than allocating work independently of his Permanent Secretary).

Home and Family

I'm glad Daddy is home. I hope he does find that he can move around more easily, although the main aim of the operation was to stop him getting worse. I am most relieved that it already seems to have done good rather than harm (or nothing).

Have I got any more nieces and nephews yet? I can't say that I feel an enormous need for more, as I am already quite uncertain about the names of the last three or four, but it's nice to know.

Friends from Botswana Days

I visited our Norwegian neighbours from Dar in Botswana. In fact I collected the wife from the airport when she arrived four days late, which surprised her, as she had no idea I was there. They seemed to have settled down to a family of two (about the same age as ours) but have now decided that since they have two years of bush work ahead, with a good Seventh Day Adventist hospital on hand, and no chance of work for Lill Anna, they might as well expand to four.

It's much hotter here than Maseru, but there's a swimming pool at the hotel.

Much love, David

Letter to parents   Mbabane, Swaziland

11/11/73

Family News

I'm pleased to hear that Sheila is safely delivered of a daughter (Juliet). The name chosen no longer causes me any embarrassment! I must admit that I am getting quite hazy as to whether Margaret's next will be the third or the fourth. I've hardly ever seen them, so they are no more than entries in the birthday book (which Nicole looks after anyway).

Forests and Mountains

We still have petrol here, although I know a delegation from here is in Pretoria to discuss rationing. The price went up 20% a few days ago, but I have not got round to converting Rand per litre to pence per gallon, so I don't know if it's cheap here – I suspect it is, which is just as well considering the distances one has to drive. I was able to go out for an extravagant Saturday ride into the gum (eucalyptus) and pine forests, and I got out and walked along one of the private forestry roads. This is a wonderful country for plants – odd little lily orchids, loganberries, wild asparagus, wild cape gooseberries, wild azaleas, huge ferns seven or eight feet tall, standing like palm trees (in Guadeloupe apparently they use the fibrous stems for plant pots). I sampled some absolutely tasteless wild strawberries, shaped like little light bulbs and bright red. Those little flowers with rather scruffy blue pompoms grow wild too.

I walked up until I got to a fire look-out tower on the top of a hill, and knowing that whites get away with a lot, I went right on and was allowed in to have a look. The watch-tower man (sounds like Jehovah's Witnesses) told me I would be cursed if I walked on the paths without permission from the company, which sounds a bit extreme, although I don't think he was implying that the Commonwealth Development Corporation employed witch doctors. In fact I think he was very pleased to have a visitor, and he let me climb the tower and look at his miles and miles of mountain and forest.

Today I walked on the hills next to the hotel. A lot of mountains here seem to be more or less smooth impermeable granite, with a thin thatch of topsoil. Some of the streams just run over single almost flat rock surfaces for long distances.

Only here for the beer!

I didn't meet many people, but one group at the roadside when I was on my way home offered me some Swazi beer from a large tin can. Apart from the taste of the metal it really wasn't bad – although rather soupy like all African beers. It's really much more palatable than the commercial version – *Heinrich's Chibuku* – which is sold all over East, Central and Southern Africa (at enormous profit to the governments and no doubt to Heinrich, alias Lonrho). Sorry to digress on beer!

Much love, David

Letter to parents   Maseru, Lesotho, 19/11/1973

I suppose Nicole and the boys will have visited you by the time you get this. I hope they are well-behaved (I think they compare quite reasonably with the average for young children).

Loss of Camera

Did I tell you I had my camera stolen? It's very annoying, but I am as fed up over the loss of film as over the loss of the camera. At first I assumed I must have left the car unlocked by mistake, but I see that an attempt has been made to force the near-side window – which is odd, because that was the side nearest the flats, and it was the other side that was left open by the thief.

Days on the Road

I'm glad to be getting to the end of this trip, although it has been very interesting. The day after tomorrow I shall drive back to Maseru for another two weeks, then probably to Johannesburg to sell back the car, and to Blantyre for a short stop on the way home.

We are still having no serious problems with petrol here. The pumps are closed over the week-end, which cuts down the number of South African tourists who come here for the gambling, and there is a speed limit of about 55 miles an hour, which is observed in the breach, but since I do not intend to travel over this weekend it doesn't really affect me. Anyway I can go about 300 miles on a full tank.

Hill Walking

I have been out walking on the hills again over the weekend. My only qualms are that I might meet one of the rather lethal snakes that are found in this part of the world, but apart from running over a small cobra on the way out of Botswana a month ago, I haven't seen any wild serpents – or tame ones either. Incidentally, I forgot to mention that red-hot pokers also grow wild here.

Manure from Sewage

I have just been to pay my respects to the British High Commissioner here; we had quite an animated discussion about the virtues of sewage sludge as manure – by way of diversion from the question of whether the U.K. would be willing to pay for water and sewerage in Swaziland. He claims that however carefully you mature the stuff, the tomato pips survive. Much love, David

Letter to parents   Maseru, Lesotho,
                                                                    1/12/1973

An Eventful Mountain Trip

I took a trip into the mountains in a four-wheel drive truck taking food and other supplies to one of the teams building roads, payment being one free meal a day! We passed one team who tried to flag us down, but when we stopped they made for the lorry with such obvious intent that we quickly started up again.

We were meant to start at 10am, but didn't get off until 6pm, and then spent one and a half hours driving around Maseru picking up odd people and things. I was one of the lucky ones in the cab, but local hitchers (who probably had to pay) returning from the South African mines had to ride on top.

The lorry had a crew of four, and needed it. The radiator leaked and had to be topped up every couple of hours, and the wheel bolts had to be tightened. Within the first two hours we had to stop twice for fuel blocks, which were cleared in the dark without a torch. We also carried forty gallons of diesel fuel in a can, and a length of hosepipe to siphon it out.

At about 1am we stopped to off-load at a hut which must have been a store. The owner was somewhat taken aback to see me stagger in with sacks of maize. At 3am we stopped for the night at what I suppose must have been a government rest-house. I'm afraid I was given the only bed (with a chicken and her chicks underneath).

We set off again on the really bad tracks at 6 o'clock, and made Thaba Tseka by noon. I helped unload there, and am still stiff as a result; I got a very dry meal in a very smart hut (always this special treatment for whites) and we ground back through the rain, with damaged suspension and a load of sheep, two of which died as a result of being tied up. Distressing. But otherwise it was an excellent trip.

Much love, David

The above is the last surviving letter from David's early adventures, all those from 1974-5 having been lost in my mother's house clearance and move (following our father's death) in 1985-6. There is one letter only from the year 1976, written in February, from London, when David was contemplating a career move. However, a large number of letters survive from the years following the family's next move, to Botswana in 1977.

Letter to parents   **London, 18/2/1976**

Looking back – and making choices

No, I wasn't in Brussels for the Cod War – I wish I had been. It would be fun to get my hands onto something new, but I seem to be fairly stuck with developing countries at the moment (not, of course, that I am not still interested in them, but there is a sameness that sometimes palls a bit).

I and a girl from the Institute are involved in a quick consultancy study for the EEC Commission, which involved going over there (Brussels) and interviewing a lot of people. Kathryn will do the bulk of the study, but I have the EEC experience – and I can interview in French! I've no doubt I say some pretty odd things, but by and large I think I manage to communicate reasonably well.

It turns out that if I had hung on a few days I would have been offered an EEC job. I suspected as much, as I got a telephone call a few days after I had given a firm "Yes" to the Ministry of Overseas Development - so I gave a firm "No" to them before they could get any further for fear of being tempted by whatever ridiculous salary they offered me for doing – probably – a ridiculous job. I would be interested to know how they would have ranked me.

I found, rather to my pleasure, that the secretary of our EEC contact spoke of Kathryn and me as *"deux jeunes chercheurs"* when she set up meetings on our behalf.

ODI Conference at Windsor

I have spent this weekend at Cumberland Lodge in Windsor Great Park. ODI was organising a conference on a vaguely Commonwealth issue, and I went along as part of the ODI equipment, though my only responsibility was to act as *rapporteur* for a study group. I am, though I say it myself, rather a good *rapporteur*; I think it's a combination of long experience taking fast summary notes in lectures and meetings, and the otherwise rather futile experience of servicing UNCTAD meetings when I was working in Geneva.

Yesterday afternoon, in a two-hour break between sessions, a group of us walked across the Park to Virginia Water. It was definitely Spring. The snowdrops in the gardens of Cumberland Lodge are already out, and the daffodils in the grass are following closely behind. This morning I slipped out for five minutes before I had to say my piece, and disturbed a rabbit on the lawn.

The Lodge itself is a rather heavy Victorian mock-Jacobean pile, on the site of a lot of other houses – a royal "Grace and Favour" residence, but the plumbing is antiquated, and the central heating woefully inadequate – all very bracing. I was glad the weather had warmed up a bit in the last couple of weeks. But the surroundings were beautiful, and the company good.

I don't think our conference was a great academic success, but it was a pleasant social occasion – very good for an institute like ours, where people live all over the place, and don't have much opportunity to relax together.

CHAPTER THREE
LETTERS 1977-1980

Letter to parents   Woodstock, 13/03/1977

Memories of student days

I am feeling rather stiff this evening. Yesterday we all had our cholera shots, which left us a bit queasy, and this afternoon I took out my rusty bicycle which has been lying idle for seven years, and cycled to Eynsham and back – a grand total of about fifteen miles. I was rather horrified at my unfitness. By the time I had completed the first mile I was reflecting on the lunacy of the attempt. I remember once setting out from College with three friends, two bicycles and a motorbike to ride to Stonehenge overnight for the summer solstice. The idea was that we would change about, taking turns on the pillion, but I and one other started off on bicycles and I was amazed and incredulous at his inability to cycle for more than five minutes without an equal rest period, so that in the end we had to give up the bicycle part (we drew lots, and I went by motorbike and fell asleep on the pillion on the way back). Anyway, I now understand what the other cyclist felt like. Strangely, I found the coming home easier than the going. Perhaps the wind was behind me. Nevertheless, I was tottering a bit when I dismounted.

House Extensions

We have the builders with us again. The mess is not as bad as last time, but there is, inevitably, a lot of dirt and grit around, as all the materials have to be brought in through the front door via kitchen and dining room. The soil pipes and manholes have had to be re-arranged, which is a bit silly, since they were put in only seven years ago, but that is now complete, and the foundation concrete has been poured, so I hope the walls will now go shooting up. My only fear is that my builder has a tendency to improve on his instructions, and is already appearing rather keen on knocking down a few more bits of wall and rebuilding them, including one in which I have laboriously installed a damp course in preparation – it remains extremely damp, but I hope it will dry out eventually now that the damp can no longer rise.

Last weekend I really wore myself out with that and other jobs, like clearing out the old bathroom before it was knocked down, and shoring up the wall around my little garden; because of the drought and then the rain, old stone walls have been toppling all over Woodstock. This weekend we have taken things comparatively easily with a bit of decorating.

Off to Africa Again

We shall be going away to Botswana on 13th April for two years. I have unpaid leave from my ministry here, so that if I want to go back after two years I can – without any accrued seniority or pension rights, but it is still a very good deal. I shall, in any case, be paid extremely well while I am away, tax-free, and with free house etc. as well. I am looking forward to it, though I know it is going to be a difficult job.
My address in Botswana will be Ministry of Agriculture, Gaborone, Botswana.

Can we come and stay with you from Easter Sunday until the 13th? I expect the best way will be for us to hire a car for a few days and leave it at the airport on the 13th. As usual, we shall have to fly at night – there are hardly any daytime flights.

The house is going to be let while we are away by a local estate agent, and we shall be putting our best furniture into store. Really we got away extremely lightly last time, considering the tenants we had.

Vine Propagation

I may have some vine cuttings for you to look after for me. I put some in under plastic, and felt very pessimistic about them, but yesterday I noticed that one had struck roots. However, I must not count my chickens too early. My friend John Mittell (who should be round for a drink in a few minutes) has got this far a couple of times, and has still produced no plants. My most promising ones came not from my very vigorous vine, that is very prone to mould, but from some far less healthy-looking cuttings rescued from quite an old vine in the walled garden of an old farm near here that belongs to the local museum and currently has some friends of ours living in it as it waits for the funds needed to turn it into a farm museum. I doubt if the vine itself is of antique stock, but I would be interested to see what it was like.

David, Nicole, and sons Bernard and Dominic 1979, at their Woodstock cottage home

Boarding School for Bernard

We have applied for a place for Bernard at Lord William School at Thame – a voluntary aided grammar school going comprehensive. They are very strong on music, and seemed more interested in the fact that Bernard could play and read music than in his scholastic accomplishments. In fact, that is his strongest point. We all (except Dominic) have an interview on the 30th.

David now commenced employment as an agricultural economist with the Ford Foundation, an American-funded organisation.

Letter to parents   Gaborone, Botswana, 17/04/1977

A Successful Journey

Here we are, via Nairobi and Johannesburg. We were met in Nairobi, to the boys' pleasure, by a Ford Foundation driver, and taken to the guest flat there, so I was able to have a long chat with my predecessor here, and with his earnest young American boss – I do find these Americans disturbingly earnest. We had lunch with Nicole's former boss from Dar es Salaam – a very nice Dutchman – and dinner with the Ford people, and left in good order at 9 o'clock the next morning.

Bernard and Dominic have enjoyed being waited on in the aeroplanes, and having a servant in Nairobi! Here, they are enjoying the luxury of a big two-double-bedded room, and an outside swimming pool, but I think they will soon tire of this hotel life if we do not get into a house. Fortunately there seems to be a house for us, which looks all right from the outside, so I hope we shall soon be installed.

Botswanan Agriculture

Botswana is still looking relatively green and pleasant after another year of good rains. I expect it will start to look a bit arid in a month or two if it turns out that the rains really have stopped for the year. We went out for a drive this afternoon, and the others were suitably surprised by the healthy appearance of the cattle. A young man to whom we gave a lift, who was employed by the government's development corporation, told us that he had "less than a hundred cattle" – very inadequate in his view. All Botswanans in government service try to accumulate cattle with their earnings, and senior civil servants and ministers sometimes own thousands of them.

We have had a very easy weekend. Tomorrow morning I shall go in to work, and also have to set about the business of setting up a bank account and completing immigration formalities.

Letter to Parents   Gaborone, 01/05/1977

A New Home

We moved into our house yesterday, with a jumble of borrowed things, as our air-freight has not yet arrived. We have quite a good house, in reasonable condition. It's an odd shape.... *(a sketch of the ground plan shows the house to be roughly H – shaped, with a swimming pool opposite a central courtyard, a verandah alongside kitchen, dining room and lounge, and a small building within the grounds as "servants' quarters")*

… it looks too grand on the plan, as it is just a concrete *"stoop"* with a roof over much of it. There are several hundred identical "Type II" houses in Gaborone, but they often do not appear identical at first sight, because they have been fitted into the plots at all sorts of angles so as to squeeze them in between the existing trees. We have lots of trees – mainly thorn acacia, but also one peach or apricot, three big thirsty eucalypts, and a couple of very untidy "syringa" trees that are planted as ornaments, but are now dropping their yellow leaves and useless yellow fruit all over the place. At least they are thornless, so the boys can climb them.

Chameleon Watching

This morning we watched a pretty, graceful little chameleon climbing on the branches of a syringa – much more graceful than the lizards, and somehow less reptilian. He climbed, gripping the small branches in a kind of scissor grip, whereas lizards seem to be able to stick on at any angle, just like flies. For extra security he wrapped his tail around the stems of leaves. His eyes were quite uncanny, swivelling independently of each other at all angles.

Preparing to Attack the Garden

I have not yet started proper gardening; it's not the best season and so far I have neither seeds nor all the tools. But today I discovered a neglected patch of sweet potatoes, and dug a small bed for them in semi-shade in the area I have decided to keep for vegetables. The soil is deep and fine, stone dry and very very hard. After lunch, with some friends, one of whom is a keen gardener, I borrowed a pick-axe to dig a compost pit. That was very heavy work, but I think the pit is almost large enough, at least for a provisional effort.

Fitting in at Work

Work is beginning to get more interesting as I start to find my feet in what is going on. In my ministry I have a rather odd position, as I fall outside the main structure of divisions and work independently to the Permanent Secretary.

Despite my good salary, we are not yet feeling very prosperous, as the Foundation takes its time making payments and reimbursing expenses. We managed to avoid paying our huge hotel bill – just as well, as we could not have done – and are still living off the money I brought, with a bank advance prepared as a fall-back reserve.

Getting to Grips with the Garden

We have now established ourselves, with a housemaid by the splendid name of "Glorious", and a couple of minute vegetable patches to show that we are serious.

I am still waiting for the first instalment of my splendid income (which has already suffered a 5% devaluation) and I am not feeling sufficiently flush to lash out on fertilizer, but the last occupants had a large rubbish heap, which consists largely of leaves and grass cuttings, so I am able to use this, once I have sorted out the plastic bags and bottles. Today I collected a garden hose and a wheelbarrow, both of which should be extremely useful. So far I have planted sweet potatoes, Chinese cabbage, dill, hot peppers, a cabbage seed-bed, and long black radishes intercropped with the cabbages. Nothing, of course, has had time to come up yet. I can't put in any of the more exotic vegetables, because we can anticipate frost in the next two months.

It is actually rather chilly at nights and early in the mornings. The *"Daily News"* is advertising coal for sale, and I think we must buy a sack. Tonight we have an electric fire on in the living room, and we are both wearing pullovers. The days, however, are pleasantly warm to positively hot, once the sun gets up high in the sky.

Bernard and Dominic Find New Friends

The boys are enjoying themselves, and looking extremely fit. They still have a month's holiday ahead, and are beginning to roam around the neighbourhood, and get to know other children. The streets are fairly quiet, and there is a network of pedestrian ways, one of which runs along the end of our garden, so there is plenty of traffic over the fence – a mixed blessing as we don't yet have either a watchman or a dog to keep out burglars.

Farming Problems

I am getting more and more involved in my work, which is at last beginning to develop some sort of shape. I spent a very interesting day out last week looking at an arable farming project being funded by the U.K. This is mainly cattle country, because of poor soils and rainfall, but arable is becoming more important as population increases, and no-one yet has done much work on systems that will use the limited rainfall to its best advantage. Fortunately for Botswana this is the third year of unusually good rains.

Letter to parents-in-law   Gaborone, 17/05/1977
from Nicole

New Place, New People, New Dog

It is very dry here and the countryside looks like the English countryside during last summer's drought. All the gardens in our area are beautifully kept and the grass is green, but it is due to the fact that they are watered a lot. Despite the fact that it does not rain much people do not seem to bother about wasting water.

Glorious, the housemaid, seems quite pleasant and she can cook more than I thought. She went home at the weekend to see her children and brought us back a chicken which she killed and cleaned this morning in no time at all. Glorious's children and her sister's daughter are looked after by an aunt who has a small farm. We have also engaged a garden boy, about fifteen years old.

We now have a dog called Cain. He was given to us by one of David's colleagues. He is fourteen months old and has adopted us quickly. After he arrived we noticed that he was not very well so yesterday I took him to the vet's. The fee was 4 *pula* (about £5) for an injection and a few tablets.

The boys are enjoying themselves and have plenty of friends.
Love, Nicole

Fuel from the Garden

We have a cheerful but very smoky fire going tonight, burning logs from trees in the garden. The chimney doesn't draw very well, and the smoke stings my eyes even one room away from the fireplace. I am still looking malevolently at the trees in the garden, that seem to take a disproportionate amount of space – four large eucalyptus, three large useless syringa trees with large crops of poisonous berries, a number of shapely but thorny acacias, and some rather undistinguished trees and bushes that seem to grow through and under most other things. It is these that I am now cutting and burning, but I have my eye on one large syringa, next to our only fruit tree – a peach I think – as a possible site for an orange tree, that I understand I should plant in June.

Trying to Control Young Joseph.....

Our fifteen-year-old gardener has no great gardening talents. He is very keen on sweeping and scraping up the grass that dares to grow in our large, bare, rear portion of the garden – where I want to make a lawn – but is less keen on digging, and his enthusiasm with the hose-pipe nearly washed all my cabbage and radish seedlings out of the ground. Glorious, the maid, is essential for keeping him in order and translating. We had a little session yesterday, because Joseph had found a spanner and tried to tighten the packing nut on one of the outside taps, but had evidently turned it the wrong way, so that the tap had come to pieces and the washer must have shot out on a jet of water. Then he had put it back together without the washer, and not said anything about the incident, which was not a very successful stratagem, as the tap continued to gush – to my puzzlement until I took it to pieces.

.....and Cain the Dog

Cain, our dog, is proving loyal, sloppy and rather silly. He is very fond of the children, and tries to sneak off after them if they go out without him. He also has a tendency to gather pieces of cloth or paper. Tonight he brought a mat of Glorious's and left it on the front porch, but luckily did not rip it up as he did one of my egg boxes full of seeds this morning. I don't think he is going to be much of a watchdog, but he is generally quite amiable.

Progress in the Veg. Patch

I am feeling nice and sleepy after a day spent largely in the garden. There's a lot to do, and we have been without a gardener for the last few days, as he complained of a bad back, so we sent him down to the hospital, who gave him some pills and ointment and told him to take four days off – just when I want him to dig more vegetable plots. My vegetables are growing slowly because of the cold – at least, I hope that's why - but I need more space to plant out cabbage, cauliflower, broccoli, and fennel seedlings, and I need a few more big holes for trees and vines. I've been trying not to do a lot of heavy digging myself because I pulled something out of joint in my neck before I left the U.K., and I want it to settle down again, but I find it hard to resist. This afternoon I put a second "band" across the garden to trap the rainwater in the wet season (there is one most years) and stop it from running into the next door garden along with my topsoil.

I'm glad you had a good holiday. It's difficult for me to think of it's being summer, though our weather is probably better than yours from about 11am to 4pm. It's the short days and nippy nights and mornings that make it evidently winter here. It hasn't rained properly since we came, although we did notice a few drops on one of our first days here, and there is sometimes a surprisingly heavy dewfall.

Dining on Goat

We had a couple of friends for lunch today – the chap I used to share an office with when I first went to ODM, and his wife. They had just been camping out in the hills near here with friends – she for two nights and he for one – and were feeling well aired. We gave them a lunch of goat and sweet potatoes and pumpkin, since Peter had told me he had never had goat or sweet potato, and we gave them plenty of South African red wine to wash it down. It was a late lunch, starting after 3 o'clock, as we had to wait for them to get back to town, and it was quite comical watching Jenny on the verge of sleep after lunch.

First Rose Bushes

While I was waiting for them, I planted out two rose trees with plenty of *kraal* manure (cow manure from a *kraal* belonging to a neighbour), composted sweepings and bone-meal. I have high hopes for the roses. Sometimes they do very well here, and I bought mine from a Norwegian who does a flourishing export business in carnations and roses, grown using seepage water from the Gaborone dam. The bone meal comes from the veterinary store at work. It is meant to be fed back to cows to combat the local phosphorous deficiency in soils and grass, and costs only about £1.50 for 50kg.

Bullies and Friends

The boys are settled in at school and seem fairly happy, although Bernard got bullied by a group of African boys on the way home on Friday, which upset him. I asked a friend whether this was common, and he said his son had had the same problem – difficult. The white boys start with an advantage – have usually started school earlier, speak better English, and generally seem to do better at school - so it is not surprising that they are resented; but we can't put up with bullying. Dominic has a girl friend (the daughter of the deputy director of veterinary services at my ministry) who spends much of the time here. I think she's quite tough, but unlike others with whom he has deigned to play, she <u>looks</u> like a little girl!

Letter to parents

Gaborone, 10/07/1977

Bernard Prepares for Boarding School

Nicole will be coming with Bernard early on 14th August. Can they stay with you? We shall give your address for the school uniform etc.

Flu Bugs, and a New Gardener

There is a nasty fluey cold around, which has kept B and D in bed for a week, and had pernicious though not disabling effects on Nicole and myself. Glorious is also out of action, and feeling very sorry for herself. The garden progresses slowly because of the cold, and the lack of attention – our gardener having given up manual labour in favour of harvesting oranges. The margin per orange is anything from 100-500%, so he ought to make a profit. We have a new gardener starting work, afternoons only, on Monday. It is time I made my projected trip to the nursery at Mafeking to buy orange trees and vines (funny idea, going to Mafeking to buy plants, but it's now a very quiet little South African town). I must first make a round of friends and neighbours who also need plants, and get a permit from another branch of my ministry to cover all reasonable needs plus some spares.

A Desert Camp

Since I last wrote, I have made a couple of trips: first by truck to a ranch in the Kgalagadi (Kalahari) desert. I slept in a tent, and in the morning there was half an inch of ice on our washing water, but I was warm enough, with a sleeping bag and a blanket, and all my clothes, plus Dominic's woolly hat. The desert was most un-desert like, with waist-high grass, and quite a lot of small trees – acacia mainly. The only livestock we saw apart from cows, were *duiker* (very small deer, about 2ft high) and warthogs.

A Luxurious Farmhouse

Second, three days later, I went to the Tuli Block, hard on the great green greasy Limpopo. That time I went by aeroplane in great comfort, and stayed at a lovely thatched farmhouse set in a beautiful garden, surrounded by lawns and tall trees. There is very little rain, but the farm I visited sits on a spit of silty soil between the Limpopo and a tributary – the Molutse – and the trees are well dug into a perennial water supply. I was helping to look after a Chinese team, and we drove around in the bush, and saw elephant, zebra, and a lot of eland. The Chinese had evidently never had such a good holiday in their lives, and were like a bunch of children on a Sunday School outing. The farm manager and his wife have to drive for one and a half hours to reach their nearest neighbours. We were, therefore, very lucky to come by air, although the airstrip, down one side of a wheat field, did not inspire great confidence.

A Puppet Show
Yesterday we all went to have a look at the Vanye agricultural show, 130km from here. It was not the greatest show I have ever seen, but it was certainly a popular event for the people of Vanye. The most successful item was a puppet show put on, somehow, by our Ministry. I was unable to gauge how educational this entertainment was. It looked like the normal business of Punch and Judy knocking each other about and boasting. There was plenty of audience participation.
P.S. – If you see any Chinese cabbage seed, please buy a couple of packets for Nicole to bring back – there is none on sale in the shops here.

Letter to Sheila and family   Gaborone, 21/07/1977

Cycle Accident in Suffolk
I hope you are in good shape and recovered from your various ills. What a pity it is that Sheila should have lost a tooth that had taken such labour to straighten out. Please get it replaced. I don't like the idea of you with a gap-toothed grin.

Four-month-old Garden
I am amazed to see that we have been here for four months. It seems like no time at all; but we are now fairly solidly dug in, me to my work and my garden, Nicole to her work and the house – and the Gaborone singers – and the children to school and friends. I take pleasure in the garden, although it is far from being a showpiece. Things are not growing particularly well, because of the frost and the birds, but I spend a lot of time looking at them to see if they are coming along. I have a new gardener, who seems fairly keen, and does things without being told to. Yesterday he planted cabbages all over a small bed that I had been intending for lettuces. I haven't the heart to pull them all out again. He is also unused to climbing beans. There I did have to pull some sticks out, twice. On his original plan, we were heading for a solid cube of bean vegetation, with short sticks planted out on a grid plan, six inches apart either way.
I also have a large yellow lawn (the grass does not like the cold either) and a brown lawn, which I water in the hope that it will produce grass.

Weather and Work
I trust that your weather is hotter than ours. It's a bit of a bad joke to see Africans trudging to work wrapped up in balaclava helmets and greatcoats to keep out the cold. It will, of course, get much hotter, and eventually much too hot. I hope to have the swimming pool in action then, but first I must invest in a pump and a filter. I like to swim in fairly clear water.
I must stop now, and see if I can re-structure the co-operative movement before going to bed (I am not entirely joking).
Much love, David

Letter from Dominic (aged 8) to cousin Stephen Wright
Dear Stephen, It is very nice here and I am on holiday. It is summer now. I have been to the Kalahari Desert two times. And I saw a lot of game.
From Dominic.

On Safari in Botswana, 1978 and 1979

Letter to Sheila and family　　　　　　　　　　　　　Gaborone, 09/1977

Thanks for my herbs. I shall have another go at things like marjoram and basil, and I need a constant supply of parsley, although the row I have at present is still looking fairly healthy.

Ready to Swim

Summer is coming on here, and the flowers have just dropped off our peach tree, leaving quite a lot of fruit set. I find it difficult to think of autumn. We are just contemplating putting the swimming pool into commission. As a friend of mine said, just paint it, buy a pump, and start pouring in money. I think that with the temperatures here one has to be a bit more particular about filtration and pouring in chlorine than in England, otherwise the water can become a soupy green within a few days. Certainly the cheapest solution is to buy a season ticket for the pool at the hotel down the road, but it lacks the snob appeal of having a pool in the back garden.

I hope you are all well, and have not had any more bicycle or horse accidents.
Much love, David

Letter to parents　　　　　　　　　　　　　　　　　Gaborone, 25/7/1977

School News

We are beginning to realise with surprise just how soon Nicole and Bernard will be off to England. The prospect does not seem to worry him at all. The academic level of his school here seems somewhat higher than Woodstock, at least for Bernard, and is a good preparation for secondary school. Dominic is still finding work very easy; I think it might have been better for him to start one year higher. They both find the level of indiscipline here startlingly high, particularly among the African students. To my disappointment, the school seems to divide fairly clearly along racial lines, and they have only one close black friend who is culturally American rather than Botswanan.

Cycling to Work

The weather continues to be cold – very cold at nights and in the mornings, warming up around mid-day, so that I need my tweed jacket when I go to work in the morning, but happily cycle to work without it in the afternoon. I am using my refurbished bicycle again for the first time in seven years. It was literally rotting away all that time in the old shed at Woodstock, but now has new back wheel, chain wheel and gears, and is enjoying a new lease of life. Unfortunately the packers took the pedals off to pack it, and I succeeded in putting them back on the wrong sides, which is rather disastrous, since one side has a reverse thread (like the top of a vacuum flask casing). The result was that I stripped the threads, and the pedals kept falling off. It is remarkably difficult to ride a bicycle with only one (wobbly) pedal. However I have bodged the thing up with a new set of pedals and some epoxy resin, and I hope it lasts. My appearance on a bicycle causes a surprising amount of merriment. Somehow, it is funnier for me to ride a bicycle than for the Rural Sociologist to do so. Perhaps I am meant to have a more august position.

Drought and Farming Problems

I am managing to find myself a great deal of work, so much so in fact that it is very difficult to do it all, although I resist working in the evenings and at weekends. To give you some idea, I am involved in trying to develop an arable farming policy (this is cattle country, although in fact more people depend on ploughing than on cattle). I am involved in trying to get some drought contingency planning done (this is drought-prone country, but people only take notice of droughts when they happen, and they have not happened for the last three years). I am involved in a whole network of committees that are trying to implement a far-reaching change in the land-tenure system. Over the last fortnight, I have been very much taken up with pushing a Bill to establish a legal framework for groups of small farmers or cattle owners who want to work together, and need a formal basis in order to borrow money or enter into any sort of contractual relationship (e.g. lease land). This weekend I have been working on a proposal to re-structure the co-operative movement, which seems to have outgrown its present structure.

Brown Lawns

The garden is a source of great pleasure to me, although the brown lawn remains as brown as ever. From time to time I go and count the tufts of grass that have succeeded in growing. I am beginning to realise, however, that I chose about the worst possible time to try and start a lawn. All the best-established lawns are yellow and threadbare now.

Piling on the Manure

As for the vegetables, we are starting to weigh into the lettuce thinnings, and today I produced one long black radish – five inches long, but it took three months to grow. I am by no means sure whether my enormous Chinese cabbages are ready. They continue to grow, but have no hearts. In terms of volume and speed, however, they are a great success. We are beginning to get spinach, which we mix with perpetual spinach. I have just put in some rows of Swiss Chard. I think I am going to get some French beans, despite frosting and bird damage (or gerbil damage). Today I had a most spectacular bonfire, burning an accumulation of dry thorn wood that had been thrown over our fence into the pedestrian way behind the house, in an attempt to get rid of gerbils. At the moment I am top-dressing everything that looks seedy with a wonderful load of horse manure in wood shavings, which I collected from the Deputy Permanent Secretary's racehorses. We do, of course, have a lot of soil deficiencies here, which may be of obscure things like zinc or boron, and the easiest way of dealing with this is to dump on a lot of manure.
Love to you both, David
(see you soon, Nicole)

Letter to parents   Gaborone, 19/09/1977

Training up Johnson the Gardener

It seems to be a long time since I last wrote to you. Blame lassitude and work, and my garden, which takes up a lot of my weekend in work and contemplation. Johnson is quite an energetic gardener, but he lacks finesse, and I keep on finding bits of remedial work that need to be done. Today I decided to water my vines until water brimmed up to the top of the small crater in which he had planted them, only to find that the water was disappearing as into a bottomless pit. The vines stand against a barrier of poles and wires that is meant to provide a sort of screen between Glorious's quarters and our house. Instead of digging holes for the poles, Johnson had produced a sort of slit trench, but somehow he always manages to backfill in such a way that he produces a seemingly flat surface that subsides later. The vines had been planted in the trench, and all the earth had fallen away around them, leaving them surrounded by enormous holes. I'm afraid this will not have done the vines any good, but at least I managed to put in some more manure. What puzzles me is what he does with all the spare earth.

The Cost of Gardening

Otherwise, the garden flourishes. We are more than self-sufficient in vegetables, although at considerable cost – 22 *pula* a month for Johnson and about 10 *pula* for water (both paid for by the Ford Foundation, so why should I worry? – but that's about £20 a month, which is a lot of veg.). We still have lots of lettuce and masses of spinach (real and "perpetual", with Swiss Chard coming along behind), but the real delicacy is my own green sprouting broccoli and cauliflower. We are getting a few crisp carrots, and a few rather stringy French beans, but lots of radishes. The first maize plants are just starting to tassel, so we should soon be getting sweetcorn, and I am very hopeful about my courgette plants, which have grown very vigorously. Tomato plants are just going in, so we shall not have any of these for some time. The weak patches in my gardening are the lawn and the flower beds. I actually have a lot of very gaudy African marigolds, but they are all in the vegetable gardens, grown from seed scattered to help ward off eel worms. I am planting a lot more flower seeds now and should get some hardy colourful plants to fill the brown spaces. Johnson has planted out a curious rectangular patch of ordinary marigolds (not African ones) in the "traffic island" in the front drive, which seems to be flourishing; and one only needs to add water for more African marigolds to appear. We should also get some canna lilies. The plants are all over the place, and really need thinning and replanting with some manure and rotting compost.

First News from Bernard

We have so far received one letter of about six lines from Bernard, which presumably means that he is happy, although his main news was that he had been sick and had had a headache, and had been sent to sleep in one of the rooms next to matron's room. I expect he was just tired, first by the excitement, then by the talking into the night of boys who find themselves in a dormitory for the first time. Mrs. Chisholm went over to the school to see him, and said he seemed to be very happy, and to be settling down well.

The parents of Bernard's best friend in Woodstock have asked if he can stay with them at half-term, as they will be going back to the U.S.A. in November, and would like to see him before they go. You won't be offended, will you?

Thankyou very much for the record of Tchaikowsky's Fifth Symphony, which you gave me for my birthday (I thought you would like to know what you had given me). Dominic insisted on putting a big candle (power-failure type) into my sponge cake and singing happy birthday, so the occasion was properly celebrated.

Dominic is, I think, missing Bernard more than he would say, or more than he realises. He goes back to school again in two days, which should keep him well occupied.

Letter to parents   Gaborone, 09/10/1977

Waiting for Rain

The weather is beginning to warm up now, and I start work half an hour earlier than in the winter – 7.30am. Dominic is on summer time too, and starts at 7.45am, but he is usually off before me so as not to miss anything, although he only has to walk down the road. This week the sky has been threatening – or promising – rain, but not producing very much of it. There is a lot of thunder and lightning around, but the water falls on someone else's garden. Last night when we were eating dinner outside at a colleague's house we had a brief downpour, which drove us inside, but this morning the ground was as hard and dry as ever. The soil here is very fine and sandy, and soaks up the rain in the top few inches, but is usually as dry as dust and as hard as cement a few inches down.

Garden Pests

My garden continues to supply us with most of our vegetables, although the supply tends to come in gluts rather than a well-balanced flow. Today I realised that the ladybird-like creatures on my spinach and Swiss Chard preferred the vegetables to the greenfly, and were making lace of all the leaves. They also produce nasty little hairy grubs with similar habits. So I picked a couple of buckets full, and sprayed the rest. It's difficult to be a biotic gardener unless you are keen on eating bugs.

I have various squash, cucumber and melon plants on the way, and am interested to see whether I can be more effective fighting the African pumpkin fly here, than I was in Tanzania. There I relied on enormous regular sprayings of systemic insecticides, but I have since learned that the little pests can be disposed of by dabbing a sugar and insecticide bait on the leaves. I have four carefully nurtured plants that were started off on blotting paper, and are meant to produce pumpkin seeds without shells, which is a great boon to people like me who enjoy pumpkin and melon seeds.

Learning from the Experts

I spent much of Thursday and Friday at a horticultural conference – strictly in line of business, although I learned more about gardening than about how we should organise horticulture in Botswana. It all made me feel very amateurish. I have been buying tomato seed as if it were just tomato seed, but I find there are varieties that produce three times as much as even the best I have, and are resistant against eelworms and two very prevalent wilt diseases. The only problem is that it is almost impossible to get the seeds of these super varieties – perhaps that overstates the problem, but one does have to get seed from Johannesburg. There is also a whole armoury of chemicals to fight different sorts of pests and diseases. My particular *bête noir* is the cutworm, which slices seedlings off at ground level, but I find I have to make up an elaborate bait for that, and I am not sure that I have an appropriate poison.

News of the Boys

We got a longer letter than usual from Bernard this week. He seems to be very happy, and to have settled in well. He said he would write to you – don't be too shocked by the spelling. I miss him, as I am sure does Dominic, although Dominic now has his own circle of friends, whereas before he was rather dependent on Bernard's circle.

Need for a Pool

Dominic is now doing a lot of swimming at school and in friends' swimming pools. Ours is still empty, except for a foot of dirty water at the deep end, but Dominic made a start at painting over the hair-cracks with pool paint today. I had thought to stop at that, but the general effect is so odd that I think I shall have to go the whole hog, and paint all of it. There is also the major expense of a pool pump, plus various other bits and pieces – and all that expensive water. I had not realised how much water was involved until the other day when a friend started filling his portable pool in the morning, and Dominic reported that they had been able to paddle at lunch-time and would be able to swim the next day. Perhaps I can connect up to my roof. Our big water-tank has already collected enough this summer to fill about a quarter of the pool, and most of it just drips away through a leaky tap.

Letter to parents   Gaborone, 30/10/1977

Adjusting to the Heat

It's beginning to get rather hot, and we are feeling the need of air conditioners and swimming pool – neither of which we have at the moment. The air conditioners were ordered six months ago, and all we can do is go on chivvying the people who were meant to supply them. The swimming pool is more a matter of us getting down to work, but there is a lot to do – cracks to fill, the whole thing to be painted, and pump and filter put into action. I have made a start on all of these jobs, but things can only be bought in working hours, which is a bit awkward. Last Monday we had a public holiday, so we drove into South Africa, thinking we could pick up a pump at the nearest medium-sized town – Zeerust, about 150km away. In the end, we went three-quarters of the way to Johannesburg, to Rustenburg about 300km away; but we got a pump and various accessories and bits of tubing.

Today I examined the existing plumbing, with a friend who has fixed up his own pool, and we came to the conclusion that there was no way that the present maze of pipes could work, so I shall have to do a lot of re-plumbing, fixing plastic pipes to the useable bits of the present steel system. Then there is bricklaying, to make the filter tank workable. I caused a small flood today by accidentally un-plumbing our garden tap. The underground plastic pipe had got mixed up with a redundant piece of tubing from the pool, which I wanted to salvage.

Garden Progress

My garden continues to supply us with almost all our vegetables. My three courgette hills give enough for us to have courgettes most days and still give some away, and I have a sporadic supply of small cucumbers. The tomatoes are not yet ripe, but I reckon we shall soon have a supply. My first lot of onions, grown from English seed, were almost a complete failure. I had not realised that onions were sensitive to day length. As a result, they simply did not form bulbs. A local variety, put in much later to form sets, is producing some quite reasonable bulbs, despite overcrowding.

I have a similar problem with the purple sprouting broccoli, which seems determined to grow to tree size, but refuses to sprout. If we have to wait much longer, it will be enormous and rather elderly.

The hot weather causes some problems, of course. All the plants look like wet rags by mid-day, but most revive. Fortunately a lot of my beds are in semi-shade. The other day, I almost lost all my curcurbits. They had not been watered over the long weekend, but they are heavily mulched, and looked all right when I did my early morning pollinating round. By lunch time, some of the leaves had gone quite crisp in the sun, so I soaked the plants, and covered them with grass to shade them (otherwise the drops of water get hot and burn the leaves); and all the mature plants recovered.

News of Bernard…

We continue to get happy letters from Bernard. He seems to have settled in very well, and says that he does not find the work too hard. I expect he was helped by the rather tough academic approach here – where he was not at all brilliant compared with his peers. Bernard says he is having regular trumpet lessons again, which pleases me.

….and Dominic

Dominic seems very happy at school here, and seems to be doing very well. He collects a lot of "stars", although I gather that a lot of them are for good writing. Apparently, in subjects like geography, everyone copies the same thing down, so the only basis for giving stars is the appearance of the work. But he gets stars for maths and English as well (despite his spelling). Once a week he goes to a French afternoon, which he enjoys, because he is effortlessly in the top group, but he is willing to work to stay there. And on Saturday afternoons he goes to swimming club. I don't quite give him cello lessons once a week, but he got one today, and seems to be making forward rather than backwards progress – can't say the same for myself.

Letter to parents   Gaborone, 13/11/1977

Success with the Pool

I am very wholesomely tired, after another weekend fixing up our swimming pool, and in the end, swimming in it. Peter and Jenny came to help yesterday, and we got the pump fitted up, and put in a new underground cable, but we had a tremendous job getting any water to

51

come through the tubes. We collected a small load of cinders from the power station for the bottom part of the filter, and Jenny had collected blocks for the bottom of the filter, and building sand for the main filter bed. We were able to fill the deep end of the pool up to the outlet pipe to the filter, but it was a meagre swim.

Clinker and Chemicals

I spent much of this morning in the sun sieving the clinker and trying to wash off the coal dust. I'm not surprised our electricity bills are so high; half the clinker was in fact coal, and I accumulated a small pile of the bigger pieces for our winter fuel, but I began to despair of the coal dust. In the end, I only put in about two inches of clinker, and put about six inches of sand on top of that. To my surprise, the water that eventually flowed out of the filter was not coal-black, but only rather cloudy from the sand, and by early afternoon it was starting to clear. So by the time Peter and Jenny arrived for their afternoon stint, they were able to actually get in and have a swim. I have to admit it is not possible to take a very long swim. The pool is only six metres long, and we need only about a quarter of the amounts of pool chemicals stipulated for "small to medium" pools; but it is very pleasant just to fall into the water, now that the weather is getting really hot. I am quite taken aback by the amounts and variety of pool chemicals needed. There is chlorine, of course, but there is also pool stabiliser, and algicide (to stop the water from turning green) and I have a little kit to test the acidity of the pool, and fuming concentrated hydrochloric acid to top up the acidity level. All the bottles and containers carry warnings, and specify antidotes. In the end, one almost wonders whether it is safe to enter the water at all.

A Scorched Garden

The hot weather is really hitting my garden. Plants shrivel up and die in a single afternoon. I am beginning to wonder if I should have a net house – literally, a house made of heavy plastic netting to keep out anything from 30 - 70% of the sunlight. I had been sceptical of the need before.

News of the Boys

Dominic is very pleased to have the pool. He is able to spend a lot of his time swimming here, because there are so many pools around. Tonight he went to bed early, or at least he meant to, because he has end-of-year exams tomorrow. These determine whether he is able to go on to the next standard. I have no real worries about Dominic, however. Apart from spelling, he seems to do very well.

Our letters from Bernard continue to be short and happy. He seems to be enjoying school, and taking part in even such un-Jones-like activities as rugby. He is having regular trumpet lessons at school. We had a short note from his housemaster recently, saying that we would be charged £15 for a large window Bernard had broken while throwing sticks for conkers. Bernard has not mentioned this in his letters, but I don't think it can be preying on his mind. One of the disadvantages of Lord William School, with which we had not reckoned, is the fact that it only has ordinary day-school holidays – only two weeks at Christmas. However, he will, of course, come here for Christmas.

Fun with Fireworks?

Last night we went to a belated firework party, at which our host took a long while to let off a number of inscrutable Chinese fireworks. One puzzling feature was the lack of blue touch-paper. The fireworks turned out to have fuses made of string, cunningly concealed. The highlight of the show was a small rocket, that had failed to light and been consigned to the fire. It managed to go off just at the same instant as a surprise firecracker, and its sudden appearance, making an erratic course through the grass towards Jenny Agar, coupled with bangs and flashes, made her leap from her chair and go rushing about, trying to escape Quite alarming!

Water Shortage

The rains are still elusive. We have had a couple of good showers today, and I have been able to raise the level of the swimming pool a couple of inches by siphoning rainwater from the roof out of our big water tank, which seems much more sensible than letting the tank fill up and overflow (I can't attach the garden hose to the tap). My garden is in a bad way at present. Two inches down, the soil is still as dry as dust and as hard as concrete. The courgettes have almost stopped producing, and are being attacked by mildew and melon-fly, and the sun is so powerful in the heat of the day that everything droops or dies, according to sensitivity. Also, I have not been able to give the garden so much attention because of pressure of work, and my weekend duties with the swimming pool.

However this evening we ate sauerkraut made from my own cabbages. It was a reasonably successful experiment, although the result was rather salty, and when the salt is washed off it is not very sauer.

New Barbecue

The barbecue was finished today and looks rather odd, as I decided to provide it with a chimney. I still have to see if it works.

Heavy Going with "the Notables"

I have had a very busy week, because on top of everything else we have had a visit by some of our Ford Foundation bosses. They take themselves very seriously, and considering the small size of their Aid programme, they managed to line up an extraordinary array of notables. In the course of just over 24 hours they managed to see the President, the Vice-President, and the Ministers of each of the four advisors. We had dinner with the Foundation bosses on Thursday, informally. On Friday we had lunch with them, the Vice-President, and an array of Ministers and Permanent Secretaries. In the afternoon I managed to fix up meetings with my Minister, my Permanent Secretary, and his Deputy. I doubt if our bosses realised how honoured they were. The problems of catching anyone senior in my ministry actually in the office, and getting him to honour an appointment, are almost legendary. In the evening I had the job of entertaining the area representative (we shared them out to expose them to Botswana) and again I got the Permanent Secretary and his Deputy. I found it all rather heavy going, but it went off all right. Yesterday morning I had an hour's exclusive chat with the three Foundation bosses.

A New Land Rover

In a most disinterested way, we seem to have persuaded them that Botswana still needs four advisors, although this decision was helped by Botswana offering to help pay for us. In a most interested way, we have also persuaded them to buy us a new shared Land Rover. The old one is steadily disintegrating, and the local (i.e. Nairobi) bosses had been very reluctant to buy us a replacement; but I understand that even the President came in on our behalf, because his advisor had had a series of breakdowns during a weekend trip to Lesotho. Having got what we wanted, I think we are all rather glad to have got rid of the "headmasters" (as a friend of mine describes them).

Planning a Christmas Trip

I'm afraid we shall probably not have the new Land Rover in time for Christmas, which is a pity. We had planned to go to Lesotho. I like the country very much, and wanted to show it off to the rest of the family, but the South Africans all take their summer holiday at Christmas, and mostly head for the sea or the mountains; so by the time we started to telephone hotels in Lesotho they were booked solid. Instead, we have been invited to go to Serowe, and possibly further north, with Peter and Jenny Agar who have their own Land Rover, and join a group of indefinite size who will be camping in a young expatriate officer's house in Serowe. We shall take the old Land Rover and travel hopefully.

Dominic is looking forward very much to Bernard's return; so are we all. Dominic has certainly missed Bernard a lot, although he has managed very well with his own circle of friends. In this weather, they are able to go round to one swimming pool after another in the afternoons.

The National Assembly

I have spent rather a lot of the last week sitting in the Officials' Box in the National Assembly, listening to the debate on the President's speech, so as to pick up anything our Minister should say in his speech. It is amusing for the first day, but quickly palls thereafter. We also have a spate of parliamentary questions that have to be answered before we have time to find out what the answers should be. I shall be glad when the session ends, and we can start working as if Parliament did not exist.

Letter to parents   Gaborone, 03/01/1978

Happy New Year, and happy birthday to Daddy.

I hope Daddy was feeling comfortable for Christmas, and that he has been well patched up. These hernia operations seem to get a bit repetitive. Your Christmas party sounds as if it must have been a lively do! The party on 27th sounds more fun, but I hope it did not tire you out.

An Adventurous Christmas

We had an excellent Christmas. We borrowed the old Ford Foundation Land Rover, which is now due to be replaced, and went up to Serowe for a communal Christmas gathering in an IVS volunteer's house, along with our friends Peter and Jenny Agar, and some half dozen others. It rained steadily much of the time, but we ate our turkey and Christmas pudding, and played games, and sang Christmas carols on Christmas night by candlelight and oil lantern (normal in Serowe) with other families and friends. The rain stopped for a while on Boxing Day, and we had a good walk.

Through Rain to Okavango

On 27th we said goodbye to most of the party, and we and the Agars set out with two Land Rovers up bush roads to a lot of places you have never heard of, and probably can't even find on the map. We camped out for two nights, and spent one mosquito-ridden night in a sort of guest house which was pressed onto us by the local police inspector, who had apparently been overdoing his celebrations a bit. It rained a great deal, though not continuously, and the roads were very bad. There was a lot of switchbacking through large pools of water, and cutting through the bush to find less muddy routes, and all in all we were extremely grateful for the four-wheel drive on the Land Rovers. The fourth night out we spent expensively at the Island Safari Hotel in Maun, on the edge of the swamps – the Okavango delta. We had a pleasant lazy day there, and went canoeing on the swamps in an interval between showers.

Floods in the Wilderness

At this point we had to set off home, so as to put Bernard on his aeroplane (yesterday), but the Agars decided to stay on to the end of the public holiday (today). So we did two 500km stints in two days, breaking the journey at Francistown, where we camped out on someone I know (quite a job finding him at 9pm on New Year's Eve without an address, and in a town I had never visited before). The main roads on both stretches were about half earth, half gravel, and in very bad condition, because of almost unprecedented amounts of rain. Today, the roads are officially closed and impassable, so I should imagine the Agars are stuck. I only hope they are stuck in a town, not on the road – or, worse, in some pan miles off the road.

We saw a fair amount of game, including giraffes, which are fairly unusual here. The other Ford Foundation people were a bit worried about us, because they knew the state of the Land Rover, but in the event we only had three small breakdowns in the course of 2,000km of very rough driving, and only one of these (a worn generator bearing) needed garage attention. We did not need to be towed once, but it was comforting to have another vehicle in sight that could have towed us, or gone to get mechanical help. I think that altogether we gave Bernard a much more interesting Christmas than most of his classmates could have had.

Saying Goodbye to Bernard

It was very pleasant having Bernard back, and a wrench to put him on the plane again yesterday. He seems quite cheerful about going back to school, although I think that for a moment he was just a little watery-eyed as he left us.

I have very much enjoyed having a holiday – I haven't really had more than the odd two or three days off since summer 1976. Today I pottered around my garden, which is looking a bit neglected and miserable, and I feel as if I am going back to school myself tomorrow.

P.S. from Nicole

Thank you very much for all the useful items you sent me, and the pair of gloves is particularly welcome. Bernard's suitcase was like Father Christmas's bag, full of interesting presents. It was great having Bernard with us and we all felt sad when he left.

Our safari was very interesting but I was glad to get home in order to have a bath and get away from the mosquitoes. It is still raining and it does not look as if it is ever going to stop. We should not complain as I am sure we shall have a very hot spell afterwards.
Love, Nicole

Letter to parents   Gaborone, 30/01/1978

Collapsing Roads and Houses

It's sounds as if you are having a real winter this year. We have read of five inches of snow in Oxfordshire, but I don't know how long it stayed around.

Here, the weather is beginning to cool down, and the nights are getting noticeably longer, but the most dramatic thing about the weather recently has been torrential downpours. As you know, we had heavy rains during our Christmas trip to the North, which washed out a nice new stretch of tarmac road the day after we travelled over it. Since then there have been more washouts and heavy rains down here, which culminated in a real downpour two nights ago, causing quite a lot of mud-brick houses to collapse. My garden would have enjoyed it if it had been fully planted, but I'm afraid it has been a bit neglected recently because Johnson has been away rather a lot, and I have not had much spare time. I did some planting this week-end – a couple of rows of *Heinz 1370* tomatoes, which are meant to grow fast, produce good firm fruit, and be nematode-resistant, which is important here. Apart from that we only have a few cabbages, some rather over-picked broccoli, my original purple-sprouting broccoli, now up to six feet tall and beginning to collapse with still no sign of any heads, green peppers, chicory (endive – looking like healthy dandelion plants), some sweet corn, and a few beans.

Christophines, Peaches and Maggots

We also have one very healthy christophine – a plant from the wet tropics which resembles a curcurbit except that it has not got seeds, and one plants the entire fruit. We had our first crop of christophines (two of them) for lunch today, but it is a difficult fruit to harvest as it is very attractive to fruit fly (or pumpkin fly) and I have to keep on spraying with systemic insecticide.

Our peaches eventually ripened and proved - virtually without exception – to contain large rotten patches full of the maggots of the wretched fruit fly. Next year I shall have to spray those. But the good bits were excellent stewed.

A Rocky Campsite

Two weekends ago we went on a small camping trip with the Agars and various other friends, plus a friend of Dominic's. We slept on a large hill about forty miles from here, where we had hoped to find a dramatic waterfall and pools to bathe in, but the rain had not yet reached that spot, and there was a bare trickle of water which tended to dry up in the heat of the day. To say "we slept" is also a bit of an exaggeration, as we mostly spent rather restless nights on uneven and bumpy pieces of rock; but we had a good time.

Ghostly Lovers and Ticks

The only other living things we met on the mountain (which is believed to be inhabited by a pair of ghostly lovers) were cattle ticks, which we had to keep on picking off each others' legs. The aftermath of the trip was that Dominic got tick-bite fever – swollen glands and fever plus headache, but easily cured with antibiotics – and infected tick-bites. This merged into what our doctor diagnosed as chickenpox (his second go at that), so he has been missing school for the whole of last week. His friend came home with several ticks still attached, and also seems to have bad tick-bite fever. However, we must go up again soon to see if the recent rains have filled the stream.

A Scary Plane Trip

Last weekend I went off to Ghanzi in the far west of the country, on the Namibian border in fact, with the Minister and Acting Permanent Secretary. They went to talk to people about foot-and-mouth. I went to "familiarise" myself. We travelled by small charter plane, so the journey was very easy, except that we took off in a violent storm, and the first half-hour out of Gaborone was more unpleasant than any flight I have ever been on. It was raining all over the Kalahari desert. We had an interesting trip, and I certainly got to know the Minister better than before.

Yesterday evening we went to celebrate the marriage of our next-door neighbour's daughter (Botswanan) to her German volunteer boyfriend. It was a very jolly occasion, with lots to eat and drink and a lot of dancing.

Letter to parents   Gaborone, 12/02/1978

A Soggy Camp on Otse Mountain

I am feeling a bit disoriented in time today. Dominic and I and eight others camped on Otse mountain last night – the place we went to last time. We had hoped to find a lot more water in our pool, after all the rain, but although there was a lot more water in the stream, the pool was much as before until we pushed mud and grass into the dam wall which the Agars and others had built under the direction of another friend who has now returned to England.

During the afternoon we had some rain, and since we only had one two-man tent between the eight of us, we set to work to build a very rough lean-to shelter against a large rock. Enthusiasm waned when the rain stopped, but we finished the structure after a fashion, cutting down live branches that we would never have touched in the ordinary way, and laying grass over the whole thing to thatch it. It was just as well that we did so, because at bed time it started to rain again, and went on patchily right through the night. Five people slept in the tent, and five in the shelter.

I think I must have got the worst place. I was last in, sleeping in the doorway at the least-finished end, although "sleeping" is only a manner of speaking, because I didn't feel as if I had slept at all. I suppose, all the same, that I must have slept some of the time, or the night would surely have seemed even longer. At the other end of the shelter two Botswana girls who were with us slept like logs right through the night, and were still quite dry in the morning. By then, my sleeping bag was beginning to get very damp, although the most disconcerting aspect was big drops of water splashing into eyes or ears at unexpected moments. I think Dominic had a fair amount of sleep, although he was getting a bit damp and plaintive by dawn.

Fortunately the rain stopped with the daylight, although this was not very evident inside the lean-to, where the thatch continued to drip. We were able to make a good fire for breakfast, and dry ourselves out. We didn't skimp on breakfast either; by tradition we always eat well on these trips, even if it means carrying rather heavier packs than would otherwise be necessary. This morning we had sausages and pancakes; by the time we had finished those, no-one felt like fried eggs – those were carried back (still unfried).

Home to Recover

We were home by lunch, as some of the party had a lunch date, although I doubt if they were very sparkling. I went to bed for a couple of hours after lunch, and haven't been sure of the time since then.

After his last experience, Dominic was a bit dubious about going up the mountain this time, although I am sure that he enjoyed it greatly, and will enjoy it even more in retrospect. We had a visiting American from the World Bank with us this time, who chatted at length with Dominic, and pronounced him "very bright". He is certainly loquacious, and enjoys chatting.

After her experiences last time, Nicole decided to forego the pleasures of trudging through tick-ridden bush with a rucksack on her back, and sleeping on hard rocks in order to view a non-existent waterfall and bathe in a stagnant pool.

Tonight, the rain is pouring down again, harder I think than last night, breaking a period of dry weather. This should refill our swimming pool, which was beginning to get a little low. We have done very well to keep it full using only rainwater since the initial filling, and to have kept the same water clean and wholesome. Otherwise, however, the garden is a bit of a mess. The lawn needs cutting, and only a few of my vegetable patches are producing. Johnson has been absent rather a lot since Christmas, ill, "ill" on holiday, or kept away by rain. I also need to collect another load of manure to put the vegetable patches back into good heart.

The English Winter

It sounds as if you are having a winter which is fun for the young rather than for your generation. On Saturday, before we left, Jenny Agar had just phoned her parents, who announced that since it was the coldest day for twenty years, they were not intending to get out of bed at all. I hope that you are keeping warm and comfortable.

Letter from Nicole to Sheila   Gaborone, 13/02/1978

Musical Pursuits

David has been meaning to write to you since Christmas but I think he will never get round to doing it. He is very busy, not only at work but he spends much of his free time (there is not a lot of it) practising the cello. He joined the orchestra of the Gaborone music society, thinking that it would be an opportunity to practise the cello once a week, but I am afraid they are aiming very high. We are having a concert on 10th March. The orchestra will perform one of the *Brandenburg* Concertos and an *Overture* by Bach. Besides that they will accompany the choir (in which I am singing) in *Missa Sancti Nicolai* by Haydn.

A Christmas Swim with Crocodiles

We spent Christmas 300 kilometres from here at a friend's. It rained all the time and reminded us very much of the English Christmas. It was ideal weather to cook the turkey. Had it been hot the kitchen would have been unbearable. On 27th December we started a five day journey towards the North. It was a very interesting trip despite the bad state of the roads. We stayed a day and a night in Maun at a hotel which is just on the edge of the river. We spent the afternoon canoeing and David had a swim. He was told afterwards by the owner of the hotel that there are crocodiles and hippopotamus in the river.

Dangerous Weather

We were back home on 1st January so that Bernard could catch his plane. We came back just in time as the road which we took was closed on Monday 2nd and for several days because it had been damaged by heavy rains. We had torrential rains and floods; mud huts have collapsed and a few people have been killed in the process. Sometimes as a roof people use corrugated iron held down with stones. When the hut collapses the roof and stones fall on the inhabitants.

School Progress

It was nice having Bernard with us. He looked very well and happy. He worked quite well last term and all his teachers are pleased with his progress although they said that he should learn to relax more. I know he worries a lot about his work and I sympathise with him as I was just the same. We are looking forward to seeing Bernard again in five weeks' time. Dominic also is doing well at school and is particularly good at Maths. He has just been promoted to a new form as the academic year here starts in January.

A Damp Camp

On Saturday David, Dominic and some friends went camping on top of a small mountain 55 kilometres from Gaborone. It rained most of the night and they came back very wet and David caught a cold. He is feeling very miserable. About a month ago we went camping there and besides the ticks we had a very restless night as we had to sleep on the rock. Three of our party, including Dominic, got tick bite fever (swollen glands, headaches and temperature) and after that Dominic developed chicken pox, which he had had when he was ten months old. These are the joys of adventure in Africa.

(Letter continued by David)
Garden Peaches

I find to my surprise that I have been here for almost a year. It's about time to start thinking about what to do next.

Thank you for having Bernard for his half term. He seems to have enjoyed himself a lot. He wrote saying that he had found one of my old school books. I'm surprised you still have any of them. They were not great works of art; perhaps they have some nostalgic value, but I expect that really you have simply not got round to throwing them out.

Flooded Deserts

I hope you are through the worst of the winter. It seems to have been pretty grim in many places. Here, the nights are closing in, and are becoming a bit cooler. By mid-day it is usually pretty warm. Much of Botswana has had unusual quantities of rain this year. We told you how wet it was during our Christmas trip, and along the eastern edge of the country to the north of Gaborone it has gone on raining. In fact, the rain has penetrated well into the desert, and the vets who are meant to be out fighting the foot-and-mouth epidemic are having a terrible time with floods in the desert. This is not so paradoxical as it might sound. A lot of Botswana has inland drainage systems, i.e. instead of running to the sea, the watercourses run into the pans, where the water evaporates, or they simply peter out. Several "lakes" now have water in them for the first time in many years, or are very much bigger than normal. This may be a bit of a problem for us, since we are planning a camping trip at Easter. John Mittel and Sue, our former neighbours at Woodstock, are coming out for a holiday, and we would like to take them around a bit, and show them some game.

Ancient Land Rover

We shall also be keeping our fingers crossed about the Land Rover, which is due for replacement, and is at the end of a six-month waiting list. In some ways this is beneficial to us, as the three other Ford Foundation families are scared to use the old vehicle, and leave it for us. Life will be far more competitive when there is a smart reliable new Land Rover available.

Giant Hailstones

My garden is still a bit of a mess, but I have a few more things growing. I am hoping to get a crop from my Witloof chicory, which looks very healthy, but I see that I ought to wait for a frost before digging it. I am a little apprehensive lest the nematodes move in before June. Today I dug what I had hoped would be a flourishing patch of sweet potatoes, and found virtually nothing. I am not sure why. My plants got knocked about rather badly by a hailstorm on Thursday. I happened to be out in it, driving around looking for a rehearsal. Out of curiosity, I got out of the car and picked up a few hailstones. They were certainly the size of marbles, very irregularly shaped, but often more than an inch long. When I got home I had neither telephone nor electricity. I reported the telephone fault, but was told I would have to wait several days. I therefore mended it myself. The problem was very obvious. Part of a tree had fallen over the line connecting our house to the nearest telephone pole, and had pulled the wires out, so I reconnected them. The telephone men came this morning, and were reluctant to believe that the job had been done.

Orchestral Debut

On Friday we had a most important cultural event: Haydn's *"Missa Sancti Nicolai"* by the Gaborone Singers, accompanied by the Gaborone Orchestra, and Bach's *Overture No. 3*, by the orchestra. The orchestra started the evening rather nervously, and made a few odd mistakes, but it was generally felt that it had never performed better (which was hardly surprising, since it had never performed before). Today, we started rehearsing for the next occasion. Nicole should have been among the singers, but went down last weekend with very complete and debilitating laryngitis, and was only just sufficiently recovered to come and listen.

Visit to Guadeloupe

Have we broken to you that we are unlikely to come to England at all this year? For once, I am in a position to afford the air fares to Guadeloupe, and since I do not know when this is likely to happen again, I think we should take advantage of the fact, and go there.
Much love, David and Nicole

On 4th April 1978, the (British) Daily Telegraph published the letter below-

ONE WHO ESCAPED IN BOTSWANA

SIR—As I am probably the last Briton to have seen 18-year-old Nicholas Love and Billy de Beer and Mike Arden alive in Botswana, and only by providential chance escaped the same brutish execution at the hands of paramilitary Botswana border guards, I have a duty to write to you.

Nicholas Love and I were on holiday together for the last two months on a "working vacation" at the Gilfillan Game Farm in Botswana, where we shared the same quarters. We both had been issued with tourist visas by the Botswana Government.

When I arrived back from South Africa yesterday I was horrified by the apparent indifference of our Foreign Secretary to the pleas of Mr and Mrs Love, that he should demand a full and independent inquiry into the killing of their son.

Equally outrageous is the failure of any Foreign Office spokesman to challenge the patently self-contradictory stories from the office of the President, Sir Seretse Khama, which try to "whitewash" this atrocity by claiming that my three friends were "spying" for Rhodesia.

From my direct knowledge I can swear that at no time was Nicholas Love (nor indeed Billy de Beer nor Mike Arden) involved in any form of political, military or intelligence-gathering activities whatever. I cannot remember any of us even discussing politics. Our conversations were always about the wild animals, game movements, home, the farm, vehicle repairs, the daily work schedules and the 15 Botswanans who also worked for Mr Gilfillan.

Deliberately, none of us ever wore military-type clothes nor camouflaged jackets. The only weapons we had were a small calibre 0·22 semi automatic "poacher's" rifle and a 0·3006 hunting rifle (for which de Beer held a licence). With these we shot for the pot rabbits and our almost staple diet of young impala deer.

Does neither the truth, the dignity of this country, nor indeed the safety of British subjects in possession of a United Kingdom passport, any longer interest Her Majesty's Government?

At this moment Dr David Owen would seem to be evading his direct responsibility by the all-too-simple expedient of saying nothing, thereby helping to give general credence to the totally false reports from Botswana.

If in such dreadful instances the Foreign Secretary timidly prefers to put expediency and short-term political considerations before principle and the human rights of British citizens abroad, then he should say so.

Then at least my friends' death will have served to warn other young Englishmen travelling overseas.
NICHOLAS C. GOODALL
London, W.8.

Letter to parents   Gaborone, 06/04/1978

An Infamous Killing

True, I haven't written for a long time. We are now in the middle of a visit from John Mittel and Sue Richards, our former next door neighbours in Woodstock. They have bought themselves a house in Eynsham – two old stone cottages knocked into one – but still managed to scrape together the money to come out here for four weeks. I took last week off work, and we went camping up in the Tuli Block – scene of the recent incident in which one British tourist and two South Africans were shot by the Botswana Defence Force (BDF). In fact we were having a drink at the Tuli Lodge, where some of these people were staying, when the BDF first turned up. They were quiet and well-behaved, and apart from asking us a few casual questions, caused us no trouble, but they did take away a house guest for questioning. I don't know if he was one of those shot the next day. Of course, Gaborone is buzzing with rumours, some of which are plain silly, but no one will ever be certain what really happened.

As it was, we were quite unaware that anything untoward had happened until after we had left the area.

A Dead Elephant

We had a very good camping place on a Development Corporation farm which I had previously visited officially, and we saw a bit of game, despite the recent heavy rains that have allowed game to disperse over normally dry areas. We also removed a very smelly tusk from a very smelly dead elephant, shot by poachers, that had chosen to die on the farm. Afterwards I stank, and had to wash very thoroughly in the river near our campsite. There were in fact two rivers, one being a "sand" river that had been in spate, but gradually disappeared in the week we were there, running into the great green greasy Limpopo, which was very muddy and swollen (the South African press suggested that two of the shot men had wandered across the border by mistake. As one of my friends remarked, they must have been exceptionally high-minded men, since the border is the Limpopo).

First Aid for the Land Rover

We had one breakdown on the way to the farm, which meant a night on the road, but we were well set up for camping and did not suffer, and John managed to patch up the Land Rover for the rest of the week. We finally left our camp on Thursday, and spent one night in the bush, before going on to the mining town of Selebi Philowe, and then south down the main road, to deliver a letter at Mahalapye. Then we turned off the main road again and took some very back roads into the Shoshong hills, where we camped for our last night out. We had intended to spend a further night in the Sandveld, but everyone was getting rather tired, and when I found there was a quicker way home we took it, and arrived here on Saturday evening. It was probably just as well, as I had an attack of diarrhoea, and John was developing tick-bite fever. Despite medication, he has been limping around all week because of a sore leg and a swollen gland. Certainly I didn't feel like any exertion resembling work on Sunday, but by Monday I was recovered and feeling very much refreshed by the holiday.

Farewell to Friends and Family

We have just seen John and Sue off on the train to Francistown. From there, they will take the bus to Maun, so as to get a look at the swamps. I was quite impressed by the comfort of the train (Rhodesia Railways). I fear that the local bus will be a bit rougher.

Tomorrow, to my great regret, we shall see Bernard off for another fourteen weeks. His holidays here really are very short. Fortunately, he doesn't seem worried or upset by the idea of going back to school.

News of a School Friend

I am interested to read about Keith Hill. He always did intend to go into politics – as indeed I did at one time. Of course, he will not win this seat, but he will probably get a better chance later. I don't think I could stand the tedium of being a back-bench MP. It really is a very low-grade job.

Letter from Nicole to   Gaborone, 10/04/1978
Sheila and Family

I hope that Spring is with you and that you have got rid of the bad weather for good. I am sure that there are lots of primroses and violets all over the place. It is still hot during the day here but the nights and the early mornings are quite chilly. There is a sort of autumn feeling in the air.

Bernard spent his two weeks' holiday with us and left last Friday. We had quite a house-full for two weeks; two friends from England are spending a month with us. We spent the first week of the holiday travelling and camping, starting with three very restful days camping on a farm which belongs to the Botswana Development Corporation. Our camp was only half a mile from the Limpopo River; we were camping very near the place where the two South Africans and the British tourist were shot two weeks ago. We only learned about the shooting when we came back to civilisation.

Bernard's School Breaks

When I saw you last September you said that you would be very happy to have Bernard for a holiday. I wonder whether it will be possible for you to have him during this coming half-term which runs from May 26th to 4th June. Bernard said that he will be very glad to come and stay with you. If it is possible for you to have him, please get in touch with our friend Margaret Chisholm at Woodstock, to arrange the day and time when you are collecting him.

Faith in Witch Doctors

Apart from a few green peppers our garden is not producing anything at the moment. The gardener was away for several days around Christmas and he does not seem to have caught up with the work. I do not think he has been feeling very well for the last few weeks. I have finally persuaded him to go and see the doctor at the local hospital. He does not believe in doctors and wanted a few days off to go to his village to see the witch doctor.

Winter Looms

The swimming pool is in a bad state; there is a leak somewhere and the water is quickly disappearing. Anyway soon we would have to empty it. The water is very cold now and at the beginning of next month it will be too cold to swim.

New Ventures

David has started to build a chicken run. We might be self-sufficient in eggs soon.
Love to you all, Nicole

P.S. from David

Nicole is nice enough not to mention that I also started to build a chicken run in Tanzania. It was very useful to hang clothes on.

A Trip to the Kalahari

We are planning another short trip to the bush this weekend – always supposing our friends return and the Land Rover goes etc. – this time to the Central Kalahari. I expect we shall find the nights very chilly there now. I went last year, a little bit later than this, and slept in all my clothes in my sleeping bag in a tent and was barely warm enough. There was ice on the washing water next day.
I hope you are all flourishing, Love, David

Letter to parents   Gaborone, 23/04/1978

Lions in the Night

We are on our own again, having said goodbye to John and Sue. I think they enjoyed themselves. Last weekend we took them out to the Central Kalahari, along with another vehicle full of acquaintances (best to travel in convoy in case of breakdowns) and we saw a few gemsbok (several times, but I think probably the same ones each time) and ostriches (almost devalued by their common-ness) and very little else. Lions were heard near our camp, but not seen. The emptiness of the place is very attractive, at least to me. Nicole came too – her first time in the Kalahari. The Land Rover behaved well, and there were no serious mishaps, although Nicole got a painful cut on her ear when John drove the Land Rover under a low tree while we were up on top (I did the same to him two weeks earlier, but I think I at least expressed contrition!)

A Day in Kanye

This weekend, Dominic is down with some bug. It's flu, or some virus thing. One of his friends has just had a similar bout of temperature and tiredness and, in Dominic's case, a sore throat. This comes at an inopportune time, since he has just started his real Easter holiday (the one we took at Easter was unofficial) and was meant to go off to Kanye for a week to stay with some former neighbours who are now involved in a rural industries project there. We tried to phone them, but in the end I went down alone, and spent most of the day there. They were very welcoming, and Ossie (Oswald Schmidt) wanted to show me all over the Centre, and talk about work; his work is not officially connected with mine but he is part of the general rural development network. I have just got back in fact – I suppose it's the best part of 100 miles each way, although that doesn't seem very far here.

Sweet Music?

Last night we had a music society evening, with a variety of high-class entertainment including the Gaborone Orchestra (all ten of them) playing a Mozart piano duet rearranged for orchestra, and variations on *"Frere Jacques"* arranged, like the Mozart, by the conductor of the orchestra. We were meant to have the affair outside, but the lighting proved temperamental. In the event, I think we would have been rather chilly. I had to borrow a pullover for the drive home tonight.

Letter to parents-in-law   Gaborone, 21/05/1978
from Nicole

New Arrivals

There is a lovely fire in the sitting room and it is really cosy. Everywhere else in the house it is freezing cold. There is an Autumn feeling in the air; the sun is only just warm and the leaves are falling. We are just harvesting our last tomatoes and green peppers. You will be interested to know that David acquired ten hens last week. They should start laying in three weeks' time. They are no trouble for the time being as long as David keeps on feeding them and giving them water. The dog does not seem very interested in them. Dominic is looking after the chickens while David is away.

50 pula for each Cow

David left on Thursday morning for Maun. Next he will be travelling in the region of the Okavango delta, the most beautiful and interesting part of Botswana. He is to investigate whether the 50-*pula* scheme is working all right. As the farmers cannot sell their cattle because of the foot-and-mouth disease, they are given 50 *pula* for each cow which they bring to be branded. It is a loan from the government and when the disease is over and the farmers can again sell their cattle, they will have to give back those 50 *pulas*. David was the instigator of this scheme. He will be home sometime next week.

An EEC Event

Dominic and I went out for lunch today. It was quite a big do given by the EEC Representative in Botswana. The food was very good and Dominic thoroughly enjoyed himself; apart from him there were two other teenage children. I was complimented on the behaviour of my son and on him being very sociable and grown up. Dominic is certainly growing up and is doing very well at school. He had to prepare an essay on pollution during the weekend, did it all on his own, and did not need any help at all.

Holiday Plans

We shall all be in England for a short stay on our way back from Guadeloupe but unfortunately we shall not all be arriving together. David will be arriving in U.K. on 2nd September. I think he will come straight to Leicester, spending the weekend with you and departing again on the Monday for London where he will be visiting ODM and other people. The children and I will be arriving on Monday 4th September. We shall go to Woodstock in order to get Bernard ready for school; I think he will be late starting school. Dominic and I will try to come and spend one night with you, 6th – 7th September. We shall have to leave England on the 8th as our ticket is a 45-day excursion ticket, and anyway Dominic is starting school again on 13th September.

Bernard will be spending his half-term holiday with Sheila and family. I am sure he will enjoy it and will be pleased to see Stephen and James again.

The President of Botswana and his wife were in England last week. I suppose you have had glimpses of them on T.V.

A Long Way to the Shoe Shop!

A friend, her daughter and I drove to Rustenburg (South Africa) on Thursday. It is 350 km from here, and is the biggest town one comes across before reaching Johannesburg. I needed a pair of shoes and took the opportunity to buy a few things which are not always available in Gaborone. I had to drive both ways as my friend, who is American, is only used to cars with automatic gear changing and as she has a chauffeur here she has not bothered to learn to drive cars with manual gear changing.

Agriculture in the Okavango District

(On the back of this letter are notes written by our father about David's visit to the Okavango swamps, where water levels were at their highest for twenty years and croplands were 3ft under water. David's department were organising the vaccination and tagging of selected cows against foot-and-mouth. Our father took great pride and interest in David's work and kept friends at Stoneygate Church well informed.)

Letter to parents-in-law
from Nicole

Gaborone, 18/06/1978

A Quiet Holiday in Guadeloupe

Thank you for the Canasta rules. We will teach Dominic to play Canasta during our holidays. We will not have a very busy social life while we are in Guadeloupe. My brother and his family are spending the summer holidays in France, so I expect we will spend the evenings quietly at home with my parents. It will be a change from our busy social life here, where we have to entertain quite a lot and are often invited out to dinner.

Amateur Dramatics

I cannot remember whether David told you that I had a small part in a play put on by the local Amateur Dramatic Group. The play was *"Private Lives"* by Noel Coward. My part was only a few lines in French; I was a French maid. The play was performed last week and was very successful. We had a full house on all four evenings. I enjoyed it very much and we all had great fun. It took a lot of my time and for several weeks I was out nearly every evening.

David Visits Lesotho

David left yesterday for Lesotho. I think he is going to take part in some negotiations for the sale of meat to EEC countries. He travelled with the Director of the Botswana Meat

Commission and some other officials. I would have liked to go with him as I have heard so much about Lesotho through David and friends who have visited that country.

Chilly Weather and Illness…

Dominic was free from coughs and colds for two weeks but now that it has turned very cold (there has been frost every night since last Monday) he is starting another cold. I hope Margaret had Becky's whooping cough treated, or she may be left with a nasty cough for quite a few years. David is feeling better now but he had a touch of bronchitis two weeks ago. It is very cold this year and it does not even get very warm during the day.

….but Healthy Hens!

Our chickens are very healthy and to our surprise one of them laid an egg yesterday, and another this morning. David had already had his breakfast when he visited the hens and found the egg, so Dominic was designated to eat the egg for breakfast as he looks after the hens. I had the second one for breakfast this morning. They are very good tasty eggs. We now have eleven hens; friends of ours were given a hen by another friend who left Botswana last Friday. As they did not want to kill it they gave it to us. At first the new hen was very belligerent towards our hens and wanted the whole place for herself, but they soon learnt to live with each other.

Holiday Address

Bernard will be going to Paris on 15th July where he will stay with my brother Denys and family for a few days. He will fly to Guadeloupe on 20th July. Our address in Guadeloupe will be: care of Mme Fortuné, La Grand Case, Sainte Anne. We shall leave Gaborone on 27th July.

Cub Scouts

Dominic is enjoying Cubs and has now passed his Bronze Arrow and his Reader Badge. I help Akela and it is hard work to keep thirty boys quiet and busy for one and a half hours. We would like to have a third helper but nobody has come forward yet.

Letter to parents   Gaborone, 25/06/1978

Chilly Africa

I am sitting in the living room, with a nice log fire, and for a change the smoke is all going up the chimney. We really need the fire; outside it is very chilly, and we have had frosts in the last few days, which have burnt up the banana trees and paw-paws. I spent the first half of last week in Lesotho, where it is even colder, but most of the time we were indoors in meetings, and I kept the air conditioner on to "warm" in my room whether I was in or not. I figured that it wouldn't make any difference to the bill, and the hotel could afford it at the rates they were charging us. ·

EEC Deals

We were working on a common Botswana, Lesotho and Swaziland approach to EEC questions. My own main concern there was beef, where we get a lot of money out of a rather precarious deal with the EEC. The trip was very interesting, because our team was really exceptionally good. The Swazi team was smaller but fairly competent; and the Lesotho team, true to form, was virtually non-existent, totally unbriefed, and extremely troublesome.

Music Hath Charms

Last night we had a Music Society members' evening at the National Museum. Our orchestra played some simple arrangements, and struggled manfully with a Bach *Fantasia and Fugue*, which was fun to play; but when I asked a friend for a frank opinion, he said it sounded as if each of us was playing a different piece of music in competition with the others. That was a very cold evening, as there is no heating in the National Museum. There were some very good contributions, particularly piano and vocal, but the hot dogs we collected afterwards were not enough to dispel the chill, and we hurried off home for hot cocoa. Nonetheless, we are all now in reasonably good form. Dominic seems to have stopped coughing, and I have shaken off the nasty bronchial cough I have had.

The Gaborone Players

Today we had an outside lunch with the families and cast of Gaborone Players' *"Private Lives"*. Did I tell you Nicole had been in this? She played a French maid, whose lines consisted mainly of shouted abuse – in French. It was a very good production, and I was amused today to find out how true to their parts the two main men were – one solidly English and unimaginative, and the other a sort of Bertie Wooster character. The sun was warm, and the whole occasion very pleasant.

An Enviable Afrikaaner Farmhouse

The chap who produced the play and hosted the lunch works at Agricultural Research, ten miles out of town, and has the house formerly occupied by the farm manager when the research station was a private farm. Just next to their little modern house stands the original Afrikaaner farmhouse, which was "condemned" by the authorities ten years ago, but still looks very sound – a big eighty-year old two-storey house, all built of unburnt clay brick. If I lived there, I would want to switch houses. They are surrounded by fields, and have inherited about ten really good orange trees along with the house. I am sure that if you lived in this sort of climate, you would want to grow orange trees. They are very attractive to look at as well as useful to have. I think there is something surreal about such bright fruit among the dark leaves. I read somewhere that in the days of orangeries, an orange scion used to be grafted onto a holly stock, and it is easy to imagine that the two trees could be close relatives.

Career Considerations

I am beginning to consider whether to cut loose from the Civil Service and take another two-year contract here. It may appear somewhat imprudent, but I am not enamoured of the British Civil Service, and I think one of the lessons of this job is that I am a saleable "Expert", and I doubt if there will be a decline in the need of developed countries for expertise on developing countries. What I really need to do is put the seal on my expertise with another book, but there is no likelihood of my doing that either here, or in the Ministry of Overseas Development.

Letter to parents

Gaborone, 09/10/1978

Looking for Lions at Khutse

Last weekend was stretched by a public holiday, and we went off to Khutse game reserve along with Peter and two of his friends, the rural sociologist from the ministry and his wife and year-old son, and a newly arrived French couple who work at the vaccine laboratory, with their three-year-old son. We were a fairly heterogenous group (four nationalities) but all got on very well. Peter remarked afterwards that we hadn't talked much, but that it hadn't seemed to matter. Dominic was very good with the two younger children, and all of them were fairly tolerable.

Our car set off on Friday evening to get an early start, and we slept out near to the road 150km from home. The others caught us up at lunch time on Saturday. I had put an elaborate series of sticks and arrows in the roadway, so that they would not drive past, but they drove past all but the last signal, which was a tall dry veld plant impossibly planted in the middle of the road.

We went further than usual, to a pass where we had heard that there was a fair amount of game, and we were rewarded by seeing very much more than on other occasions, although still no lions. As usual, we heard lions during the night, and we went for a drive around in the bush on Sunday morning and found a fresh kill, but no sign of the lion. In fact had we not been rather afraid of his reappearance we might have got down and helped ourselves to a leg of kudu.

We had some fuel worries, since neither Peter nor I had brought as much as usual, but my combination of two tanks plus two jerry cans was more than adequate. I had to give both the cans to Peter, and arrived home with more than half a tank myself. As it turned out, mechanical worries would have been more justified, as the steering mechanism started to shake loose. Fortunately Mac (the sociologist) is a better mechanic than I, and had brought a good set of spanners with him, so we were able to stop and fix things en route.

Having a four-day weekend makes all the difference to these trips. It meant that we were able to spend two nights at the same camp, and have a leisurely trip, instead of rushing all the while. I could quite happily have spent a whole week there, once we had got established with a big wood-pile, tents up for those who wanted to sleep indoors, sleeping places, rubbish tip etc. Most of the day there was some game on the pan, coming to lick salt, as the surface water had long dried up, but the game was most plentiful in the morning when we woke up – kudu, hartebeeste, gemsbok, springbok, and even one big heavy eland, like a cow gone wrong (funny that we mostly have to use Afrikaans names).

One other party drove onto the pan while we were there. We knew one of them, and we looked at each other through binoculars, but apart from that we had several hundred (probably several thousand) square km to ourselves.

On Safari at Khutse Game Park, Botswana

Dug-out canoe, Motloutse River near Francistown, Botswana

Paid Employment for Nicole

Nicole is working again, this time for the Ministry of Agriculture. The new vaccine factory is being established and run by a French company, and Nicole has been recruited as translator/secretary. She is also working very hard in all her "spare" time finishing some typing she had taken on when she thought she was unemployed, for an economic consultant whose writing is ten times worse than my own.

Another New Gardener, and a New Contract

We have had another change of gardeners. The new one is not so bright as the old (who took offence when I told him off for letting my plants die while we were on leave) but is a fairly cheery soul. He has watered most of my seedling tomatoes right out of their box. The garden is not in great heart, and could do with a load of manure, but is slowly picking up. Today I bought a very expensive expanse of plastic netting to make a net-house (to reduce the sunlight as well as the birds). I hope I get round to it before next winter.

I am in the process of renewing my contract until 1981.

P.S. Our Woodstock tenants have stopped paying rent, and I have just told my solicitors to give them notice to quit. I hope it works.

Letter to parents

Gaborone, 15/10/1978

Overtime for Nicole

Nicole is tapping away on the typewriter in my study, which she has completely taken over for the last three weeks. An economic consultant whose handwriting is even worse than mine had arranged for her to type his report when she got her job with the vets. Unfortunately, the report keeps on getting longer. The author has repeatedly thanked me fulsomely for my useful comments and good advice, but keeps on ignoring one of my main points, which is that he is writing too much, and the longer his report gets, the less impact it will have. I have said this of two successive drafts, the second of which was about three times as long as the first, and the final report promises to be twice as long again.

The consultant is, in fact, one of the qualities of life in Gaborone as far as I am concerned, and I shall be very sorry when he goes in a month's time (not so, I think, Nicole). He is academically extremely good, but is also a mine of ideas on all subjects. That's really the trouble with his report – he can't resist putting all his ideas down.

Dramatic Weather and Rat Droppings

We have had our first real rains of this season, accompanied by spectacular lightning and explosive thunderclaps. It was as if the house was being shelled on Friday night. Also, the weather is getting hotter, and the garden calls, so I have spent most of the weekend in it, putting up my net house, digging, collecting and fetching manure (rat droppings in sawdust from the vet. lab.) and mending cracks in our invalid swimming pool. Next week I plan to go out and get a whole lot of manure with two friends.

Chungalolos

Dominic spent a lot of today collecting "chungalolos" – big black centipedes – from the garden, and throwing them to the chickens, and found it difficult to get to sleep tonight, because he had chungalolos on his mind. I know the feeling. I remember not being able to sleep after an afternoon surrounded by a cloud of flies in Bradgate Park.

Welcoming the Officials

I am not looking forward to a Ford Foundation visitation next week, not because I fear inspection or other unpleasant surprises, but because I am the *de facto* Ford Foundation representative, and I shall have to waste a lot of time chauffeuring and arranging social things for the visitors. I shall be pleased to see them onto the plane on Wednesday, even though it will involve a 65km drive, since the airport here is out of commission, as seems to happen at least once a year. I have to get up early to collect them tomorrow. They'll really feel they have landed in a bush post, coming down on a gravel runway, going through immigration in a tent, and then being picked up in my increasingly battered and tatty car.

Letter to Sheila and Ron from Nicole   Gaborone, 15/10/1978

Overworked and Exhausted!

I enclose a birthday cheque for Stephen and Juliet. Once again their birthday cards and present will be late, although I have been thinking about it for days but I do not have much spare time, in fact I have no spare time at all. I am working more or less full time day and night. Besides my job in the morning I have been asked by an economic consultant, friend of David, to type a very lengthy report which is going on and on. I have been at it for the last three weeks and there are still eight more chapters to come. I am really fed up as I spend all my afternoons and my evenings typing away.

It is getting hot again but the evenings and early mornings are still pleasant. On Friday night we had a terrific storm which lasted all night. We hardly slept as the combination of thunder and raindrops on the roof made a lot of noise; as soon as we shut our eyes and fell asleep there would be a loud crash of thunder and we would wake up. Our swimming pool is not fixed yet (it is leaking) as David and I are too busy to do any repairs. All the same David started to fill in some cracks today, with epoxy resin.

I am worn out and need another holiday!
Love from Nicole

A Successful Operation, and an Invitation

We're very pleased to hear that Daddy's hip operation is safely completed. Despite what the doctors say, I bet it will give him greater mobility, because he is active and mobile anyway. I'm sure the important thing is to use it as much as possible as soon as this is allowed. Perhaps when you are feeling all fit and bouncy again, you would like to come out here for a spot of warm weather. I'm sure you would like it, and it's not yet too late to think of coming here for Christmas. If the connections from Johannesburg didn't meet up, we would always be ready to come down by car to fetch you, although probably you would find the air connection more comfortable simply because it involves less sitting still – one hour, instead of four driving. Or you could take the train to Mafeking – slow, but comfortable – and we could pick you up there. Alternatively, we shall probably come to the U.K. in April, and you could come back with us. Please treat this suggestion seriously.

Another Vanishing Gardener

I have spent much of this weekend gardening, and enlarging my net house. I like to potter, and exasperate Nicole by looking at my seedlings several times a day (which I think is a sensible thing to do here, since they can suddenly dry up and die, or get eaten by something, if not watched). But recently I have had little time to potter at weekends. My latest gardener has been coming to work less and less frequently, and was obviously quite happy to be given the sack two days ago, so I have to rush around with the hose, as well as spraying everything in sight with the nastiest insecticides I can find, and fill in the gaps with hard manual labour on the net house. I am so satisfied with the latter that I am now making it bigger; formerly, it was box-like. Now I am spreading the walls out like a tent. By adding 18% more net I can get 40% more ground under netting. Of course, I may feel differently if everything collapses and dies, which is a danger, since one does create a damper climate inside the net.

Cherished Results

The productive parts of the garden are fairly satisfactory. I have a tight patch of nice little cabbages heading up, and some rather small onions beginning to form bulbs. My sweet corn is rather poor. I am only just beginning to appreciate the importance of digging over this dense soil, just to allow plants to get their roots through. It's no use trying to use one thorough cultivation for two successive crops. The spinach has served well, but is beginning to get eaten by ravenous ladybirds, so I have just sprayed that. I have a patch of very hefty transplanted self-sown tomatoes, just forming fruit. My two new apple trees have transplanted well, and one actually has an apple on it. There are grapes on one of my two-year-old vines. My two surviving delicate citrus trees (grapefruit and tangerine) are growing well, as are the two tough rough lemons – but still no fruit. And the great big useless peach tree has about a dozen peaches on it – going to go well into the fruit-fly season before they ripen. The chickens are laying 7-9 eggs a day, and are beginning to earn their keep.

Dominic's Progress

Dominic has exams tomorrow, to see if he can move into the next standard. Apart from atrocious spelling, he causes little anxiety. His teacher says he's a pleasure to teach, which I find rather extraordinary. All the same, he is a very nice helpful, cheerful easy child now (I don't think parenthood biases my judgement on that point).

Christmas Approaches

Nicole says that if you are at a loose end for presents, she would like *"The Human Factor"* by Graham Green as combined birthday plus Christmas. I would like *"In Extremity"* (a book on Gerard Manley Hopkins) by John Robinson. They must be sent by book post, and wrapped in some special way if they are to avoid quite heavy duty. The easiest way of dealing with this is probably to order from Blackwells, Broad Street, Oxford, and ask them to look after

wrapping and postage. If other members of the family want to know what to send, we need drying up cloths. Bernard would appreciate some felt pens. What would you like?
Much love, David

P.S. from Nicole – We would love to have you here and Dominic would be particularly thrilled. The house is cooled and as we do not pay electricity charges we can have the air-conditioners day and night. I am sure you would love it.

I left Dominic's duffle coat in the front bedroom cupboard. As it will be too small for him when we come back to U.K. I think you can give it to either Sheila or Margaret for one of their children.
Love from Nicole

Letter to parents   Gaborone, 11/12/1978

Greetings and Congratulations

Happy Christmas, happy birthday (Daddy), and happy New Year! I hope you are in good shape for the festivities, and that Daddy's new hip is limbering up. I heard recently of someone who took up mountain climbing after getting a new hip, so I have great expectations of Daddy now that he is all hipped up. At least, I'm sure you will be able to drive again, and I expect you are already doing so, although I do think it is sensible for Mummy to keep her hand in. The traffic really hasn't suddenly got much worse; and anyway, the worse it is the slower it is.

The Joys of Air Travel

We didn't really expect to persuade you to come to Botswana for Christmas, but the invitation stands. Remember that it is quite unnecessary for you to carry any luggage at all once you have been delivered to the airport. The airline will do it all for you, and deliver you and your luggage to us at Gaborone airport. At the drop of a hat, they'll dump you both into wheel chairs and give you the same automatic treatment as the luggage (but a bit gentler), although I am sure you would neither want nor enjoy such attentions. Mind you, I did come across one muddled old lady last time I was at Johannesburg airport who had been shepherded onto a variety of flights, and thought she was already in London where she would be met by her son, whereas in fact I think she had only managed to get back to where she started out. Of course, most people do lug baggage around with them, but that's only because they will insist on trying to carry more than a perfectly adequate travel allowance, by pretending that those two enormous holdalls contain the little odds and ends that they have to have with them on the flight.

As for having "done" Africa – I am lost for words, or would be if I thought you were serious. I expect you have done Europe too. It's all the same isn't it? Anyway, "our" Africa is quite unlike the bits you did in 1967.

Visit to Kanye

We have had one of Dominic's friends, a Canadian ex-neighbour whose parents are good friends of ours, with us for the last week, and yesterday we took them both back to the friend's home in Kanye for the return visit. We stayed the night in a guest *rondavel* they have at Rural Innovation Centre where they live and work. Yesterday afternoon I took the children crab fishing in some irrigation ditches fed from a large and generally fairly useless dam that was built as part of the war effort. The Taiwan Chinese had an irrigation scheme going there for a few years, but were kicked out when Botswana decided to recognise the mainland Chinese.

A Virulent Weed

Now a harassed Canadian volunteer is trying to run the scheme for a local development trust, but his main crop appears to be nut-sedge grass. This crafty plant produces lots of little nuts which get left in the ground when the parent plant is pulled out or cultivated, and which then sprout with great vigour. It seems extraordinary that a weed like this should appear to be totally uncontrollable.

Too Many Tiny Crabs!

The wages of our self-indulgence in crab fishing was the penance of spending the entire morning removing the meat from nineteen crabs – small crabs by your standards. I made a Guadeloupean dish of stuffed crabs for lunch, which went down well.

Back to the Garden

We left Kanye fairly early this afternoon, because I wanted to be home in time to care for my garden. We have been having very hot and totally rain-less weather (105′ F in the shade) which simply knocks the plants down and shrivels them up (it has a similar effect on Nicole; I, strangely, am more heat-resistant). However, we were surprised to find that Gaborone had evidently had a good downpour while we in Kanye had been lamenting the continued drought. I didn't have to do any watering. Unfortunately, I suspect that the rain was very local, and tomorrow my Permanent Secretary will again be complaining that his little farm ten miles down the road has been missed, in favour of the town gardeners who don't really need rain anyway.

My net house is flourishing, and is beginning to produce some crops, despite the heat and the usual crop of bugs and diseases. We are getting a fair quantity of French beans. My sweet corn seems to have been stunted by the heat, and is tasselling too early, but I hope to get something from that. I have a nice decorative/ utilitarian patch of sunflowers coming up by the chicken run. The plan is that the chickens will eat the seed heads.

My one local hen has gone broody, and is sitting on six duck eggs which I got from a friend. I do not have high hopes, but I thought it would be interesting and educative (to me as well as Dominic) to try the experiment. We are still getting enough for our own needs, and a few to sell, although my hens are not commercially minded.

The Dangers of Drought

I fear that work here has suffered from the heat. We need a few good rainstorms to wake people up, although perhaps a drought would also have a stimulating effect. The rains have been so good for the last five years that people find it difficult to remember that droughts still happen. When we do have a drought, it will probably be very unpleasant, as the cattle population is at an all-time high, and a nation-wide drought could easily lead to the death of half the livestock herd (in drought, most cattle die from lack of grazing within reach of their water source, not lack of water). There is far too much complacency engendered by good years, and far too little preparedness for bad years.

Bernard's Progress

We are expecting Bernard on the 19th. From his letters, he seems to keep cheerful and enjoy school. I hope the school is good for him. It has a good reputation, but we really have very little way of telling. I shall be interested to see his report. His letters to us are greatly improved (seldom more than half a page), but writing is clearly still a struggle. It is odd that both he and Dominic are such good readers, and yet are dyslectic spellers.

Letter to Sheila and family   Gaborone, 14/01/1979

Hopeful Plans

I begin to think that weekends are the times when I make plans for things that don't get done. I always bring a bag full of papers home, and have projects for the garden, but rarely get beyond paying the week's bills. About once in two months I make a supreme effort and send off what is meant to be a monthly financial account to the Ford Foundation of all the things that they are meant to reimburse, and there are various other semi-official things like that to be done, but I don't often accomplish anything more substantial.

I tend to spend spare daylight time viewing the garden, removing the odd tuft of weeds (usually a case of random victimisation, as there are so many weeds happily growing where I am trying to grow other things) or pondering why this or that piece of lawn/ tree/ flower/ vegetable/ chicken is ailing when in my view it has had all the necessary attention to keep it in good form. My gardening is a bit like Mr. Englander's – philosophical rather than active. However, we have managed courgettes, lettuce, cucumbers, tomatoes, beetroot, *mange-tout* peas, plenty of beans, Chinese cabbage and probably one or two other things as well, so I ain't complaining.

Musical Pastimes

I am also leading a musical life of a fullness which puzzles and slightly worries me. I'm not sure that music really commands as much of my affections as it is managing to take of my time. I practise once a week with a quartet, and once with an orchestra. Next weekend we are giving a performance, so there is unusual activity – rehearsals yesterday, today, tomorrow, and Thursday. Probably the main reason I do all this is that we have an extremely good solo violinist - unfortunately leaving in two months – and a very good conductor, who does a lot of his own orchestration. For the next concert he has done us a very lively orchestration of Scott Joplin's *"Entertainer"*, which rather threw the orchestra at first, because we are totally unused to stressing the second beat in a bar, but I reckon it will be OK on the night – certainly up to the Francistown standard, because I doubt if they have ever had an orchestra there before. We shall be going up on the sleeper train, which should be fun (Rhodesia Railway – they run our railway!)

Family News

Mummy and Daddy said that you all seemed to be fit and well, and that your David (Wright) seemed to be enjoying university – despite his problem friend.

I hope all your farming activities are prospering; ditto yourselves. It seems silly to stop at the top of a page, but I am feeling sleepy. Perhaps Nicole will fill it up tomorrow.
Lots of love, David

Letter to parents   Gaborone, 14/01/1979

Weather Home and Abroad

I hope your weather is easing off a bit. Snow and ice are nice to look at, but the pleasure can soon pall, particularly if compounded by seasonal strikes and power cuts.

We are still sweltering. We also had a good thunderstorm two days ago, but sorely need more. This is meant to be the rainy season, and the crucial months for ploughing and planting are November – December. Crops planted in January generally get stopped before maturity by the frosts and cold weather, and after this month there's little point in planting. So far, however, very little land has been ploughed. It's the same for grazing. The warm months are the key ones for re-growth of pasture (one can hardly call our stuff "pasture" – "veld" is a better description). So far, the cattle are still in fair condition, because there was good growth last year. But there is very little new growth, and we shall probably see big losses later in the year if there is not plenty of rain in the next two months. In some ways, this won't be such a bad thing. The present cattle population is probably more than the veld can stand in the long run, and without a violent reduction in cattle numbers, it will get badly hammered, and may even be reduced to real desert.

Garden Battles

My own garden is not exactly blooming like a rose. I have had quite good success with my net-house, which has provided courgettes, lettuce, tomatoes and *mange-tout* peas. But I have a lot of nematodes in the soil, and I am preparing to clear half of the net-house completely, so that I can treat the soil. I also have downy mildew, cutworms, and pumpkin fly, grey aphids, red spider-mite, bacterial wilt, blossom-end rot, fruit fly, and various viral infections here and there. As Nicole said in some exasperation, having a garden here is more demanding than having a child.

Poultry News

My chickens are in good nick, except for one which surprised us (and doubtless herself) by dying. One keeps on laying eggs in the water trough, which seems a bit careless; it can't be such a surprise. The one which was sitting on duck eggs eventually got fed up, and broke the eggs, thus losing her honoured status as expectant foster-mother. She has therefore been sent back inside to join the common throng. Our cock has not yet thought of crowing, which is as we should wish – although I don't expect that will last.

Letter to parents   Gaborone, 18/02/1979

Drought

The "rains" are almost over now, but very little rain has fallen, and we are preparing for a hard year with little harvest or grazing. The only thing one can do about drought in the livestock industry is to kill animals before they go beyond the point of no return. Unfortunately one of the worst affected parts of the country is the north, which still cannot market because of the long ban imposed after a foot-and-mouth disease outbreak. Even so, I am still worried about the capacity of the export abbatoir to take the cattle that may be offered for sale in the rest of the country, let alone the numbers that ought to be marketed. We ought to kill at least a million head this year, but the most that the abattoir has ever handled to date is 220,000.

Virulent Weeds

Red spider-mites have even tried the leaves of the one feverfew plant that I have managed to grow; it's really very irresponsible of me to introduce a new weed, but judging by the difficulties I have had, I don't think that feverfew is going to become the next scourge of the Botswana veld. Actually, there are lots of useless weeds, and some that are very poisonous, and these tend to increase with grazing pressure, as the cattle eat the nutritious plants and leave the poisonous and indigestible plants. One always finds a wide circle of more or less unpleasant plants around a watering point.   In Maun, I was told that one of the plants, *acanthus spermum*, was known as "petition", because its arrival coincided with a petition to the authorities complaining about the harshness of their chief. There is another one called "mogau", which is so poisonous that a girl working on a research project for the Ministry ended up in hospital after simply picking some. We have a nasty newcomer, a grass which is also found in Europe, called "Nassela tussock", which is so fibrous and indigestible that if the cattle do try and eat it, they literally die of constipation.

Official Tourism

The weekend before last, Nicole and I flew up to Maun with some Ford Foundation visitors for some official tourism – looking at irrigation sites, research stations, and cows. We spent a short time on the water, and saw fish eagles, kingfishers, pelicans and storks. We had meant to go back on Sunday evening, but it was so hot that our little plane wouldn't start, so we spent another night there at the expense of the charter company, and flew back in the cool of the morning.

The Boys

Dominic is in good form. He now goes riding once a week, and yesterday he passed his grade two swimmer's badge. He is now a very good swimmer, still more under the water than on it, but able to make good speed with several strokes. Bernard seems to be happy, and he writes cheerful letters.

Letter to Sheila and Ron Gaborone, 14/03/1979

Guardianship

I'm afraid it has taken me rather a long time to send you my Christmas "Thank you letter" (enclosed), mainly because I put it aside while I wondered how I should ask you what I am about to ask you.

Are you willing to take on formal guardianship of Bernard, so far as his school is concerned, while we are away? This is not, of course, legal guardianship; we have no intention of renouncing parenthood duties. But the school wants to know that there is someone to deal with in emergencies, to look after clothes purchases, and to ensure that he has somewhere to go on out-weekends. Mrs. Chisholm has done this conscientiously – perhaps too conscientiously because she now feels she can't cope with that and looking after a semi-invalid parent. We pay all costs of travelling (including collecting, fetching, carrying), clothes, laundry etc.

Of course it's a bit of a problem you being so far from Thame, but I don't think it will normally be necessary for you to visit Thame or collect him from there. He is old enough now to get into Oxford and buy himself coach tickets, and, for that matter, to buy some of his clothes himself. And we do manage to rotate him between various friends and relatives for out-weekends. However, I don't like loading any extra responsibilities on Mummy and Daddy, and I think Bernard fits comfortably into your family.

Perhaps you can think about it, and give me an answer when we are home on leave in April.

I do hope we can see you this time – but of course we must: we shall have a whole month to do it in.

Much love, David

Letter to Sheila and Ron Woodstock, 07/05/1979

Guardianship, and Old Carpentry Tools!

Excuse the paper, but we don't have much choice now. I hope we shall have spoken on the phone before you get this, but since I am sending a cheque, I can also profit from the opportunity to write.

The cheque is for two things: first, £50 for costs of guardian-ing Bernard. Please do charge realistically highly for all costs including petrol. When you run short, tell me. The other £50 is a speculation. Please buy me any interesting old carpenters' tools you see, either at the junk yard, or at the stripped furniture place – things like wooden (not metal) moulding planes, spokeshaves, long saws for pit sawing, etc. I want to test a hunch that there is money to be made from these (I have actually seen tools for sale around here at £7+ which might have come out of a box at the junk yard labelled "£5 for the lot"). The tools should be hand made, involving blacksmith work and/or shaped wood – (that may confuse you because good tools don't look hand made!) Try and get a varied selection, avoiding broken tools or tools with bits missing. If I make any profit on the transaction, I shall give you a third – if that seems fair. Any loss I keep for myself.

Also, if you see any chairs like those I bought with the initials F.C. stamped on the back of the seat, I would like up to three more and a similar chair with arms. They won't come out of the £50, but if you see them, buy them and pay out of any money you have of mine. I will repay immediately.

That sounds very complicated. If you don't like to do it, don't bother, but I think it should be rather fun to poke around from time to time with someone else's money to spend.

Holiday Arrangements

Coming back to Bernard, a friend of Nicole's, Mrs. Ruth Johnson, will look after travel, train and plane bookings etc. Another close friend in the locality in case of emergency is Mrs. Jill Shishtawi.

We did enjoy our stay with you. This has been a hectic holiday, and although it may not have seemed so to you, our stay in Suffolk was a patch of peace and calm, without a lot of social calls or jobs to do around the house (I more or less finished patching up the house this morning).

House Hunting in Oxfordshire

We expended a lot of nervous energy trying to rustle up money to buy a big and beautiful house two miles from Woodstock, but the building societies thought it all very odd, and either said no, or that money would be very expensive (18% one said) or that the Bank of England would object because I am non-resident. When we finally gave up, I was both very relieved and very disappointed. It sounds as if David and Margaret (Pearce) are also going to have problems with their house-buying.

I am afraid this is a ramshackle letter, interrupted by the sad job of delivering Bernard back to school. We do miss him.

Dominic and Bernard with Grandparents Bert and Marjorie, Morland Avenue, Leicester, 1980 and 1982

Letter to parents   Gaborone, 03/06/1979

Trade Talks at Lobatse

I'm afraid it is a long while since I've written. I tend to be busy with work in the week, and with socialising at weekends. For example, yesterday morning (Saturday) I went to Lobatse with the Permanent Secretary to help talk to the Belgian Vice-Prime Minister about meat. The Vice-PM was here to shoot lions, and I suspect to have a quiet week with a lady friend, but he also did the political rounds, and as he also happened to be a big meat-importer, we took the opportunity to talk business. We want to get more meat into the EEC, and we would like a foothold in the Belgian market. The Vice-PM fairly clearly asked us to give him a special deal if he could help on these matters, but to my surprise (and to the surprise of the Permanent Secretary), the marketing people from the Meat Commission didn't seem to understand at all. We both felt that their failure to take up the proposal arose from stupidity, not business ethics. I found myself as the main two-way interpreter.

A Secure Duck-house

We got back from Lobatse at lunch time. After lunch, Dominic and I put finishing touches to our new duck-house, hanging cement-soaked sacks up against the wire-mesh fence that forms the back wall of the house, to make at least a psychological barrier for would-be poultry thieves, who really have rather easy access. We then had friends in for dinner.

Children's Orchestra

Today, Dominic and I made it out of bed just in time to get to the children's section of the Gaborone orchestra. As it happened, there were only four children, including me, and a viola player rather older than myself, so I temporarily joined the section. Dominic then stayed on to try the "grown up" orchestra. He made a valiant try, although his intonation is still far from perfect, and he is rather indifferent of sharps and flats. We then had just time before lunch to move the three ducks and the outgoing flock of hens to the duck-house, leaving the chicken house vacant for our new arrivals.

Mixing Building with Pleasure

After lunch I spent a vigorous hour or two with pick, hammer and cold chisel undoing the work of a man I have hired to mend and enlarge our swimming pool. The work he had done was unfortunately very solid, but his technique was that of a house-builder, not a pool-builder. He had made a foundation for the walls, instead of building them on the base slab of the pool. This would have meant that slight movement would have opened a crack. Since concrete gets harder every day, and since I was afraid that the builder would turn up tomorrow and continue where he had left off, I thought that the best thing to do was to smash enough to make the work easier and the purpose clearer. I expect to have to do some hard explaining tomorrow.

In the course of this work, I had to collect some planks to make a bit of shuttering for poured concrete so I collected our joint Land Rover from a Ford Foundation colleague. That meant one chat and a beer. Then I went to some French friends to pick up the planks, and it took me at least an hour and a half, plus another beer, before I could escape without seeming uncivil. An hour later, they came to us for a chat and a drink, and with but a pause to read Dominic a story, eat dinner, and listen to the news, here I am at 10pm writing to Bernard and to yourselves.

Surviving Drought

We have had a sociologist friend, Chris, staying with us for the last few days. He's from Oxford, although I only know him from here (not my generation). Chris is doing work to find out what people really do to keep alive in a drought. We shall, of course, also be trying to keep them alive, but we really do need to know more about who is hit by a drought, and how, so as to be better prepared in future. Chris moved out today, to share an empty flat with another sociologist, but we may have another guest on Tuesday – an American college student on vacation assignment to the Ministry – if I cannot find a flat for him in the next 48 hours.

Wine into Water

Since I last wrote, we have had the trauma of sacking our maid, for performing an inverse miracle – wine into water – for the third time. She was a good worker, and loyal to us in a strange way; but I was fed up, felt my authority was becoming very suspect, and no longer trusted her to be honest in more important matters. We have a new lady, Anna, who hasn't much idea of the work, but seems to be trying hard. Fortunately, she speaks enough English to get by with.

Letter to parents   Gaborone, 17/06/1979

Enduring Drought

We are going through a very cold spell – chilly nights, slight frosts, and only an hour of warm weather around mid-day. We even felt one or two spots of rain, but there was nothing that would show up on a rain gauge, let alone help droughts. We are in deep drought, with no prospect of rain before October. A lot of my work is now taken up with reactions to the drought – projects to buy seed, and to move cattle from worst affected areas for slaughter. Really, the only thing to do with cattle in drought is to kill as many as possible while they are still worth something. Feeding them is quite impracticable, and only increases ecological damage.

Petrol Problems Due to Sanctions

Like everyone else, we are having petrol worries. This week our petrol went up overnight from 38 *thebe* a litre to over 52 *thebe*, and there are prospects of more rises to come, and possible shortages. Apart from everything else, we feel the full brunt of oil sanctions against South Africa, which used to rely heavily on supplies from Iran. This has immediately led to other price rises, since almost everything we use has to be transported long distances. Increases in transport and fuel costs are really going to hit commercial ranchers who depend on diesel to run their boreholes, and who have to move cattle over very long distances.

Swimming Pool Saga

I have spent the weekend working on our swimming pool, with the assistance of an American student who is staying with us (he is here on a Ford Foundation scheme; next week he should be able to move into a borrowed house). As you know, our pool let us down last year. I got my last-gardener-but-one to knock out a wall, so that I could diagnose the problem, and enlarge the pool. The problem was pretty obvious once the wall was removed – virtually no structural link between the floor and the walls of the pool. Our maid (whom we have at last sacked for stealing our drinks, and filling the bottles with water – a disgusting habit!) found us a would-be builder, whom I hired to do the rebuilding. He proved to have little or no building experience, and no building knowledge. Our gardener has since told us that his experience consisted of painting and thatching. Anyway, I got rid of him about Wednesday last week. At least I had managed to get him to put in an acceptable new concrete floor, and bring in some of the materials we needed, but I had to dismantle quite a lot of his brickwork, and waste a lot of time compromising by straightening things out and working out the real line without the bulges and bends. We are now well on track, with half the brickwork completed, and the thing really looks quite businesslike, although I wouldn't wish to show off my work to a bricklayer.

Rabbit and Poultry Husbandry

Last week Dominic bought himself a rabbit, which is eventually intended to multiply, although for the moment it is too young. This week, I bought fifteen replacement hens. We still have about eight of the last lot, in with the ducks, but they are due for the pot when the new ones get into the habit of laying. That should not be long now, as they have already started producing a few eggs. Nicole does the marketing, and has no difficulty finding customers. I am not a good agricultural economist; I have never worked out whether the chickens pay for their keep. My main interest is getting all those nice fresh eggs.

Bernard's Travels

We have heard that Bernard managed to get to Sheila's and back at half term, despite reading the arrivals board instead of the departures board, and thereby missing a couple of trains. We were also told that he was "swotting like mad" for his end of term exams. I hope such diligence is rewarded, for his sake. His teachers actually seem a bit concerned that he is so worried about his work. So like his father!

Letter to Sheila from Nicole   Gaborone, 25/06/1979

Visit to Suffolk by Régis, Schoolmate of Dominic

Régis and his father will arrive in London on 30th June. Régis is very keen to come and stay with you although he is anxious, as he has never been to a foreign country without his parents. I think Liliane, Régis' mother, would like to come and fetch him at the end of July and meet you. It would be nice for Régis if he could go camping with James. I took him on a day's outing with the cubs a few weeks ago and he thoroughly enjoyed it.

Thank you very much for having Bernard. He wrote last week and said that he enjoyed his stay with you very much. He seems to have done a lot of revising for his end of year exams and I hope his efforts will be rewarded. We are looking forward to seeing him soon.

Nicole's Domestic Difficulties

We have only been back for a month but already we feel in need of another holiday. Life is very hectic: music rehearsals, work and lately we seem to have done a lot of entertaining. I was also without a maid for a while. I sacked Glorious - for the third time she watered the drinks. I was sorry to see her go and I miss her but there had to be an end to it. I have now recruited somebody else, but she is useless and does not register quickly. For instance if I ask her to put the mustard on the table for a meal, she will then put the mustard on the table for all the other meals, even for breakfast. She is also very slow.

David has been working hard on the swimming pool for the last two weeks. At first he employed somebody who said he was a bricklayer but his work showed that he knew nothing about bricklaying. Our gardener told us later that in fact he was a carpenter. We have had an American student staying with us since the beginning of the month and he has helped David a lot. The maid's husband or boyfriend offered his services yesterday and he looks as if he knows what he is doing; he apparently works as a bricklayer. The funny thing is that the maid was very cross when David paid the husband; she said it was not right for him to accept money. We could not find out what her motives were.

Snow in Africa

Winter arrived suddenly two weeks ago; until then it was still warm during the day and cool at night. Apparently it even snowed in Johannesburg which has not happened for years. In the morning the temperature is usually 6 degrees centigrade. After such a long cold winter I hope that your summer is hot and pleasant. I enjoy the weather we are having now and already dread the long summer to come.
Love to you all, Nicole

P.S. from David

I'm off on a trip up-country on Monday, and hope to get back on Friday in time to jump into the new Land Rover and head off to the desert with friends. Camping promises to be chilly.
Much love, David

Letter to parents   Gaborone, 22/07/1979

House Guests

We have had a series of people staying in the house; first, a sociologist whom I helped to recruit for a consultancy on how people are dealing with the drought, then a Ford Foundation "intern" – i.e. a university student doing a project in his vacation. Both of these are extremely pleasant people. I am particularly impressed by the intern, whom I find extraordinarily mature and knowledgeable for his twenty-three years (two previously spent in Botswana). These two ended up sharing a borrowed house, although we see quite a lot of them. They were followed by our friends the Agars, who had returned from a six-week trip around Botswana and Namibia, and needed a roof over their heads until they left, which they did last week, going out on the plane that brought Bernard in.

Protecting Cattle

In the meantime, I have spent a week in the North with a whole troop of people from our Ministry, to consult with the district council, the *kgotlas* ("grass-roots" meetings) on tsetse clearance and a fence that is meant to separate cattle from wildlife in the swamps. We also had to talk about a scheme to move 30,000 cattle out of an area still affected by foot-and-mouth restrictions (and drought), and a foot-and-mouth panic that, to our enormous relief, turned out to be a false alarm.

Desert Camping Trip

As soon as I got back, we packed up and went off to the desert with Peter and Jenny, our two other erstwhile guests, and six others, to look at wilderness and several thousand hartebeeste which came to lick salt at the pan where we camped. I was feeling a bit the worse for wear by then, but was back on form within about 24 hours. We had a very restful camp, with three nights in the same spot, marred only by the fact that we could see three other vehicles! Between us, we probably had a thousand square miles.

Bernard missed all that unfortunately, but is here now, and in good form. Dominic is very pleased to have him here, and they seem to get on as well as ever. Next month we plan to spend a week in the swamps with him – expensive, but something to do once in a visit (or a lifetime!)

A Royal Visit

Yes, I shall see the Queen. I was a bit miffed not to be invited to the assembly of British people, but found I was invited to the State House Garden Party, which is one up. No, I have not lost my republican views, but I am a bit of a politician, and will make no unseemly gestures.

Nights here remain very cold, but days are warming up. In the desert we needed two sleeping bags each.

Letter to parents
Gaborone, 28/08/1979

A Long Drive

I'm afraid it's ages since I last wrote; we have been away. I took a week off, and we went up north to the swamps. We made a leisurely journey up, as we had no fixed dates until the Tuesday, and it is a long way (about 1,000km); and also we got caught up in the weekend petrol pump closures (1pm Saturday to noon Sunday), which can be quite hazardous when there is only a petrol station every 200km or so. We camped comfortably in a dry river bed just off the road on Saturday, making a slow run into Francistown the next morning, giving ourselves time for coffee with friends before the pumps opened, after which we went haring off. Generally, we refused hitch-hikers; we were full, and they are almost impossible to ditch if you tire of their company. However, we did pick up a British teacher whom we knew slightly, and therefore could not refuse a roads foreman who was hitching at the same spot. Fortunately he was only going about 25 miles.

Wilderness Camp

I had planned a night stop in a game reserve which is bordered by a perennial river, off our route, but was surprised how long it took to get there, and only left the main road around twilight. Almost immediately we saw gemsbok, zebra, and a baby wildebeeste who fled down the track before us. Eventually, well after nightfall, we came to a strange dusty sort of clearing, which looked almost like the trampled ground of a cattle post. I looked around for a *kraal* or water tank, but saw neither, nor were there any cattle, but there was firewood lying around, so we camped there – with our hitch-hiker who had no other arrangements, and was heading for exactly the same destination as us. It was quite pleasant to have another adult to help with the camping.

In the morning all became clear; we had camped about half a kilometre from the banks of the river, and the ground was trampled and overgrazed by wildebeeste and zebra going to water. Unfortunately they did not all troop through our camp in the dawn; even in the reserves, Botswana's wildlife is sufficiently conditioned by poachers to give anything human a wide berth. However, it was quite clear from the grisly remains that lions were active as well as poachers. On the way out we saw a couple of very large mixed herds of zebra and hartebeeste, and I tried to sneak up close enough to take pictures, but got nothing better than a very good memory of thundering hooves and fleeing rumps.

Bush Telegraph

We saw more wildlife all along the main road (often very close) until we were quite near to Maun. There we had a comfortable night in a hotel – expensive, but some of us become a bit frazzled with too many successive nights of poor-to-middling sleep, and washing in a cupful of shared water. The local information exchange system was remarkable. Our hitchhiker was trying to locate a friend who had come the same way a few days earlier, and kept on being surprised to receive messages via people she had never met before. As a result, she was able to share the small aeroplane that took us out to the camp we were to stay at in the swamps.

Game Spotting by Dug-out Canoe

We spent a comfortable night in camp, then went out for a three-day, two-night trip in a couple of *mekoro* – dug-out canoes with flat bottoms that are poled along through the water-grass and reeds, like punts. Of course, we did not have to do the poling. We just lay back *"comme les rois fainéants"*, as Nicole says, brushing off the tsetse flies, and wondering whether the polers would really manage to drive a way through the next patch of grass (river courses are avoided because of hippos and crocodiles).

Normally, we had to leave the boats and walk on land to see the game, although sometimes we saw animals from the boats, and more often we heard tremendous splashing noises and were told that somewhere out of view we had disturbed a herd of linchwe. We saw traces of elephants, and heard lion, but saw neither; but I had an excellent close-up of three huge buffalo charging out (happily in the opposite direction) from behind a bush, and another time we got very close to a whole family of warthogs who seemed more curious than afraid of our presence. Our guides caught a lot of fish, simply by leaving a net out overnight, so we were able to supplement our diet of tinned food with a fair quota of grilled fish.

Crocs and Birds by Night

We had one more night in camp before we left. We also had an intriguing motor-boat trip at night to look at crocodiles, spear fish, and watch birds. When the boaters find a small enough crocodile they pull it into the boat, but the little ones are starting to get wise, and the only one we managed to catch unawares was about seven feet long. Curiously, the birds roosting in the reeds were not disturbed by the motor-boat or the lights. We were able to get really close to a brilliant little malachite kingfisher, about two inches high, who just perched, blinking and looking dazed. Another quite extraordinary sight was a group of six green and yellow little bee-eaters, so squashed up together on the same reed that they looked like a single oddly-shaped leaf.

A Weary Return

We left the camp on Saturday afternoon, recovered our Land Rover, and made a leisurely start back, camping for the first night only 120km down the road. I had a sneaking wish to see some more game, but we saw nothing that night. We rose, literally, at dawn – 5.30am – but it was about 8 o'clock by the time we had finished a hurried breakfast. In fact, we did see more game: giraffe, only a few hundred yards from the main road, and a family of leopards (or possibly cheetahs) making a leisurely entry to a Ministry of Agriculture ranch. I was told later that they cause no bother there, as the ranch holds only mature animals, and leopards prefer game (also in the ranch) and calves.

Nicole and I drove in shifts for the rest of the day, with only half an hour off for coffee in Francistown while we waited for the petrol pumps to open, and we arrived back home, very weary, around 8pm.

Home to the Garden

The weather here is getting warmer, and we have even had a couple of unseasonable storms, which have added a welcome touch of green to the brown earth. My refurbished swimming pool is completed and full of water, which stays in, notwithstanding Nicole's scepticism. However, so far it has been a bit too cold for more than one or two brief symbolic plunges.

Our peach tree is beautifully in flower, and I can see a welcome number of flower buds on the citrus trees that I have planted: two lemons, a grapefruit, a *"naartje"* (tangerine), and an orange. Only the orange, which is a late replacement, does not have flower buds. However one really cannot expect to get a significant amount of fruit off citrus in the first four years. I also have three apple trees, none of which has yet got around to shedding last year's leaves. They are even newer than the citrus, and I don't really think I can expect anything off them, but that isn't going to stop me from hoping. I am very optimistic about my two grape vines. One has already borne fruit last year, and I can see that it has a lot of flower buds this year. The other, which is a more delicate white variety, stood still for its first year, but burst into life last year, and I am hoping it too will come up to scratch. I successfully took half a dozen cuttings from these vines last year, and I have planted five outside the kitchen in a hot area where most plants refuse to grow, and the sixth against the trellis with the two parent plants.

Success with Vegetables!

We have had some excellent pickings of broccoli, and half a dozen good cauliflower. I always feel rather clever when I produce cauliflower, since my efforts in Tanzania and Woodstock were markedly unsuccessful. I could have had a few asparagus spears, but decided to follow the advice of the books, and let them grow strong for a second season. I have some very impressive-looking globe artichoke plants in my net house, but fear they will suffer badly when the hot weather comes. I am also becoming a bit more successful with flowers than I used to be, as a result of some urging by Nicole. Some of last season's chrysanthemums are still flowering, and I have managed to raise ranunculus and six carnations from seed; they too will suffer when the sun gets hotter.

Livestock News

The livestock is flourishing, although the ducks still have not laid a single egg, let alone raised a brood. We have fourteen new chickens, and two old ones (in with the ducks) and quite often get sixteen eggs a day. The new hens are called "tetras" – probably a recent hybrid – and are much healthier, greedier, stupider and more productive than their predecessors. Perhaps these characteristics generally go together. We are rabbit-sitting for some French friends, and Dominic's doe today produced her first litter of three little pink pigs. This is very satisfactory, because Bernard goes tomorrow, and he has also been closely involved in rabbit husbandry.

A Painful Mishap

Today has been marred by a mishap of Dominic's. He was cutting a piece of wire with my pliers, and the cut end jumped into his eye. It actually marked the conjunctiva, and has been very sore and irritating. I phoned the eye doctor, who told me to put a patch over the eye, and come to him if it continued to be painful tomorrow. I do not think there is any damage done, but Dominic has been feeling tired and headachy, and didn't really enjoy this afternoon's picnic outing as he would usually have done.

Musical Enterprises

I think Bernard has had a really good stay, but he doesn't seem to be particularly depressed by the prospect of going back to school. Yesterday both he and Dominic took part in a small concert by the Junior Orchestra. This is composed mainly of recorders, with a smattering of other instruments. Bernard was able to shine in a piece chosen for him and another good cornet player. Dominic also comes regularly to the Senior Orchestra, where, at the moment, he plays the double bass part in a piece by Schumann, that gives me (as the real cello) some very crucial and difficult romantic high notes.

Death of a Friend

We had some very sad news the other day: Mrs. Jill Shishtawi, Nicole's friend who lived across the road from us in Woodstock, has died. This was not totally unexpected. She appeared to be perfectly well when we were last home, but we heard she was being treated for a very fast-growing brain tumour. The treatment appeared to do some good, and she was able to live normally at home, but in the end she died very quickly of septicaemia – presumably a result of the illness and treatment. She had two children: a boy about the same age as Dominic, and a younger girl. Jill used to help arrange Bernard's travel and holidays, and is a great loss as a sensible practical person we could always turn to in Woodstock.

Letter to parents   **Gaborone, 30/09/1979**

A Gloomy Weekend

We are in the middle of a long weekend – Independence celebrations. This time we have stayed at home. Someone else has the Ford Foundation Land Rover, and anyway we seem to be a bit thin on friends who both want to go on trips, and appear to us as congenial enough to be good company for several days on end. Peter and Jenny have gone (and split up again after reuniting for a long safari around South Africa), and this weekend is under a bit of a cloud, since another couple we have been out with (and with whom we were planning a Christmas trip) have been summoned back in disgrace by their firm – possibly to be sacked, but certainly not to return (the disgrace is professional, not any sort of misconduct, but that doesn't help them greatly).

More Fruit Trees

I have taken a small citrus tree from their garden, and have also rather foolishly purchased three more – an apricot, a plum and a peach – from which I may conceivably get one small crop before leaving in eighteen months. But I enjoy growing and planting fruit trees, even for the benefit of someone else. I have a lot of flowers on one of my one-year-old apple trees, but do not really expect apples, because I doubt if there is another apple tree to pollinate it anywhere in the neighbourhood. One of my lemons has set fruit for the first time, and my peach tree was a wonderful sight two weeks ago, when it was covered with blossom. It also has set quite a lot of fruit, but I know that I shall have to spray them with a nasty systemic insecticide later on if I am to get any peaches that are not riddled with maggots.

My two vines are very healthy and have lots of flowers, and I have grown globe artichokes in the net house. So far we have eaten only four, but I think we can have another four tomorrow.

It's a very good children's garden. We often have Dominic's friends in to help with the rabbits and swim in the pool, which is functioning splendidly.

A Notable Nose!

We're going to the Independence Day Cocktail Party at State House tomorrow, which reminds me that you mentioned seeing what looked like my nose on television during the Queen's visit! You might have done, but not at the banquet, because I wasn't invited to that.

Observing the Royals....

However, we were among the select hundreds invited to drinks on the lawns of State House. It was rather a ridiculous occasion. It would have been quite pleasant had it not been for the socialising Royalty. I had no wish to shake them by the hand, and make inane conversation, but despite my anti-royalist beliefs (not, you will notice, strong enough to make me refuse the invite) it did seem excessively rude to too obviously head the other way when they suddenly popped up, as they constantly did. At one point I thought I was trapped, when Prince Andrew suddenly appeared almost at my elbow; but he chatted with a rather tartish-looking girl who turned out to sort diamonds, which he found extraordinarily interesting and absolutely fascinating in the two minutes he allotted to her. I manfully stood my ground, and when he had finished, he turned towards me and said *"I say, can we clear a little space here,"* which we did, and he walked away through it. I didn't feel it was one of those occasions that added value to my life.

.....and a President

I was flattered a couple of days earlier when I was strolling around the agricultural section of the Trade Fair with my Permanent Secretary, and he was hailed by the President who had come to take first pick of the bulls on show. The P.S. said *"You do know David Jones, don't you?"* and the President said *"Of course!"* which shows either that he has a good memory, or is an easy liar. I like to think it's the former.

Giant Hailstones

I suppose you are sliding into Autumn as we slide into Summer. I bet your end is wetter than ours, although we have had a couple of welcome storms, which have added a bit of green to the ground. We had a hailstorm which seemed heavy to me, but was much heavier elsewhere. I was at Molepolole Brigades Trust two days ago, and commented on the ragged state of their net house. The answer was that tennis-ball-sized hailstones had punched holes through the nets, and even through a number of tin roofs.

Letter from Nicole to parents-in-law   Gaborone, 07/10/1979

A Riotous Party

We spent yesterday afternoon with friends who live in a village on the outskirts of Gaborone. They live in a *rondavel* owned by a Motswana, and the owner, as well as his parents and another couple, have houses in the same compound. The landlord had decided to celebrate Wendy's mother's arrival (our friends Wendy and Paul are British) by killing a goat. There were quite a few guests (African and expatriates). There was also an unwanted guest, a drunken lady carrying her baby on her back. She had had a few drinks before (somewhere else I presume) and after a few drinks at our party she had great difficulty keeping on her feet. Our friends' landlord was very shocked by this lady's attitude, and after some struggling managed to throw her out of the compound. At one time somebody even brought out a whip to give a good correction to the lady, but somebody else stopped him. I was very concerned about the baby on the lady's back; he or she nearly fell off the mother's back in the process.

Letter to parents   Gaborone, 11/11/1979

Money Matters

You do have my London Bank details, don't you? Thank you for paying in for me, it will be nice to have funds paid in without all the fuss of getting foreign exchange transferred from here. Not that there is any difficulty – Botswana has almost more foreign exchange than it knows what to do with, and it is just a question of spending half an hour filling in the right forms. However I manage to spend a lot of money in the U.K., what with insurance, and Bernard's school boarding fees which I get reimbursed in *pula*.

Bernard's Growing Independence

Thank you for your letter, and for looking after Bernard over his weekend. It's good that he is now able to look after himself, and to get around without depending too much on other people. Do you realise I had probably never made a train journey on my own until I went to university (or rather, to university interviews)? Of course, Bernard does enjoy being back in a family atmosphere. This evening, we are trying to phone him up to say happy birthday, but so far we have not managed to get through. I think Sunday evenings must be a busy time on the boarding house telephone.

Malnutrition - a Tragedy

We have had a tragedy in our household. The maid's baby died last week. What makes it worse is that I am now almost certain that it died of malnutrition. In fact, I recognised the symptoms two or three days before the child died. Previously I had just thought it was feeble-minded, because it looked plump, but was rather peculiar, and was singularly lacking in interest in anything going on in the world around it. Afterwards, Anna told us that she was feeding the baby on potatoes and milk. I am sure it must really have been maize meal (which is a lot more nourishing than potatoes, but still a very poor diet on its own) plus a little skim milk powder in water. She had been leaving the children with her mother, which is a well-established route to malnutrition; but she brought them here a couple of months ago because she said that her mother was not feeding them properly. She and her husband went home at the beginning of the week to bury the baby, and only arrived back this evening. If I understood her right, she stayed longer than she had intended, because another child at her parents' home had also died.

The Perils of Buying Property

I'm interested to hear that at last Margaret and David are making progress with their house-buying. As you say, it will be very awkward if they complete a sale before a purchase. The more I think of it, the more I am appalled by the complication and expense of house-purchase. I know it is the largest single expense that most people make, but it is not so much larger than, for example, the price of a new car, that one can justify all the fuss and bother that is part and parcel of house-buying. Of course, only part of it is the fault of the lawyers and the law (in particular, the apparent lack of a land registry). The building societies are difficult chiefly because they get funds below the market rate, and have less money to lend than demands from secured borrowers. Perhaps if I find myself unemployed in Britain in sixteen months time, I should look more carefully at this area. Up to now, it seems mainly to have attracted crooks and loan sharks. Just a thought.

Tedious Speeches

We are now into the hot weather, with some quite uncomfortably warm afternoons, but also some surprisingly cool days when the sky is overcast. Yesterday I attended the opening of a new grain storage facility, and I sat shivering in the shadow of the new silos while my new minister read a long and extremely boring speech which was haltingly translated into Setswana. I compared notes afterwards with Nicole, and found that we had both been impatiently counting the pages he had already read, and trying to compare them with the thickness of pages still to be read. The ceremony was about 120km from here, and on the way home we passed through heavy rain, but the road was completely dry for the last 40km before Gaborone.

Garden Triumphs and Failures

My garden is a bit discouraging at the moment. I have had a bad attack of red spider-mites, which are about the most difficult pests to dislodge. In fact, I doubt if they will disappear until the first frosts. They are almost too small to see, yet they do a tremendous amount of damage to plants, and they like almost everything broad-leaved; not just beans, tomatoes, aubergines and curcurbits, but also chrysanthemums and weeds. Add to that the (sitting) ducks, which broke all their eggs but one (which I then threw out), and Dominic's rabbit, which produced its litter of eight about two weeks early, so that they all died. The only really healthy-looking things at the moment are the grape vines, which have a lot of fruit, and the fruit trees, which have very little but still look fine. I might possibly get one or two apples on one of my little trees. Last week I bought myself a pear tree, which is completely stupid since I shall certainly not get any fruit from it; but I do enjoy planting trees, and with any luck someone else will keep them alive and enjoy them.

School News

At the moment, Dominic is very much occupied with end of year examinations. Passing from one form to the next is a serious business here, particularly in Government schools. I suspect that we may well find that Dominic is well ahead of many English children when he gets back into the U.K. system, which will be a very mixed blessing. He will probably also find the U.K. system surprisingly uncompetitive. Generally, I think he is well taught here, in a way that would be regarded as rather old-fashioned at home.

Hobnobbing with Russians

Last night we went to an excellent concert given by a lady pianist from the U.S.S.R., and then had the honour of hosting a rather chaotic buffet dinner for her and the Russian Ambassador, on behalf of the music society. Her playing was better than her company, because she spoke no English. The Russian Ambassador made up by speaking quite a lot, as did his wife, who is the subject of some interesting stories about enterprising attempts at spying and planting electronic "bugs" while on a social visit to the U.S. Ambassador's house. With us, she ranged from grandmotherly conversation about Dominic, to attempts to pump me on the trial of my former Acting Permanent Secretary for corruption. If she planted any bugs here, she will be disappointed by the standard of information obtained.

Letter to parents   Gaborone, 17/12/1979

Christmas Plans

Happy Christmas! Nicole says I haven't written to you for weeks and weeks, which I feel must be an exaggeration. On the other side, I can't find any letters from you since mid-November, and am sure you have written since then.

Dominic is on holiday, and spent last week at Kanye with friends, and this week has his friend from Kanye here. Bernard arrives Wednesday (I think). We are not planning to do anything special over Christmas. I had hoped to go camping in the Tuli Block, but Nicole is feeling rather worn out with the heat and a heavy work load, and doesn't feel like doing anything tiring. I hope, all the same, that we get out for a few days camping. It is tiring, but all the same, tremendously relaxing (at least for me).

Farming Difficulties

The rains here started well, at least in the south of the country, but there has been a rather worrying two-week gap, now getting on for three weeks, which could well cause havoc with the growing crop. However, at least there is a reasonable new growth of grass down here, and the cattle are looking well again. Up north, where the going has been toughest with foot-and-mouth and two years' marketing embargo, the rains have so far been rather poor. I fear we shall at best have a patchily good year, and at worst, a mixture of moderate and severe drought. However, I am regarded as a pessimist on these matters. Gaborone's water supply looks secure for next year, which is a relief.

Home Husbandry

My gardening this year is not very successful. We have a lot of green peppers, and pigeon peas (bush peas, grown with seed gathered in Guadeloupe and planted last year – the bushes are ten feet tall and still growing). One of our lawns has been covered with self-seeded pumpkins, and my christophines (a sort of climbing cucumber, common in Guadeloupe but exotic here) have produced enough fruit for a meal. But other things are suffering badly from heat and red spider-mites. I have bought two new ducks, and put an old one in the fridge for Christmas because she wouldn't lay; and we had two chickens for a big dinner the other day. Dominic's rabbits flourish but do not reproduce.

Letter to Sheila and family   Khartoum Hilton, Sudan, 11/01/1980

Impressions of the Sudan

Greetings from Khartoum. I have been here for the last week for a meeting of Ford Foundation agricultural people. Thanks to the airlines, I have had some time here before and after my official stay. It is a strange country, although of course I haven't seen the half of it, and couldn't in less than a year. I have only been to Khartoum, and to Wad Medami some 150km away, where we went to look at a huge new irrigation scheme. But what I have seen has been interesting.

Racial Groups

The people are of all sorts, except blond European types. There are very black Africans from the south, with patterns of scars all over their faces, and quite a lot of very Egyptian-looking people, but most come somewhere in between, with Arabic features and fuzzy hair. In long nightgowns and turbans they all look very similar.

Bargains in the Souk

The atmosphere is very friendly – probably partly because there are too few tourists around to spoil the place and make a nuisance of themselves. In the *souk*, no-one opportunes the visitors to buy, and all the traders are friendly, dignified and polite. Of course they ask high prices, but the margin they leave for bargaining down seems to be quite reasonable. I went to the *souk* with two colleagues and we each bought a *Djellebah* and white skull cap, and put them on. In some countries people might have been rather insulted. Here they are just pleased.

Weather, and Hotels

At the moment, it is Khartoum's cold season. For many of us "Africans" it was quite chilly at times, but in a month or so it will start getting hotter, eventually reaching 50' Centigrade (120' F – i.e. HOT). I have been here once in that sort of weather, just out of an aeroplane and back in again, but it was like walking into an oven. This hotel is, of course, totally cut off from the outside atmosphere. It's impossible even to open the window in my bedroom (from which I have a pleasant view of the Blue Nile converging with the White Nile). I find this artificial atmosphere rather oppressive. I am also glad that I am not personally responsible for the hotel bill; after our Foundation discount it comes out at about £40 a night, exclusive of meals. A small beer costs £2, and my coffee and toast in the morning is about the same – not a place to bring the family.

Our hotel in Wad Medami was very different, but it was clean, and the meals were served much faster than here. Specialities are Nile perch, lamb kebabs, and roast pigeon.

Irrigation Pros and Cons

The trip to Wad Medami took us past mile after mile of completely barren soil, with surprisingly large herds of goats and cattle. This was because the road ran parallel to the Gezira irrigation scheme, and the settlers on the scheme are not allowed to keep cattle there. Probably a few miles back from the scheme there was savannah woodland and grazing, similar to that in Botswana, but I have never seen quite such large areas of completely devastated land.

The irrigation schemes are impressive, but a bit worrying. The scheme we looked at was starting with 300,000 acres, to rise later to 800,000, with the first stage costing about 150 million dollars. The administration required is enormous. The scheme tells the tenants what to plant and when; it does all the ploughing and land preparation; it maintains a pest control service which depends on radio links between field teams and a fleet of spraying aircraft; it markets the crop and gins the cotton. And on top of this it has to look after huge pumps (the water is pump-lifted from the Nile) and miles of irrigation canals. The cost of dealing with the malaria and bilharzia created by the scheme is about as great as the value of output. Still, one must give great credit to the Sudanese for managing to run several schemes of this size without substantial help from outside. Not many developing countries could.

Whirling Dervishes

This evening (Friday – mosque day) we went to the outskirts of Khartoum to see the whirling dervishes. They really do exist. Only a few of them whirled, but there was a great deal of dancing and "inspired" activity – people apparently in trances rushing around and falling down. The dancers are all men of course, but women stand around and ululate. Some of the dancers were obviously show-offs; others seemed to be having great fun. There were some very jolly little fat men looking like the sultan of Baghdad dancing as if they were at the discotheque.

I have one more day here, and then I am due to spend most of Sunday travelling, starting out at 1.30am – not a joyful prospect.

Language Frustrations

I have just tried to listen to the TV news in Arabic, but found it rather difficult as I only understand names and numbers and the odd word that is the same in Swahili (the numbers are similar to Swahili and very easy to learn). I almost got caught up in an Egyptian romantic thriller, which was easier to understand than the news, but again I felt I might be missing the finer points.

However I think I have told you all the important points about the Sudan, and it's time for bed. Unfortunately someone seems to be having a party in the next-door room – not what I expect from the Hilton. I shall have to remember to drop a line to the manager.

Letter to parents   Gaborone, 27/01/1980

The Khartoum Trip

I think I told you I was going to Khartoum for a Ford Foundation policy review meeting for the Middle East/ Africa staff. We met in the Hilton Hotel, and at the conclusion of business, one of the senior New York guys gave a little speech in which he said how inspiring it had been to have such a meeting *"in an African setting"*. We were all too polite to laugh, although I think he would have been able to see the humour if we had. It was an interesting and enjoyable break, except that the flights, or the air conditioning, or the dryness, or a combination of all, gave me most uncomfortable nose/ throat/ sinuses.

Gaborone Agricultural Problems....

Life is very busy, although agriculture is not looking terribly prosperous just at the moment. We have had strange patchy rains, which have improved grazing, in the south but not in the north, but which have not been steady enough for good crops. Lots of fields are ploughed but empty of crops, or have even worse-than-usual crop stands. On top of this, we have a persistent foot-and-mouth outbreak in the north, where people haven't been able to sell their cattle for two years (when an area has foot-and-mouth it is "closed" and no sales can take place).

... and Garden Problems

My garden is a mixture of moderate successes and total failures at the moment. The best part is the livestock. Dominic is very pleased because his rabbit has just produced five "kittens". My ducks are less successful. They lay eggs, but nothing ever hatches. I think the male may end up in the pot soon. However, this may be unjust, as I gather that fat ducks lay infertile eggs, and I have always fed mine *ad lib*. I did kill one of Dominic's rabbits the other day, at his request, but I find I lack the phlegm for this bloodthirsty trade. He was a very friendly little rabbit. I think the secret is to have enough so that one doesn't get to know them. Dominic was very pleased with the price he got, which at last puts him on top financially – i.e. he paid me back for the feed I had bought. Mind you, he still benefits from the other feed that is bought for ducks or chickens, but I think that he earns it by looking after poultry.

Mountain Walks and a Hog-Roast

We have had a healthy weekend. I was beginning to feel a bit podgy and unfit, so yesterday Dominic and Cain and I (Cain is the dog) took a brisk one-hour walk up and down the highest hill in the neighbourhood of Gaborone – Kgale mountain. My achievement looks unimpressive compared with the annual "Up Kgale" race, but it got the blood circulating well. We then went on to a party, complete with roast pig – underdone as is usually the case at barbecues. People are very reluctant to believe that a pig cooked on a spit takes at least eight hours. From a practical point of view, I have decided that spit-cooking went out of fashion none too early. It is inefficient of fuel, inefficient of meat (the inside is never cooked until the outside is black and uneatable), messy, and time-consuming. In fact the food at the party was a bit of a flop. Our hostess (a young Frenchwoman) had gone to great trouble to prepare great quantities, but she had used a lot of shrimps, unaware that they were all uncooked. I gathered up those I could, and put them into the barbecue in silver paper, which was a good improvement.

Ghostly Lovers, Baboons and Ticks

Today we, plus three friends from last night and two extra children, went to another lot of hills, about 45km away, where we have sometimes camped in the past. There is a small stream (usually very small) leading up into a range of hills, and we normally leave the main valley and scramble up a rock-slope – steep but manageable by all but the most sensitive to heights – to a smaller valley above which leads into a circle of hills. If there were more water, it would be a bit like Derbyshire, except that at Edale we would have been surprised to see baboons' heads poking up over rocks as they kept an eye on us, and barked warnings to their tribes.

We never see anyone on the hills. Botswanans are not fond of hills, and particularly dislike this one, which has a legend attached to it. A long while ago a couple of lovers, whose parents opposed their match, are said to have run away up the mountain and disappeared, and since then it is said that people who climb *Lentswe la Baratani* (Lovers' Rock) may also fail to come down. This superstition is not shared by cattle, which go up there for water and grass when it is scarce elsewhere. We found a trickle of water in parts of the stream, but enough to fill a number of pools. In the past we have swum in some of the pools, but at present they are low and muddy. Despite this, the place is beautiful, and I am determined to make another camping trip up there again soon.

Apart from the baboons, there is hardly any wildlife larger than a cattle-tick, but there are lots of those of all shapes and sizes, mostly of the pin-head variety. The four dots glued to the first page of this letter were turned up by Nicole on a brief re-examination of my right arm, which in theory had already been picked over. They had also survived a bath and a swim. They look fairly innocuous, but they are the ones that normally seem to carry tick-bite fever – a form of typhus. So far, Nicole and Bernard have escaped this; Dominic and I may have acquired some immunity, but there are several varieties of the fever so we may be running to the doctor later this week. Dominic produced a greater crop than me, through wearing his trousers outside his socks and playing hide and seek in the long grass. He kept a score as they were picked off – 286 I believe including some bigger types. I don't think that will deter him from going back. He's rather proud of his score and may try and do better next time.

We are all feeling healthily tired after the outing, and are ready for an early bed. I hope you are keeping well and can see the end of winter.

Letter from David to Bernard   Gaborone, 02/03/1980

Dominic's Party

We had Dominic's birthday party on Friday. Dominic organised games until Mummy and I came home. I then divided up the party into two teams, and told them to find ways of crossing from the tree house to the earth ridge by the eucalyptus trees without touching the ground. The first team did little more than jump from chair to chair, and wanted to walk along a pole on the ground. I took points off them for being too close to the earth. Dominic's team came next. They had the advantage of having the time to make plans, but they had two big disadvantages: N..., who was unwilling to take his feet off the ground for fear of breaking his neck; and S....., who messed up all Dominic's plans by insisting on stretching the rope they were to swing along from the very top of the syringa tree. I had to allow Dominic extra time to put things right, and let one person go twice to take the place of N..... When they did get their feet off the ground, Dominic's team was the faster, but I penalised it for the mess up, and was able to judge that there had been a draw.

After that, there was a barbecue for the younger members, then *"King Kong"* hired from Home Movies. The film was scratched and battered, but it held together for us. I had never seen it before. It is a sort of classic for photographic effects, although I am sure that I would have been ashamed to be seen going to such a film when it was first re-issued (this was the second *"King Kong"* – there was a much earlier film which was less well made; Dominic says he has seen it on TV).

A Leap Year Birthday

Mummy and I then had a second barbecue with Michel, Agnes, Pascal and Veronique (it was Veronique's birthday too; she was only having her sixth birthday since she was born on 29th February. When you come to think of it, if people are born at the same rate throughout the year, only one person in every 1,461 (i.e. 4 X 365+1) is born on 29th February.

Worrying Police Tactics

Pascal is much happier than he has been for a long time. I can't remember if we told you that the police had arrested him and said they would charge him with having killed a child in a hit and run accident on the Francistown road near Mahalapye before Christmas. Their evidence was only the fact that he had been driving the same sort of vehicle as the one in the accident, and that it had been slightly damaged (by hitting a cow) the same day. Anyway, they have now told him that they cannot tell him when he will be called for identification, and although we dare not raise his hopes too much, we think that this probably means that they have realised that they do not have enough evidence to bring a case.

The Fascination of the Operating Table!

Yesterday morning I went to Pascal and Veronique's to watch an operation on a cat. They are helping the veterinary practice of a vet employed by the Ministry, who has been moved from Gaborone to Lobatse, and they run a surgery from the garage of the house that the Ostrogradskys used to live in. I have never seen an operation of any sort on anything. This was a very routine affair: sterilisation of a female cat. It was made a bit more interesting by the fact that the cat turned out to be pregnant. I was impressed by the efficiency of the operation. The cut was only about 3cm long, and there was hardly any blood. I think the skill consists of knowing where to make the cut, and how deeply, and in being able to recognise what is inside. I have heard of doctors trying to play at being a vet, and taking out all the wrong pieces, with disastrous results.

I brought home the removed uterus in a jar of formalin to show it to Dominic. I had hoped to be able to show the foeti (foetuses – baby kittens in the uterus) but they were still less than 1cm long, and barely distinguishable – little more than white tadpoles with tiny limbs and a visible almost human face.

An Unwelcome Appointment

I have to go out in a minute, as I have a totally unwanted dinner with a visiting World Bank mission. To make matters worse, their arrangements somehow didn't register with the management of the Holiday Inn, and I had to re-make them from scratch, so that if anything now goes wrong it will be my fault; and something is almost bound to go wrong, since it is, after all, the Holiday Inn. In fact, my first attempt to make the dinner booking, done face to face with the manager, also seems to have disappeared from human records, and was re-done yesterday when I went in to order the wine.

Letter to parents   Gaborone, 16/03/1980

Khutse Game Reserve

Last weekend we took off to Khutse game reserve with a bunch of French friends who had never been there before. We are always a bit surprised when people ask us questions like *"Should we bring charcoal to cook on?"* (to which the answer is *"No, we shall pull down a few dead trees"*) – but we were equally naïve ourselves not so long ago. We left on Friday afternoon and camped along the way on Friday night. It's not an ideal arrangement to go to that park over a normal weekend, because it takes eight hours hard driving to get to the place where we camp. In fact, once we were inside the park, we made very slow progress, because there had been good rains recently, and the grass growing between the two wheel tracks was flowering and kept on blocking the radiators, particularly of the leading car.

Confrontation with a Lion

We had a very good weekend all the same. Because of all the rain, we did not see a great deal of game. That may sound paradoxical, but good grazing means that herds disperse. There was, however, enough to satisfy the novices, and the high point – retrospectively at least – was when one of the party wandered over a ridge behind our camp to take photographs, and came face to face with a lion, which stood its ground until he panicked and ran, dropping his camera on the way. We gave the lion time to go away, and then went out to search for the camera, armed with a variety of totally ridiculous weapons (axes, spades) and twice beat a hasty retreat, having met up with the lion again. At one point, she came within about twenty yards of the camp, and watched from behind a bush, as we watched from the top of the Land Rover. Unfortunately, we couldn't find the camera, as the guy who dropped it was understandably vague about the exact route he had taken through the bush.

Cub Camp

This weekend we went out again, on a much more domestic jaunt to a ranch outside Kanye for a one-night camp with twenty-five cub scouts. As you probably know, Nicole helps with the cubs in an attempt to keep the pack going. We had a lot of helpers, and fortunately it did not rain. The cubs are not particularly well organised or well behaved, but I think that for many of them camping is not such a novel experience as for most English children of the same age. They are a lot of little litter-bugs though, including (or perhaps particularly) the European children, who form the majority since the pack comes from Dominic's English-medium school. There are no lions around Kanye, although there are certainly hyenas and leopard, and there must be a lot of poisonous snakes, although we rarely see them. The most savage beast I saw was one small scorpion, when I lifted up a stone in the course of trail-laying. Nicole and I slept very well in our tent, with a sheet of foam under our sleeping bag and a blanket on top (it is hot in daytime but not at night).

Margaret's New Home

It sounds as if Margaret has at last solved her housing problem – or at least, moved from the buying problem to the re-building problem. The situation of the house sounds excellent. I have always wanted to have a stream in my garden. I suppose David (Pearce) will find somewhere to cut himself off from the re-building, which doesn't strike me as his scene, and leave it to Margaret, who wished it on herself.

Boarding School for Dominic

Will you be in Leicester in August? We shall be going to Guadeloupe this summer, but shall travel back via England as we did two years ago, and would like to spend a few days with you. Nicole will be putting Dominic into school. I do hope he enjoys it. He has such high hopes, and may find it rather surprising to be one of the very little ones again; also, he may well not see nearly as much of Bernard as he expects. I shall feel rather bereft without a child around. He has become quite a sturdy character – I don't mean physically, although he's growing well and is a fit wiry little boy – but he's very good at getting on with other children, and exceptionally good with younger children. He's imaginative, and able to express himself well, and he's got quite a competitive streak. He just won a prize in a stamp-collectors' show – his entry in the stamp exhibition was his own work and his own idea.

Garden and Livestock

My garden is still a bit of a mess. We have had a rapid turnover of gardeners recently, and with the weekends away, I haven't spent much time on it. We had a good crop of sweet corn, and we have had lots of green peppers, and small quantities of various other things, but the soil gets tired very quickly here, and even with chicken manure and rabbit manure and lots of compost, it is difficult to keep it producing well. However we have had a good crop of white guavas from one of the trees I planted, and lots of pigeon peas – tree peas – from seed gathered in Guadeloupe. Next year, before we leave, I am hoping to get fruit from all my citrus trees. At present we have one grapefruit, about half a dozen mandarins, and a dozen lemons ripening on the trees.

My ducks have still only produced one duckling between the five of them, and have stopped laying as the days have got shorter. I replaced all my chickens about a month ago with twenty new ones, and five little cockerels to fatten for the pot. Two days ago I found one of the new hens near death with what appeared to be the symptoms of Newcastle's disease (an epidemic disease), or possibly, leucosis, since on examination I discovered the liver and kidneys were grossly enlarged. It is now in the freezer, looking perfectly healthy (but dead!). I am keeping an eye on all the others. I deloused them all yesterday, which is an unpleasant chore, but not half so unpleasant as plucking a bird that is crawling with lice (as was the sick one that I culled). Dominic has two rabbits ready for the pot, and four babies to take their place, but the nasty work of killing and skinning keeps on being deferred. I feel much worse about killing them than I do about the chickens.

Speeches for Others

I wrote a "major" speech for our Assistant Minister last week. I calculated it would take him about fifteen minutes. Afterwards he told me that, translating as he went along, it took him one and a half hours. This week I have done a much more modest job for the Minister (opening a Convention of Bank employees) because I know he reads slowly. I always find it fun to see my words reported in the paper, attributed to someone else – sometimes bits of Presidential speeches.

Letter to Sheila and family   Gaborone, 23/03/1980

Tricks of Time

You see from the date (year altered) that I, at least, am still in 1979. But then, perhaps you are still 21. Happy Birthday!

Coping with Foot-and-Mouth

We are rolling on towards winter, with fine days, cold nights, a good harvest expected, and the agricultural scene only marred by persistent foot-and-mouth disease, which has at least the virtue of providing a job for Nicole. It is extraordinarily difficult to control foot-and-mouth in a country the size of France with three million cattle, and lots of game that are carriers of the disease. Mind you, I think the game are usually innocent scapegoats (if you see what I mean) because I understand that it is experimentally difficult to infect cattle from game, and I suspect that most of our problems arise from ineffective vaccination procedures and movement control, combined with persistent low-level infections in cattle; but we are not meant to say that.

The Khutse Lioness

We visited Khutse a few weeks ago. Inside the park, the grass was so high that we had to keep stopping to unblock the radiators of the cars, as they clogged up with a solid mat of grass seeds. We did not see a great deal of game, but had our first close brush with a lion. One of the party went out over a ridge behind the camp, to take photographs of the savannah plain, and came face to face with a lioness. He held his ground for some time, but when the lion trotted around to get a look at him from another angle, he broke and ran, dropping his camera in the process. We went back to look for the camera, but twice met the lion and had to retreat. In the end she disappeared, but we still didn't find the lost camera. Possibly there is a lion roaming around Khutse, wearing a camera in order to be mistaken for a tourist.

Becoming Second Cellist

Gaborone has acquired another cellist, who is certainly better than me, so I am not doing quite so much music as before, but we are practising for the *Messiah* next weekend (Nicole in the choir, I in the orchestra) and another concert only a few days later. Dominic is in the second concert, but not in the *Messiah*.

Tool Buying Project

Have you yet spent all the money I sent you for buying tools? Don't worry if the prices are going up. That's the intention. I should be far more worried if you said that they were going down.

Enclosed with this letter was an article from the "Leicester Mercury" daily newspaper, date February 7th 1980, by Victor Collin. The subject was old carpenters' tools. The writer had recently been buying at market stalls in East Anglia and a photograph shows "a plough-plane made by Griffiths of Norwich about 1900, mounted in brass.... and under-priced at £18. Such pieces will certainly increase in stature over the next few years." This information was intended to spur me on with the search for bargains.

Letter to parents   Gaborone, 18/05/1980

Vetting the Boys' Letters

Dominic's thank you letter went through three drafts before being judged fit for release, although there was not much to choose between the three. Every time I look at anything written by my boys I get an appalling feeling of *déjà vu – encore vu* if you like, because my writing certainly doesn't improve. Also, I still find that almost everything I write starts with a correction; - but at least I can spell. Yes, I know, *"he paced his trunc"*, but that was some time ago.

Working Safari

While Dominic was away on his exciting safari I managed a short working safari of my own, which took me past hippo pools and giraffe, not to mention wildebeeste, buffalo, impala, water-buck and elephants by the score, although the rarest sighting was a honey-badger (looks very much like our badger, but has a particular fondness for wild honeycombs). In more serious moments I was discussing the boundaries of forest reserves with Land Boards, looking at a Brigades Trust (local development/ training trust) that had been grossly run down and mismanaged by American Baptist Missionaries, and studying *bunds* (dykes) being built by famine relief labour to keep floods out of seasonally flooded crop areas. After the latter exercise, I shall make sure that I ask for a bilharzia screening when I have my next medical check. The Permanent Secretary (who is a sufficiently good friend to be thoroughly rude and not to mind when I reply in the same vein) grumbled a bit at my P160 travel bill. It actually costs more now to pay an officer mileage allowance to travel to a place like Maun or Kasane in his own car than to let him go by plane. I did the first leg of my journey by train, the next two by catching (cadging) lifts with other officers, and the return by plane, carrying my sleeping bag and blankets with me so that I could sleep out on floors or – if necessary – in the bush.

Future Work Prospects

Thanks for having Bernard for the holiday. He does enjoy being at home, even when it is not this home. You are right, I shall hate having both of them away from home, but I don't see the alternative. I still don't know what (if anything) I shall be doing next year, but I don't think there's much chance that I shall be doing it in the U.K. There just don't seem to be any jobs. The funny thing is that the U.K. people here keep on getting enormous pay rises. In the last months, they have combined a big local rise with an even bigger increase in the U.K. component. The non-civil-servant expatriates working for statutory corporations etc. are on a parity arrangement and have had really enormous increases to match the civil servant expatriates.

I think Dominic will miss Africa more than Bernard. He's always been more at ease here and, like me, enjoys the spaces, and things like camping and riding. I'm beginning to wonder if I ought to learn to ride. I went down to the stables last weekend to collect manure for the garden, and suddenly found the idea very attractive.

Gardens and Farms

My garden does not flourish greatly. The soil here gets tired very fast. So do the gardeners, including me. However, I have a pleasant patch of chrysanthemums, and some carnations (grown from seed). Someone picked our one grapefruit, but so far no-one has found the tangerines, and I am expecting great things – or at least things – from my asparagus bed next spring. My present batch of chickens is without doubt the worst so far – even the poultry officer admits that, and he sold them to me – but, they more than fill our needs. At least one of my ducks is laying, which is unseasonal, but I feel that such enthusiasm deserves to be rewarded, so I am going to let her sit.

Some acquaintances have just bought themselves a farm on the Limpopo – 2,500 *Morgan* (6,200 acres) plus 200 cattle plus a house plus fences (expensive now – P300 for 600km) plus 100 orange trees, all for P50,000 – a very tempting proposition although I think they have got an unusual bargain – but Nicole doesn't seem to think that cattle farming on the Limpopo is quite her style. She might put it more forcibly.

Letter from Nicole to parents-in-law   Gaborone, 01/06/1980

Winter Chills

David left yesterday for Tanzania where he will spend a week. He is attending a conference at Arusha in the north of the country. He spent the night at Lusaka and flew to Arusha today. He will certainly be less cold than here although it is the cool season in Tanzania. Arusha has a very pleasant climate and it is cool most of the year.

It is winter now and for the last two weeks the weather has been very cold, especially at night. We have to turn on the heating in the morning and evening. I bought 100 kg of wood three weeks ago and thought we would have enough to last us until July when we go on leave, but it is nearly all gone. I went to buy some more yesterday but the hardware shop where I get the wood had run out. In the meantime we shall use the air conditioner but electricity is expensive here.

The Mikado

I have been very busy lately with the rehearsals of *"The Mikado"*. I am in the chorus. We are rather an old lot and are not little maids of under eighteen. Most of us are forty and above. Anyway it is fun. *"The Mikado"* will be on for two weeks. Tickets are selling well.

Sick Hens

Our chickens are a dead loss. They lay very few eggs and the few that David has killed because they look thin and ill had cancer of the liver; one which he killed last week not only had cancer of the liver but growths all over its skin. David will kill the ones which are left before we go on leave and will start with a fresh batch on our return. The last two litters of rabbits are really doing well. There are a few lettuces and Chinese cabbages growing but it is really too cold for anything to grow at the moment.

School and Holiday Preparations

I have asked my friend Ruth Johnson to despatch Bernard's trunk to your address by British Rail or British Road. I hope it will survive the journey as it is rather battered. When I am in England I shall buy him a new one. I am going to write to Cash's to order name tapes for the children and I shall ask them to address the parcel to you.

We shall leave for our holiday on 9th July. We first fly to New York where we shall spend three days, and from New York will fly direct to Guadeloupe. We shall arrive in Guadeloupe on 13th July but I think we shall land a few hours before Bernard.

I am enclosing a photo of Dominic and David taken at the last concert of the music society.

Letter to Sheila and family   Gaborone, 25/06/1980

(Nicole writing)

I do apologise for not sending David (Wright) birthday wishes and a cheque but life has been hectic since Easter. I was acting in *"The Mikado"* and for about three months I hardly spent an evening at home. It was fun but very demanding. It is over now after eight very successful shows. I appreciate spending the evening at home, in the warmth. Winter is here and for the last week it has really been very cold, even during the day. The temperature has been one or two degrees centigrade every night, all this week.

Orchestral Concert, Gabarone, 1980. David and Dominic

Kenya 1982, Bernard, David, Dominic and Nicole

Complex Travel Plans

We are leaving for Guadeloupe next week, but are stopping in the States first. I am leaving with Dominic on 4th July. We are flying to New York and from there will take a bus or train to go to Williamstown (MA.) to stay with a friend. We shall return to New York on 10th to meet David who will be flying to New York via Nairobi. We fly to Guadeloupe on 13th July. We shall meet Bernard in Guadeloupe; he is arriving a few hours after us.

We shall be in Leicester on 16th August and hope to see you while we are there.

I enclose a cheque for David and Thomas.

Love to you all, Nicole

(David writing) Hello!

I've just been making pig's head brawn and my fingers are impregnated with grease, so my pen keeps giving out. No, we haven't taken up pig husbandry, but we have just bought a pig and shared it with someone else, and we were left with the head. Over the next week we should be killing about thirteen here, so we should have a full freezer when we get back. Mind you, I shall sell most of those at work. I shall try and find time to write a proper letter from Guadeloupe.

Lots of love, David

Tropical Lassitude

I know I should have written before. My excuse is that I have lost the habit of the tropics. I'm surprised to find that I need to sleep about one and a half times as much as usual – and still wake up feeling weary. However, apart from one time when I found I had a temperature of 102', it's not a debilitating weariness, but the comfortable lassitude of the tropics.

We all travelled without incident by our different routes – Bernard via Paris; Nicole and Dominic via Williamstown, Massachussetts, where they stayed with old friends; myself via Nairobi, meeting D and N in New York, where we spent three days.

Beach Days and Octopus Stew

Here, we spend our time sleeping, eating, and going to the beach. None of us has yet been too painfully sunburned; all of us are peeling. Predictably, I turned a pinker hue than the others, and I think that was probably the reason for my temperature. The small boy of an old friend of Nicole's, also staying here (and partly Guadeloupean so he should have some immunity), was so badly burned that he came up in blisters that broke into raw flesh, so that for a week after he arrived he was unable to swim and had to wear bandages all over his shoulders. Dominic is the member of our party who has so far suffered the greatest natural injury; M. Fortuné gave him a huge (land) crab that he had found in the garden, and when Dominic poked it, it took off all the skin from the tip of his index finger, and part of the nail. However, that too is now cured.

We have been on one sailing expedition for two days in Denys' new boat, and may go on another. I have fished four baby octopus from a bank of conch shells off the beach, and intend to get a couple more so as to make a reasonable octopus stew.

Today we all went off for a swim in the thermal baths on the other side of the island – water 70-80' Fahrenheit, which is very relaxing, but not very conducive to energetic swimming.

Guadeloupe, July 1980

Left,
Nicole and brother
Denys with Great
Grandmother Fortuné

Right
Trekking across the
island - Bernard,
Dominic and Denys

Assorted Relatives

We have paid two visits to Nicole's ninety-seven year old grandmother, who was remarkably sprightly, although she is getting deafer, and sometimes has difficulty placing people she hasn't seen for some time (we didn't fall into that category).

All in all, we made up a household of fourteen, including Denys' family, of whom seven are young persons between the ages of eleven and seventeen. You can imagine that it is not always a peaceful household. Without too much self-deception, I think I can say that our two are the easiest of the younger guests. Denys' Davyd is now fourteen. His sister Sylvie is of pleasant disposition but somewhat untrained, and has grown up too fast for comfort. It's almost impossible to conceive that she is about the same age as Dominic; at eleven there is no doubt that she is a young woman, if not a young lady. Genevieve, whom I have met several times in Paris, as far back as 1961, has two large girls of fourteen and seventeen, and a boy who is a few months younger than Dominic, and is a shrimp, just about the same size and build as he is. The girls generally do as they are told (asked) but with a very ill grace when it doesn't suit them. There was smouldering rebellion the other day when they were herded off to the other side of the island to meet elderly friends and relatives whom they had never seen or heard of before, and whom they would evidently wish to plunge back into the same oblivion. Genevieve, who has never before visited Guadeloupe, was more interested than they were in finding her roots. Mind you, their idea of a good day seems to consist of wandering up and down the beach and seafront of Ste Anne, which strikes me as even more boring than meeting elderly relatives.

Back to England

I have just received your letter of 21st July. If this letter makes equal speed, it should reach you before we do, but I may telegram you just to make sure. We should arrive in London on 16th, and stay the night with Ruth Johnson, then we would like to go to Leicester. I shall have to speed back to Botswana after a very brief stay. Nicole will stay longer to put Dominic into school – but not necessarily in Leicester.

Death of a President

I am completely out of touch with events in Botswana after the death of the President, which was expected when we left. My Permanent Secretary had already been seconded to the Office of the President to make funeral arrangements.

Letter to parents   Gaborone, 12/10/1980

Farewell to the Garden

We have grapes on the vine, plums beginning to form on the plum tree, apricots ditto, lots of little peaches, a few sprays of apple blossom, and a variety of citrus all flowering. Very little of this will be for us. I think I must write out a guide to the garden for the benefit of the next occupant, although I shall be neither surprised nor heartbroken to find that the garden has been reduced to a dusty desert by the time I visit it again. My enjoyment is in doing things, not sitting back and contemplating them when done.

Dressing for the Climate

The weather is getting really hot. Tonight I put on a Sudanese cotton *jallaba*, which seems the right sort of garment for this weather. Unfortunately, I think it would cause an unseemly stir if I were to wear it to work.

Tomorrow I am going to a meeting in Kasane – 900-plus kilometres as the light aeroplane flies. I hope to be home again for dinner! I shall be talking to the local Land Board about timber concessions on tribal land.

A Desert Trip

Two weekends ago we took advantage of a public holiday to take a more leisurely trip into the desert. There was not much game, because there had been recent rain. The high points of the trip were a pair of lions, who mated noisily all night mildly terrifying one of our party who had never been out there before (sleeping in the Land Rover, wondering whether she dared get out to spend a penny), and a Kori bustard, which is (I am told) the heaviest flying bird (the Condor has a wider wing-span, but is lighter). One of our party was a very keen ornithologist; he kept on pointing out birds and bird songs that I would not otherwise have noticed. We found a plover's nest – which is really not a nest, just three speckled eggs on the

ground in a very shallow depression. The best small bird was a little swallow-tailed bee-eater. It was a good weekend without mishaps, and we took it leisurely enough to come back feeling rested. Time for bed.
Lots of love, David

Christmas Letter to all friends   Gaborone, 28/12/1980

Reflections on Gaborone

I feel I owe rather a lot of people an updating letter, so I hope they will not mind sharing one. There would not have been any chance of my writing at this length to each of you for months, because of our forthcoming move to Nairobi.

I am already feeling nostalgic for Gaborone and my job. I have greatly enjoyed both. I am sorry I didn't manage to persuade more friends to come here and have a look. Physically, Gaborone is not a very inspiring place; just a pleasant small town, growing very fast. I find our piece of it very pleasant because there are lots of trees and bourgainvillias in the gardens of the older houses (maximum age about 16 years).

New Suburbs

New suburbs are growing out at an extraordinary pace, taking up old ranching areas. They are of a very much higher quality than the old low-cost housing areas put up around the time of Independence, but those areas have a vitality about them which is still missing from the new areas. The site and service schemes where people put up their own houses on serviced plots, and the privately owned low-cost housing areas are interesting, because of all the activity to up-grade houses. At weekends everyone seems to be adding an extra room, or stripping off an old roof and putting on a new one to bring all the piece-meal extensions under one roof. In the south of the town, the squatter area, "Old Naledi" (*naledi* means "star") is still growing, but roads have been punched through it, stand-pipes are being put in, and people are getting title to land and improving their plots. In two other places, the town is reaching out to pre-existing villages: Tlokweng ("among the Tlokwa" – the chief town of the small tribe of Chief Gaborone) and Mogoditshane (*"mo go ditshane"* – "where there are baboons"). People from town with an eye on the future have been getting building plots from the tribal authorities in these villages, and building modern houses among the *rondavels*, but the villagers are now beginning to resent this, and refuse them plots, because these townspeople play no part in local affairs.

A Hungry Party

Last weekend we went to a party in Tlokweng given in honour of some friends who have been renting a house in a compound for the past two years, but are now returning home to the U.K. It was quite an occasion. There were three parties going on at the same time. The landlord, a tall solemn man, had bought a lot of beef for stewing, but it melted away before the crowds that came to eat it, and the children, who naturally came last in the queue for food, received only a dribble of gravy on their *bogobe* (sorghum porridge), rice, potatoes, and cabbage salad.

Idyllic Country Living

Some other ex-patriates live even further out of town. We have several friends living in a village about 15km out; one couple have built themselves a beautiful stone and thatch house in the hills above the village, where they keep their pigs, hens and ducks. Life there seems very pleasant. People are friendly, and honest, and the only inconveniences are the distance, and the fact that the water keeps giving up. During the dry weather this year they were frequent visitors with a truck full of water drums and containers of various sorts. Some of the more permanent expatriates, like David Finlay, my Permanent Secretary, live in splendid isolation on freehold farms, where they control their own small communities of domestic servants, workers, and their families.

Practical Husbandry

We did not feel that we could sacrifice the time needed to live outside Gaborone, or justify giving up our rent-free house, free water and free electricity, but I managed to bring part of the rural area into our garden. It started off with the chickens, and we went on to rabbits (Dominic's, not mine) and ducks. I went into this with some apprehension, since I had never really kept any animals before. In theory I once owned a whole rabbit, and various other pets, but I never felt that they depended on my stewardship. In practice, things worked out very well. We have almost always had very fresh eggs, and a surplus to sell, and we have been quite cold-blooded about killing and eating old hens. Dominic's rabbits bred and made him a nice chunk of pocket money. The ducks were the least successful part of the venture. They laid lots of eggs, but until this year they hatched only one. I think the drake was to blame. This year we ate him, had a short and unproductive interlude with a very elderly drake from a friend, who went the same way, and then replaced him with a young and vigorous one from our friends in the village. Since then, the ducks have not looked back. We have had three successful hatchings, the last only a week ago. Unfortunately someone broke in and stole him and one of the ducks, about a month ago; but he had done his work, and was only waiting for a final appearance on our table.

Experimental Construction

I doubt if the ducks have really broken even, but they gave me a good excuse to try out various schemes. I made a duck pond by digging a hole, lining it with wire mesh, and smearing that with a strong cement mixture. So far, that has held water for two years. The only disadvantage that I can see is that the smearing of cement is best done by hand, and leaves one with cement-filled sores that take ages to heal. Incidentally, the main thing wrong with the ponds we made when we were children was that they had no reinforcement, that's why they cracked and leaked. A thin skin (3cm) with reinforcement evidently can hold water and last. I thatched part of the roof of the pen with stalks of elephant grass, maize and sunflower; it didn't keep the rain out, but it kept the ducks in. I made a *pozzolanic* cement of rotten bricks and builder's lime for the floor, and that has stayed very solid. And I arranged a run-off to take surplus dirty water to my vegetables, which appreciated this flow of liquid manure. I also learned a lot about building, and building supervision, by rebuilding our leaky old swimming pool. This involved concreting and bricklaying, and so far has held water for two seasons.

Leafy Gardens

As for the plants, my gardens will never look like Abbey Park, (Leicestershire) and I have never had the nerve to use scarce water on the lawn, but I have planted about sixty trees and shrubs, and picked at least some peaches, lemons, tangerines, guavas, figs, plums, apricots and grapes from them, and I hope my successor will get grapefruit, oranges and maybe even apples as well, from trees I have planted. I have grown a lot of vegetables, with very mixed success, but my two main triumphs have been asparagus (from seed) and globe artichokes.

Regretful Parting

I shall be very sorry to leave the Ministry of Agriculture here. I feel there is a great deal still to be done, and I do not have full confidence that it will be done as I would have wished. Of course, this is always the case, and it cannot be a reason for staying put. Generally, I have greatly enjoyed my work, which has given me an opportunity both to get involved in policy, and in the detail of implementation. The country is small enough for one to be able to see the effects of decisions on the ground. I also feel I have achieved quite a lot; it is satisfying to be able to identify policies and decisions which would not have been taken if I had not been there. I hope that I shall be able to find my next job as an aid administrator in the Ford Foundation's Nairobi office equally satisfying.

Nicole has also enjoyed her work here with the vaccine institute, and doesn't look forward to the prospect of unemployment in Nairobi, but I think something will turn up for her; it always has so far.

Moving to Nairobi

When we tell people we are leaving, the reaction is almost invariably the same. First, they look a bit anxious, and say cautiously *"Are you going back to the U.K.?"* When we say that we are going to Nairobi, they brighten, and say *"Ah! You'll enjoy that, won't you?"* For many people here, Nairobi has been a memorable stop in a series of moves and localisations; the next step after Botswana is often the Solomon Islands, or Fiji, or Papua New Guinea (known among the migrant expats. as "PNG".

Absent Sons

The other big change in the last year has been, of course, sending Dominic to Lord William's School along with Bernard, leaving us childless here. To be honest, I was dreading it. I very much enjoyed having the boys with us, and felt I was able to make up for being a bit of an absentee father when I was working in London. Certainly, I do miss them, yet the change was less traumatic than I had feared. Also, it is good that we generally get short and happy letters from both of them. Dominic seems to have settled in well. He wrote early on that some people teased him for his lisp, which is hardly noticeable now, but he took it philosophically and asked for speech therapy classes. He has just written asking if he can join the local scouts. And of course Bernard is now well settled in.

Travel Plans

The boys will come out to Gaborone this week, for a final visit. We shall spend Christmas here, and on New Year's Eve, Bernard, Dominic, the dog Cain and I will travel to Nairobi. Nicole has volunteered to stay here until January third to supervise loading of sea-freight (air-freight leaves this week). We shall step into a house that I know, that is already furnished and staffed, and has two or three bathrooms, and a large unkempt hillside garden. We shall have lots of room for guests....

Nostalgia for Safari Life

Unfortunately I do not think we shall have an opportunity to go on a last safari. We have taken much greater advantage of game parks and the "bush" than we did in Tanzania. There are several reasons for this: we know more, we were well introduced to camping here by friends, the boys are bigger, we have the Ford Foundation Land Rover at our disposal, and we have more local leave than before. We have been out quite a few times, to the Khutse park, north to Maun and Kasane, or east to the Tuli block. Nicole's parents can hardly believe that I have induced her to camp out in lion-infested waterless bush for the fun of it. All in all, we have seen a very good selection of Southern African mammals and birds – including the kori bustard, the largest bird, and of course, lion and elephant. In his last term Dominic went on an excellent safari organised by the school including night outings and tracking. Despite carrying snake serum, and frequent encounters with scorpions and tsetse fly, we have suffered nothing worse than tick-bite fever (tick typhus).

Compensations of Ex-Pat. Life

I'm glad I don't have to endure the English winter, or the frequent sight and sound of Mrs. Thatcher on the box. Here the weather is warm – occasionally uncomfortably so, but I still prefer that to the cold. And Mrs. Thatcher is at a comfortable distance, capable of being classed with Mr. Reagan as a general disaster of democratic choice.

(Personal P.S.)

We are very busy now packing, and being invited around to people who ply us with food and drinks, so that when we get home we feel like sleeping it off rather than doing necessary things. In the rush, we have not yet had time to do your puzzle, but thank you in anticipation.

I think the boys are pleased to be back in the sun and the warmth. The swimming pool is having a last fling of heavy use.

See you in Nairobi?!

Lots of love, David and Nicole

CHAPTER FOUR
LETTERS 1981–1985

Letter to parents

The Ford Foundation, Nairobi,
Kenya, 25/01/1981

An Easy Move to Nairobi

I am afraid I haven't written to you for ages, even to say thank you for Christmas presents, which I do now. Thank you! I hope the boys have written. I haven't monitored their performance in this area.

We are now comfortably settled in after the easiest move we have ever made. The house was fully furnished and servanted in preparation for our arrival. Our air freight arrived about ten days after us, giving us a few more clothes, cups and saucers, and the radio, record player, etc. We are still waiting for sea freight, which among other things contains a large selection of good quality seeds. I hope they don't get seized by customs. The seeds commonly available here are appalling – just as bad as when we were in Dar es Salaam ten years ago. I feel like writing to the seed company and congratulating them for providing a point of stability in a changing world.

New House....

Our house (like many Kenyan houses, including those still being built by the Kenyan elite) is rather like something out of Manor Road or the posh part of Oadby Hill. It has a pleasant atmosphere, and the boys were quite impressed. From a security point of view, it is like a sieve, with eight outside doors, including sets of French windows, and doors onto roofs and the balcony (easily climbable), and lots of old-fashioned windows. The crime rate is said to have gone down since Kenyatta's death (helped by one or two bloody shoot-outs), but I am afraid we are still going to have to deface the house with the usual paraphernalia of bars.

New Garden

You would love our garden. It has been allowed to run down by the last two tenants, but has survived because it was originally well laid out and planted. Francis, the gardener, is a big friendly chap, who seems to enjoy being told to shift tons of earth around, and although he doesn't have much nous about gardening, he has the muscle-power to complement my instructions. Of course, what makes it a bit difficult is that my instructions all have to be given in Swahili, which is a language I still speak more of than Setswana, but I am by no means fluent.

The garden runs down quite a steep hillside, and is laid out in a series of terraces. The top one is dominated by a huge kapok tree, which overshadows the house, and provides a place for plants like anthuriums that like shade. Then you go down stone steps to the next two layers, which have small lawns and flower gardens. There must be three dozen rose bushes, all old and rather sick-looking, and mostly suffering from scale insects (not, I think, an English problem; primitive sucking insects that don't walk about, but fix on like little limpets). Despite this, the bushes manage to produce a regular supply of roses for the house, so I reckon this is a good place for roses. I have just bought another fourteen bushes from a really excellent nursery outside town – apparently all Kenyan-run, which is one of the surprises of life here. I have re-made the next two layers (or Francis has), using tree-thinnings and a lot of spade-work to recreate narrow terraces on a very steep bit. The first has half a dozen coffee seedlings, just as a touch of fantasy, and will have five newly-planted citrus (planting trees for someone else again!) and the next has about ten assorted bananas, begged from a Kenyan colleague. Then there is a large but completely dilapidated wire-netting house for vegetables and soft fruit, on a series of three shallow terraces, and a gentle slope with rough lawn, black wattle trees (mimosa trees) and jacaranda. Of the three Ford houses here, I feel I have got the most interesting garden.

Letter to sister Margaret and
family, from Nicole
Nairobi, 28/01/1981

I hope that life at your house is now more comfortable and that all the building work is over. I cannot think of anything more annoying than living among dust, plaster etc. How is your livestock?

A Month in Nairobi

We have now been in Nairobi for 28 days and I must say it has been one of our less troublesome moves. When we arrived a fully furnished house was waiting for us and also a houseboy and a gardener. It is sometimes quite difficult to take over other people's staff (the houseboy and gardener had been working for David's predecessor) but the change over was very easy and I quickly told the houseboy what was expected of him. He is quite an old man (67) and if he were a European he would now be enjoying retired life. The house is vast and palatial but with only the two of us there is not much to do.

The garden is very big and David's first priority was to chop some trees down in order to prepare a vegetable garden. We have been buying quite a lot of plants and today the gardener planted thirteen rose trees.

City Life

Nairobi is a big, modern city and for the first few days we were quite scared to drive around and what made it worse was that I did not know where I was going. I was pleased to have the children with me to direct me. Bernard has a very good sense of orientation. Driving is very fast and drivers are not very courteous; one must have eyes everywhere when driving. The shops are quite well stocked and there is a profusion of fruit and vegetables which we lacked in Botswana. The only dark cloud is a permanent shortage (it seems) of flour and rice.

As regard to entertainment we are rather spoiled: there are several cinemas and two theatres. The *Maison Francaise* is very dynamic and organises film shows, concerts and exhibitions. The Music Society is also very active; once a week they have lunch-time concerts; there is a larger concert every three months, and social evenings for members. I have of course joined the choir. David has not made up his mind whether he should join the orchestra. He doesn't have his cello yet (it is in the sea freight) and it depends of course on how much time he will have free; he will have to travel quite a lot and already this year he will have to be away sometime in March and then in May.

School Holiday Plans

Margaret did say when I saw her in September that you would welcome the children for this coming half-term. I am afraid their half-term is very short (20th-25th February) having had three weeks holiday at Christmas. I have left it to my friend Ruth Johnson to decide where they should go for half-term (either to you or to Sheila) - it all depends on which place is the easiest to get to transport-wise. If you have any suggestions please phone her... perhaps you could phone Ruth in a week's time to see what she has decided.

Dominic has settled down very well at school and his work has been very good. Having Bernard with him has helped a lot.
Love to you all, Nicole

A Busy City

We have now been in Nairobi for one month. Coming from Gaborone we had quite a shock particularly as regards traffic. There are very few cars in Gaborone, no traffic jams. But here it is a different story. Driving here is like driving in any big city in England. It is easy when one knows one's way but being new, we get in the wrong lane, and also get lost. Nairobi is a very pleasant city; there are lots of shops and supermarkets, and a profusion of fruit and vegetables. People are also more practical and take initiatives. There is also more corruption.

Empty Rooms

We have a very big house, too big for us really. On the ground floor there are a big sitting room, big dining room (rather stately), breakfast room, kitchen, pantry, laundry room. Upstairs: four bedrooms, a study, two bathrooms. The garden is huge and David has been very busy fixing the wire netting over the vegetable garden to stop the birds from eating the plants. We have also been buying plants and roses. David's predecessor was not interested in gardening and did not bother to plant anything during the three years he lived here.

Work versus Leisure

I am enjoying a day of leisure for the time being. It is nice to be able to relax and read. I do not think it will be possible for me to get a job here because there are a lot of secretaries (Indians and Kenyans) who are citizens. Besides I do not want to work full-time, at least during the holiday, as I feel I should give some of my time to the children; I see so little of them. We live quite a long way from town and I should be available to take them swimming, riding etc. while they are here. Not to worry, something might turn up. The only thing I miss when I am unemployed is not having my own money to do what I want with it.

An Equable Climate

The climate here is very pleasant and I understand why the English liked this country when they first came here. The temperature does not go above 27' during the day and in the evening it is between 14'-10'. It is a pleasant change after the heat of Gaborone.

Letter to parents   Nairobi, 07/03/1981

Crossed Wires Across Continents

Thanks for your letter. I hope I remember to put a cheque with this one for Dominic's cello repairs. Yes, of course I approve. In fact I wish his teacher were not so cautious. It's so silly that Dominic's practice should be messed around because his cello needs fixing. When I realised this was happening, I sent the teacher a cheque and a letter giving her general authorisation for repairs up to £20, or some figure like that, but apparently that will not work either because she is not allowed to hold balances on behalf of pupils. She is in some sort of uncomfortable hybrid position between being a private teacher and a public servant. She sent me a rather defensive letter back saying she "certainly hadn't undertaken the repairs without proper authorisation" – which is, of course, exactly what I tried to tell her she could do.

New Agricultural Advisor Role

From your letter, I am not sure if I have fully explained to you what I am now doing. I am at present not working for any government, not even in a quasi-official capacity as I was in Botswana. I am now the agricultural programme advisor of the Ford Foundation office here. As an aid organisation, we are very small by conventional standards. Our office covers eighteen countries in the region, and spends between 2 and 2.5 million dollars a year. Our main areas of activity are agriculture / rural development / food policy / programmes to raise the status of women, law, human and civil rights, indigenous social science capacity, health, nutrition, population and refugees. Because we are small and relatively highly staffed, we are an innovative and experimental donor. We try to avoid direct administration of projects, and work through government agencies, universities, private researchers, and local and foreign non-government organisations.

Projects to Improve Food Production and Diet

For example, I am currently dealing with a prospective project initiated by Catholic Relief Service to develop a system by which sunflower, and possibly other oilseeds grown in semi-arid areas, can be de-hulled and processed locally, so that they make a direct contribution to the diet. Another project with a private Kenyan environmental organisation will experiment with agro-forestry using schools and local organisations. This is particularly relevant to the fragile ecologies of overcrowded uplands (many farms in high rainfall areas of Kenya are less than one acre of steep hillside) and semi-arid rangeland (say, 100-600mm rainfall a year plus high evapo-transpiration, and easily turned into shifting sand-desert). I also deal with what is left of the Botswana Technical Assistance project (which is what I was part of), but we are running that down over the next eighteen months.

Range of Political Philosophies

The region is very varied. A lot of countries are extremely difficult to work in, generally because their governments have decided they know all the answers, and are patently making a terrible mess of things. These include Tanzania, Ethiopia, and Zambia. A few countries however are very exciting, because of a wealth of creative talent inside and outside government. Kenya and Zimbabwe are the best examples. Coming from countries where one has to develop an instinct for dealing with fragile psyches and general intellectual insecurity, it is a delightful shock to come across lots of self-confident and articulate professional Africans – and I don't mean the sort of brash aggressive articulateness that comes from insecurity. These are people who are reflective and open to ideas.

Brassiéres Open Doors to Co-operation!

On Friday, I am off on a trip to Tanzania and Ethiopia – two problem children. Both countries are in a terrible mess. Some Ethiopians are expecting a worse famine soon than that which brought down the Emperor. Tanzania already has serious food shortages. I have to take a lot of presents with me for friends and relatives of Goran Hyden's wife (Goran is the Representative) who comes from Tanzania (including a couple of brassiéres!)

"Wish You Were Here"

You really ought to come out here for a holiday. You would have liked Botswana, but in some ways I think you would like Kenya even more. Mummy would love our garden, and I need her advice on roses. I have about a hundred, but most of them are poor weak old things. I hope they will perk up when the rains come. They do occasionally produce some very beautiful flowers, and periodically I count the buds to see if I am making progress. I think I must be, because I am now approaching twenty buds, whereas at first I seldom had more than six or seven. I have bought a few more, about half of which promptly died, but they are cheap enough – from 8-16sh. I keep on looking out of the window at a new bed that I am preparing for floribundas. I have been pouring water into it for hours, but its absorbtive capacity seems to be almost infinite. The soil is heavy red clay – quite structureless below the first few inches, and rock hard. I got Francis to dig me a trench about eighteen inches deep and the same wide. We have put two inches of gravel into the bottom for drainage, and I have filled the rest with the excavated soil, mixed with a sack of chicken manure and a great pile of unrotted acacia leaves and pods, plus about fifteen kg. of builders' lime. The leaves may drain the soil of nitrogen as they rot, but I can replace that from a packet, and they should improve the structure. I aim to have at least one really healthy bed of roses. I am also taking cuttings of canina and a multiflora rootstock that has taken over one of the old rose plants, in the fond belief that I may be able to bud my own roses. Why not? I have yet to get one of my budding attempts to work, but it is very easy to make rootstocks, and in principle budding is straightforward enough.

Exotic Birds

The other thing that you would like here is the bird life. I have just been reminded of this by the sight of a large dark-green crested bird with solid scarlet wings gliding across the garden below me. I am in the sun-room, a sort of lighthouse stuck onto one corner of our bedroom, and the garden slopes down the hill in front of me. We don't yet know the name of this bird, but he comes to eat the ripe guavas. Earlier, I saw three buzzards or hawks circling above the garden. One was evidently in someone else's air space, and kept on being tackled in flight. When those guys come out, the other birds disappear. Other birds we hear rather than see. There are some that really sing "songs" – simple tunes of several different notes, over and over again, but not always the same, so I think different birds have different songs.

Spectacular Trees and Creepers

Outside the window, our huge bombax tree is coming into flower, but we cannot see it to great advantage since the canopy of the tree is well above the level of the roof. I think it is a variety of kapok, and like kapok the bark is studded with enormous cone-shaped thorns up to an inch long – not a climbing tree. The white and rose flowers are about five inches across, with a long pistil in the centre. The little nectar-sucking birds are able to have a field day.

One plant of salmon-pink bourgainvillea has managed to get up into the tree. On the other side of the house, a big flame-of-the-forest tree (much taller than the house) is completely smothered with purple bourgainvillea.

Murder too Close for Comfort

I shouldn't give the impression that we live on a huge estate. I suppose we have about two acres, and I have a good view of the neighbour's wall and his swimming pool, which is now empty because he allowed it to go green and stagnant; but if you look in the right directions you are in the middle of a forest. An Asian businessman was kidnapped in the middle of town, and strangled there last week – so not everything in the garden is lovely! Murders do not make great news value in this city.

On that last idyllic note!
– lots of love, David

P.S. from Nicole - a New Job

I started work at the Belgian Embassy last Monday. My first week at work was rather quiet as my boss is still on leave, therefore I have not met him yet. The Belgian Embassy is in the same building as the Ford Foundation office, but David's working hours and mine do not always coincide, hence a lot of driving to and from town.

Letter to parents   Nairobi, 26/04/1981

Ancient Arab Settlements

We have been home for two days after a very pleasant and interesting trip to Lamu. You may have had a card from us there, although I expect that the Lamu postal services are probably a bit slower than those from Nairobi. Lamu is one of the oldest settlements in Kenya, starting life as an Arab colony over a thousand years ago. At various times there have been quite a lot of these settlements up and down the coast, most of which are now defunct, while a few, including Zanzibar and Mombassa, have grown into something different. Dar es Salaam is a very late Arab settlement, although it more or less covers two or three much older sites. Around Lamu, which is one of a group of islands, there is quite a complex of sites, which used to be flourishing towns trading between East Africa and the Gulf, Persia, India and even China. The Swahili language came from this area. With the development of ports and industries on the mainland, these towns have been declining for the last one hundred and fifty years, and Lamu is the only one which is still largely intact.

Historic Island Buildings

Our hotel was partly made up of old buildings in what was left of another old town, Shela, about two miles from Lamu on the same island. There were still some fine buildings left there, but the only ones being well preserved were those that had been bought by Europeans, Americans, and various wealthy stateless people. We visited a beautiful one, which was being rented by a German family we met. It actually had an upstairs bathroom (an open tank fed from a cistern, from which you scooped out water to pour over yourself). The original sanitary arrangements were not still in use, but they also had indoor lavatories, leading to a sort of septic tank. The old buildings are cool, because they have very thick lime mortar walls, and the flat roofs are thick, with very heavy limestone cement on mangrove poles (normally the first source of collapse).

Lamu Town – a Rare Survivor

Lamu itself is a network of narrow passages between tall buildings. The only road that can take vehicles is along the sea front, and I doubt if there are more than two or three government vehicles on the island. All traffic comes in by *dhow*, even from the airport, which is on a neighbouring island, and if you want to go to Shela you either walk or take a *dhow*. I felt that the *raison d'être* of the place was probably tourism, and that without it, Lamu would die; but it was not badly corrupted by tourism.

A Meeting with Noah?

A few people are involved in boat building, and we saw two extraordinary speculative ventures: wooden motor vessels built by traditional methods, but over a hundred feet long and about thirty feet high. An old man was still working on one, and told me that he and his son had been building it for three years. A local estimated the price at 300,000sh. (£15,000). No-one really knew whether or not they could be operated profitably, because the whole thing was a completely new venture. A local bus-owner had invested all his money in one of them. As the boys said, these huge rather crude wooden vessels, studded with great iron nails, looked like Noah's ark under construction (the gaps between the planks are caulked with cotton, mixed with lime and oil, preferably shark oil).

Rare Culture on Isolated Islands

We visited Pate, another old town, that used to be greater than Lamu, but had declined into a large village surrounded by ruins. In a way, it was more lively than Lamu; it had stopped declining. Most of the remaining buildings had reverted to thatched roofs, and people were cultivating maize, tobacco and sesame among the ruins. We picked up lots of fragments of Chinese pottery and porcelain. I expect they are mostly two hundred or more years old, and I hope the boys will be able to check on this. The people were a lighter mixture of Arab and African than in Lamu, where most are basically African; but they had kept more to traditional jewellery. For example, some of them had the top part of their ears pierced about ten times for small gold rings, and large plugs about the size of a domino in the extended lobe of the ear. It took us six hours to get there by *dhow*, starting at about 3am, because there was hardly any wind, with the result that we arrived at low tide and stuck on a sandbank about a mile out. We then waded in, with the boatmen carrying all our belongings on their heads. It was an exhausting day, but interesting.

Creating Novel Four-Posters

Otherwise, we ate well (mainly fish), bathed, and slept extremely well despite the heat, which took us a bit by surprise at first. I bought two beds – at least, I bought the legs of two beds, bits of other beds to make into the superstructure of a four-poster (I think one of my beds was basically single-storey originally) and various long bits of wood for the bed frames, which are meant to reach me by bus, but which are easily replaceable if they don't arrive. I still don't know how my four-poster will work out. It is quite possible that when it is cleaned up, I shall have a mixture of about three different woods. However I liked the idea of acquiring something so exotic, and even by the time I have finished repairs I doubt if I shall be much over £100 on the pair. The simpler of the two beds came from one of our boatmen. Most of my work on that will be making good the damage he caused while dismantling it!

Count Your Blossoms!

All was well at home when we got back. My garden is really in very good shape. I repeated my rosebud count and found almost eighty, which is ten times what I used to get. My latest ten plantings have all taken (floribundas and two climbers) and some are near to flowering. We have plenty of vegetables: beans, spinach, courgettes, squash, Chinese cabbage. Francis keeps on telling me how surprised my predecessor would be to see the garden now. Honestly however, I don't think he would be surprised at all, he probably wouldn't notice.

Letter to parents   Nairobi, 24/05/1981

Off Into the Unknown

I am going away for a long trip to Zambia, Zimbabwe and Botswana on Tuesday, so you may get a card from one of those exotic places. I don't mind travelling, but I don't find it very exciting either. One is never sure how things are going to turn out. Zambia is said to be a dreadful place at the moment – paranoia plus shortages. Of course, it is still a lot better than Uganda, which is a pleasure yet to come. Of course, I shall be pleased to be back in Botswana, and I expect Zimbabwe to be quite interesting.

The Kenyatta Legacy

The atmosphere here has been a bit strained recently. The present government has still not really buried the problems of the Kenyatta succession, and a number of otherwise trivial incidents have come in a heap, and made it jittery. Government doctors went on strike, and have been arrested; university students staged a protest meeting on a number of issues (mostly trivial, but one quite reasonable, which is that the government had decided to give them a nine-month holiday so as to get terms back on a sequence that had been disrupted by a previous punitive university closure). The demonstrations were broken up by the police, and the university was closed down immediately. My secretary is very put out because one of her daughters was due to take her first exams in four weeks' time. There has been an abortive and somewhat farcical treason trial, enlivened by an apparent ploy by the Special Branch to smear the Minister for Constitutional and Home Affairs .... and so on. And the financial and economic situation is not good, Kenya is running short on food, and using all its foreign exchange on petrol. Mind you, none of this affects us, apart from irritants like hardly ever being able to buy wheat flour or rice.

Running Battle with Moles

My own efforts at self-sufficiency are being blighted by moles. They have taken a liking to the bottom half inch of my maize plants, which is the most important half inch from a number of points of view (particularly that of the moles!) They are crafty little beasts, and had me completely foxed at first because they come up under the plant, do their dirty work more or less under cover, and block up the hole behind them as they retreat. My maize garden is beginning to look more like a badly kept cemetery. I still have not caught any moles, but this afternoon I unearthed an elaborate nest, about the size of a small washing-up bowl, about a foot under a maize plant. It was full of grass, bits of old plastic bags, and bits of my maize plants, plus a substantial quantity of old manure and rubbish neatly stashed away in side passages. Apparently there are itinerant mole-catchers who make traps out of old tin cans, but they do not come our way. I realise though, that these are super-moles, not the charming little characters one sometimes finds blundering around in an English garden; for a start, they must be about the size of rats.

Garden Successes

Otherwise, we are doing rather well on the vegetable front. We now have a lot of drumhead cabbages, and a lot of small cauliflowers are beginning to head; and of course we have lots of beans. There is also lettuce, and several rows of carrots are almost ready.

My roses are really doing well, and Nathan (houseboy) is now allowed to pick almost *ad lib*. My experiments with budding roses seem to be succeeding beyond my expectations. It's amazingly simple. I have a number of sources of old multiflora – two plants gone wild in the hedges, and one cultivated rose that has died back and suckered - it's really nothing but the old mildew-prone pink small-flowered rambler that you have (or probably used to have) at the end of the garden. Anyway, you cut nine-inch lengths of that, and stick them in the ground, and when they have rooted and started to sprout you tie in a bud with a strip cut from an old plastic bag. There are some fairly simple techniques of cutting and inserting the bud which I read up. For instance, I think the one or two attempts I made when I was a boy failed because I did not realise that the woody tissue had to be peeled off, leaving just the bud on a little patch of soft green bark. This is all done at ground level, and the bud is covered with earth to keep it moist. About a month later, the multiflora stock is cut just above the new bud, and new growth is forced from the bud.

I am now at the stage where the new buds are just beginning to grow on the first of my new roses, but it seems to be almost 100% successful and should give more vigorous plants than cuttings, as well as plants of varieties that will not strike cuttings. I am now going to try and make a standard rose. This just involves getting a long cane to root, "de-eyeing" it, and grafting on a new rose at the top. Moles, of course, do not like roses!

Sea Freight Arrives

All our luggage has arrived at last, and the house seems very full. One or two odd little things don't seem to be here (an extension flex, for instance) but I expect that such things will either turn up, or were given away or forgotten in packing; they are not the things that intelligent packers would steal. Nothing seems to be broken.

Half Term with Grandparents

Thank you for looking after Bernard and Dominic this week. I hope you find time for a few games of bridge. We considered whether to send their weekly letter to Morland Avenue, but decided that if it arrived in time they would probably be able to share this one, and still have the pleasure (I hope) of an almost identical letter awaiting them when they return to school.

Post Card from Zimbabwe to Sheila and family, showing a photograph of "Zimbabwe ruins – View of the Temple from the Acropolis"

Dear Sheila, Ron and family, I am at the end of a visit to Zambia, Botswana and Zimbabwe, whose common feature has been that I have been cold all the time! As Nicole tells me, I have a short memory when it comes to climate. My suitcase is full of safari suits that I have not worn at all.

I have hardly managed to get out of town at all in any of the places I have visited, and am still saving up the Great Zimbabwe Ruins for some future trip. They had great significance in the Independence War, as historic proof that African achievements were not limited to mud huts! The visit has brought home to me just how unpleasant the war was in its closing months, and how fast the old government was losing control.

Love, David

Letter from Nicole to parents-in-law   Nairobi, Spring 1981

Cheap Orange Marmalade

I have spent most of the afternoon making orange marmalade. Unlike in Botswana where several friends had orange trees and I got the oranges free, here I have to buy them but they are still cheap and grow most of the year. When I gather more jars I shall make more marmalade.

Burglar Bars

The house is upside down for the moment, as the burglar bars are being fixed on windows and doors. I shall feel more secure when I am on my own. David advises me to lock the bedroom door at night but there are two windows and a door looking onto the balcony and anybody can climb from downstairs onto the balcony (at least Bernard and Dominic can).

A Trip to Mombassa

I had a very pleasant weekend in Mombassa. I was on the south coast and the weather was good, not too hot but enough to get sunburnt. It rained a lot on the north coast. The hotel was very comfortable and the train journey on the way to Mombassa was restful. Coming back, that was another story. We had a breakdown, so had to wait for the engine to be mended and arrived three hours late in Nairobi. We had to let an African man sleep in our compartment (in Kenya there are separate compartments for men and women on the night trains). He was rather drunk and did not want to leave his dear lady. I tried to call the inspector but he was not to be found. This man snored all night so nobody in the compartment got any sleep at all. From time to time I would poke him or jump on his bed to make him change position and we would then have a few minutes' silence but it did not last. Anyway we had a good laugh!

Old Friends in Gaborone

David phoned on Wednesday evening from Gaborone. All the friends were pleased to see him and he is invited out every night. He said that it was very cold in Botswana. David should be back on 17th June. As for me, I have not been too lonely. Working helps a lot! I had supper with David's boss and family one evening; my neighbours also invited me on another evening. I am going to the theatre tonight to see *"Macbeth"*. I had to learn by heart pages of it when I was at school but I have not seen the play. I am having lunch with a friend tomorrow and in the evening I am going to a concert – so I am not doing too badly.

I hope that the children had a pleasant week and that you are not too worn out. I have not heard from them for some time. They write often at the beginning of term (I suppose that they feel rather homesick) but as the term draws to its end we get less and less letters.

Goodbye to the Moles

The garden is doing well. The pest firm seems to have got rid of the moles. I picked at least ten cauliflowers last week but I do not know what to do with the cabbages, as they cannot be frozen. I give quite a lot of the lettuce away. I always tell David that he sees too big; a small vegetable patch would be enough for us.

Canadian Friends

I am enclosing a few photos taken by David during the summer and in Nairobi. On some of the photos you will see two children whom you do not know, as well as a man with glasses. They are Dana and David Schmidt and Ossie Schmidt, their father. They are our Canadian friends from Botswana and for some time used to be our neighbours. On their way back to Canada they stopped in Nairobi to visit us. Dana and Dominic are very good friends.

Letters to parents-in-law from Nicole   Nairobi, June 1981

New Purchases

I bought a deep freeze and it is proving useful to store and freeze all the vegetables from the garden. It is a second hand one (new ones are very expensive here) and rather big but I think it is a good bargain.

As you know, David is interested in roses and I would like to give him for his birthday a really good book on roses. As you know more on this subject than I do I would be very grateful if you could buy the book for me and let me know the price. I think I would pay up to £15. Keep it and I shall collect it when we are in England during the summer.

I have ordered a cassette, Verdi's *"Requiem"* and asked the firm to send it to your address. If I have it sent here I might have to pay a lot of duty on it.

Thank you for having the children.

Love, Nicole

Chilly South Africa!

David has just phoned from Salisbury; he says that it is very cold and he wishes that he had more warm clothes with him. I advised him to take lots of warm clothes as it is now winter in southern Africa, but he did not want to listen. I remember being quite cold in Bulawayo last April, when it was still summer. The evenings are quite cool here but lately we have had very warm sunny days.

A Good Carrot Crop

I started harvesting carrots today; they are not very big but have no bugs or nematodes for a change. Usually David's carrot crop is very bad and we only get a very few good ones. I shall even be able to freeze some. My deep-freeze is getting quite full now.

An Irish Holiday

We have booked for a canal holiday in Ireland from 15th to 29th August. We shall arrive in U.K. on 8th August and we shall be grateful if you could accommodate us during the week 8th-15th August and again for two or three days at the end of August. I know the boys are finishing school on 17th July but because of my job I shall not be able to come to U.K. before 8th August. I have explained this to them and I think they understand. I am going to write to Sheila and Margaret to ask whether it will be possible to have them for two or three weeks. There is also a possibility that they might go to France and stay with my mother who is travelling to France with her sister who is not very well. Is it possible to have the boys' trunks and bicycles sent to you? At the end of term I think they should come to you to sort out their belongings and carry their trunks upstairs. Could you let me know as soon as possible if this is all right with you.

Careless Workmen

The workers have just finished fixing the burglar bars; the house has been in a real mess and they have made a lot of scratches on the parquet floor by pushing their big machine everywhere. They also made the walls very dirty but fortunately they re-painted the places where they had made dirty marks. I feel more secure now. Part of the house is without electricity tonight; there is a short-circuit somewhere. I shall have to ask the Foundation to send somebody to see to it on Monday.

Irish canal holiday, 1981 – Dominic

Family picnic, Kenya

Letter from Nicole to parents-in-law

An Absent Husband

David came back on 17th June, spent one week at home and left again on Sunday morning. This time he will be away for one week and is travelling in Kenya. His trip will take him to the north of the country, east of Lake Turkana (now Lake Rudolph) to see whether it is in the interests of the Foundation to fund a project there. If I were not working life would be very lonely. David will certainly write to you next week and tell you all about his trip which should be very interesting.

I hope your Evergreen party went well. I am sure the garden looks lovely even if it was raining.

Love, Nicole

Letter from Nicole to Sheila
Nairobi, 16/07/1981

The Boys' Travels

I hope the children will have an easy journey to Wickham Skeith and that they will not meet with rioters on the way to Leicester.

Once again thank you for having the children, I am very grateful to you. If you or Ron have a free moment I would be grateful if you would make Bernard practise the piano. It is not often that he gets the opportunity to have the use of a piano during the long holidays. I seem to remember that you have your grandmother's cello but I am afraid it will be too big for Dominic; he can always try.

Camping Plans

It is rather chilly and grey – real English summer weather at its worst. It has been raining which is unusual for the time of year, but it will help David's maize to grow.
We hope to go camping this weekend. It has not been possible until now as we did not have a suitable car (the Foundation has now purchased a Land Rover) and the sea freight which contained our camping equipment has arrived very recently.

Best wishes to you all and love. See you soon, Nicole

Letter to parents
Addis Ababa Hilton,
July 1981

Tanzanian Recollections from Ethiopia

Me voila en Ethiopie! I have just spent ten days in Tanzania, which is its normal amiable tatty self. I got out of town for the first three or four days to the Faculty of Agriculture, and was able to visit some villages as well as talk to university and government people. Everything was 5-10 times as expensive as it used to be ten years ago. I bought myself one nice carving which was, despite heavy bargaining, several times as expensive as anything similar I had bought in the past. In fact I was disappointed in the carvings. Either my standards have gone up or theirs have gone down; probably both. I got the impression that people were working almost on a production-line basis. I did see two enormous carvings, fortunately already sold, that were so good that they merited a place in an ethnographic museum: excellent details of clothing, scarification, face decoration, guns, animals etc – the sort of thing that does raise one's personal standards.

Temptation to Buy – and a Gift of Jeans

I was very tempted by some really outstanding antique Zanzibari furniture – a carved table and bookcase bureau, for which the owner wanted an illegal direct payment into a foreign account. Expensive - £1,000 for the bookcase bureau – but I'm still tempted!

Luckily I could not make a *rendez-vous* to view the piece (I saw it only from photographs) because my driver from my last visit to Arusha in June came over to see me. I was bringing him a pair of jeans from Botswana as a present from myself and the Assistant Minister who was with me. It was meant to be a three-way present, but the other Motswana, who is an amiable rogue, failed to subscribe. Jeans are difficult to get in Tanzania, so I think the gift was appreciated.

Renewed Friendship, and Search for Weapons

The driver, Juma Abdulla, is a pleasant, squat, stocky coastal Moslem. Our conversation is limited, because my Swahili is still pretty awful and his English is worse, but he really seemed pleased to see me as well as the gift, and turned out at 3am this morning with his Ministry Land Rover to take me to the airport. We came across two road blocks on the way, and I feared that Juma might get some awkward questions about whether he was on government business, but we were waved through both times. The blocks were armed soldiers and police searching cars for weapons. I cannot see any good reason for exempting a government vehicle from such a search, since they are so widely misused (as in my case) but perhaps they thought that a white man in a government vehicle was above suspicion

Exploring Addis

.   I have spent quite a lot of the day sleeping, because I had such a poor night. In fact in dribs and drabs I am sure I have now made up a whole night. After a late lunch I went out for a walk in the city, which is much as I remember it: a strange mixture of modernity and slums. The streets are full of life, and filth. Here and there deep gorges run through the city carrying polluted water. One was full of quite large dead fish. Perhaps someone higher up had been poisoning the water to get a catch, or maybe they had been caught in a torrent after the rains. There was certainly not enough water to sustain them alive where I saw them.

People sell firewood a few sticks at a time – just enough to boil one pot of water. Pack-donkeys bring it into town. Banana-like trees are planted near the houses for their leaves, which are used in baking bread. They produce no bananas on this particular variety. Being Sunday there was little commerce, except in the Moslem and black Jewish quarters. The only class of shops that seemed to stay open were the coffin makers. One had a sign in English: *"Box Shop"*.

Many of the people are very good-looking – particularly the girls. The children are attractive but importunate. In some of these streets a European is quite a show!

Letter to parents   Nairobi, 22/07/1981

An Expensive Call

I have just spoken to you, but so briefly that I feel I should write as well. I hope the boys didn't feel they had been short-changed. The costs of making phone calls are quite horrendous. That one was about £10 U.K. equivalent for four minutes.

I didn't know B and D were with you. Are they staying there awaiting their luggage, or is there an epidemic at Wickham Skeith – or did they want to be somewhere where there were some decent riots? At least I know that you and they are all right.

Thank you for agreeing to try to make our holiday train bookings. It's difficult to do from here, and we left it too late to do easily by post. I have written to Chris Woods, and expect to meet up briefly with him and his wife in Ireland.

Stone Age Sites in the Rift Valley

We had an outing last weekend. A colleague has had a little four-wheel-drive Suzuki bought for her as her working car, and we borrowed it to go down into the Rift Valley. First we went to a Stone Age site (400,000 – 500,000 BC) at Olegasailu (spelling fairly optional – everything starting *"Ole.."* is Masai, not Spanish). This was a strange place investigated for years by the Leakeys without ever turning up a single identifiable human bone, but literally littered with stone axes, cleavers and hammer-stones – and yet no trace either of fire or post-holes for huts. We slept at a *banda*.

A Soda Lake Experience

We went on to Lake Magadi on Sunday. Magadi is a soda lake. The manager of the ICI plant there (who came to dinner here last night) says they have several million tonnes of "flack" – about 600 feet deep and 80 km long – a slushy semi-solid mixture of crystals and thick solution. We had been there before, but this time we drove almost round the lake, and saw giraffe, gerenuk, Thomson's gazelle, duiker, brindled gnu and oryx, all mixed up with Masai and their cattle. We shall go back – only real chagrin of such trips is wishing the boys were with us to enjoy them!

Rough Sleeping with Lions

I had been regretting the Kalahari, which took a day to get to, and now find that something just as good is just two miles down the road – only snag, temperatures over 100'F for much of the year. We even have friends there – but that may be a snag too, because they are such friendly people that they may want us to stay with them or camp in their garden when I would rather be out sleeping under a bush and listening to the lions.

My garden flourisheth. Grafted my first standard rose yesterday. See you soon.
Much love, David

Letter to Sheila and Ron   Woodstock, 02/09/1981

Antique Furniture

Thank you for having us and for looking after the boys. I hope by the time you get this, you will have had a good holiday.

I was stimulated to write this by popping into a local antique shop and seeing a grand piano almost identical to the one in your sitting room, with the price tag £1,250. The shop specialises a bit in pianos and had a piano directory giving details etc. The piano they had was a rosewood Broadwood (I think) – yours is also rosewood, but I can't remember the make. Apparently they are quite rare. Date is about 1830. If you want to know more, write to the shop (card enclosed) giving make, details of any maker's mark, dimension and (most important) the serial number (yes, they had serial numbers). Of course as an antique yours has been a bit spoiled by having the keyboard messed around to bring it to approximate concert pitch, but I suppose that could be put right again without too much difficulty. I must say, I am not surprised by the value. It always looked to me like an exceptionally nice piece.

I also had a look at barometers. Those similar to Grannie and Grandpa's were priced around £265 – so it probably is worth getting yours repaired – certainly worth looking after it.

On a similar subject, I have decided I would like two more chairs. Your neighbour who sold us the tools had two that I want: a carver with arms, matching our dining room chairs, and a Regency "country" desk chair, also with arms, and with a curved wooden seat. The latter was in the shop. I think he was asking about £35 each. Could you see if he still has them, and try to get the pair for £55, or at a maximum, £60. Tell me if and when this is done and I'll send a cheque.

Irish Barge Holiday

We had a lovely holiday. Friends had said "water below; water above" when they heard we were going to be on Irish canals. In fact we only had one grey day with a spattering of rain in the whole fortnight, and for the rest, the weather was the best Ireland could offer. In fact we heard that officially one of our weeks was the best in four years! The canal boat was very well fitted and comfortable, and the canals had enough water in them to be fun. In fact, only half the journey was on canal proper, the rest being on the Barrow navigation and the River Barrow, raised by weirs that are by-passed by short stretches of canal with locks. The river was wide and wound through beautiful countryside – farmland and wooded hilly areas. Most of the while the waters were very clear. The boys caught a fish, which they immediately dropped into the oily bilges. They also caught a large eel, which we ate.

We managed all the locks, although some of them were very dilapidated and/ or stiff, particularly on the Barrow, which is little used. A gang of workmen was in the course of removing one of the gates as we went down, but assured us we would still be able to get back up if we arrived before Monday lunch-time, which fortunately proved to be the case; and another lock was in such a state of dilapidation that we were scarcely able to sneak through the one functioning gate. Fortunately, Irish locks are much larger than their U.K. equivalents, and the standard boat was about 60 feet long and 12 feet wide (we had a boat of U.K. dimensions). The Royal Canal (now abandoned) was able to take even bigger boats – 80 feet long – almost large enough, I would have thought, to be a commercial proposition now.

I think we did well to choose Irish rather than English canals. The countryside is so much more unspoiled and the canals very much less crowded (sounds silly, but English canals are quite crowded and it is commonplace to queue for locks).

At Home in Woodstock

Our house is in reasonable nick – a bit shabbier than when we left, but still quite tolerable. When we first arrived, it seemed very small, but it has grown considerably in the last two days.

The boys go back to school tomorrow. We shall see them at the weekend, and then not again until Christmas.

Love to you, David

Letter to parents-in-law
from Nicole
Nairobi, 14/09/1981

Back to Work

I hope that you had a pleasant week in Clacton and that the hot weather continued. I thought of you on Saturday morning, the day you left; it was a very hot day.

I arrived back in Nairobi last Monday, in time to go back to work at 10am. It was a tiring day and all day I felt very sleepy. David arrived safely on Thursday and went straight back to work. He left for Kampala yesterday morning; I do not think he was looking forward to this trip. When I came back from the airport I turned on the radio (BBC World News) and heard that twenty-five people travelling on a bus in Uganda were killed by a land mine explosion. It was not very reassuring news.

Nostalgia for Woodstock

It was pleasant staying in our little house in Woodstock; we were getting used to it again when we had to leave. I do think the kitchen is the best investment we have made in the house – it is very pleasant. We have ordered a carpet for the living room – the blue one which we have had for the last seventeen years looked shabby. It will be transferred to the attic room; the attic carpet is very threadbare. The house has not been too badly looked after, although two pairs of sheets have disappeared.

I did a "Patience" last night and it was successful; the second time since I have learned the game, It is like a drug, one really gets hooked on it.

Thank you very much for having us. Love to you both, Nicole

Letter to parents
Nairobi, 20/09/1981

The Uganda Trip, and Budding Roses!

You will see that I am back in my old box again, after a very interesting and really quite pleasant week in Uganda. I was there mainly for a conference on rehabilitation and development that we were sponsoring at the University (at Makerere), but I also visited a possible rural development project – i.e. possible for sponsorship; the project already existed. I left on Sunday, which of course hardly gave me time to unpack, start clearing my desk, and bud my various rose cuttings from your garden and Margaret's, before packing and setting off again. Incidentally, I budded about ten or twelve roses from the snippets I had brought back, and generally the buds are still looking green and healthy, so that in six months' time I should be starting to get the first flowers.

Danger in Uganda, and Water Shortages

As I walked out to the plane, a fellow passenger told me that the early morning BBC had reported a bus full of passengers blown up about ten miles from Kampala, which was not an auspicious start, but in fact the visit went by without anything untoward happening to me. The University was really in surprisingly good shape. Buildings needed painting, but were otherwise reasonably well maintained. The main problem is lack of water, as a consequence of which the main buildings smelled of their lavatories, but even there (surprisingly) someone must regularly have done the rather horrible job of cleaning them out. I stayed at the guesthouse at the University, and most mornings I had a dribble of water from the cold tap of the bath, and enough water to flush the lavatory at least once in the day. There was also a bottle in the bathroom, which I filled up with water to wash in for the rest of the day.

Power for the whole of the country comes from Thompson's Falls, and only occasionally goes off because of old cables snapping. One student hostel on the campus is eleven storeys high, with lifts permanently out of order. Heaven knows how they manage for water etc. (particularly etc!)

Correct Etiquette Under Fire!

Apart from these minor problems, we were really very well looked after, with simple but quite adequate food. The conference itself was academically no great shakes, but there were plenty of papers by Ugandans, and it was the first occasion of its sort for almost ten years, which was an achievement in itself. The local staff worked extraordinarily hard to make it a success.

We did hear the odd popping of guns most nights, and on Thursday at lunch time there was a great deal of shooting from the bottom of the hill on which the University stands. It is a surprisingly innocent sound, just like a lot of jumping jacks going off. I looked around to see if everyone was going to dive to the ground and take cover, but instead most of them strolled out onto the steps to see if they could see anything. From where we were, there was little to be seen except a little cloud of white smoke, and people running up the hill towards us to get away from the shooting. This happened twice, but we never found out what it was all about. One version was that it was just police shooting at a stolen car.

Out and About with the Bishop

Yesterday morning I was collected by the Busoga Diocese, and driven to Jinja, which used to be the main industrial centre of Uganda. The roads, of course, are terrible, but there was quite a lot of traffic, including very heavy trucks. On the way we passed sugar and tea estates that had been allowed to go to bush after the Asians were driven out, and were slowly being brought back into cultivation by their former owners.

I spent the rest of yesterday visiting villages with the Bishop, and had to make a couple of little speeches. At one village they put on a dance for us. My general impression is that just now there is no shortage of food in the villages, although there is a great shortage of everything manufactured, in particular clothes and blankets. People were literally wearing rags; although it is a warmer area than here, the nights without blankets must be very chilly.

Prices of things that are manufactured sound silly, even after our recent inflationary experiences. The one that sounded most ridiculous was a deposit on a bottle of beer of fifty to eighty shillings. A cup of tea at the airport cost fifty shillings too.

Very many thanks to you for having us. I hope we did not wear you out.
Love, David

Letter to parents   Nairobi, 18/10/1981

Fun in the Garden

The weather here is warming up. We had some good rain about three weeks ago, but it has now stopped, and I am anxiously waiting for some more for the maize and beans that I planted then. I also planted out about seven roses of my own grafting when the rain came, and these seem to be recovering from that shock to their system. About eight or ten of the grafts I took from shoots of your roses, and the one from Margaret's (kept in the refrigerator for three weeks) have taken, and the most advanced are about six inches high; the least advanced is about a quarter inch, because something chewed it. In fact I had a lot more success with them than with some attractive red cut roses that I bought here after our return, which have yielded perhaps three successful grafts out of about ten attempts.

Trouble in Uganda

I can't remember if I wrote to you after my Uganda trip. If I did, I'm going to bore you. I had an easy time, with no unpleasantness (if having no water to flush the toilet or to wash in does not count as an unpleasantness). I heard only one sustained period of gunfire, although there were the odd pops in the night. Since then, the local newspapers have almost daily regaled us with tales of Kenyan lorry drivers who have either been shot dead by Ugandan soldiers, or have had miraculous escapes – in two cases having been left for dead. Of course, the normal motive in their case is to steal their vehicles or the loads they are carrying. The two vehicles given to Makerere University by the Foundation have both been stolen, the second at gun-point while it was carrying someone I know, who then had to listen to the thieves debating whether to kill him or let him go.

"The Beggar's Opera" and a Broken Toe

Nicole has been very busy rehearsing for, and playing in, the *"Beggar's Opera"*, which finished last weekend. It was extremely well done. Since then, she has managed to break one of her little toes, while doing nothing more adventurous than getting up off the settee. It was very painful, but I strapped the toe to the next one along, which was apparently the right thing to do since the doctor did not even trouble to remove my strapping. It's much less painful now than it was, and we are able to sleep without a bent wire coat-hanger down the bed to keep the weight of bedclothes off her foot.

Storm Drains

We are having storm water drainage channels put in to my design down one side of the house. The men have been at work for a week already, and have at least another week to go. It is quite a substantial job, and is being done well by a local contractor, so that as well as giving gardening instructions in Swahili every morning, I now also try to fit in a short survey of the works with the builder, also in Swahili. A real Swahili-speaker from the coast would probably double up with laughter if he heard us, as we all speak absolutely dreadful Swahili – the others are Luya and Kikuyu, respectively, and their local languages bear only occasional resemblances to Swahili, which by origin is not a pure African language at all. The cost of all this building activity will be the equivalent of about £200 (paid, I should add, by the Foundation). How many man-weeks' work could you get for that in Leicester? (that excludes materials, which will probably cost as much as the work).

A Busy Day of Rest

For the last two Sundays we have been swimming before lunch, which leaves us feeling like a nice nap after lunch. Today, partly because of Nicole's foot, we stayed in and did odd jobs: painting the garden table, and clearing up some of the odd spots left by the previous lot of workmen, who welded burglar bars onto all of our windows. I have almost finished a rabbit hutch, because I feel the need for some garden livestock, and also a source of home-grown manure.

Bee Husbandry

After that, I may have a shot at a beehive. We are surrounded by bees, and this seems to be a swarming season. Last week we had a swarm outside the kitchen, and tried to tempt them into a hive owned by our next-door neighbour, but they took off and went somewhere else. He (or rather his workmen) put the hive up a tree, and within a week a swarm of bees moved in. I'm not sure if bees have moved back into the space above me in the sun-room, from which they have been evicted twice so far; but if not, they are prospecting busily. Yesterday morning there was an active swarm above a tall tree just next to the house. I think all this activity is because the rain has brought a lot of trees into flower at once; we have jacaranda and "flame of the forest" all around us, and just at the bottom of the garden there is a huge eucalyptus forest, which must also be an excellent source of nectar (you might have thought eucalyptus would produce honey that tasted of "Vicks" – it is not so).

A Visit to India

At the end of the month I shall go to India for a fortnight, which should be pleasant. Mind you, at the seminar I am going to, I shall have to put up with and pretend to enjoy the company of the Botswana expatriate whom I probably like least; a man who did everything he could to make my job difficult when I first came to Botswana. I hope my presence imposes an equal strain upon him.

Sojourn in France

We have arranged for the boys to spend half-term in Le Havre with Suzy and Robert, who are back there again. It would be good for their French, which needs some forced brushing-up. Agnes and Bruno are about their age. I wonder how they will get on together. Agnes is really rather stunning; Bruno seemed very sensible and mature last time I met him, which must be two years ago.

Christmas Arrangements

The boys are coming here for Christmas on separate planes, and returning separately, because Bernard is involved in a play at the end of term, and will be going back early for a skiing trip. If you should need a Christmas courier, use Dominic, who is leaving on 18th, as he will have the emptier suitcase.

Letter to Sheila and Ron   Nairobi, 25/10/1981

Update on Furniture

Thank you for putting us up, and for buying my two latest chairs. I hope you don't feel your house is getting too much like a chair repository. Yes, please do put woodworm killer on them if you can find the time. I hate to think that things I like are slowly being eaten from the inside.

I didn't really expect you to want to sell the piano; I never sell anything I like, whether it makes sense or not, although if I did I think I would sell on the principle that I would use the proceeds to buy something I liked even more. However, it is sensible to know how much a thing like that is worth. For example, it really is worth going to some trouble to treat the woodworm in it, and keep it in good order, whereas if it was just a pleasant piece of junk, you might let it fall to pieces gently.

Comparative Living Standards

I'm glad your holiday in France was such a success. I'm amused by your comments about the Fargeaud's house. I'm afraid you soon come to realise what poor relations we English are by Common Market standards. However, we are still pretty rich by African standards. A pleasant young enumerator came to see me yesterday from the Central Statistical bureau, because we had somehow got into one of their sample surveys. One of the questions he had to ask me was my monthly income, and when I told him he queried it twice, because he thought I must be giving him an annual income figure. My servants are doing pretty well on £35 a month, plus a room to live in (and free electric light!).

Mutual Colleagues

I expect Mummy has told you that Ruth Johnson's husband Andy is presently posted at the place where your David works (Ruth, in case the name is unfamiliar, is Nicole's friend, who arranges Bernard and Dominic's collection and despatch). Andy is a professional officer, but I find him very pleasant all the same – and very bright. I am sure that if David introduces himself, he would be very ready to be friendly, although that may be the last thing David wants.

From Roses to Orchids

Quite a lot of the buddings I made with roses from Mummy's and Margaret's gardens took, although a few have since been chewed back to nothing by some nasty little pest. The cutting from Margaret's garden survived three weeks in the refrigerator, wrapped up in polythene, so it's possible that if I had taken a cutting from you, that would have survived too. I am now beginning to plant out some of my first lot of budded plants.

Today I started a new venture. The local orchid society had one of its rare sales. It was rather like the Christmas sales. I arrived only half an hour before the doors opened, and there must have been about a hundred people there ahead of me. When the doors opened, it was obvious that the only thing to do was to grab anything that looked nice, and reconsider later. With one small tussle, I quickly got my hands on three plants that turned out to be more expensive than any other plants I have ever bought – by a factor of about five. They are cymbidium orchids, which in principle should grow in the open air in this very temperate climate. We shall see. They are grown in pots full of granulated fir tree bark, and when they do flower, they are quite spectacular.

Action Shots

I enclose a cheque for the chairs, and two photos taken by Dominic at your house: one of Bernard wondering what to do with a croquet mallet, and a second one taken a few moments later of Bernard hitting Grandpa on the head with it. I can't think why Dominic didn't take a third picture to complete this dramatic action series.
Lot of love, David

P.S. from Nicole

Thank you very much for having the children during the summer. They should be in France this week, staying with my cousin. Dominic went to Dunkirk for a day trip last week; they are doing rather well.

I have now recovered from the rehearsals and performances of *"The Beggar's Opera"*. It was a good show but the rehearsals were rather strenuous. We never finished rehearsing before 12.30pm and rehearsed nearly every evening.

The short rains have started and it is cool again, but as soon as there is a ray of sun the bees swarm around the bedroom roof. They are dislodged every time they nest there, but always come back.
Love to you all, Nicole

| Letter from Nicole to parents-in-law | Nairobi, 07/11/1981 |

Home Alone

David left last Sunday for Hyderabad in India. I do not think I shall hear from him, unless he sends a postcard, as it is not possible to phone to or from India, except to Delhi. When he is in Delhi next week perhaps he will get in touch. I could have gone with him (all expenses paid by ICRISAT, the organisation which is arranging the conference David is attending) but we are short of staff at work and I think I owe it to the children to spend as much time as possible with them during their holidays. Had I gone with David I would have had to subtract two weeks from my annual holiday. I hope the opportunity will present itself again. David thought the trip to India would be his last trip abroad this year, but unfortunately he will have to go away for another two weeks at the beginning of December.

Competitive "Patience"

I have just won a game of Patience, after several unsuccessful attempts. An acquaintance who stayed with us recently taught us another kind of Patience; it is called "Racing Demon". It is played with two persons and one has to be very quick as both players have to add to the ace piles. I find it very frustrating as David wins every time; I think I have only won twice. It is rather nerve-wracking. I prefer the other Patience game as it is relaxing and one can play at one's own pace.

Bernard and Dominic, and Christmas Plans

I think you know that the children spent the week of half-term (last week) in France, at Le Havre. They were staying with my cousin, Anick's sister (I think you met Anick in the past). They enjoyed themselves very much and got on well with my cousin's children. Denys' wife, who is in France at the moment, had them for the week-end and she phoned me on Sunday, so I spoke to the children. Bernard's voice is really deep now.

The children will be here in six weeks' time. Dominic will leave before Bernard as Bernard is in a play and the last performance will be on 19th. Bernard will travel on 20th and will not stay very long as he is leaving again on 1st January in order to join the school skiing party. Dominic will be with us for more than three weeks and I think he will enjoy getting spoilt a little. I am trying to get a house on the coast so that we can spend a few days with him at the sea-side. I should have started looking around earlier. Everything is booked by now.

A Night Out

Yesterday I went to the theatre to see *"Hay Fever"*. The intrigues in Coward's plays are more or less the same but the play was well acted and we had a good laugh. The friends I went with took me to their club for dinner afterwards. *"The Muthaiga Club"* is a sport / social club, very much sought after by diplomats and expatriates. It is very English and very much like it was fifty or sixty years ago. I do not think it would be David's cup of tea at all. Tonight I am going to a concert.

Vegetables for One, and a Quick Knit

I have just been down to the garden to see what there was. I got a good crop of green peppers, broccoli, salad, radishes, fennel, and two cucumbers (not very healthy). A lot of vegetables just for one person! I shall freeze the broccoli and share the lettuce with my English neighbours who have invited me for lunch today.

I have finished knitting for Bernard a polo-neck jumper and a woolly hat for skiing. I bought the wool in England and Bernard chose it himself; the jumper is made of chunky "Pattons" wool, it was quick to knit. To make it more interesting I wanted to knit something with a Fair Isle design but Bernard wanted it plain.

Love to you both, Nicole

Letter to parents

Banjara Hotel, Hyderabad,
India, 08/11/1981

A New Use for Water Pipes

What a strange continent this is! A new water main has been laid to Hyderabad town, parallel to the road our bus followed every day from the hotel to the research station where the conference was held. I have never seen a pipeline like it. The cement pipes are well over a metre in diameter, look hand-made, and leak all over the place creating new water sources which people use to drink and wash in – and of course to wash themselves after they have been to the lavatory in it! For this reason, all surface water is suspect and washing can be dangerous. The reject pipes have often had walls built at both ends and are inhabited.

Life in Hyderabad

In Hyderabad the streets are always crowded with people, bicycles, families on scooters, cycle-rickshaws, scooter rickshaws, bullock carts, cars, lorries painted in bright greens and reds, and densely-packed buses, but I have yet to see a serious accident. Everyone drives on the horn. There are many beggars, those with the most spectacular deformities simply being laid on mats in the road, where they palpate. Food is good. About half the meals I have had at the International Centre for Research in the Semi-Arid Tropics have been vegetarian, and quite acceptable.

Despite everything, there is a tremendous sense of vitality in the place. Hyderabad is growing at an enormous pace, because it has been chosen as an industrial centre, and everywhere buildings are going up with enormous gangs of labourers – many of them women. When they make a road here, the granite rocks are delivered to the site, and labourers with hammers break it up into gravel. Anyone with a hammer and chisel can make building blocks from the granite outcrops that dominate the landscape. It is actually cheaper to buy hand-made granite rock fence-posts than to buy concrete posts.

Acclaim at the Sorghum Conference

The conference was interesting, although I never really made up the sleep I lost on the journey, and kept dropping off to sleep when they turned the lights off to show exceedingly dull "visual aid" slides – often just pages of print reproducing what the speaker was saying. I gave a short paper myself at the end, which went down extremely well, rather to my surprise, since I was really telling off the natural scientists for not doing research which was relevant to small farmers. In fact there must have been only about ten social scientists of various sorts in the company of 240 agriculturalists and natural scientists, of whom the largest contingent were plant breeders and geneticists.

I shall spend a couple of days here next week to talk with people at the Centre, then go on to New Delhi to meet our program people there – although it seems only too likely that by the time I get there, the people I want to meet will be here.
Love, David

Letter to Sheila and Ron   Hyderabad, 08/11/1981

All about Sorghum

I meant to send you a postcard, but there are none immediately to hand, and it's almost lunch-time, so you'll have to admire the stamps instead.

I've been at a conference on sorghum for the last week. I mentioned this to an economist friend, and he burst out laughing, which shows how far I've come. Sorghum seems quite a sensible subject to me now. In case you don't know, it's a "coarse grain" grown for cattle food in the U.S. and Australia, but eaten by lots of people in drier areas of Africa and India – a bit like the millet that we used to feed the budgerigars, but with bigger grain. Most of the people attending were natural scientists – particularly breeders – and I told them fairly bluntly that they were doing the wrong sort of research. To my surprise, most of them loved it.

Impressions of India

India is interesting. It's so different from anywhere else I have ever been. Dirty, noisy, crowded and yet full of vitality. It's possible to find all the dirt and smells rather revolting, but generally expatriates who live here enjoy the place because it also has a lot to offer. Apart from anything else it's interesting to find people who don't feel that they need to be westernised or assimilated into another more developed culture.

Hyderabad

Hyderabad is a big city (2.5 million) growing and industrialising very fast. It's built on rocky, hilly country with lots of granite outcrops, which otherwise unemployed people are steadily reducing to building blocks, fence posts and even gravel. When they make a road here, the lorries bring great chunks of rock, and piece-work labourers with hammers break it up into the right sizes of aggregate and gravel. A lot of the building workers are women, including gypsies – *"bhajmins"* – who carry their wealth as heavy silver ornaments.
Love to you all, David

Moving Countries

As last year, I hope that I'm forgiven for writing a circular letter. We have so many friends and relatives that it's really impossible to write to all of them.

We moved from Botswana to Nairobi at the turn of the year. I was actually meant to arrive on New Year's Eve, and had been hoping to find a party waiting for me, but because of the normal problems with flights, I and the boys spent New Year's Eve in the Southern Suns Hotel at Jan Smuts airport (Johannesburg), feeling less than festive. Nicole came on a day later, having seen off the last of the packing. That was the last we saw of our household goods for another four months.

A Flying Dog

Our first task when Nicole arrived was to release Cain, our dog, who had come on the same flight. Having been consigned as freight, he was taken off to the freight depot, locked miserably in a kennel that looked quite big until we tried to put him in it. It took all my powers of persuasiveness and awkwardness, plus a few shillings, to get him out of bond that night.

Change of Role

My job here is not the same as in Botswana. There I was advising the Ministry of Agriculture on anything from grain marketing to staff movements. It's difficult to say in which area my advice was least often rejected, but I had a very good relationship with my Permanent Secretary and Ministers, and the job was very exciting.

Here, I am mainly the agricultural advisor in the Ford Foundation's office; "mainly" because I have other responsibilities, even including human rights. We make grants – mainly now to non-government bodies. "My" projects include one with Catholic Relief, one with the African Inland Church, and possibly in future one with an Anglican Diocese in Uganda, as well as secular organisations. The Foundation is completely secular, but has no objection to using religious organisations as a basis for development work. In Africa they are one of the commonest and solidest forms of indigenous organisation at national or local level. In general, our philosophy is that we are not primarily in the business of financing development, but of financing experiments and studies aimed at finding out how to achieve development in a number of areas which include agriculture, health, nutrition, and population.

Dancing Ex-Guerillas

In addition we do some legal and human rights work and even some work in the cultural area. One of the more unusual projects I have to look at next time I am in Zimbabwe is a proposal to form a dance troupe consisting of former female guerrillas, who have often done nothing but train and fight since their early teens, and are now untrained for anything else and not wanted in the national army. But we will not fund something like school or hospital construction just because it is a good cause, and we give very few scholarships, though there is a constant anguished search for scholarships and educational support by young people throughout the region.

A Huge Region to Cover

Our region covers about eighteen countries in East, Central and Southern Africa. We really only work in about five of these, but it does mean that we (that is, myself and two colleagues, not Nicole I'm afraid) travel quite a lot. I have been to Botswana, Zimbabwe, Zambia, Ethiopia, Tanzania and Uganda in the past year, and have also had the treat of a trip to India two weeks back. That was a remnant of my previous job; I went to an international seminar on sorghum. The odd thing is that many of you will not even know what sorghum is. It's a so-called "coarse grain" that is a staple food in many drought-prone areas. I find it very interesting, since it is an undeveloped crop, with literally thousands of different varieties, but it is difficult to mill and process and there are few really good cultivars for human use. It happens to be one of Botswana's main crops, which is why I know about it.

Life in Uganda

My trip to Uganda was useful too. I stayed on the university campus, where the main hardship was lack of water. This made the public buildings a bit smelly, although the staff of Makerere really managed extraordinarily well just keeping things going. All university staff need some other source of income (or to be involved in some sorts of fiddles), because their salary is not enough to live on after the incredible inflation they have had. My favourite "silly" price was the deposit on a beer bottle: anything from fifty to eighty shillings (until Amin, the shilling was roughly on a par with the old U.K. shilling). I did hear occasional shots in the night, and there was a regular fusillade from the police station just down the road one lunch-time. I looked around to see whether the correct behaviour was to get down behind a wall to escape stray bullets, but the locals just strolled out onto the verandah to see if they could see anything.

General Shortages

This left me a bit apprehensive about a planned trip to Jinja, but in fact the only really alarming thing about that trip was the driving of the young American social worker who took me. We went out with the bishop into villages in Busoga, and there appeared to be no real food shortage. In fact, the shortages that hurt are of other things: hoes, clothes, medicines. People wear the most fantastic rags. At one homestead, a small boy spent the whole of our visit trying to find some way of wearing an old cotton jacket – greenish brown and full of holes – as a pair of trousers, to cover his perfectly decent nakedness; but that which he tried to hide always managed to emerge through some gap or other. Old men wore layers of rags or ladies' dresses whose evanescent transparency reminded me of the oldest regimental colours hung up in some cathedral, where you know that a touch – certainly a wash – would reduce them to powder. With regard to health, the bishop remarked in a matter of fact manner that they really must do something about this high mortality, because people were spending so much time at funerals. We were given a slap-up meal, and at one village they even put on a dance for us. Funnily enough, they were Moslems, but they seemed pleased enough to see the bishop.

Ethiopian Conflicts

Ethiopia was another fascinating place. The heartland of the country is now peaceful, although militiamen with rifles guard all public buildings, including agricultural colleges, to the irritation of the staff. They are not a nuisance, they just get in the way. The separatist wars go on expensively in Eritrea and Ogaden. One of my visits was to a nutritional institution in the grounds of the military hospital (formerly the Swedish Children's Hospital) which is mainly staffed by Russians, and there were plenty of maimed and injured soldiers in evidence. It is difficult to take any sides in these wars. The Amharic Ethiopians extended a zone of influence into an empire; lost some of it to the Italians; retrieved it again. When the central structure came apart in the revolution, separatist tendencies had their day. Now the central government is, in its own view, simply putting the country back together again.

Surviving Under Difficulties

Impressively, institutions go on functioning, though often under great stress. The schools, for example, operate three shifts a day with different sets of pupils. The relatively well-off make great sacrifices to send their children to the private "foreign" schools: French, German, American. I was taken by friends to a traditional restaurant on the outskirts of town. A praise-singer with a bow-played instrument, which he played with great skill, came round from group to group and improvised flattering songs, getting good payment in return by local standards. I was *"Meester Dawitt, the handsome young Englishman"*. It's probably just as well I was not told what else he said.

Kenya – Nomads and Larva Fields

My only other real field trip was to Marsabit in northern Kenya, the African Inland Church project which is bringing both livestock husbandry advice and an involvement in Kenyan social and political life to nomadic Borana, Gabbra and Khonso tribesmen. These partly semitic people have little respect for frontiers, and almost no links with the predominantly agricultural Bantu tribes who dominate Kenyan political life. The drive there was exciting. Marsabit itself is a long way, but beyond Marsabit we had to cross a larva field and the salt-covered Chalbi desert, which was a whole day's slow driving to Kalacha. The missionary in charge there, "Dilly" Anderson, is ideal for the job; a Kenyan-born engineer, who can fix almost anything without getting flustered. He told me he once broke the axle on his truck on the larva field, so he burnt charcoal, made an impromptu furnace, and hammer-welded a brace to allow him to get back to base. Mind you, I think he was just a little bit proud of that episode. *Shifta* (bandits) raid in this area from time to time, but so far not around Kalacha. I only suffered from the hospitality: bowls full of smoke-flavoured grey-coloured curdled milk, which had a dramatic effect on my digestion.

Family Excursions

The boys are at school in Thame, but have been here twice so far. At Easter we took them to Lamu, an old Swahili (part Arab/ African/ Omani) settlement on an island off the coast, above Mombassa. That was delightful. We stayed at a hotel improvised out of old buildings on the sea front, in a small settlement about 4km from Lamu town itself. There are about two motor vehicles on the island, but we could walk into town and take the hotel *dhow* back. The heat plastered us to our beds after lunch, but we don't really mind heat so long as we don't have to do anything in it. We slept like logs (at Nairobi altitudes, we find we sleep lightly). Bernard and Dominic will be here again for Christmas, and we plan to get out into the bush, and to the coast. Nairobi has few charms for them. They don't have the same circle of friends as in Gaborone, and they can't get around easily in this big security-conscious town. Bernard is going off early after Christmas for a skiing holiday with the school.

We all had a really enjoyable summer holiday in the U.K. and the Irish Republic, the latter on a narrow boat on the Irish Grand Canal and the River Barrow. Ireland put on its best weather for years; one afternoon of drizzle in two weeks. It was both restful and interesting (one of the interesting things was wondering whether decrepit lock gates would allow us back through, or whether they would be closed for repairs before we returned) and were able to renew acquaintance with Chris Woods, my former Young Liberal friend of twenty-four years standing (is it really that long?) Incidentally, I am now a paid-up Social Democrat.

Life in Nairobi

In Nairobi, we live in great comfort. We have an oldish house in about two and a half acres, with a beautiful garden that stretches down a hill in about six terraces, with lawns and flower beds on the top levels, and my banana trees and vegetable *shamba* (garden) at the bottom. I took over about a hundred elderly and ailing roses, and have nursed some back to strength and replaced others. I now make my own replacement roses by budding onto floribunda cuttings from the hedges. With this climate, it's probably a much quicker business than in the U.K. I already have several flowers from budstock I sneaked back in from England this summer. Francis, my gardener, is a very hard and willing worker, and I think he really appreciates the fact that I go round the garden every morning, and tell him what to do. It is also a very good way of keeping up my pidgin Swahili. We buy no vegetables, and give quite a lot away.

Social life is good. Today, for instance, we went out to lunch to Lake Magadi eighty miles away in the Rift Valley. It's a soda lake, rather like the Dead Sea, only deader. In fact it is so solid with soda that heavy equipment can be driven over the top. It's also one of our favourite getaway places, where we can see game without going to a game park. We do quite a lot of entertaining, much of it work-related, but I don't mind that.

Nicole does a lot of singing with the Nairobi Music Society. It's varied. The last production was Gay's *"Beggar's Opera"* – very beautifully staged. The next is *"The Messiah"*. I have so far managed to get to two orchestra rehearsals, but usually contrive to be out of the country for the rehearsals, the performance, or both. However, we are always pleased to see visitors, and usually have some spare beds in the house.

Happy Christmas, Happy New Year,
With love from David and Nicole Jones

Letter from Nicole
to parents-in-law

Nairobi, 06/12/1981

A Birthday Treat

Thank you very much for your birthday wishes and present. On my birthday last Sunday we drove to Magadi (80 miles from here) to a lunch party. It was not in my honour, but friends had invited us and several other people from Nairobi to have lunch there, where they live and work. Magadi is at sea level and of course is very hot. We had a lovely day there and the other guests were very pleasant. After lunch we all went swimming, not in the lake but in the club pool. Last night David took me out for a meal.

Home Alone Again

Once again I took David to the airport this morning. He is going to be away for the next two weeks (in Zimbabwe and Botswana). He will be back in the early hours of the morning on 19th December, just a few hours before Dominic arrives.

David came back from India three weeks ago with a very bad cold which I caught within 24 hours. For two weeks we were sniffling, coughing and feeling rather sorry for ourselves. We have just got rid of the cold and I hope he does not come back with another one.

Busy Times at the Embassy

I have been very busy for the last week, as a Belgian Economic Mission is visiting Kenya and the department of the Embassy where I work is responsible for the organisation. I have been going to work at odd hours and coming back home very late in the evening. The delegates are being accommodated at the Intercontinental Hotel, and we have moved our offices there so that we are on the spot to give them all the help they need and fix all their appointments. This week will not be quiet either, as the Music Society is presenting *"The Messiah"* on 11th, 12th and 13th, and most evenings we will be rehearsing.

Cold and Rain

Last night David was saying that the garden could do with some rain and obviously his wish was heard. It started to rain during the night and it has not stopped since (it is now 5pm). Of course it is chilly; at lunch time I felt so cold that I lit a fire. Apparently the short rains were not very good this year but I have the impression that it has rained often for the last two months.

Christmas is Coming

I am not too behind this year for all the Xmas preparations. I shall post the Xmas cards next week; David took with him the mail for Botswana and David's boss posted, in the States, the mail destined for friends in the States. I made a few mince pies several weeks ago. I do not think I shall make an Xmas pudding this year; we only eat very little of the Xmas pud and never finish it.

We shall take two short holidays during the Xmas vacation. We shall spend Xmas and Boxing Day in Tsavo Game Park, which is about three hours' drive from here. We shall not camp but shall stay at a self-catering *banda* which is equipped with a kitchenette and a bathroom (with hot and cold water and shower) which is very appreciable. I have booked a cottage at the sea-side from 7th to 10th January just before Dominic goes back. This will take the place of a skiing holiday for Dominic. I am sure it will be just as exciting for him and he will have the advantage of going back to school very sunburnt and brown.

I wish you a very happy Xmas.

Love, Nicole

Letter to parents   Nairobi, 31/12/1981

New Year Plans

Happy New Year! Bernard will be seeing the New Year in care of British Airways, and I'll give him this letter to post. As you probably know, he's off on a school skiing holiday in Italy. I hope he doesn't break himself up too much, or come back thoroughly disillusioned with skiing. One week is about enough time to learn to coast down very gentle slopes with only the occasional twisted ankle.

Health Worries

We had a very bad start to Christmas. The afternoon he arrived, Dominic had a small fit. Neither Nicole nor I was on the scene at the time, but he apparently had slight convulsions. Naturally, we were very worried, and he has since had quite a lot of tests and seen a neurologist here. The conclusion seems to be that there is probably very little wrong. He was under unusual stress at the time, since he had been up for about 24 hours, or on the aeroplane, and he also had a bad cold, but didn't feel sleepy and went on with us to a very active party. For the time being, he will take pills to reduce the likelihood of another fit, and will have to go on taking them until told to stop, but his electro-encephalogram appears to be OK, and people who have a single fit are very common.

It was almost Christmas Eve before we eventually got to the neurologist – a very pleasant and reassuring young Ugandan – and we were so relieved by what he told us that we had a very relaxed and somewhat euphoric Christmas.

Celebrating Christmas

We had our Christmas dinner on Christmas Eve, and on Christmas morning we took the office Land Rover and drove off to Tsavo national park, where we stayed in a thatched *banda* (with mod. cons.) and spent two and a half days driving around looking at, or for, animals.

Elephants and Rhinos at Risk

There's a hefty population around the park which is fond of meat and even fonder of ivory, but we saw quite a lot of different types of beastie, including a fair number of elephants with quite respectable tusks. The real slaughter occurred in the last years of Kenyatta's rule; his relatives were involved, and the number of elephants in the park is said to have fallen from 30,000 to 10,000. Providing the population is allowed to recover this may not turn out to have been such a bad thing. The elephant numbers had reached such a level that most of the trees in the plain areas had been destroyed, and now they may recover. The rhinos are a different matter. They have almost been exterminated. One estimate is that only seventy are left in the whole of Kenya.

Family Adventures

In a few minutes we shall go to the airport to say goodbye to Bernard. Then tomorrow Nicole and I and Dominic will set off for a couple of nights at Magadi – if we can all fit in our little Suzuki four-wheel drive with all our luggage and camping gear. And the week-end 7th through 10th we shall make another trip, this time to Mombassa for a weekend, and after that we shall be on our own again. It is nice having the boys with us. I expect we appreciate them more for their absence.

Otherwise, life goes on. The rains have ended for now, and the only vegetable we have in abundance is green maize, which will soon get too hard to be pleasant, but we have lots of other things in the fridge. Tonight we had a special Chinese meal (at home) which included two exotics from my garden: a jicama bean tuber (used as water chestnut, stays crisp when cooked) and scorzerona.

Too Much Seaside Sun

We had a very pleasant four days at the coast, although I burnt so rapidly and dramatically that I had to spend a lot of time indoors, only coming out for quick dips when the sun was coming up or going down. The first day we were there, I went out snorkelling with a mask with Dominic, for a first easy run, and later walked along the brilliant white beach with him for about a mile, and back again. That evening my back was only mildly warm, but my legs, feet and thighs were burning. I think it was the reflection from the beach that really did the damage. I concluded that my back was the tough part of me, and that it was safe to go for a longer snorkelling trip the next day. So Dominic and I both spent about an hour and a half face down in the water, going out to the reef and back. Naturally, after that my back was very sore too, but strangely, my thighs were substantially more burnt than before, so I suppose that this time I was being burnt by reflected sunlight from the bottom of the shallows. You can't win, can you? Dominic, of course, was very little affected by comparison, but even he complained of a sore back. Now I'm peeling nicely, and itching terribly.

Dominic and Bernard – Lone Flights and Skiing

All told, we had a very good holiday, apart from the alarms and excursions over Dominic. I think he was a little bit more chagrined than usual when he left. Of course, he was on his own for the long journey, which isn't much fun. Apparently on the way here, the stewardess in Zurich ushered him into a room full of moody and silent youngsters, who had been similarly parked, with a cheery *"Come and play with all these children!"* which fortunately he found hilarious.

We don't know at all how Bernard's skiing holiday went. I hope it wasn't a disillusionment. Skiing is really much harder than it looks for a beginner, and is sometimes both painful and rather terrifying. I remember taking what I thought was a short ski-lift up to the top of a moderate slope, and instead we went on and on and on up narrow paths between pine trees, and were deposited on hard packed snow at the top of a steep slope, with experienced skiers whistling down about our ears. It took me about half an hour to get down, by skiing from left to right across the slope, falling down, waiting for a clear patch, and then doing the same thing from right to left.

No Rain, No Water

This letter has now spent four days in the typewriter, and has started to get dusty and gritty. We have not had rain for about two months, and everything is beginning to get rather dry. Yesterday evening we came home to find that the water had failed. We went out to dinner, for some Foundation visitors, with our camping trip water containers in the back of the car, but by the time we came back (having cadged a shower) the water was back on. Some areas of Nairobi have been having enormous water problems for weeks already, but our part is not normally affected.

I feel really lazy today. Perhaps we should go out and have a swim to keep us in good shape.

Magadi Lake with Friends

French friends from Botswana have been with us for the week, so we have had more outings than usual. Yesterday we went to Magadi in our little Citroen, and gave it some rough treatment on the dirt roads around the lake. There was no game to be seen around the lake, but we had excellent views of lots of giraffe both coming and going. Here there is (fortunately) a lot of prejudice against game meat, so people seldom poach, and the animals are able to graze within sight of habitation. I could not resist the opportunity to fill a large plastic bag with a good quantity of game manure collected under the tree where we stopped for lunch. Animals tend to shelter under the fairly rare spreading trees in the heat of the day. I think my collection was contributed to by buffalo, wildebeeste, gazelle, zebra and some very small buck.

Welcome Reassurance

Dominic's school doctor has written to us (which is more than the boys have done) saying that in his view one fit does not warrant any medication or periodic surveillance, and he will take him off the present pills over a six-month period. Reassuring – but do doctors really know anything at all?

Human Archeology Collection

I forgot the highlight of last week, which was a tour of the strong room of the Kenyan museum (to which we have made a loan) to see the best of the East African source materials on human archaeology – practically everything from East Africa used in Leakey's *"Making of Mankind"*.

Letter to parents   Nairobi, 14/02/1982

Constructing a Biltong Box

This evening we have had the first rain of the long rains – just an intermittent light drizzle, not enough even to start to bring the grass back to green, but at least a promise of more to come. I had decided to make a biltong box: an open box of fly mesh, which I can hang in a breezy place to dry out raw beef in the South African manner, because we are very fond of biltong but find that here it is scarce, expensive, and of poor quality. Over the last two days I have put in a lot of work, and now have the basic frame, made out of the solid timber of the packing case in which our luggage arrived (a pleasant practice, to start us off at each new place with a stock of timber for odd jobs!). But if the rains are about to begin, my efforts will have been in vain – at least for another three or four months. Once the rains start, there would be a good chance of ending up with a load of mouldy smelly meat.

An Exhausting Climb on the Ngong Hills

Nicole and I spent this afternoon out on the Ngong hills, with a party of 10-11 year olds and their teachers who are training for a climb up Mount Kenya next weekend. We are both fairly stiff and exhausted, having walked not many miles, but climbed a series of hills all of which would I suppose qualify as mountains in Britain, since we ended up around 7,500 feet – but remember we live at 4,000 feet. The weather was ideal – dry, breezy and slightly overcast, despite which my arms, legs and neck now glow a healthy pink. You will be pleased to hear that I wear a straw hat (local type) for such jaunts, and even for most of my gardening.

The Body Rebels!

If I want to, and can find the time, I can go on the Mount Kenya trip next week. The only thing that gives slight pause for thought is whether my knees will make it. Everything else about me seems to be pretty fit, but ever since my last walk across the centre of Guadeloupe two years ago (a really gruelling exercise that, in fogs, bogs, tropical rainstorms, as well as a lot of up and down, or edging along mountainsides that frequently disappeared in landslides) my right knee hasn't been absolutely sure of itself. I noticed that one of the climbers today was wearing an elastic knee stocking. Actually a number of my more sporting contemporaries at City Boys were already sporting them at age 18 or 19. Perhaps that's what I need.

Diplomacy Over Servants' Health

Having got into a medical vein, one of the high spots of this week was our decision that Francis and Nathan should go off and have a proper medical check-up. The Foundation pays for these – annually for "inside" servants, and on appointment for "outside" ones; but many people, ourselves included, never bother. Because what do you do if they are sick? Sack them? What really prompted us this time is that Nathan, who is sixty-eight, insists that he has perfect eyesight, but somehow manages to overlook cobwebs, and more distressingly, the huge bugs that occasionally infest our cabbages and cauliflowers. So since we couldn't send him off to have his eyes tested without doubting his word and bruising his dignity, we sent the pair of them off for the whole shooting match.

The pair of them are quite a joke in town. They don't know their way around at all; but we got them there, and they got themselves back, and they have to pay a second visit on Tuesday next week. I do hope I am going to be able to get them there a second time. When I was working with Francis in the garden yesterday he poured out a great recital which I had trouble tuning in to at first. He was both incredulous and indignant. What sort of doctor was this? He wanted to look at all sorts of things, and took some very unpleasant samples (I'm glad he managed to do this at the surgery; I was bracing myself to receive a collection of bottles and jam jars). Worst of all, he took a large amount of blood, at which point Francis felt like giving him a good punch! And then to add insult to injury HE DID NOT GIVE THEM ANY MEDICINE AT ALL!

News from the Boys

Bernard and Dominic have sent us two cheery letters (the first did not arrive until we had sent them a fairly stiff letter of complaint). Bernard really enjoyed the skiing holiday, and felt he had excelled. He also got a good mark in his English Lit. O-level, and "middling" marks for other things (a bit reticent on actual grades). Dominic spoke in the Debating Society against a motion to the effect that women are still discriminated against, and although he lost, because more girls turned up than boys he claimed a moral victory, since five girls voted for him.

The rain has started again, quite heavily this time. I could hear it advancing up the garden until it reached the house. Definitely not biltong-curing weather.

The lights have gone out, so this may be quite illegible.

Lots of love, David and Nicole

Letter to parents   Nairobi, 22/03/1982

Baking Heat in the Rift Valley

Two weekends ago we went camping in our usual spot down by Lake Magadi, taking with us Sarah, the twelve-year-old daughter of a colleague. It's difficult to say how much she enjoyed the trip. She was absolutely worn out and inarticulate on our return, but did her best to be helpful, and was pleasant company.

It is extraordinarily hot down in the basin of the Rift Valley. The wind blows hot. However, we know now that the stream where we camp is reputed to be free of bilharzia, so at least we were spared the frustration of seeing it and hearing it, but not daring to touch the water until it had been boiled. Our friends came over from Magadi Soda for drinks and dinner. They had been having a fraught week, having just sacked their Kenyan chief engineer for corruption and incompetence, and were awaiting a local board meeting the next day, with big-wigs from I.C.I. (U.K.) whom they regard as a lot of pompous fools. There was a spattering of rain as we sat outside over our drinks, which was quite pleasant; but in expectation of more, I put the waterproof fly-sheets over our tents. In fact it did not rain again, but our tent was so hot that we couldn't sleep at all until I had struggled out again and removed the fly-sheet.

High Altitude Camping

It was all very different from the week before, when we camped in the Aberdares at about 10,000 feet, and woke up to find frost on the grass, and three buffaloes quietly grazing on the short grass of the fishing camp.

Social Life

Last weekend, the Parrishes came over from Magadi to visit us, so we had a dinner party for them on Friday. On Sunday we went to play bridge with our next door neighbours. Nicole and I started out with two fantastic hands, which could have given us two games (and rubber) straight off, but which we underbid badly. We then went on to lose heavily on everything else.

Cattle and Camel Breeding

Yesterday was quite busy for a Saturday, but also a bit frustrating. I had to see some people at work, which I don't like doing on a Saturday, but these were quite interesting people with a sort of missionary background (Mennonite and something else) who were interested in training pastoralists in the semi-arid north east, and at the same time, in breeding cattle and camels for drought conditions. One of the things that worried them was that the people in positions of influence – primarily the Kikuyu – are not cattle-keeping people, and although they have bought up lots of ranches, they have little interest in cattle or ranching, and have sent a lot of carefully built up herds to the abattoir, so that there's a danger of losing something like eighty years of breeding work – particularly on Boran cattle. However, they also want to pick up on camel breeding work which is being done mainly by old white Kenyan families. This is both for meat and milk. Camels complement cattle, being upper-storey grazers (like giraffe). It is interesting that there are no recognised camel breeds yet.

Reckless Bidding

After this lot I went to an auction, which was fun, and wasted about 450sh on a mah-jong set (I have played once), an ice-cream bucket, and what was described as an old army vacuum flask – to hold about two quarts – but on closer inspection it turned out to be insulated with little pieces of cork, such as we used to have in our bran tub. Never mind! It cost only 30sh.

A Tedious Wedding Ceremony...

After a hurried lunch, we went off to the Anglican cathedral for the wedding of a Kenyan economist who receives a grant from us. In fact, he had regarded himself as married for some time, but was intending to take his wife back to the U.S. with him, and needed a certificate for U.S. immigration. We needn't have hurried. They didn't get started until at least an hour after the time stated on the invitation, and everything was quite extraordinarily ponderous. It took about three playings of the wedding march to get the bride up from the door to the altar steps. The white clergyman, who has an extraordinary resemblance to John Odling-Smee, kept on having little whispered *tête-a-têtes* with the bride and groom; and when he mentioned that he had discussed with them their mutual duties and obligations, I couldn't help wondering whether these conversations had been held during the service, rather than before it. Worst of all were the hymns. Half the congregation hadn't been issued with hymn books anyway, and probably a fair proportion were either illiterate, or couldn't read English. It would have made you weep to hear how they sang *"Guide me, O thou great Jehovah"*. It really took me aback, because I am used to Africans singing enthusiastically and unaccompanied.

...and a Boring Reception!

We then went on to the reception. By this time I was hot, thirsty, and tired of sitting, so I was looking forward to a beer and a bit of a party. However, they sat us down on rows of chairs in an assembly hall, and processed the wedding party at the same snail's pace to a long table on the stage, where they sat solemnly like the Last Supper. Then they opened with a prayer, and started long speeches, the gist of which was what an obedient child Willis had been, and how brilliantly he had done at school. I regret that I don't know how the occasion ended, because I couldn't stand any more. I murmured "another urgent appointment" to the couple sitting next to us (whom I knew slightly), pressed my gift on them for onward transmission, and walked out, feeling as I did so a great sense of liberation.

Rascals with Bows and Arrows

Today, for light relief, we picnicked at a tiny national park, Ol Donyo Sabuk, beyond Thika, about thirty miles from here. As we settled down to open our basket, a game warden strolled up with a gun and warned me not to go too far from the car *"because there are sometimes rascals about"*. I asked whether the rascals had knives. No, he said, usually not knives but sometimes bows and arrows. However, we ate in peace and were not troubled by any falling arrows. On the road we came across two different kinds of blackberry: one apricot yellow, and the other a more conventional colour, but about a quarter the usual size. Both had a pleasant flavour, although not knowing them I only tasted, and did not eat any.

Demanding Music

I have talked only of weekends. Weeks too are very busy – the choir and orchestra are now coming together for joint rehearsals of Haydn's *"Creation"*. Lots of very nice music; much of it technically very difficult – or at least beyond my level. However, there are five other cellos, and some of them are excellent. I also spent one evening last week playing cello, flute and piano trios with two Dutch ladies – with some trepidation, but they turned out to be not embarrassingly expert.

At the end of the week I'm off to Zimbabwe for about five days, arriving back just in time for the boys, and the concert.

Letter from Nicole to Sheila and Ron   Nairobi, 28/03/1982

Concert Rehearsals

First of all, Happy Birthday Sheila, and many happy returns. I thought David was going to write but he left for Zimbabwe yesterday and did not have time to do it. In fact we have been rather busy lately, mostly with music rehearsals. Our Easter Concert will be held next week (there will be three performances). The Music Society has invited the choir master of King's College, London, to come here and conduct (he is a friend of a couple who are members of the Society). This man arrived on Tuesday and we have had rehearsals with him daily so that we can get used to his way of conducting and he has enough time to make good all the mistakes we have been making. David hopes to be back on Friday, just in time for the first performance. There are very few cellists, and although he is the worst, his services are needed.

Desperate for Rain

The rains are now three weeks late and I am sure farmers are getting quite desperate. Some districts of Nairobi have been without water for weeks. We have been lucky, although twice the water cut off in our area, but not for very long. The garden is looking very sad, especially the lawns, which we do not water.

7.30pm – Hurray it rains! And I hope it is going to last. The streets are already flooded and cars were stuck on the road because their engines were flooded. David has ordered a thousand-gallon water tank which is sitting in our drive waiting to be placed somewhere convenient in order to get rain water from the roof. It is a pity that he has not had time to fix it before he went away; there is a lot of water falling from the sky this evening.

Illusions of Scotland

We recently visited the Aberdares Mountains, where we camped at 10,000 feet. It was pretty cold during the night and there was frost on the grass in the morning. The scenery is very beautiful up there and one has the impression of being somewhere in Scotland. The Aberdares National Park is huge and as there are lots of water points the animals are rather dispersed and one does not see many of them. We saw three buffaloes and some gazelles, and also three waterbucks enjoying a swim in a stream.

Letter from Dominic to Grandparents   Nairobi, 13/04/1982

Dear Granny and Grandpa,

I am very sorry that I did not write to you thanking you for the money you gave me and the two star bars. Here in Nairobi there is nothing to do except for work or feeding the rabbits and playing cards. But for Easter we went to Mombassa. While at the coast we went out quite some way and saw quite a few fish and Daddy saw a couple of sting-rays.
Lots of love, Dominic

Letter from Nicole Nairobi, 24/04/1982
to parents-in-law

Family Outings

The children left last Sunday at 2am; they had a pleasant holiday although there is not a lot for them to do here. Twice I booked a riding lesson for them and both times we had to cancel the lesson because of the rain. They had an enjoyable time in Mombassa and did a lot of swimming with David, going far away to the reef. Bernard of course was busy revising the whole time he was here, and I hope he gets fairly good results, as he is taking his exams very seriously.

David is away for two days on a field trip; he will be back some time today. He went to see a project run by the Catholic Relief Services, which the Ford Foundation is financing. He went to see another project last Friday and took the children with him; they were very interested.

Letter from Nicole Nairobi, 24/06/1982
to Sheila and Ron

A Hectic Schedule

I have not forgotten Anne's and Thomas' birthdays; I seem to have less and less time, although I do not have any housework to do. I must admit that lately we have been entertaining a lot and we have also been to a lot of dinner parties and cocktails, so many things that I would do in the evening do not get done. We had two lots of friends from Botswana staying with us last month. Actually one family, Margaret and Bobby Rowe, live in your part of the world and they might come and visit you sometime. They are a very pleasant couple; their youngest son was very friendly with Dominic in Botswana.

Music Society

The Music Society also takes a great deal of my time, as I have been nominated secretary. I have to keep the subscriptions up to date (300 members), and the newsletter once a month, attend meetings etc. Our latest production was *"Dido and Aeneas"* which was performed at the Kenya National Theatre. We had four performances and it was a success considering the fact that Purcell is not very well known. Everybody I know who has been to see the opera said that it was enchanting. Somebody made a video tape of it and I must say I was very impressed; the singing came out well and the décor and costumes look quite professional.

Conferences

David is away again this week – in Angola this time. He should be back on Monday morning and his boss told me that he is going to have another very busy week as he has to attend another conference. Last week David was also attending a conference and we hardly saw each other. Anyway in a month's time we shall be on leave and we shall have plenty of time with each other and the children. We are going to Guadeloupe this year. The children will fly direct from Paris and we shall meet them in Guadeloupe a week later.

A Visitor from U.K.

One of Auntie Phyllis's sons is in Nairobi this week on business. Patrick phoned me on Monday evening to say that he was here. I had not met him before. I remember that at Sheila's parents' wedding anniversary one or two of his brothers were there. I have invited Patrick for supper tomorrow evening and I shall take him to the National Park to see some animals on Saturday afternoon. David will be sorry to miss him.

Home Grown Bananas

The garden looks beautiful after the rains; we have a profusion of roses. We always have more vegetables than we can eat. We had our first banana crop, three different types – green to be eaten as vegetables, small sweet ones, and big sweet ones which are good for frying and are eaten as a dessert with cream and rum – *"bananes flambées"*.

A New Puppy

We have acquired a puppy to keep company to Cain, our old dog. She is called Cleo and is of Labrador mother and Alsatian father (both parents are pure pedigree). She is four months and not fully house-trained yet, although she is getting better and does not make as many messes as she used to. I think it is easier to bring up a child than a dog. Perhaps we shall see you in Leicester when we are staying there in August.

Letter from Nicole Nairobi, June 1982
to parents-in –law

Complex Journeys

David has now been away for a week, this time in Angola, and all being well he should be back tomorrow morning. I received a telegram yesterday to say that he had arrived safely. I hope the telegram was delayed, and it does not mean that he only arrived in Luanda yesterday. David is coming back via Paris and should have spent the day with my cousin Anick, before flying back to Nairobi tonight.

An Independent Mother

Although on my own, the week went very fast; most evenings I was invited out by friends. Today I had lunch with David's new colleague who is here on her own for two years, with her one-year-old child. She did not run away from her husband and is not divorced or separated but the job at the Ford Foundation office here appealed to her and she thought it would be good experience for her future career; obviously she was a strong candidate as she was offered the job. It will not be easy for her as she will have to travel from time to time and now that the child is mobile she cannot really take her on trips. She is looking for a good children's maid and half her problems will be solved if she finds one.

Patrick's Visit

As you know, last week Patrick Childs was in Nairobi. He phoned me on Monday to say that he was here. I had never met him before. I found him a very pleasant young man, very easy to get on with. I invited him for supper on Friday. I had planned to go and buy some baskets from a village a few kilometres outside Nairobi on Saturday, and I invited him to join me. He was very pleased as it gave him an opportunity to see a bit of the countryside and he found the baskets so beautifully woven that he decided to buy two. I took him to the Nairobi National Park yesterday although unfortunately we saw very few animals; they are all over the place as there is plenty of water everywhere. All the same, we saw two hippos in the river. I had warned him that hippos do not show themselves very much so he was delighted at the sight of them. I think there is a great resemblance between David and Patrick, and even with Bernard.

"Dido and Aeneas"

The four performances of *"Dido and Aeneas"* went very well and the attendance was better than expected. Everybody who saw the opera thought it was delightful. We were able to see and hear ourselves at a lunch last Sunday, when somebody showed a video of our performance. I am going to a concert of the Nairobi Orchestra tonight; once again because of his travelling commitments David is not able to take part.

Letter from Nicole Nairobi, 01/09/1982
to parents-in-law

Leicestershire Visit

Thank you for having us, and I hope we did not leave too much mess behind us. Dominic and I had a game of golf on Saturday (it was the first time for me) and had a pleasant walk in Bradgate on Monday; we must have walked at least four km. It was very hot.

I have seen some very pretty flower-pot holders in Marks and Spencer and I thought you would like to treat yourself to one for Christmas; I enclose £5. It is very difficult to get good presents in Kenya.

I phoned Sheila yesterday. They are all well. Bernard and Dominic will go and spend half-term with her.

Love, Nicole and the boys

Letter to parents   Meikles Hotel, Harare, Zimbabwe,
                                                                    19/09/1982

Always on the Move

I'm really at home at the moment, not at the Meikles, but I shall be back there again tomorrow afternoon, so why not use the airmail forms they provide so liberally?

I was in Zimbabwe from 7th – 11th, will return from 20th – 28th, and again from 1st – 6th October. The reason for this is that we are expecting all our Foundation trustees to arrive for a meeting in Nairobi, and many of them will profit from a visit to Zimbabwe before or after the meeting. I have to be there with another staff member to conduct them around; not a job I look forward to. These may not be particularly easy tourists, and they may not appreciate how many things can go wrong with time-tables in Africa. For instance, in one remarkable day, a group of trustees (which will include Robert McNamara) is meant to meet the Prime Minister, the Minister for Lands and Settlement, the Minister for Economic Planning, and the Minister of Justice; but only one of these appointments is in any way confirmed, or has a definite time to it. The rest are on stand-by, and the Prime minister takes precedence.

Nervous Days in Harare

I really quite like Zimbabwe, although for me it has a feeling of not being really Africa – at least, Harare, the capital, does, and that's all I know. However, even in Harare people are a bit uncertain and nervous at the moment. A fairly sizeable part of the army has taken to the bush, and there have been a lot of incidents in the south. The problem is basically tribal, although some of Mugabe's former ZANLA guerrillas have become disaffected because of what they see as a too cautious approach by the government, plus self-enrichment by the new elite, and have joined the dissidents. So far, all the trouble is in the south, not in Harare. All we need is for some of the trustees to be kidnapped!

Rumours in Nairobi

Here too there is some uncertainty, and a lot of rumours, but little news of what is going on behind the scenes. It seems there is a lot of pressure on the President to resign and let someone stronger take over, but he is fighting back and trying to rally public support.

While I was away, Nicole had a visit from a lady whose father built our house in 1952. We thought it was much older than that, judging by the style, and by the quality of much of the detailed work (excellent). We really are very lucky with this house. I do wish you would come and visit while we are still here.

A Cool Climate

At the moment it is raining, which is very pleasant; not that we need cooling down. If I have one serious complaint about the climate of Nairobi, it is that it is too cool for comfort much of the time; never cold or frosty of course, but there are many evenings when we enjoy a good fire.

Garden Delights

My garden can do with some rain. I have let the roses die back, because the books all say they need a rest period, although I really cannot see why. For the present, too, there are very few vegetables, and I am fighting a running battle with the caterpillars (tiny and insidious) for my cauliflower and broccoli plants. This afternoon I planted a variety of other seeds around my newest planting of brassicas, to test out the theory that variety confuses the insects.

The rain will also benefit my orchid collection: mostly little local epiphytes, struggling to survive. I shall be delighted if any of them do flower. I also have one beautiful flower spray on an exotic cymbidium orchid – a foot high, and still in quite good shape after more than a month in flower.

Friendly Neighbours

Last night we played bridge with our neighbours. They're better than us, but not distressingly so. They are both very fond of our dogs, and while we were away they often invited them for the afternoon (of course, they spoiled them atrociously). Unfortunately they will be leaving fairly soon. There is also a very pleasant Cypriot couple from London adjoining on another side, he Greek, she Turkish – but he's a civil engineer and will be leaving even sooner for a job in Bahrain. Our relationship with the remaining neighbours, very well-heeled Kenyans, is amicable but distant.

Music from Childhood

Many thanks for the Sibelius symphonies – an inspired choice! Actually *Finlandia* by Sibelius was about the first piece of serious music I ever really liked – you had it in your collection of 78 rpm records.
Much love, David

Letter from Nicole   Nairobi, 09/1982
to Sheila

David's Activities

David is now back from Zimbabwe where he spent most of September. He had to be there to organise the visit of the Ford Foundation Board of Trustees, also to welcome them and accompany them on official visits, field trips and sight-seeing trips. They also came to Kenya to attend their four-yearly meeting, and various receptions and meetings with Kenyan officials. I had the opportunity to visit David while he was in Zimbabwe and spent a weekend in Harare. I did not see much of Harare but I thought it was a very impersonal town, without any life. Nairobi is such an interesting and lively city that one gets very spoilt here and finds other African cities (with the exception of West Africa) very uninteresting. Anyway I must get used to the idea of living there as we might be moving there next year.

Unorthodox African transport

1982, Ascent of Mount Kenya – Lenana Point (16,000 ft)

The Boys' Half-Term

I have asked Bernard to let you know when Dominic and he will be arriving at Stowmarket (I believe it is the nearest station to Wickham Skeith). Bernard and Dominic are now in the same building (the boarding house) as Bernard is in charge of the First Year dormitory.

Aftermath of a Coup

Life is back to normal after the coup. Soldiers and government officials as well as university lecturers and students who took part are still being tried. There must be at least 3,000 to 4,000 people in prisons by now and life inside there must be very uncomfortable.
Love, Nicole

(Continues with letter from David)

Music Making

I am feeling quite virtuous, as I have played my cello twice in two days, first with a mainly Dutch group (organised by a lady whose first name is Joke), and tonight with the Nairobi orchestra. Joke's group is more fun, because I can play the music. Mind you, the Dutch in general are strange serious people – almost as strange as Swedes – and they also speak a strange language which, when you listen carefully, is like a mixture of bad English and bad German. The orchestra, by contrast, is fairly light-hearted, but is determined to play very difficult pieces of music. This time we have Brahms' second *Symphony* and Walton's *"Façade"* as well as a variety of other things. It doesn't help that I am also away for most of the rehearsals.

Orchids

Nicole has mentioned my orchids. I am not feeling very proud of them today, since I spent lunch-time at the Nairobi orchid exhibition, which was spectacular. Nairobi has a reasonable climate for growing quite a number of types of orchids, and a few people have enormous collections, mainly of exotic types. However, we also have large numbers of indigenous East African orchids, often with rather small flowers compared with those from Brazil and south east Asia, but interesting in their own right. Most of my little collection is indigenous, but I have a few exotics, and have sneaked in a few Guadeloupean varieties. Most grow on trees, or pieces of fibre from the giant fern. So far, I have managed a single flower, and since flowering is an annual event, I have a long while to wait for anything else. However, growing them at all is something of an achievement – rather like my teenage hobby of growing cacti.

Dogs and Rabbits on the Operating Table

Our two dogs are back with us today, having both been in-patients at the university veterinary clinic (boarding fee 75p a day). Cain has been nipping through the barbed wire fence to go on night prowls, and in the end mis-judged the jump and tore his backside. We didn't notice until the cuts were infected, and one had abcessed, and had to be cleaned out before being stitched. Cleo just went to be spayed. I recently stitched one of our rabbits. Her son and husband had taken a large bite out of her rump, so I cleaned the hole, and sewed it up again with a needle and some strong thread. She seems to be all right again, although strangely I can't find any stitches to remove.

From Mugabe to Robert McNamara

I shall be back in Zimbabwe again in two weeks' time, and shall visit Bulawayo this time, as well as Harare, and then go on to Botswana. The other recent visits left no time for real work, and were really rather a drag, although there were some compensations, including two visits to Victoria Falls, and the possibility of sitting in on interesting interviews with several ministers, and with Prime Minister Mugabe. Also, I shall savour the memory of Robert McNamara referring to me as "our leader".
Love, David

A Strange Shapeless Chewed Object!

We have had a very lazy week-end. It's 8pm now and we have just woken up from our Sunday afternoon nap. I have been outside feeding the rabbits in the dark, and chastising Cleo, our young dog, for taking a tin in which I had just planted some seeds, and tipping it out in one of the dog baskets. She is very affectionate, and when she is lonely she gathers up a variety of things and chews them. She is at a chewing stage, and has almost destroyed the doormat and both dog baskets. None will be replaced until she stops chewing, although I occasionally feel a bit self-conscious about the strange shapeless object outside the front door.

Culture Differences over Pets and Wildlife

Both dogs are convalescent, having been in-patients at the University clinic. Cain had been slipping out through the barbed-wire fence, and must have slipped a bit less adroitly than usual. He had a whole string of cuts around his rear end. Cleo went in to be spayed. Nicole did not feel like coping with hordes of amorous dogs, or puppies. Boarding fees at the clinic are 15shillings a day, which I think must compare very favourably with anything in the U.K. Most of the owners at the small animal clinic are Europeans, but a fair number of Kenyans also turn up with sick pets. This may not seem odd to you, but traditionally even among those tribes (and religions – dogs are unclean to Moslems) that tolerate dogs, it is most unusual to feed them at all regularly, let alone spend money looking after them. It is interesting how much the Kenyan upper class has been Europeanised in such cultural matters. Another example is the existence of wildlife clubs in Kenyan schools. Again, this may not seem odd, but wildlife competes with farming and grazier activities, and the wildlife parks were set up by Europeans for Europeans. Where necessary, Africans were simply told to move their villages to make way for the parks. If there is a traditional view, it is that wildlife are a damned nuisance, except as meat and skins, in which respect they are free for all. However, Kenyan school-children (and not just the rich ones) write letters to the wildlife journal about the need to preserve their wildlife heritage.

Planning a Move to Zimbabwe

We have got rid of our visiting trustees, and are now able to get back to normal routine. I have visited Zimbabwe three times in a month. Getting back to normal means that I shall be back there again in two weeks. I must also start looking at the property market there, because we intend to set up a sub-office as soon as we get the necessary agreement on "privileges" - i.e. not paying income tax, being able to import cars and office equipment duty-free, and so on. This is taking longer than it should, because they have no experience of dealing with international non-governmental organisations; also because the two ministries principally concerned (Finance and Planning, and Foreign Affairs) are still squabbling over each other's turf. The other day the American ambassador who had turned up for the ceremonial signing of a large aid agreement, was sent away again while the ministries argued which of them was the principal signatory on the Government side.

Trouble Brewing in Zimbabwe

Zimbabwe is not in a very good state at the moment, because the two main independence parties, whose support coincides with the two main tribal groups, are on poor terms. Mugabe's group is in control, and has a "reconciliation" cabinet with ministers from Nkomo's ZAPU, and from the white community, but ZAPU continues to insist that it was cheated; it has certainly itself cheated by holding on to arms, and is scared about suggestions that it might be absorbed into a single party with ZANU. A lot of ZAPU/ ZIPRA soldiers have deserted; rumour says that 10% of the army is AWOL. It is not clear whether they have any unified leadership. ZAPU denies that it controls them, and Nkomo, whatever his other faults, does not want civil war (he certainly could not win one, with 20% of the population). It is a distressing situation, and the fault is certainly not only on one side. White friends of mine, who have a long-standing relationship with ZAPU (the first independence party) say rather bitterly that "reconciliation is for whites, not for ZAPU". Life in Harare is still pretty normal, however. It is down south in the Ndebele (Matabele to you) areas that the situation is really tense.

The Kenyan Coup

In Kenya, we still do not think that all the trouble is over. Many people believe that there was more than one coup attempt going on, and that senior cabinet ministers were involved, but that the lower-ranks coup (which took place because the senior ministers were as unpopular as the President) temporarily drew all the fire by going off at half-cock. If this is so, there is a lot of sorting out still to be done.

Tension over Somalis in Kenya

There also appear to be some *shifta* troubles up north. We don't hear much about these, because the Somalis have no good political links, and no-one seems very interested in them; but in the area which I visited a year ago (and must visit again) one now has to travel in convoy between Isiolo and Marsarbit. However, I'm sure there are no convoys from Marsarbit to the Hurri Hills. I should explain that although Somalia is another country, a large part of Kenya is also populated by Somali peoples, who are generally suspected of being more loyal to Somalia than they are to Kenya. This may well be true, but the measures taken against them are not such as to increase their loyalty to Kenya.

Relaxing in the Garden

Meanwhile, I cultivate my garden. I now have about a dozen types of indigenous orchid – perhaps more, perhaps less. Many of them look very similar at the stage of having only two or three leaves and a length of stem. Most are epiphytic, and I tape them onto pieces of bark or tree-fern, and mist-spray them once or twice a day. They are seldom very showy, and none of mine has yet produced a flower, but one I gave our next-door neighbour has already flowered. I think hers has been stimulated into flower by hardship; it had almost been dried up by exposure to direct sun. My interest has just been boosted by the annual Nairobi orchid show, most of which is devoted to exotic orchids, but there is also a good showing of the indigenous ones - naturally all in flower. Yesterday I found a new one: tiny, with no leaves at all, just a mass of coiled roots clinging to a dead twig.

The garden proper is in quite good shape, since we have been getting intermittent rain for more than a fortnight. I have also found a nearby source of horse manure, which should help the cabbages along. Tomorrow I shall invest in half a sack of seed potatoes. I have a lot of maize coming up, but I shall have to replant the beans that go with them since I used old stock and they failed to germinate. This is a constant problem, since I tend to lay in stocks of seed when available, and they quite often fail to come up when they are used months or years later.

Gigantic Radishes

We are finishing broccoli and cauliflower, and I have planted lettuce, tomato, cabbage (standard and Chinese), cauliflower, broccoli, leeks, fennel, onions, chicory, and Japanese radishes that are said to grow to a colossal size. We normally grow foot-long Indian radishes; they last in the ground much better than the little red ones.

I have been downstairs to chastise Cleo again. She seems to have forgotten her house-training while at the kennels.

Lots of love, David

Letter to Sheila and Ron   Nairobi, 28/11/1982

A Birthday Thank You

Thank you very much for my birthday wallet. It arrived last week, and was a very pleasant surprise. I think that in spite of the horrific postage, it travelled surface mail. I hope you didn't think I was ungrateful not to reply earlier.

I was sorry to miss Wickham Skeith this year. I do think of it as one of the (few) places where I can turn up any time in the knowledge that you will be pleased to see me and will find me somewhere to sleep. I hope too many other people don't feel the same way about your welcoming house! Although really I think that is what a house should be like. We are always very happy to have people drop in on us, although of course it doesn't happen very often here, since we are rather a long way from those of our friends who do not live in Nairobi.

Thanks, too, for looking after the boys. I think they feel very at home with you. I hope they are easy guests (I believe they are, but then parents usually do, don't they?).

We are looking forward very much to having them with us again in three weeks' time.

Preparing to Climb Mount Kenya

This holiday we are planning to climb Mount Kenya; not to the very top, because one has to be a real rock climber to do that, but to Lenana point, which is quite high enough to give us all altitude sickness. Nicole doesn't intend to make the ascent. I'm sure she could manage it, but there's no point in doing something you don't want to do, and it is true that she has much more limited lung capacity than the rest of us. In fact I was quite taken aback when I saw our routine chest x-rays recently to realise that I must be able to hold about four times as much in my lungs as she can!

My weak point these days is my knees. They were extremely painful by the time I finished our two-day Guadeloupe walk this year. I find this very irritating. Fortunately there doesn't seem to be anything structurally wrong with them; I suppose I just lack exercise. Here we go everywhere by car. I suppose I could cycle to work, but I doubt if I would live very long in the Nairobi traffic. Anyway, I have decided that I must give my knees some serious exercise before Mount Kenya, so I run up the six flights of stairs at work at least once a day, and am considering giving up the lift completely.

Walking in the Rain

Today we took rather more serious exercise, and took the dogs (Cleo and Cain) out for a long walk through the outskirts of Nairobi. When we had almost finished the first third of our circle, it started to rain gently, and it went on raining steadily for the next two hours. We and the dogs were absolutely soaked through, and took great pleasure in soaking ourselves in a hot bath.

Plenteous Rains

The short rains this year have been terrific, and threaten to merge into the long rains. Some old settlers we met at lunch today say that this last happened in 1962. My maize plants are flourishing (without thinking, I planted a long-rains variety that reaches ten feet, so if the rains do stop, that will be a complete failure – maize must have rains through to flowering, otherwise the heads don't form). My potatoes are being picked off one by one by some sort of fungal or bacterial blight. I sent one to a horticultural advisory service to have the disease identified, and they came back with the message that they had wilt and blight! I could have told them that myself. It's rather like going to the doctor, and explaining your symptoms in order to be advised you must have an upset tummy!

Deterring Burglars

There has been a spate of burglaries in our area, and while I was last away thieves came through our garden twice in order to rob the house next door; however, so far they have not visited us. Our guards are fairly incompetent, and probably try to follow the first two wise monkeys: *"hear no evil, see no evil"*; our dogs are altogether too friendly to humans, although we noticed today that they seem to have a reputation with the neighbourhood dogs, who disappeared behind their hedges or simply turned tail and ran, when ours hove into view.
Bed time.
Love, David

P.S. from Nicole

Thank you for having the children; they enjoyed their stay with you. Through them we heard all about David (Wright's) house. I hope the tenants are satisfactory.

Your folk singing sounds very interesting. Perhaps one of these days I shall hear the name of your group mentioned on the BBC; I often listen to the folk singing programme on the *World News* on Wednesday mornings.

Christmas Music

The Nairobi Music Society has just performed Britten's *"Ceremony of Carols"* and Kodaly's *"Te Deum"* – two quite unusual works. I had already sung the Britten in Botswana, but although I knew of Kodaly, his music was completely new to me as to most other people. We gave three performances and from what I have heard most people enjoyed the *"Te Deum"* even more than the *"Ceremony of Carols"*. The orchestra was very small, only brass instruments, so David did not play. The orchestra will join us when we perform *"The Messiah"* just before Christmas. I think *"The Messiah"* is a well-known work all over English-speaking Africa and always attracts a big crowd. Quite a lot of Africans join the choir on this occasion.

A Quiet Christmas

I suppose that all your family will be back at home for Christmas. We shall spend a quiet Christmas at home this year. We were invited to spend Christmas with friends at a game park but the men (David, Bernard and Dominic) have to take things easy before they start on their difficult journey to Mount Kenya. We shall spend a weekend at a game park before the children go back to school.
Love, Nicole

Letter to parents   Nairobi, 28/12/1982
from Nicole

Climbing the Mountain

We left Nairobi yesterday at 6am and reached Naro Mour, a small village at the foot of Mount Kenya, at 9.30am. We went to the lodge in order to get porters, guides and extra rucksacks, and then drove another 10km to the Park Gate (Mount Kenya is a National Park) where David and the children started their climb. Most people drive to the Meteorological Station (10km from the gate) and start climbing from there, but it is advisable to walk those first 10km in order to progressively get used to the altitude. The porters were not very keen on walking the first 10km but I was not going to use my precious petrol to take them there. Yesterday was a beautiful hot clear day, therefore they had a good start. Today will be the real test for David and the children and if by the end of the day they are not rushed down because of pulmonary oedema or other respiratory troubles, I think they will have made it.

While they are climbing I am staying at the lodge which consists of a main house (an old farmhouse I suppose) and several cottages scattered in the garden. There is a stream running through the garden and one has the impression of being somewhere in Scotland or Wales.

Christmas Thanks

Thank you very much for the Christmas presents which were very much appreciated. The stainless steel dish will be useful, as when I have a dinner party I always realise that I have not got enough dishes. It will also be difficult for Nathan to break it.

We had a very pleasant Christmas on our own. We were promised a duck, but did not get it, so I had to buy two halves of a turkey in the end. One half was enough for us and we had finished it by the time we left yesterday. The Christmas pudding, made by Dominic and me, was very good.

Petrol Panic

It was just as well that we had not planned to go anywhere for Christmas as there was a big fire on Christmas Eve at the Nairobi main petrol depot, which accentuated the petrol shortage already experienced here and resulted in people panicking and rushing to buy petrol. There were long queues at every petrol station. The pipe-line has been damaged, so petrol is now being ferried from Mombassa by tankers and trains.

P.S. From David – a Successful Climb

We made it without great difficulty up Mount Kenya. The tented camp at 14,000ft was very chilly, and we were in our down sleeping bags shortly after 6pm, by which time the sun had gone down and the wind was getting up, and the climate outside the sleeping bag was pretty unbearable. Our guides, wanting to cut a day off their work, tried to persuade us to start for the top at 2am, which would have been fairly grim, but we wisely stayed under wraps until the sun came up at 6am, then had breakfast. The final stretch was very tiring, because of the altitude and the need to keep stopping and resting; but none of us felt really ill until we were almost back to the tented camp for another delightful night, at which point Dominic got a bad headache and temporary loss of morale. Fortunately he recovered after an hour or two resting in the camp. The next day we went back to the Meteorological Station in time to be picked up by Nicole for a good lunch.

Orchids and Holidays

Many thanks for the orchid book. My collection grows slowly, but I now really need some sort of orchid house to get them growing well - only one small flower at present.

Can Dominic spend the half-term with you please? Feb. 18th-23rd. Bernard will probably be in France this time.

Lots of love, David

Letter to all friends
Nairobi, 12/1982

Past and Future

1982 is almost over, we are only twelve months from 1984, Brezhnev is dead, and I am over forty. I am not suggesting that these indicators of the passage of time are of equal importance, but they make me conscious of change, and of a need to do something new. What should it be? As a safeguard I have signed on with the Ford Foundation for another two years.

The Boys' Progress

Bernard and Dominic are still at Lord William's School in Thame. Bernard has passed five O-Levels, which is a relief to us all, and he is now a sixth former, in charge of a junior dormitory; an onerous honour. Dominic's letters are mainly about rugby, which I understand even less than football and cricket. So far, to our relief, no-one has kicked out any of his teeth.

Bernard went back early for a skiing holiday, which he greatly enjoyed. I was afraid it would be a disillusioning experience, having memories of my own first terrified attempts at skiing, which often ended with foot-wrenching falls. Fortunately Bernard seems to be a better natural skier than me.

A Failed Coup

The big event in Kenya this year was the attempted coup on 1st August. We were home on leave at the time, which was fortunate in one sense, but rather irritating in another. I have never experienced a coup or coup attempt, and when one comes, I have to be on holiday.

The attempt was led by privates and junior officers in the Kenya air force, an elite branch of the armed forces. They briefly controlled two air force bases, the airport and the broadcasting service. They also assisted mobs to break open shops and loot them in town. This may have been their undoing; certainly it was an amateurish waste of time, when they could have been establishing control of key points. By mid-morning the army, police and General Service Unit

(GSU – a heavily armed special police unit with some British officers) - had come out against the coup and were systematically mopping up centres of resistance.

Death and Damage

Quite a lot of looters, air force men and university students (who joined the coup attempt) were shot, but it is still not at all clear how many, and probably never will be. One Japanese tourist was shot at the Hilton Hotel as he tried to take photographs (quite likely mistaken for a sniper). Several Asian women were raped and Asian-owned shops suffered more than African-owned shops. This has made the Asian community very jittery. Europeans generally seem to have had few special problems, although a number had their cars commandeered. Francis, our gardener, gave me a dramatic account of how he drove back the invading hordes from the gateway to our house, but I know that really nothing at all untoward happened in our residential area.

Underlying Discontent

Many people believe that plotting was not confined to the air force, but included the army, police, GSU and some politicians. The subsequent dismissal of the heads of the GSU and police "in the public interest" lends credence to such rumours.

The coup attempt reflected fairly widespread discontent: with the poor performance of the economy (a reflection of global depression); with corruption in high places; with the vast gap between (Kenyans) rich and poor; with the harassment and detention of left-wing figures (a very recent phenomenon under the present leadership - more serious under Kenyatta); with interference in the democratic process; with the newly-proclaimed one-party state; and with the lack of dignity of the leadership. None of these causes of grievance has been removed, and resentment has probably been heightened by the heavy-handed way the police and army conducted searches for dissidents and for looted goods. People without identity cards were summarily beaten; the houses and luggage of the poor were searched, and much legitimately acquired property – shoes, cassette recorders, sewing machines, radios etc - was seized and either simply stolen, or held for identification by shopkeepers.

I think further changes are inevitable, but I do not know what they will be or how they will come about.

An Arduous Trek in Guadeloupe

While the coup was going on, we were having a very pleasant and relaxing holiday in Guadeloupe. The high point (at least in terms of altitude) was a two-day walk across the island with the boys. The centre of the island is very rarely visited by Guadeloupeans, but some tracks are maintained. First we went to the summit of the Soufriere volcano, which was chilly and misty, then we took an extraordinary "path" through mountain mangroves – an almost impenetrable network of roots and branches. The path had been cut out, but mostly involved clambering from branch to branch, several feet above the ground. This was preferable to the *"Savane aux Ananas"* which came next: a shallow bog overlying rock. Botanically it is very interesting, because it is full of ground orchids and *bromidiaceae* (the *"ananas"*). One can inspect these from close quarters, as one is in the mud. We bivouacked for the night in the middle of this bog, in a tent improvised from poles and plastic sheeting. As the light faded, the rain started. Our tent kept out 99% of the rain, but the remaining 1% and rising damp slowly soaked into our sleeping bags. In the morning we wrung them out. The next day was somewhat drier, and by 4pm we were able to bathe in a stream and change into dry clothes in the belief that the road, and a waiting car, were only minutes away. Sure enough, two hours later, there was the car, and we were greeted with "You were lucky it did not rain last night!" The boys announced that they had now had enough of this sort of pleasure; however, faced with a choice of the coast or Mount Kenya at Christmas, they have chosen Mount Kenya.

Kenyan Camping

Nicole and I have spent a number of weekends out camping here, sometimes in national parks and sometimes just out in the wild. Of course this is fully equipped camping with a four-wheel-drive vehicle (preferably two, just in case). I would like to do a foot safari, but that takes a lot of organising and a lot of time; nor am I very attracted by the highly organised foot safaris. I feel it should be something you do yourselves.

Getting to Know Zimbabwe

A place I have seen a lot of this year is Zimbabwe. Apart from ordinary working trips, I and a colleague had to show three groups of Ford Foundation trustees around there when they came to Africa for a board meeting in Nairobi. In some ways this was very tedious; I would not choose to be a tour guide. However our tourists were a bit out of the ordinary. I would have liked some sort of permanent record of Robert McNamara (Kennedy's and Johnson's Secretary of State for Defence, and ex-President of the World Bank) referring to me as "our leader". He was exceptionally alert, but was almost matched by some of the others. We had a good half hour with Prime Minister Mugabe, and meetings with several other ministers – and I was able to visit Victoria Falls twice.

Positive / Negative Aspects of Zimbabwe

Zimbabwe is very interesting, because it has the most advanced and industrialised economy in Africa (other than South Africa). Also it has come to independence with a huge number of highly trained Africans. There is a remarkable lack of bitterness among Africans, despite the fact that hundreds were summarily shot or hung (no prisoner of war status; being a terrorist was a capital offence), and many of the present leadership have spent years in detention. But despite these assets, many elementary mistakes are being made for political reasons or through political pressure, such as rapid increases in minimum wages, confused signals to the private sector, and chaotic land resettlement programmes (which will disrupt agricultural production). On top of this there is deliberate South African economic and political sabotage, an exodus of skilled whites, and the world depression. Not surprisingly the economy is reeling, but it could be worse. The end of the war and the huge increase in African spending power gave a tremendous boost to industrial production, and very high maize prices have led to bumper crops. In fact for the time being at least, they do not know what to do with the stuff. They can only export it at a loss, and anyway South African-backed dissidents keep on blowing up the railways through Mozambique.

Dangerous Factions

The most serious problem, however, is the continued and even deepening distrust between the Shona and the Matabele: Mugabe's ZANU and Nkomo's ZAPU (although neither party intended to be ethnic). I blame both sides. The ZAPU leadership felt cheated in the election (although they lost convincingly) and held back large stocks of weapons. However, Mugabe first threatened them with the prospect of a one-party state (so that they could never hope to win), then when they reacted, hammered them. He has also discredited Nkomo, which seems foolish, because Nkomo's vice and virtue was always a willingness to negotiate with anyone. Now there is no-one obvious to negotiate with, which is much more dangerous. The Matabele are only a third of the population, but they are capable of causing havoc, and they are solidly united. Really, the South Africans could not ask for more!

The Solace of Music, and the Garden

Meanwhile, I cultivate my garden and my orchids. Over the past year I have picked up a couple of dozen orchids, including a few of the big cultivated cymbidiums, but most of them are local ground or tree orchids, mainly of botanical interest. We are also both involved in musical activities. Nicole sings a lot and is honorary secretary of the Music Society. I play in the orchestra, and also sometimes with a small and pleasantly amateurish group (in which I am the only non-Dutch member, but they kindly speak English for me).

Wishing you all peace in 1983.

Love, David and Nicole

Family News

David left this morning for Lesotho where he will spend a week; from there he will fly to
Harare and will be back here on 11th February. He has already been away twice in the last two
weeks, to Kenya.

I have not heard from the children yet, but we had a letter from the Boarding Housemaster
saying that they arrived safely.

Swimming, and Knitting

The dry weather is with us again and I am afraid before very long the grass will be yellow
and scorched. But it is nice to wake up every morning to a beautiful sunny day. I went to the
swimming pool on Friday; the water was lovely. From now on I shall try to go every day after
work, it is good exercise.

I gave Dominic the Arran jersey for Christmas. Bernard was very envious, but he will have to
wait for one like it until the summer, as I cannot get decent wool here. I bought locally made
acrylic wool to knit a jersey for Bernard, as he seems not to have very many, especially for
school.

01/02/1983

A Health Alarm for Nicole

David is still away and he will not be back before 11th February. I have just spent a few days
in hospital having suffered severe chest pains. It happened during the night last Thursday and
as I was on my own and had difficulty breathing I got very scared. I managed to call my
neighbours, the Weavers, who called in the doctor. The doctor came and advised to have me
admitted straight away to hospital. Of course I was afraid that it was a thrombosis or
something of the sort, but apparently I am suffering from an inflammation of the lining of the
stomach and of course I must watch my diet. I am out of hospital now, feeling tired but
better. I was admitted to the intensive care unit so that they could do all the heart tests straight
away. I have been well looked after and doctors and staff at the Nairobi hospital (a private
hospital) are very good and competent, but I had to pay a pretty packet. Now a young
American lady who is doing research here and who has nowhere to stay yet, is staying with me
until David comes back.

A Woodland Campsite

We are on our way to a comparatively early bed (9.30pm) after two pleasant but tiring days
camping. We took the Land Rover, and went with the Byrne family to a very beautiful spot at
the foot of Mount Kenya. The camp site was a huge glade in the middle of giant pencil cedars
(an indigenous tree, being felled out outside the national parks) and podocarpus trees.
Elephant and fire had left us an abundance of firewood, and it was evident that zebra and
buffalo also used the glade, but we saw neither – fortunately, perhaps, since the buffalo can be
very dangerous. I went into the forest to look for orchids (found nothing of note) and found
it very uncanny on my own, but all I saw was a couple of large buck and some colobus
monkeys high up in the trees. There really is a very European feel about this sort of highland
forest. I went back to gather moss for my plants, and apart from the greater height of the trees
it was just like gathering moss in Swithland Woods, with the major exception that in
Swithland you are not always wondering whether there is going to be a buffalo or an elephant
hiding in the undergrowth.

A Noisy Night

Last night most of us ate too well, so we were more than usually conscious of the animal
calls. Nicole, because of her diet, ate more sensibly than the rest of us, and probably slept

better as a result. I also got one of my nasty sinus headaches – a mixture of altitude effect (9,500 feet) and unaccustomed exposure to cold winds – so I got up earlier than the others to make tea, and was wide awake when the elephants trumpeted down below us.

Bird Spotting

After breakfast, we went for a walk, and probably climbed another 1,000 feet or more, which left us much improved for lunch. The Byrnes are keen bird-watchers – have spotted 249 species over the last two years, and are looking for the 250th. Most of the more interesting birds we saw, however, were Hartlaub's Turaco – a beautiful green pheasant-sized bird with bright red underwing; lovely, but not a rarity. We get them in the garden. We also saw the cinnamon bee-eater, another beauty of the kingfisher family, that we also get in the garden.

Frustration in Zimbabwe

I returned only last week from a three-week trip to Lesotho and Zimbabwe. This was interesting, but not wholly satisfying, as I spent much of my time in Zimbabwe looking for a house, and eventually found one only to be told that the time was not ripe to buy. Evidently there was some lack of communication between my boss and his boss in New York. Also, I don't think Goran (my boss) knows anything about buying houses. On things like this he is sometimes very impractical, and I suspect he thought we could locate a house, and then put things on ice until we were ready to buy. So I was wasting time with estate agents while Nicole was being ill in Nairobi. Fortunately, as you can see from the weekend trip, she is now pretty well back to normal, although it is unclear when or whether she will be able to resume eating a lot of the food she really enjoys most.

Garden Experiments

In Nairobi, the rainy season seems to have started earlier than usual, and I have planted my maize and beans, like any good Kenyan. If I am unlucky, the rain will stop again and everything will die. This season I have more or less given up potatoes, since they seem to do so badly in our clay soil. So I have planted a large bed of carrots, which do well, and an experimental bed of soya beans. If these do well, I shall have to think of some way to eat them. Several of my little orchids appear to be putting out flower spikes, so I may be lucky, particularly if this is a wet season; they like humidity.
Lots of love, David

Letter to parents   Nairobi, 20/03/1983

Three Days to Wait

We are expecting the boys in three days, which is something we always look forward to. At least one good aspect of their being away at school is that we don't get tired of each other.

A Busy Weekend

This has been "one of those weekends" - not bad, but just busy. By the end of a week, I often feel it would be nice to have a lazy weekend, but it seldom seems to work out like that. We went out on Friday evening, getting back rather late. On Saturday we went to a reception, then came back to give a dinner party for ten people, then when we had got rid of those, we sat and read the paper, waiting for the visiting conductor who is to conduct Verdi's *"Requiem"* for the Music Society. He is staying with us for the next ten days. He arrived in good form, so we sat up and chatted with him and the people who had collected him until 3am. This morning we had our first guests to discuss arrangements with the conductor. I then went out to a farewell luncheon about fifteen miles away, got back in time to sleep for about an hour, and currently we have more visitors to talk about concert plans until it is time to go out to a concert.

I wonder if Michael knows the conductor. He is a professor of civil engineering from Imperial College, London, called Eric Brown. His professional interest is the behaviour of materials, which I think was one of Michael's interests. Anyway, he is a very pleasant person and I think he will be a very easy guest, or would be if he were not continually having to be carted to and fro and having meetings.

Looking Forward to a Concert…

I am not involved in this particular musical venture. The music is extremely difficult and I was away for most of the rehearsals; so not too unwillingly I decided to give it a miss. Of course, come the day I shall wish I were involved, because I enjoy this sort of thing. It should be good, too. Apart from Eric Brown, we have imported a number of professional vocal soloists, and have beefed up the orchestra with about half a dozen professional instrumentalists.

…and Reminiscing After the Performance

The concert consisted of our three Italian soloists, who conformed perfectly to everyone's idea of what an Italian soloist should be like. The bass and tenor were both about 5'2" tall, with curly hair, while the soprano (of uncertain age) was about five inches taller and generously built. All sang very loudly and extremely dramatically, with a lot of very expressive gestures. Unfortunately, since all the arias were in Italian, very few people in the audience had any idea what the drama was about. It was easier to make out the titles in the programme, for instance *"ecce il orrido campo!"* We were surely beholding a horrid field, but we did not know where or why. However the audience (99% white, unfortunately) was most appreciative. Both the tenor and the soprano seemed to be having slight difficulties with the climate, and worried our guest by coughing, and the bass and soprano also sang some notes which were pretty clearly out of tune, but with such aplomb that one started to wonder if it was one's own ear which was at fault.

An Un-Cooperative Climate

I hope their voices hold out. However, it's not surprising if they do have some problems. The rains have not yet come, and the atmosphere is very dry. Also, at our altitude, the physics of making notes must be slightly different. In fact, this is very noticeable with the wind instruments, which have great difficulty getting to concert pitch here because tuning consists of making the body of the instrument longer or shorter by adjusting one of the places where the instrument is joined together, and here they have to make their instruments so much longer that they threaten to fall asunder. This problem does not affect string instruments. These fall apart for quite different reasons, and far more ominously. Someone has kindly stuck the back of my cello up again, no better than I would have done it, although I thought he was some sort of expert; but at least it no longer buzzes on so many of the low notes.

I have been playing from time to time, mainly rather simple 18th century music, with a group in which I am the only English member. Furthermore, all the rest are Dutch, so occasionally I have to ask for a translation.

Countryside and Seaside

I can't remember if I have written since our last camping weekend on the lower slopes of Mount Kenya, which was delightful; the place was beautiful – a long glade in the cedar forest.

We shall spend Easter with the boys in a rented bungalow at the seaside. Actually, it doesn't seem right to call it "the seaside" – it is "The Coast". I expect it will be extremely hot and humid, since we are even feeling the heat up here in Nairobi. There has been no rain for about a month, since a short period of heavy rain that proved to be a false start. However, we have a garden lunch for the Music Society at the end of the week, so I have given orders for the roses to be watered regularly, and not to be picked, so that we can have at least a few flowers for the visitors. My vegetable patch is in poor shape. More water for the roses means less for the vegetables, and in any case I have let it run down in anticipation of the rainy season, which is the right time to plant things, or at least to plant them out.

Mombassa, 1982 – Opening shellfish

1983, Relaxing days in Nairobi

Zimbabwe Prospects and Atrocities

Another reason for neglecting the veg. was anticipation of an early departure for Zimbabwe. The trouble in Matabeleland, however, makes it seem likely that we shall, at the least, give ourselves a short time to judge what is going on, and what the trend is. At present I have no fears for our own personal safety. Harare is still a much safer place for Europeans than Nairobi. However, the Foundation does claim to have principles about human rights, and it seems somewhat inconsistent with such principles to sign an agreement for the government that is currently letting its army torture, intimidate and kill large numbers of its own population.

From the evidence we have gathered, it would not be fair to accuse the government of genocide, but it certainly seems to have been prepared to use callous and brutal methods to try and destroy dissident support in Matabeleland, and may well have killed upwards of a thousand people in the process. At the moment the problem seems to be somewhat less serious than it was. The most brutal army unit has been withdrawn, and there are no new reports of atrocities. However, this does not necessarily prove that the government has relented and will not use the same methods again if it feels they are necessary.

Work Colleagues and Home Comforts

Goran is away in New York at the moment talking to our trustees, who may have their own views on the matter, although (like most Americans) they usually seem very poorly informed on Africa.

I am sitting in my study area writing this by the light of a table lamp, and insects keep on squeezing in through the windows and landing on me. Meanwhile, downstairs, a glass of beer is getting warm and losing its head. I think I had better go down and finish it.
Lots of love, David and Nicole

Letter to parents   **Nairobi, 13/04/1983**

Crabs, Rabbits and Bridge

We are just about to put Bernard and Dominic on the plane after a very pleasant holiday together. We had an easy time at the Coast, swimming, sleeping, and eating. One day we bought two enormous black crabs, so big we could hardly get them into the saucepan to cook them – they were of course still struggling. Fortunately their claws had bits of raffia tied to them, so that we could handle them without being nipped, because their nip really is something to avoid.

Today (Sunday) we were very busy making a new rabbit hutch. We now have ten little ones, and their accommodation is getting rather cramped. Dominic wanted to get it finished before he left, and we almost succeeded.

We have also played a lot of bridge. In fact we have just finished about five hands which we played very badly, nobody managing to win a single below-the-line point.
Lots of love, David and Nicole

Letter from Nicole
to Sheila

An Exhausting Musical Week

Sorry for forgetting your birthday, I suppose David forgot, but I did not. I was just too busy at the time with rehearsals and organising our Easter concert which was rather special this year. We performed Verdi's *"Requiem"* and invited soloists and instrumentalists from abroad (namely Germany, Italy, France, Holland) to reinforce our choir and orchestra. In fact the Italian singers did not turn out to be very good and our local mezzo-soprano surpassed them all. Our guest conductor from Britain, a teacher from Imperial College London, was staying with us. He was very good company but talked a lot and kept us awake late at night. The guest singers and instrumentalists gave several concerts, so it was quite a musical week.

Holidays

The children were here for two and a half weeks; they went back to school last Sunday evening. While they were here we spent four days in Mombassa, at the seaside. It was very relaxing and although the days were hot the nights were cool, as it rained at night.

We shall be in U.K. in August, the last two weeks as we hope to spend two weeks in France. We have not managed to book anything yet. People are dreadful at answering letters.
Love, Nicole

P.S. from David

Fancy suggesting that I could forget your birthday! But we really have been very busy. It takes me ages to catch up with my desk when I get back from a trip or a workshop. I have never dealt with as much paper (much of it rather dull stuff) as I do here. I shall just about be back in control by next month, when I go to Cairo for ten days.

We have not had much news of you recently, but I suppose that means you are all well. On our side, we are in pretty good shape. The boys were in excellent form, and to my relief do not seem to be going "off" as they get older. They are more independent, but very pleasant company. I hope your livestock and garden are flourishing. I am waiting for rain, but currently have thirteen rabbits, of which ten are destined for the table.
Lots of love, David

Letter to parents

Self-Sufficiency

We are back on our own again after a very pleasant time with the boys. It's funny that I am never in the least nervous about my own air travel, but I am always tremendously relieved to know that they have arrived safely. On our last day together, we built a new mobile rabbit hutch, so that the young ones can eat the lawn. Dominic was very keen to get the rabbits in before he left, but we did not quite manage that. I added the finishing touches yesterday. We are now waiting to see if dogs or other night prowlers will break in and take the rabbits.

The rains have started, half-heartedly and very late. My garden is in reasonable shape, because Francis spends a lot of time watering it, although we do not have our usual abundance of beans. For every rains I plant a mixture of maize and green beans in some of the large beds. We eat the beans green, and put a lot in the freezer, and at the end of the season the remaining beans are left to dry out to give us a stock of dry beans for stews. We store them in the freezer, even when they are dried, since otherwise they are soon riddled with weevils. The same applies to rice, flour, etc. The maize is also eaten green, and frozen, and anything left when it starts to go hard is given to the servants, who prefer their maize rather more solid than we like ours to be. This year I have planted half a bed with soya beans, just for a change. I don't know what I shall do with them. I have put carrots in another big bed, and these are just germinating. If the rains keep up (a big "if") I shall have lots and lots of carrots. And in another bed I have planted lucerne around my maize instead of beans. This is for the rabbits. The logic of this is that the soil gets "sick" after repeated bean plantings.

A Hard Childhood

Yesterday I went to get a load of horse manure, accompanied by Francis, Nathan's small son, and Eliud, whose school fees I pay. Eliud's father died a long time ago; his mother was mentally disturbed and hung herself about eight months ago. However in a Kenyan setting it seems hardly correct to call Eliud an orphan, since he has a family structure that clothes and feeds him. The real orphans here are urban children whose mothers are slum prostitutes and *"changaa"* brewers, and who have no family structure to receive them. I can't say that having many hands really made the work lighter, but everyone enjoyed the ride. Francis complains almost daily about the quality of the manure, which is mixed up with sawdust (or as we would say in our bad Swahili, with *"planks"*). This makes it much more difficult to use than good *kraal* or *boma* (cow) manure, because incompletely decomposed sawdust takes nitrogen out of the soil, and attracts termites; but over the long run the garden benefits.

To Go or Not To Go

Our move to Zimbabwe remains in the air. The situation there has improved somewhat, but the Government is still taking a very hard line on areas that are believed to support dissidents, apparently in the hope that those who really do provide support will be pressured by their communities into withholding it, or will be informed on by their neighbours. However, there is very little evidence that communities under pressure do behave like this. There will, of course, be informers, but that is another matter, and is certainly not sufficient to achieve the ends of the Government. In fact, informers supply martyrs, which may help to fuel the fire. Don't suppose from this that I am a supporter of ZAPU as opposed to ZANU; rather the contrary. I do not think that ZANU has any justification for rebellion, and I think what the dissidents have done has been very harmful to Zimbabwe, but I doubt if the problem can now be solved militarily. Even if it is successfully suppressed now, it will probably break out again. Nor do I think there is justification for a policy of communal punishment which uses injustice as a weapon.

Holiday On Hold

Our summer holiday is also in the air. We had decided to go to France this year, and tried to get information from the *"Gîtes de France"*, which co-ordinates privately owned self-catering accommodation (including the two flats in Nicole's parents' house); but we simply have not had a reply. We have now asked Yves to book something for us, but he says that the first fortnight of August, which was the period we had been aiming for, is completely booked out. This means that we shall probably now take our holiday in the second fortnight, and try and visit our U.K. friends and relatives from about 1st - 13th August. Will you be around at that time?

Much love, David and Nicole

P.S. from Nicole

Perhaps I should let you know of the children's plans between the time school finishes (19th July) and the beginning of August, when we arrive. They would like to go on a hike for a few days and walk the Chilterns. Will it be possible for them to come to Leicester at the end of term and leave all their belongings with you? I suppose it will take them a few days to gather all their equipment before they start on their walk. Bernard intends to buy a few things when he is in Leicester at half-term.

Love, Nicole

Letter to Sheila and Ron   Nairobi, 04/05/1983

Independent Travel

Nicole and I are just back from a very strenuous working safari in Northern Kenya, to visit a project in a very remote area just south of the Ethiopian border. We drove all the way in a little four-wheel-drive Suzuki, with just enough room for the two of us and our luggage, which consisted largely of food, water, petrol, a second spare tyre, camping gear, and various emergency items. At the last minute I tried to switch to a light aircraft belonging to the Mission Aviation services, that was going in the same general direction. It would have been much tamer, but did not work out because the mission flight was switched to an even smaller plane that did not have room both for us and for the extra fuel that our add-on flight would have entailed, so we headed back home, and packed in a record time of about half an hour.

An Elusive Military Convoy

The reason for trying to make the switch was the rather late discovery that we would have to travel in military convoy from Isiolo (less than half way to our destination) to Marsarbit; and worse, that the convoy was leaving a day later than us.

I did my best to talk our way through at Isiolo, and go either without a convoy, or with a special escort; but the local police commander was very resistant to such ideas. He talked to us for ages, to no avail. I was not sure if he was fishing obscurely for a bribe, but if he was, he was very obscure and did not get one. In the end we decided to sleep in the Samburu game reserve and try again the next day. They let us through the barrier for that, and had I had the nerve I could simply have pushed ahead to the next barrier (on the other side of the supposedly insecure area) to try again from there (saying that I had come from Samburu I suppose); but I was not quite ready to risk it. In the event we enjoyed our night in Samburu, and it was doubtless there that we filled our tyres up with small thorns.

The next day we went back to our police barrier at Isiolo, and tried again. Around 11am we were told that a special escort was being provided for a big truck, and that we could go on ahead of it, without getting out of sight. In fact we never saw the truck again, despite making occasional attempts to dawdle, and no *shifta* attacked us. I had some hard explaining to do at the two check-points on the other side. They were very keen to know what the convoy consisted of, and I really didn't know, which made my claim that I was part of the convoy seem rather thin. Oh, and we also had to stop and change two tyres on the way. The road was in rather poor shape after the rains and our little car was almost jolted to pieces on the corrugations. Dirt roads develop very pronounced corrugations from the vibration of the vehicles going over them – like a tin roof, but spaced out at 20-30cm intervals. If one goes fast enough, one can get a fairly smooth ride, but unfortunately at such speeds the car almost loses contact with the road, which is rather dangerous, especially when the tyres keep bursting.

Civilisation!

We slept at Marsarbit, which is an odd place to find after 270km of semi-desert and black volcanic plains. It is high enough to be cool and green and misty, with an area of cool tropical forest. We stayed the night in a local *"hoteli"* which provided a reasonably clean but rather cell-like double room, rudimentary sanitation, and a diet of goat stew, sweet "fat cakes" (sort of doughnuts without the jam) and tea.

Larva Plain and Desert

After Marsarbit came the really rough part of the trip - a hundred miles of real desert. This included some of the most inhospitable landscapes I have ever seen: black larva plains – black volcanic outcrops where the larva had been forced up through fissures and split into piles of huge rocks as it solidified. The road was a track made by pushing the larger rocks to both sides. There was one good stretch of hard flat sandy desert, where we could go as fast as we liked (in almost any direction), and in dry times there's an even better stretch of salt desert beyond. But we came after good rains, and had to take the slow track through the hills. To our dismay, the people we were looking for were not where we had expected to find them (in a village on the edge of the desert), but had moved up into the hills. So we had to back-track and head off towards Ethiopia along a track that looked as if it was hardly ever used. We were just about to give up when we saw roofs ahead.

Troubled Project in the Hills

The hills were much pleasanter than the village would have been: cool, with misty mornings, instead of hot and dusty. The project itself was a mess. The missionary who had started it had gone on a year's furlough, leaving it in the hands of a younger man who had no talent for dealing with local people. The mission administration in Nairobi had very little interest in development projects, and the African bishop for Kenya had tried to misappropriate the mission's assets. Although the bishop had since died, the missionary society, finding itself without liquid assets, had diverted the project funds to other uses.

Fervent Hosts, and Fleas

Our hosts, however, were very pleasant, if somewhat excessively given to praying, and a rather simplistic form of Christianity (*"Joy! Joy! We're on our way to heaven!"*) And there they sat, up in the hills, in a neat little pre-fab with a wind-generator, digging small dams and looking after trees. The only real inconvenience was fleas, which were all over the house. One of my favourite memories is the wife bowing her head to say grace, and saying instead *"Oh! There's a flea in my soup!"*

Confined to Convoy

On the way back, we had the full rigours of the convoy, with one big truck behind and another in front, each with about ten soldiers carrying automatic weapons sitting on top of all the non-military passengers and baggage. We travelled uncomfortably and fast, with one obligatory stop for goat stew and chapatti at a *hoteli* en route. Nicole didn't want to take the risk of eating in such a place, and arrived home tired, hungry, and with an upset tummy. Total trip 1,500km, mostly on dirt.

Future Plans

Tomorrow I head off again, this time for a week in Cairo. I hear the temperature there is about 100′ F. What fun!

Bernard has decided he wants to study farm management, or agriculture, and will eventually have to have a year's practical work. Any ideas?

Lots of love, David and Nicole

Postcard to parents
showing Sailboats on the Nile

Aswan, Egypt, May 1983

It really is like this, although the people in the boats are probably English or German. I'm taking twenty-four hours off here while waiting for the plane back to Nairobi after a Ford Foundation staff workshop. I almost didn't get here at all, because sandstorms at Aswan made landing impossible, but having woken at 3am this morning, we finally took off at 1.30pm.

Much love, David

Letter to parents

Nairobi, 29/05/1983

Dams, Drought and Flood in Egypt

Thanks for your letter. Egypt is a very odd place. The greenery you saw on the card was fairly genuine (given normal allowances for slight touching up) but extends only one or two kilometres on either side of the Nile, as far as the irrigation canals reach out into the flood plain. Actually, I had a good look at that photo, and wondered whether it was taken before the building of the High Dam, when there was an annual Nile flood, because I recognised the place and it now looks a bit dry and sandy. The flood must really have been an extraordinary thing to see. The benefits of doing away with it are rather more questionable than they probably appeared when it was built. The new lands above Aswan have proved difficult and unpopular, and the absence of a flood silt load has led to declining soil fertility below the Dam, on Egypt's traditional lands. It has also led to a lot of building construction on the best agricultural lands, for previous construction was confined to higher, generally useless, land. I would not like to be asked to manage Egypt now. Population is growing very fast, and it simply cannot feed itself, and depends on aid from the U.S.

Standards of Literacy
Thank you for looking after Bernard (and Dominic?) over the weekend. I hope they were both there, because they tend to entertain each other. However, I think that by and large they are pretty easy guests. Bernard's letters to us have suddenly become much more literate, which is a relief. Dominic's are still dreadful, full of peculiar spelling mistakes and incomplete sentences, and compared to his handwriting mine would win prizes for orthography. However, when he has something to say (and no distractions) he is sometimes quite amusing, so maybe there will be a transformation there eventually. I don't think the boys do nearly as much critically scrutinised essay writing as we used to. I think I usually had at least one essay a week, which I generally enjoyed doing because it came fairly easily to me. Maybe their curriculum has been Americanised. I find that a lot of Americans write extraordinarily badly, because they have never been required to learn to write whole paragraphs. One of my two American colleagues, who has a Ph.D. in sociology, writes such poor project proposals that the New York staff (who have rather fussily high standards) simply send them back. I suspect I may be asked to look at one tomorrow, and I'm afraid that even after a painful re-write it will still be painfully bad (even her secretary sometimes sends them back!)

Orchid Watching
I have spent a very lazy weekend watching my orchids grow (and orchids grow very slowly). I have one or two little flowers on local orchids, but nothing spectacular at the moment. However, they are interesting things, and because they are so slow-growing and so demanding, even a new root showing on a dormant plant becomes quite exciting. A slug or snail may then come along and bite off the new root and then one waits several more weeks for a new one to appear. However mine are now generally healthy, and even plants that I had been pessimistic about, because they came from warmer places than Nairobi, seem to be progressing. I picked up a few more last time we were at the coast, and some more in our recent safari to the north.

D.I.Y. in the Rain
I like the thought of you cementing the path in the rain. I know just how frustrating it can be. I enjoy using cement, but have always insisted on mixing my own, because I remember just how poor the ready-mixed packs from Woolworths used to be. I think it was always stale. There must also be a great temptation to keep the proportion of cement to a minimum because it costs a lot, while sand costs next to nothing. I have not done any big jobs around the house recently because I am still biding my time in case we get sent to Zimbabwe. If I were sure of spending more time here I would make an orchid house – basically just poles and plastic, but it helps to get a slightly higher temperature and more humid conditions.

Rich and Poor
We are eating a lot of green maize from the garden. So, I think, are our staff. I got very cross the other day because I reckon I am getting only about half of what I grow; but given their wage levels it is hard to be self-righteous.

Unsavoury Election Candidates
We too are in the very long run-up to a September election, although it is hard to see how it will change anything. Moi does not command great respect, but there is also a fear of change. There are lots of rumours. This weekend some people thought there would be a coup, and there is also a rumour that Moi's chief putative successor/ rival, Charles Njonjo, has been arrested, following a political and press campaign against an un-named "traitor". Njonjo is much liked by many Asians and Europeans, but I think he is a very nasty bit of work. He has certainly been behind a lot of meddling with the electoral process to exclude people he does

not like from Parliament, and he is certainly as guilty as anybody of getting rake-offs on contracts, and accumulating assets abroad (he farms in the U.K.). Early last week our local administrator telephoned us at 2am to tell us she had heard there was fighting going on in our neighbourhood, and ask if we could give her any news. We had heard nothing, but were told the next day that there had been a shoot-out between police and armed robbers. And on that reassuring note, goodnight!
Lots of Love, David

P.S. - I should be in England for a conference from 3rd – 8th July. I shall try and get twenty-four hours with the boys at the end, but probably won't be able to get to Leicester – will give you a ring - David.

Letter to Bernard and Dominic   Nairobi, 22/07//1983

A Bit of Boasting!

I'm afraid I've been holding up your letter, but we have had a hard week. This was the only evening we did not either go out to dinner or have guests here.

I'm feeling quite cocky, because I showed off successfully this evening. On Wednesday, Tony Byrne was telling us how fit he was getting with all his jogging. He could almost run three miles non-stop.

"Oh!" I said, without thinking too hard –"I think I could run three miles without stopping." So for the last two days I have been in training, which means that I cut out breakfast cereals and half a slice of toast, and I ran up the office stairs instead of taking the lift; and I ran three miles without stopping, while poor Tony had to drop our after half a mile with a torn muscle. I'm only a little bit stiff this evening.

We received good Boarding House reports for you. I hope your walk goes well. If you do get this letter before we leave Nairobi, see if you can give us a quick ring.
Lots of love from your athletic Daddy

Letter to parents   Nairobi, 24/07/1983

Anxious Parents

If the boys telephone you to tell you that they have finished their Ridgeway walk, please call us and let us know. I feel strongly that they have to be encouraged to do such things, but that does not prevent us from worrying about them, as you must remember only too well. At least, I suppose you must have been worried when I first took off with a rucksack and (as I still remember) too little bedding for sleeping out without a tent. At least they are much better equipped with tent, and sleeping bags superior to the one I thought necessary at that time. And they are really very much more experienced than I was at that sort of camping, because of all the camping we have done in Africa. The stationary style of camping I learned with the scouts involved different skills.

Entertaining Nicole's Mother

We have had Madame Fortuné with us for the last two weeks. Last week we took her to a tented camp, and she slept in a tent for the first time in her life, and I think she enjoyed it. This weekend we decided to be rather more extravagant, and took her to a lodge in the Amboseli Game Park. We had a small problem getting there, because we took the office Peugeot 504 – more spacious than our car, and better on rough roads; less good for game-viewing than the Land Rover (too low) but more comfortable.

Resourceful Repairs

Anyway, the exhaust pipe broke in two in an apparently deserted bit of Maasai steppe about 150km from Nairobi, so I wriggled underneath and tied it back into place as best I could with miscellaneous bits of wire and a couple of pipe clips, and about 2km down the road we found a Sikh enterprise making concrete blocks, and they let their welder join the exhaust pipe back together again, for which he charged me all of 70 shillings (£3.50). I think he thought he was over-charging!

Abundant Game

We saw hundreds and hundreds of zebra and wildebeeste (gnu) in the park, and a good selection of other things: lots of elephants, gazelle, impala, ostrich, giraffe, reedbuck, oryx, warthog, hartebeeste, one leopard, and four lions eating a freshly killed buffalo (oh yes, and buffalo). So it was a good trip.

The weather here has been uniformly cold and cloudy everywhere we have been with Madame Fortuné, giving her a rather strange view of the climate in tropical Africa. Every night we sit in front of a good wood fire.

Surprise Visitors?

I hope it's all right for us to come and land on you for a few days in August. If by any mischance I have got it all wrong, just leave a front door key in the outside lavatory, and warn the neighbours so that they don't call the police.

Lots of love, David and Nicole

Letter to parents Nairobi, 31/08/1983
(written on headed paper from a Suffolk Estate Agent)

Don't you like my headed paper? We did look at a house in Suffolk – with many warnings to the children not to run around upstairs, because the whole structure appeared to be in imminent danger of collapsing around us (we did not make an offer).

Gratitude towards Parents

Thank you for your hospitality. I hope you don't think we just take it for granted. It is very nice to have a "home" still in England, although having said that please don't feel that we expect you to keep the house indefinitely as a convenience to family, even when it gets too big and inconvenient for you. I should add that I see no sign of this at the moment. You seem to be keeping remarkably well, nor am I encouraging you to move. I know you like the house, and it keeps you among the people you know.

Keeping in Touch

We had a very pleasant and easy holiday all told, and I am pleased we managed to see all the immediate family. Sheila's lot appeared in good form. We saw our friends from Botswana who live near Norwich. We also stopped in at some other Botswana friends at Stiffkey near Wells-next-the-Sea on the way home. They are just off to Nigeria after about three years in England with intermittent consultancy jobs. In their case I don't think there is any pressing financial need. James is a retired Nigerian colonial civil servant (English not Nigerian!) but I think he just wants to get stuck into a job.

I spent my last two days at Wickham Skeith mending a Windsor chair which has been hanging in the roof of the barn since I bought it two (or four?) years ago – a very satisfying job. I was even able to use one of my antique tools to shape a new arm for the chair.

Lots of love, David

P.S. from Nicole

Thank you for having us and I hope we did not wear you out. Can you give Sheila the packet of tea next time you see her, also give Sheila and Ron the tea cosy for Christmas on our behalf. The pair of sheets is a present from us to you. I hope you had a pleasant and sunny holiday. I enclose £5 for the telephone calls.

Love, Nicole

NOTE – David's visits to us were always great fun. He totally changed the atmosphere in our home during his brief visits – I tend to be relaxed and dreamy, letting weeds blossom and dust settle. David was always, by contrast, full of restless energy. It may have been on this visit that I watched in admiration as he mended an antique chair with great skill, encouraged me to try budding and grafting roses, and then experimented with re-hairing a cello bow (the cello that our grandmother had played) using long white tail-hairs from the fat little Welsh pony we owned at the time! I cannot say the re-hairing was a total success but I was amazed by David's creative inventiveness. I was also thrilled that he and Nicole at that time had ideas about making Suffolk their English base, rather than Oxfordshire.

Letter to Sheila and Ron   Nairobi, 11/09/1983

Back in Work Mode

Thanks again for your hospitality, and for letting me turn your house into a chair workshop for forty-eight hours. I really do enjoy your house and household, and find it very relaxing (not just because I let you do all the work either).

I have had a fairly hectic time since leaving, and have only really found time to settle a bit this weekend. As I probably told you, I had to leave for Zimbabwe the same day I arrived back in Nairobi. However, I had expected to have half a day to change my clothes, gather my wits, and pick up the most urgent threads in the office. As it turned out, the flight left three hours later the same morning, and since my office messed up on meeting me, I had spent most of that time at the airport, just managing half an hour in the office before my colleagues came in to work, and literally five minutes at home – not even long enough to drink the cup of coffee Nathan made me.

Enterprising Dogs

Of course, we are still catching up, but we are now both back, and at work, and no major disasters occurred while we were away. The dogs were very pleased to see us, and the younger one who is part Labrador – a very greedy race of scavengers – has become very fat. I think I have found the reason. A lot of our neighbours (unfortunately not us) have avocado trees in their gardens, and she sneaks in to steal the windfalls during the night (she's an "outside" dog).

Finding a New Home Base

With many backward glances, we decided not to buy a house in France. However, in family conclave, we have decided we should be looking for a bigger house in Britain to serve as a long-term home base, and we like your area. Will you look for me? At least, get agents to put you on their lists, and send us details of anything particularly tempting. I reckon we can go into the £60,000 to £70,000 range (depending on condition: less if extensive repairs have to be done, but we don't really want to have to do urgent repairs at a distance). You have a fairly good idea of the sort of house I like. I suppose we are looking for something rather like your own house with two good reception rooms, study, big kitchen, 3-4 bedrooms with two bathrooms or space for a second bathroom, and two acres (or more). The quality of the basic house is important. Generally, I would look for something old which had originally been well built. I am not very enthusiastic for myself about converted barns or rows of cottages. If I were going to live in a barn I would want to do the conversion myself; converted cottages usually remain rather poky, and usually were rather badly built in the first place. Structural soundness is of course extremely important for a possibly absentee owner – even with you around! I will (seriously) pay any costs arising from the search, including a surveyor's fee if it seems urgent to move fast. About half the money would be dependent on the sale of our Woodstock house, presently let until February next year.

Suffolk Village Life

I am reading *"Akenfield"*, which is probably not a *nom de plume* for Wickham Skeith, but is certainly very close to you. *"Framlingham, Woodbridge and Wickham Market are almost within walking distance..."* But you don't have a Baptist Chapel, or a church with a red-brick tower; nor, I think, are you on *"an isthmus of London (Eocene) clay"* .

(The first page of the letter ends here. The remainder is lost.)
NOTE - Since I never tire of looking at ancient houses – particularly remote farmhouses, the more ramshackle and unrestored the better – I jumped at this invitation to bother Estate Agents and search for a suitable Suffolk base for David and family. I found some beauties, and got as far as asking David how I should pay the deposit on a wonderful Tudor oak-frame farmhouse set in two acres near Cratfield, when I heard of a change of plan. The search would now take place, not in Suffolk, but in sunny south-west France. It was not really a surprise, since Nicole hates cold damp weather and grew up in sunny Guadeloupe.

David in fact asked us whether we would like to contribute to the purchase and share the French acquisition. Of course, the answer had to be "No thanks". With his inflated Ex-Pat. Salary, I don't think he ever realised how hard up we were with seven children on a school teacher's salary.

However, the seed of an idea was planted in my wild imagination that never quite left me; buying a ruin in rural France gradually grew into a dream I could not ignore, as time would tell.

Letter to parents   Nairobi, 26/09/1983

Revelling Evergreeners!
. We were pleased to hear that you got back from your Evergreen holiday with all the party intact (more or less; hangovers don't really count as an illness, even though the sufferer might have thought otherwise).

A Weekend in the Forest
Today is General Election day in Kenya, and our office was closed for the occasion, so Nicole and I made a lazy weekend of it and camped in Mount Kenya National Park. We stayed in a very good "official" camping place, near one of the park entrances, which we had visited once before with friends. I hasten to add that an official campsite here is nothing like those one finds at the seaside in England. Our site consisted of a glade in the forest, running down through giant pencil cedar and podocarpus trees to a stream about a mile below. I think there was a pit latrine somewhere at the top (we used our own shovel) and there was a tap at the park gates. We had the whole area to ourselves, apart from zebra which ran away every time they saw us, but kept coming back again. On Saturday night we heard lion mating nearby (the warden told us they had been on the track outside his hut). There was also plentiful evidence of elephant and buffalo, but we didn't see them. In fact we generally kept away from dark woodland where the buffalo tend to spend the daylight hours, because they are by far the most dangerous animals around (not counting crocodiles but they are easily avoided by keeping out of deep water). There have been two tourist deaths from buffalo in the last three months.

A Sunday Morning Stroll!
Yesterday we took our thermos flask and went for a Sunday morning walk – a few miles up the mountain and down again. We started at 8,600 feet, and I suppose we climbed (on a motorable track) to about 10,000 feet, by which time Nicole was feeling very out of breath. One truck full of tourist climbers passed us, driven by an old Swedish settler who has a tourist business (Karen Blixen/ Isaak Dineson's godson if that means anything to you; if it doesn't, buy the paperback version of her book *"Out of Africa"*). Four members of another party struggled up with binoculars and bird-watching gear while we sat on a hillock at the point where the forest finally faded out (like my pen) into moorland, and drank our coffee. We slept very well after that – both enjoying a luxurious afternoon nap and a very good long night's sleep, despite some extraordinary night calls of birds and animals from the forests all around us.

Seasoned Campers

As usual, we camped in considerable comfort. We have this to a fine art now, and can only just fit all the things we really need for a weekend into the back of our (the office's) little four-wheel-drive Suzuki: a cool box for frozen food and cold drinks, a tin trunk full of food, cutlery etc., thirty litres of water and a siphon, paraffin and calor gas lamps, folding stools and a table, a nice big tent with a one-inch foam sheet to cover the floor, etc. - there's no reason to be uncomfortable.

Fresh Trout for Lunch

Today we both walked a bit stiffly, showing that we had benefited from yesterday's walk. We got up late (after 8am!), had a leisurely breakfast, read a bit, and spent about an hour and a half putting everything back in the Suzuki, then we went to Kenya's only trout farm for a fresh trout lunch, and back home in time for me to spray my orchids and feed the rabbits.

Nasty Hairy Caterpillars

We are, as you can gather, back in the routine of Kenya again. I found my plants and garden in reasonable condition. A nasty hairy caterpillar had got in with my orchids, and had chewed off all the growing root tips. This is a recurring problem. I suppose I should be pleased that the tastiest thing about orchids is the roots, not the shoots (although they do eat those too) but slugs, snails, moths and caterpillars all make a beeline (by land, air and sea!) for the root tips, and naturally this sets the plants back no end. Anyway I have sprayed and scattered slug pellets around, and I have recommenced my normal battle against over-watering. This evening I found the plants in my greenhouse box (a box-like contraption nailed to a tree, and covered in plastic) standing in water, and siphoned out a pint or two with a plastic tube. Tomorrow I shall explain again that too much water is worse than too little.

Kenyan Elections

I haven't said anything about the elections, but there really isn't much to say. It's a good thing that they have elections here (not many countries around here have them quite so regularly) and despite all sorts of cynicism and abuses, they do mean something. It's predictable that a lot of ministers will lose their seats (that was the reason given for calling the elections this year not next). However the issues are far from clear, since all the candidates belong to the same party and compete with each other in their loyalty to the President. Apart from this, and throwing accusations at each other, the electoral battle concentrates very heavily on who can do most for the constituency, so that "redistributive" local issues play more of a role – at least in public debate – than national policy issues. I wait with interest to see what the outcome is.

Lots of love, David and Nicole

Letter from Nicole to   Nairobi, 12/10/1983
parents-in-law

Called to Zimbabwe

David is leaving this morning for Zimbabwe; it is an unexpected trip but the colleague who was meant to do this trip had to go to the States (his father is dying) so David had to go instead. He will be back on Saturday 15th, which is not too far away.

Boys' Plans

The children's half-term starts on October 21st. I hope that they have got in touch with you. They should be back at school on the evening of 30th and I suppose they will travel back by the morning bus. Thank you very much for having them. I think that they find it easier to work when they are staying with you. Bernard has to start doing revision for the mock exams which will be held in January. As he is going skiing he will not have much time to revise during the Christmas holidays. Dominic should have revision to do for the end of term tests.

Luxury Camp on an Island – with Snakes!

We spent last weekend at Island Camp which is the biggest island on Lake Baringo. Lake Baringo is one of the lakes of the Rift Valley and I think it is the largest. The others are Lake Navaisha, Lake Nakuru and Lake Bogoria. There is a tented camp on the island (where we stayed). It is very comfortable camping as each tent is simply but nicely furnished and has a bathroom. There are people living on the island and they have masses of goats, therefore there are not many trees left. It is a charming and restful place and there is still a lot of vegetation around the camp compound and the bird life is very abundant. While there I saw a snake in the toilets. I was very frightened and quickly went out to call for help. One of the servants came and told me that the snake was harmless; he even touched it. It was a vivid green colour. After that I was watching everywhere for snakes. Love, Nicole

Letter from David to   Nairobi, 23/10/1983
his sons

A Politician's Life

Despite what Mummy says, I have always been attracted by politics, but I think that to get anywhere it is normally necessary to possess a driving ambition (maybe two driving ambitions) and possibly a somewhat deficient personality. You will note that Neil Kinnock has not taken anything except politics seriously in his whole life. Having proved that he was bright in his primary school, he struggled into university, got a poor degree, and chose to become a teacher in a place where he could reasonably hope to take over a safe Labour seat when the elderly sitting member retired. During the last Labour government, Michael Foot had him appointed a "Parliamentary Private Secretary" (a sort of political assistant to a minister) and later told him *"You must be about the worst P.P.S. in the history of Parliament"*. As a potential national leader, he does not inspire great confidence in me. He looks too much like the sort of politician who knows how to manoeuvre the system and who will adopt any position he thinks will win votes in the short term; in other words, a less-intelligent Harold Wilson.

Walk with a Conservationist

This afternoon we are going to walk in Karura Forest with the Wanyekis who live there. Frances Wanyeki, who is with the Forest Department, has recently joined the Orchid Society, because he is interested in conservation aspects. I wonder if that means he will not let me remove plants from trees.

Don't forget the element for our electric iron and the big jar of Marmite.
Lots of love, Daddy

Letter from Nicole   Nairobi, 14/11/1983
to parents-in-law

More Travels

David has now been away for two weeks; he should be back on 17th November at 1am. This time, his travels took him to Zimbabwe, Zambia and Botswana. He wanted to go to Swaziland, but it looks as if he will not make it. Goran Hyden, the Representative, wants him back here for a meeting on 17th in the morning.

Goose-Eating Mongoose

While David has been away I have been very busy and I have been invited a lot by friends, so the time has not seemed too long. I have spent the weekend in Karen (the district of Nairobi named after Karen Blixen, where she had her coffee plantation) with friends from Botswana. They moved to Nairobi five months ago. They have a house surrounded by three acres and had two geese. Unfortunately the sitting goose was eaten by a mongoose on Friday night. They purchased two ducks yesterday.

Music

We went to a concert given by the Nairobi Orchestra last night. Unfortunately David could not take part. He was very sorry, as for once, he had practised a lot and had been to most of the rehearsals.

The month of November will be a very busy month as regards music. We are having our Christmas concert on 24th, 25th and 26th. We are performing Rossini's *"Petite Messe Solemnelle"* and Bernstein's *"Chichester Psalms"*, which is a difficult work but it is a challenge. There is the children's carol concert on 23rd November; it is organised by the Society but I am responsible. Then on 16th, 17th and 18th December we shall perform (as every year) extracts from the *Messiah*. The orchestra will accompany the choir.

Belgian Visitors

I am spending the afternoon at the Serena Hotel, helping a delegation of Belgian businessmen. They are all textile traders. Kenyan traders interested in textiles have been invited to contact them at the Serena Hotel and my colleague and I are there to direct the visitors around. A change from the day to day office work.

The children will be flying to Kenya on 16th December.
Love, Nicole

Letter from Nicole   Nairobi, 28/11/1983

More Music

We had a very busy week as we had our concert on Thursday, Friday and Saturday, and after the concert on Saturday I invited the committee members and a few others home for a drink. The party went on until 3am so we were rather tired yesterday. We started the rehearsals for the *"Messiah"* on Thursday. David will join the orchestra this time.

Orchids in Bloom

David has two orchids in full bloom at the moment and he has proudly exhibited them on the desk in the sun room. The desk is fairly big but those two orchids are quite big plants, therefore there is just enough room for the typewriter. He took some photos yesterday and if they are good we shall send you a print. Love, Nicole

Letter to parents   Nairobi, 27/12/1983

Christmas Thanks

Thank you very much for the whole array of gifts. All are greatly appreciated. I was going to say that I had never had a Parker pen before, but delving into the dim recesses of my memory, I think I may once have found a slightly cracked one which someone else had thrown away – not, I hasten to add, a handsome one like this. We have also enjoyed the house-hunting Thelwell, but most of all we have enjoyed *"The Secret Diary"*. We did, however, wonder whether you had read it, or whether you would have sent it if you had, as it is somewhat indecent in parts. Needless to say, this has not deterred the boys.

Unseasonal Rain

We spent Christmas at Amboseli national park, reading our Christmas presents, and looking at game in a rather desultory way. Usually Amboseli is three-quarters land and one quarter lake, although one cannot really see the lake because the land is flat, and there is a fringe of tall reeds around it. Presently, Amboseli seems to be three-quarters lake, because of the unseasonal rain which is falling everywhere (including here in Nairobi). This must have been rather a nuisance for tourists who were having a once-in-a-lifetime chance to visit the game parks, but it didn't cause us any great anguish. We slept in under our mosquito nets, sloshed off once a day to see game, and cooked our duck (very tender) in an ancient wood-fired dover stove, with the help of a Maasai fire-maker and washer-up who was part of the establishment.

Orchid Enthusiast

Yesterday we splashed back to Nairobi, and had a few more games of bridge, and today we have read our Christmas books, looked at our orchid plants (me only) and played non-demanding games.

A propos orchids, it's silly of me to think of this now, after Christmas, but I am trying to put my collecting on a more scientific basis, which means maintaining a proper record of each plant, including photographs where possible, and I would also like to be able to do some drawings. I'm not nearly as good at this as you are, but I am also lacking in materials. Since you know about these things, please could you find me a large pad (say 100 sheets) of good, white, durable drawing paper of approximately A4 size (about the size of this notepaper) and an up-to-date drawing pen for Indian ink, with a fairly fine tip. Tell me how much they cost, and either send them, or give them to the boys to bring out to me at Easter.
Lots of love, David

Circular letter to all friends at Christmas

Nairobi, December 1983

Benefits of Life in Kenya

We're still here. If we stay much longer we shall become part of the landscape. While Botswana holds a higher place in our affections, there is something undeniably catching about Kenya, and bit by bit one learns how to find the comforts of life. There will be someone at Naivasha who makes good Camembert cheese, or a workshop at Limuru turning out Windsor chairs. There was nothing like that in Botswana, where virtually everything manufactured came from South Africa (as well as most of the food). We have now joined a milk run with two friends, so that we do not have to rely on the thin and partly reconstituted milk produced by Kenya Co-operative Creameries. Instead we get Jersey milk from a little dairy at Ngong. The supply varies erratically with the rains, but the milk is rich enough to supply most of our butter requirements – from the skimmings we get when we boil it (it is not pasteurised). We supplement that by being members of a dairy co-operative operating from a holding not much larger than our own garden. The "co-operative" gets around the restrictions on selling milk, but I suppose it also means we are part owners.

Black Kenyan Endeavours

A lot of these entrepreneurial activities belong to white Kenyans – but by no means all of them. The Ngong dairy is Kikuyu, for example. Other prominent black Kenyans are involved in such unusual businesses as growing orchids for export to Germany and Japan. There is a strong entrepreneurial streak in this country.

White Kenyans

The white Kenyans are a strange lot. Although they have African business associates and of necessity speak one or more African languages, they mostly continue to live in an almost exclusively white social circle. I find many of them frankly rather racialist, in a paternalistic way. Some go, but others come. We met one the other day who had only recently become a Kenyan citizen. I think he came originally from Lancashire. He was a partner in a small factory, and the "Kenyanisation" of the firm, which was completed with his change of citizenship, made it easier for them to get import licences. The factory sounded rather unlike anything found in Lancashire. Most of the work was done in the open air; the boilers were wood-fired; and the entire workforce was body-searched four times a day to cut down pilfering.

White Transients

The majority of whites here, however, are not Kenyans. Like us, they are transients. This is a constant problem for the choir and the orchestra, in which we are both involved (Nicole now as secretary to the choir; I still as a humble second cellist). Over the three years we have been here, the orchestra must have changed about three-quarters of its members. It also grows and shrinks alarmingly according to the popularity of the pieces being rehearsed and the current conductor.

The National Assembly

Another local institution that has recently changed a lot of its members is the National Assembly. However, it kept more of the old lot than is usually the case here: almost a quarter of the sitting M.P.s were returned, including the one white M.P. (Philip Leakey, son of the archeologist). Our seat had nine candidates (not the record) so the happy winner only needed about 15% of the votes. There will now be a succession of election petition hearings, which may last almost through the life of the current Parliament.

Anticipating Zimbabwe

We had expected to be in Zimbabwe by now to open a Ford Foundation office there, but it has taken much longer than we had expected to finalise an agreement with the government there. The main problem is simply that the bureaucracy there lacks experience, and is painfully, painfully slow. We still expect a move early next year.

Bernard and Dominic

The boys are in good form. Bernard, now eighteen, is coming up to A-Levels and hoping to go into some form of agricultural management. Dominic, fourteen, has no career plans, and his letters are mostly about rugby, where apparently he makes up for lack of size with plenty of aggression. We are relieved that he still has all his front teeth. This Christmas they will spend only ten days with us, then go skiing with the school.

There's lots more we could tell you, but that will have to do for this year.
Merry Christmas and Happy New Year.
With love from Nicole and David

P.S. to Parents on Future Possibilities

I should explain about the move to Harare and various other moves we have thought about. Our Harare plans were held up because the government there took an extraordinarily long time to pass our draft agreement with them around the various interested departments, and then made a number of important changes, of which the most important from the Foundation's viewpoint was to remove exemption from local income tax from the draft. This has been a sticking point in their negotiations with a number of non-government organisations, so I was not surprised, although our New York people were. However, when we told the civil servants concerned that this would mean bringing out our vice-president to negotiate with the Minister of Economic Affairs all over again, there was a flurry of activity, and they changed their minds; so with any luck the agreement will be signed soon. We have mixed feelings about the move. It will be a step up for me, but we are very comfortable in Nairobi, and do not expect Harare to be so congenial. It is a country at a silly age!

Letter to Parents   Nairobi, 15/01/1984

Serious Swimming

After a spell of unseasonable rainy weather around New Year and Christmas, we are now once again enjoying sun and warm weather. This weekend Nicole and I went swimming twice at a local hotel: serious stuff, no messing around, battling from one end of the pool and back dodging the more frivolous swimmers who prefer to swim from side to side, or stand still in the middle of the shallow end. I do twenty-five or thirty lengths while Nicole does twenty, and it certainly leaves me feeling better than when I started.

Tea Plantations

We went to western Kenya for New Year, staying, for once, in hotels at Kericho and Kisumu. At Kericho there is the "Tea Hotel" which stands among huge tea plantations. I knew they were there, of course, but never having seen them had no idea how impressive they would be. Tea, as you know, is a tree, which will grow to quite a height if allowed to do so, but on the estates it is constantly pruned back to a height of three to four feet, and forms an apparently unbroken expanse, rather like a huge privet hedge. Because it is constantly topped with new leaves, the predominant colour is very pale green. The pluckers have to push their way between the bushes, plucking two leaves and a bud (no more) from each new shoot. Stretching for miles over the rolling uplands, the estates form an attractive though clearly artificial landscape.

Kisumu Town

Kisumu is a pleasant though grubby little town on the edge of Lake Victoria – a little bit reminiscent of Dar es Salaam with its colonial bungalows and high humidity. Before the East African community broke up, it used to be the chief port for Kenyan lake trade with Uganda and Tanzania, and the large passenger ferries and train ferry of the defunct East African Railways and Harbours are tied up and rusting away slowly in the railway port.

Orchid Collecting

We went walking in one of the remaining patches of indigenous forest, and I was able to collect several small local orchids. I should explain that many of the local orchids are not at all showy, although a few are very attractive. One that I collected this time had a pleasant spray of little pink flowers arising from a single broad leaf, and was somewhat similar in general form to a lily of the valley – except of course that it was growing up a tree. In general, epiphytic orchids are far commoner here than terrestrial ones – in fact I have only two local terrestrial orchids, one of which is a very faithful flowerer, and is just coming out again. Most of the epiphytes, however, are quite easy to keep alive, though rather more difficult to flower.

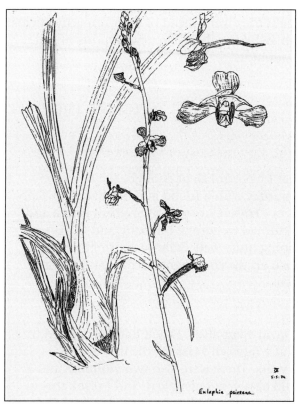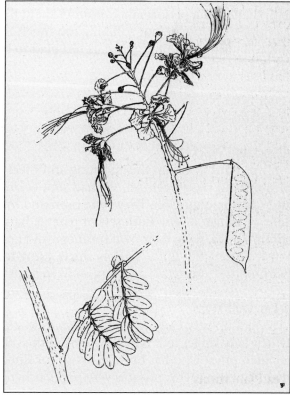

David's pen-and-ink drawings of orchids

Supporting Pastoralists

As luck would have it, we had to dinner the other day a man whose grandfather helped build the first tea factory in Kenya, at a time when Kericho was still almost all forest. He, like his grandfather, is an engineer missionary with the African Inland Church, and runs a project which I like, but which has given me greater problems than almost any other. The project involves providing extension (agricultural advisory) services to pastoralists in the far north of Kenya, developing water supplies, and assisting these people, who are rather unsure of their nationality, to play a part in governing themselves. So far so good. However, Dilly Anderson did not think to tell me that he would be away on furlough for the second year of the project, with no prospect of leaving an equally experienced person in charge.

Dubious Morals of a Bishop

Even he couldn't really be expected to know that the church's African bishop would decide to blue the church's reserves, including our grant, on some properties that strangely seemed to be in the process of being converted to his own name. The bishop is now, as the Botswana would say, "late" - (*"Have you heard about so-and-so?" "No." "He's late!"*) - amid dark rumours that his dubious conduct and surprisingly early lateness are connected. However, in consequence, the project we have funded cannot get its hands on the funds we gave it. We are assured that all will come right in the end, when the late bishop's widow can be persuaded to move out of the house that she maintains is hers, so that the property can be sold. However, I shall be more cautious with churches in future.

A Present from Cousin Patrick

We got a beautiful book on Tanzanian cave paintings from Patrick Childs, with a short letter saying that he had given up his publishing job in order to go back to University to train as an architect, in order to restore historic buildings. He is both a pleasant and an interesting person.

Plans

Nicole has asked me to tell you that the boys' half term will be from 17th to 26th February. We had a card from them, written in Italy but posted in England, expressing great satisfaction with their skiing performance. Both of them thought they were ahead of their respective fields.

I hope that you are not suffering too much from awful weather. The news reports of gales and collapsing buildings make us feel glad to be out of it.
Much love, David

Letter from Nicole to parents-in-law

Nairobi, 13/02/1984

A Sociable Weekend

It was hard to get up this morning and I feel that I have not slept enough. We had a very pleasant but busy weekend. We had supper on Saturday with a friend and her husband, Sally and Christe Johansson. They were born and bred in Kenya: Christe is of Swedish origin and Sally of British origin. Both sets of parents have returned to Europe but Sally and Christe are still in Kenya, have their own business, and are doing quite well. Sally is chairman of the Music Society but unfortunately she is going to give up the chairmanship this year as she is her husband's secretary and cannot fit in both jobs.

A Farewell Mass

We got up very early yesterday to go to Mass (David went also). David had been asked by a Dutch lady singer to accompany her on the cello at a farewell Mass for the university chaplain, a Dutch priest who has been in Kenya for fifteen years. There were also two violinists and a flautist playing. This priest is very popular here and also very outspoken, and I think this is one of the reasons why his lectureship at the University has not been renewed. The church was packed. He is also a very good preacher, his sermons are excellent.

Barbecue, and More Music

We got home at 11.30am and had to prepare a barbecue for eight guests (colleagues of mine at the Embassy). Our guests left at about 4pm and at 6pm we went out again. David was playing the cello with one of his musical groups. Apart from the orchestra he plays with a Dutch group, and with a mixed group of Americans and British. He was playing with the American/ British group last night. Janet is of American origin but now has Kenyan citizenship. She married a Kenyan eighteen years ago but is now divorced and is living with a pleasant Ismaili/ Kenyan. They are both vegetarians but I must say that we always eat very well at their house.

To Tanzania, and Guadeloupe

Next weekend we shall be in Tanzania where David will be attending the last day of a conference. We shall leave on Thursday afternoon and will be back on Sunday. The Tanzanian border is only two hours' drive from Nairobi, and it will take another two hours to get to Arusha. I have not been to Tanzania for eleven years.

We shall certainly go to Guadeloupe for our summer holidays this year. For your information, we plan to be in England from 28th August to 5th September. I know that at about that time you are away with the Evergreens and I hope all the same that we shall be able to see you. Can we use your house if you are away?

The weather is very hot and pleasant at the moment and we are making the most of it as the rains will certainly start at the end of next month.

We wish Mummy a very happy birthday.

Love, Nicole

Letter to parents   Nairobi, 25/03/1984

Disrupted Plans

I'm taking advantage of an involuntary delay at Nairobi airport – a delay to an involuntary flight too. I'm on my way to Harare to sit on the doorsteps of the civil servants who are meant to be processing our agreement with the Government of Zimbabwe, on orders from our New York office who are overwhelmed with naïve amazement and shocked disbelief at the one-step-forward-two-steps-back bureaucratic process. This is a great nuisance, as I shall miss a concert I was to play in, tonight and tomorrow (not that I feel I am indispensable, there are five other cellists of which four are certainly more proficient than me, but I've done a lot of work and I don't like throwing it away). But after a lot of running around yesterday afternoon and this morning I managed to get a ticket without producing any money (this is Sunday).

Alarming Flights

Half an hour ago we were half way down the runway, and I was just nodding off, when the pilot put the brakes on and brought us back to our starting point. One learns to be phlegmatic about these things. Last week I was on a plane that started to backfire – an alarming experience, since one could hear those very strange banging and bumping noises, and see the whole wing and engine jumping up and down each time.

"Elijah"

Otherwise, we are in good order. Nicole is practising hard for *"Elijah"*, which follows hot on the tracks of the Orchestra's concert. I'm meant to be playing in that too. With luck I shall manage three rehearsals. I just hope the choir sings loudly enough to drown the noises from the Orchestra.

Future Plans

The boys, as you know, are expected on the 13th. I'm meant to be in Bangladesh then (I can't think why the Foundation decided to schedule a workshop so close to Easter) but I should be back by 18th April, in time to join the others at the coast for several days.

We are planning to spend our summer holidays in Guadeloupe this year with Nicole's parents. I feel that from a long-term planning point of view, I should really be in Europe (U.K. or France) looking for a house, and maybe sounding out job prospects (dim!), but we realise that we shall now have very few more opportunities for family holidays all together, because the boys are growing up, also that opportunities for holidays in Guadeloupe may also be rather limited. I don't envisage staying with the Foundation very much longer, and without their home leave system, travel to the West Indies becomes rather expensive. So we shall enjoy this holiday while we have the chance, and postpone more serious decisions.

A New Home Base

As for Europe, my feeling is that we probably should still think of buying something small and not too expensive somewhere pleasant where we can expect to meet up over the coming years. The Bordeaux/ Dordogne region remains a possibility. Property there is much cheaper than anywhere in England, and I have developed a taste for places that are both warmer and emptier than England normally is. The problem in this equation is not knowing what I shall do next.

Running Repairs

Our "one hour perhaps" delay here is almost achieved. I expect we shall now start a "second hour perhaps" as the technicians replace the tyres that burst when the plane braked, and repair the wing flaps. Unfortunately the seats in the waiting area are not designed for sleeping.

Troubled Nights

We've had a run of rather bad nights. Three nights ago, a low class burglar cut our garden fence and stole our hosepipe (no doubt the night guard was asleep, as he normally is). Two nights ago, we went out to dinner with a visiting ex-Botswana friend, naturally came back rather late, and were woken up about 5.30am, because the guard had decided to demonstrate his vigilance by pressing the radio alarm to report the previous night's theft of the hosepipe. Last night we went out for a musical evening with friends and came back at midnight for phone calls to New York, but at least we were able to get a decent night's sleep.

We are being called. Amazing!

Lots of love, David

Letter from Nicole   Nairobi, 11/04/1984
to parents-in-law

Unpredictable Changes

I know that David wrote to you two weeks ago when he was stuck at the airport. In fact he spent all the day at the airport; his plane left at 8pm so he had to spend the night at Jo'burg airport.

David came back on 24th and left again on 28th, so he was only four days at home. Once again he missed the three performances of *"Elijah"* which were held on 6th, 7th and 8th April. Of course he had to cancel his trip to Bangladesh. One good thing about the unexpected trip to Zimbabwe is that he will be here while the children are on holidays. Had he been in Bangladesh he would have been away part of the children's holidays.

Kind Friends, and a Tired Houseboy

As you can see I have been on my own quite a lot lately, but I was so busy with the rehearsals of *"Elijah"* that I did not have much time to feel miserable. Friends are always very good when I am on my own and I am often invited for a meal; I had two invitations for lunch on Sunday, for instance.

I took the opportunity while David was away to send my houseboy, Nathan, to see his family and have a rest. He is getting rather old and he needs more than one annual holiday. Besides, when the children are here there is more work to do and he needs to get some strength before they arrive.

With Old Friends in Mombassa

We shall be going to Mombassa for five days next week. Another family whom we knew in Botswana (the husband is now working here) will accompany us. Their children, six and three, are of course rather smaller than ours but they are two nice little girls and I think it is good for our children to have to cope with smaller children from time to time.

Tree Tomatoes

The rains are late this year but it seems that it is going to rain in earnest now; we have had rain for the last three nights but not enough yet to make the lawn green. The gardener brought me lots of tree tomatoes and vegetables from the garden today. We have had a very good harvest of tree tomatoes lately and I have spent many hours peeling and stewing them. One has to pour boiling water on them before peeling them. They are very pleasant to eat.

The children should be here Friday morning at 6am and I will have to leave the house at 5.45am to go to the airport, which is very early to get out of bed, but on the eve of their arrival I get so excited that I can hardly sleep.

On the desk in front of me I have two beautiful African violets (purple and pale pink) which are in full bloom. There is also one with white flowers, just beginning to open. Until very recently we were unlucky with African violets but suddenly they have started to like their environment and they now look very healthy.

I wish you a happy Easter.
Love, Nicole

Letter to parents   Nairobi, 01/05/1984

Easter at the Coast

We have had a very agreeable time together for the last two weeks. Over Easter we went to the coast with some ex-Botswana friends, and took two beach cottages. It rained more than we would have liked, but at the coast one does not feel like doing very much anyway. We swam and sunbathed in moderation, slept immoderately, and ate very well. As usual, fish came to our door, and a lot of time was spent preparing fiddly things like crabs and octopus. We have just eaten the last crab, and there is still a deep-frozen octopus in the refrigerator. On the last day of our holiday, however, we discovered a fishing station where we could buy superb fresh fish for very low prices.

Wind Surfing

The weekend just past we had another outing – this time to Lake Baringo where a friend of ours runs a renewable energy project. The project houses are all on the lake shore – a strange dry volcanic landscape tumbling down over the rocks into a huge expanse of brown water. The boys said it was better than Mombassa; it didn't rain in the daytime (although there was some rain at night), and one could get directly into swimming depth water, without picking one's way through seaweed and sharp coral rocks. Best of all, we had the use of a wind surfboard, and the light winds that we needed as beginners. Bernard made very good progress with this. Dominic made progress, and enjoyed himself, but because of his size and low weight had problems pulling the sail out of the water, and controlling it in the wind. Everything on a wind surfer floats, but any mistake capsizes the thing, and the sailor has to climb back onto the floating board, and haul the waterlogged sail out of the water – exhausting even in warm water. Even Nicole was persuaded to stand upright on the board and capsize it a few times! I had already done my apprenticeship, but I still find it very difficult to end up where I want to go, and spent a lot of time in the water (which contains crocodiles and hippo, but for some reason these do not seem to molest people- I hasten to add that we saw neither, and that if we had, we would have been out of the water in a flash).

Limping Home

We had a minor breakdown on our return trip, but managed to limp back to Baringo, where by great good luck we found an Asian garage owner from Nairobi who mended our car.

We arrived back to find old friends from Botswana waiting for us at home. They were on their way to Uganda to spend a few days with their youngest son, who is a volunteer there. I hope they return safely! They are resourceful people, but even resourcefulness has its limits when one meets up with armed bandits.

Thank you very much for the drawing materials. I have received both sets, and enclose £6, which I think is approximately what it cost you to buy and send them. Perhaps I do need some colour paints as well, but for identification line drawings are hard to beat. I have been practising with various degrees of success. I shall send you one or two of the better results in due course!

I think we still have time for a quick game of bridge.

Lots of love, David and Nicole

Letter from Nicole to parents-in-law

Nairobi, 22/05/1984

Visiting Tea Plantations

David left this morning for Embu district, about 200/300 km from Nairobi, where he was going to visit small tea plantations with a view to donating money to those small farmers. He will spend the night in Meru, I suppose, and will be back tomorrow. He does not often have the opportunity to travel in Kenya, so he is always pleased to do so. Since Easter he has not been away and it is nice to have him at home. He will go away around mid-June.

Drought, Hungry Cattle, and Baboons

We are experiencing a very serious drought. It has hardly rained in and around Nairobi and there is hardly any grass for the cattle to graze; usually at this time of year the vegetation is very lush. We still get a lot of vegetables from the garden because we water, although we shall not have any maize or beans this year as the baboons eat them as soon as they come out of the ground. It is forbidden to destroy them as they are wild animals and protected by the wildlife people. They are a real pest and killing a few would not harm anybody as there are so many of them.

Books, Films, and Nomads

I am very pleased you are enjoying reading *"Nellie"*. I thought Nellie was a tremendous woman and very lively. The film you have seen on Kenya sounds like a film I saw a few months ago at the Museum called *"A season in the sun"* and made by Alan Root and his wife Joan. They make films on Kenya for Anglia TV. It was a very good film. If you have the opportunity to watch *"Two in the bush"*, do not miss it. I saw a very good film last week on the various tribes who live in the desert. The slides shown have been used to illustrate a book called *"Shepherds of the desert"*. The author of the book took the photos and gave a commentary. It was very interesting, as he is of the opinion that the nomads are less and less able to live their nomadic life as they are enticed to settle. As they are not able to travel any more the soil where their animals graze gets eroded. By moving from one place to another it gives the soil time to recuperate. It is a very difficult problem and there are several schools of thought on the matter. Of course by being in one place they get water, health facilities and schools, but is it the life they want?

Love, Nicole

Letter to parents

Nairobi, 24/05/1984

A Welcome Payment!

Thanks for looking after the boys during their half-term It seems incredible that they are already past half-term. We've only just put them on the plane back (and received a very nice little *ex-gratia* payment of £100 per delayed child for the inconvenience caused by B.A. over-booking the flight – a contribution to our summer holiday fares).

A Tea-Picking Agency

We are extremely busy on one thing or another. I spent Tuesday and Wednesday morning on a safari to a smallholder tea-growing area to see a potential employment project. Incredibly, smallholders with between one-third and one and a half hectares of tea are often short of tea-picking labour, and an enterprising young man from the area proposes to develop a tea-picking agency that will put casual labour onto something resembling a payroll – to be paid by a check-off system from the Tea Development Authority's computerised payments to farmers – an interesting combination of old and new systems.

A Musical Evening

Anyway, I got back in time for an afternoon's work yesterday, then straight on to orchestra, and straight on from that to a music group evening, with a brief pause for an omelette provided by our Dutch pianist and host. In fact we turned out to be a very small group – two cellists and a piano – and spent the whole evening playing some very difficult Vaughan Williams folk song arrangements, which was Haydn Hopkins' final attempt to interest me in my cello. Alas, it didn't work! Incidentally, I'm sorry to say that Dominic is now giving up his lessons. I'm afraid he doesn't find his teacher very exciting.

Planning Ahead

This evening we had a sort of meeting to arrange catering etc. for a long weekend two weekends hence for about thirteen people – mainly from the Belgian Embassy. We shall go to Lake Baringo, and on to Maralal– a highlands area well to the North of us. Actually, we shall pass an area where there has recently been a lot of fighting, but somehow this doesn't seem to affect Europeans. Nicole went on from our meeting to her *"Gondoliers"* rehearsal and is just back.

This weekend we plan to stay in a cottage belonging to someone I know, in his parents-in-law's garden in the forest at the bottom of the Aberdares mountain. We've never been there, but apparently they have a trout stream and an icy pool to bathe in.

The New Orchid House

This will be a change from the previous two weekends, which have been devoted to building an orchid house, assisted by my gardener and the orphan schoolboy I sponsor. We have made very solid progress, and the whole frame is now finished, but it doesn't yet have its door, plastic greenhouse skin, or plant shelves. The whole structure is about nine feet by nine feet, with staging for two long plant shelves, each about three feet wide, and is very solidly made out of local cedar poles (rot and insect proof for many years) and creosoted softwood. I wouldn't be surprised if some future tenant of this house decided to convert it into a garden shed, or even living quarters.

Lots of love, David

Letter from Nicole
to parents-in-law

Nairobi, 17/06/1984

Exams for the Boys

Thank you very much for having the children once again. I believe the weather was not very good that week but as Bernard said it allowed them to do a lot of work as there was no incentive to venture outside. Both children are doing exams this week. Bernard should have finished on 23rd June and after that I do not know what he will do. He wanted to go walking. I have asked him to let you know, as well as Mr. Adams, of his whereabouts. I have been thinking of him a lot and I wish I were there to give him some moral support at least.

Uganda

David is in Uganda for a few days; he should be back tomorrow but when one goes to that country one is never sure whether one's programme will work as scheduled. He has not been to Uganda for the last two years, and it was high time he went to supervise the project the Foundation is funding. Things are much better here but from time to time people are killed. Friends of ours have just spent two weeks in Uganda visiting their son who is working there. They came back very pleased and full of praise for the Ugandans.

Helping a Friend

All the same I have had a very busy weekend looking after two little girls (six and three years old) who are daughters of friends of ours. The mother is pregnant and is very tired. She does not usually have very much stamina and being pregnant does not make things better. She has asked me to have the children for the weekend so that she could have a rest and stay in bed a bit longer in the morning. Sarah and Ruth, the daughters, have been very good and they were no trouble at all. They did not object when I put them in bed this afternoon, Ruth did not wake up at night (she often does at home) and they did not wake me early. They played in their room until I got out of bed. I took them to the animal orphanage this morning and we saw lions, tigers, hippopotamus, zebras, monkeys etc. They were thrilled.

Shortages

We still have no rain and I do not think it will rain any more now, it is not hot enough. I have been told that there will be shortages soon, especially dairy products and potatoes. The price of vegetables has already gone up. We have not had any electricity cuts but it will not be long before it happens, as the main river which provides electricity to most of Kenya is very dry. People who get their water from boreholes experience shortages of water. The McDonalds (Ruth's and Sarah's parents) were telling me today that the pressure of water is so low in their area that the water tank which is in their loft has not been filling up for days; it means that they do not get any water in the house. They bathed the girls here before they left tonight.

"The Gondoliers"

I am very busy with rehearsals of *"The Gondoliers"*. The first performance will be on 29th June and the show will run until 7th July. Of course I am out every night. David considered at one time joining us, but when I told him that there would be rehearsals every night he changed his mind. It is very demanding but fun.

David has been a bit under the weather last week. He had a tummy bug and a very bad cold. He was feeling better when he left for Uganda, but he was still coughing a lot. Love, Nicole

Letter to parents   Nairobi, 30/09/1984

Addis Ababa

I'm writing from Addis Ababa airport, where I am waiting for a plane back to Nairobi after a week at a conference. We were worked fairly hard, so I had little opportunity to see the town, let alone the country, but as before, I find it a strangely attractive place. The landscape around Addis consists of green volcanic hills and densely farmed valleys – although I still have no real experience of the Ethiopian countryside. Research Stations I have seen, but they are much the same everywhere. Addis itself has well laid out streets (without street names apparently) linking some grandiose "squares" ("places" is a better description) – *Black Lion Square. Revolution Square*, and so on). The main roads are flanked by modern buildings, and the spaces in-between are filled with alleyways and insanitary (the Ethiopians are VERY insanitary) shacks.

Unwelcome Attentions

The people themselves are very attractive and – at their best – very gracious. At their worst they are a pest. Yesterday hotel staff who realised I was leaving soon, kept on insinuating themselves into my room; one porter accompanied me into the lift, which is the French style – matchbox sized so it is hard to keep an aloof distance – and plied me with silly questions: *"Was I English? Ah good!" "Was I leaving tomorrow, tomorrow yes? Ah good!" "Was my room single or double? Ah good!"* – with a ghastly ingratiating smile accompanying every *"Ah good!"* I did not tip him, and to my pleasure, he was not on duty today.

To be fair, I should add that other Ethiopians I have met have been extremely pleasant hosts, with a leisurely, generous and old-fashioned sense of hospitality.

Family News

We have had a fairly up-beat letter from Bernard. He finds the work tiring but manageable, and quite interesting. I think he mentioned that he had come to see you. Dominic has also written, proving that Bernard's presence is not absolutely necessary to get communication out of him. It remains to be seen whether he can keep up the routine weekly letter.

Since my return from holiday twenty-five days ago, I have managed to spend about one week at work. I hope now to have a reasonably un-interrupted month in Nairobi, looking after my plants. I lost one or two, but only one that I really set any store by.

Drought and Famine in Ethiopia

The whole region remains very dry. Ethiopia is entering a worse drought than that which precipitated the revolution ten years ago. It is better equipped to deal with drought than it was then, but there will still be a great deal of hardship and many deaths. Even if food aid were available in adequate amounts, the supply system could not handle it. I spoke yesterday to the co-ordinator of the Christian Relief and Development Association – an impressive organisation grouping all the churches and some non-church bodies like Oxfam and the Red Cross. The co-ordinator, Brother Augustine O'Keefe – extremely Irish – was cheerfully pessimistic. He sees his job essentially as providing a fill-in, fast-moving addition to Government services, about which he was quite complimentary, but he says that the official donors, though given good warning of the situation, are unwilling to take any notice until pictures of wizened babies start appearing in the international press, by which time it is rather late in the day.

We have nothing as competent linking the non-governmental organisations in Kenya – although I doubt if our drought is anything like as serious.

Lots of love, David

Letter to Sons   Nairobi, 30/09/1984

A Lucky Raffle

Mummy and I won three prizes between us at the Orchid Society raffle. I calculate that we came quite close to recovering the Shs.150 that we spent on tickets. I won a gift voucher for Shs.100 at a plant and pet shop (which I have never patronised, so I doubt if it will really be worth that amount of cash) plus a quite remarkably ugly black, green and red handbag, which must I suppose have been priced at about Shs.50-100, but is really worth nothing at all to us. Mummy won a large plant pot, which is of value to me, but not to her.

Illegal Imports

I have planted two ears of triticale (a cross between wheat and rye) in my garden. So far I have about seventeen plants, but if it doesn't rain I shall lose them all. I am not actually planning to go into large-scale grain production this year, but I am interested to see if I can multiply up this stock (purloined from a research station in Ethiopia). I am afraid that although I am generally an honest person, I like my gardening activities to have a little element of illegality. For example, I am very particularly careful about my irregularly imported orchids. Most of these still look healthy, and Bernard's *Epidendrum Ciliare* actually has the beginnings of a flower shoot. I also have a very attractive plant in flower at the moment – a Nairobi purchase.

Lots of love, Daddy

Biomass Fuel, and a House Party

Thanks for your letter. I don't think I've written to you for a long time. Since our holiday, I have visited three countries, but I'm now having a rest (!) in Nairobi in order to get some solid work done. We spent a weekend at a house-party on Lake Baringo. Our friend Jacques, who runs the "Euphorbia Project" (an experiment at growing succulent euphorbia plants as biomass fuel in semi-arid conditions) has the remains of a road construction camp at his disposal, and was able to lodge about twenty people. As usual in French/Belgian company, a large part of our time and energy was devoted to eating. However, I managed to spend quite a lot of my time on his wind-surf. After Guadeloupe, I realise that Baringo is not the ideal place for this, although it's probably as good as can be hoped for in a semi-arid inland area. The wind is unpredictable, but is generally very gentle in the morning, dropping off to dead calm around mid-day, and coming back rather suddenly to an uncomfortable level around 5pm. Unfortunately, it does not keep to a strict routine, and several times I was tempted out by a rising wind, only to be deposited in a dead calm in the middle of the lake. Once I was so utterly becalmed that I rolled up the sail, and paddled back using the centre-board (adjustable keel) as a paddle.

Welcome Showers

We have had a few very welcome showers rather earlier than usual. They have not really been good enough for planting, although I am sure that many hungry people will have tried to plant, and may lose their seed. The rain will help cattle, but otherwise the drought continues. Maize flour seems to be still available, although the price has risen. Supplies of bread are precarious, and cooking oil is very hard to find. Otherwise, it is difficult to find out what is happening to people in remote areas. I suspect that the going is very tough.

Tough Gardening

My garden looks more attractive than it did immediately on our return, although it will take more rain than this to give us back real lawns. At the moment I am not cutting the grass, because I suspect that I shall need it for my rabbits; anyway, we do not have a functioning lawn-mower. At least the rain seems to have given the baboons something to eat other than my garden. Most of my orchids from Guadeloupe appear to have survived, although I did not have anything to exhibit at the Orchid Show. Since then, one of my hot-house plants has come into flower, and another has produced two strong flower shoots.

Action Aid Sponsorship

I'm interested to hear that Friedl sponsors someone through Action Aid. They seem to do quite a good job. Some friends of ours sponsored a girl in Kisumu through Action Aid. The only thing which irritated and annoyed them was that when the girl dropped out of school (very few make it right through the school system, which is NOT to say that they have failed to benefit) Action Aid simply substituted someone else, and lost all contact with the original beneficiary.

Lots of love, David and Nicole

Famine in Ethiopia

We are now well into the short rains, and the garden is greening up nicely, but of course there is still a shortage of basic foodstuffs, and this probably will continue until at least May next year. It's interesting how Ethiopia has suddenly hit all the headlines as news. Of course it should, but the Ethiopians are right to be somewhat cynical, since they announced the famine when there was still time to organise relief properly; but no-one took any notice until people started starving on a large scale, by which time it was necessary to take panic measures. We are not so hard hit here for several reasons: the drought is less severe; fewer people really live perpetually on the edge of famine; administration and communication are better (Ethiopia is still astonishingly short of roads); and we have no major civil wars going on.

Baboon Vandals

My own garden is still famine prone because of the baboons, which pull up all my maize and bean seedlings – infuriating! Yesterday I painted a maize cob with a strong insecticide and hung it up over my beans. Within five minutes a baboon had taken it, but I am pessimistic about the chances of doing more than giving the wretched animal a tummy ache. In case you are appalled by this piece of interference with wild life, you must realise that baboons are completely un-endearing animals. Although they are officially protected (as is virtually everything apart from rats and mice), conserving them is about as attractive a proposition as conserving rats.

Orchids from the Comorro Islands

I have a very fine cymbidium orchid with eleven two-and-a-half inch flowers on a single stem (pink and white), and two others in flower. A friend has just brought me a bundle of large terrestrial orchids from the Comorro Islands – badly hacked around, but I think most of them will recover.

Rich Food

On Friday we went out to dinner with my old friend from Botswana and ODA, Peter Agar, who has now left the civil service and is working as a consultant with Coopers and Lybrand. With him was another former colleague who has become a tax expert and is working for a year with a government commission in Zimbabwe.

We gave a West Indian party last night. I think Nicole was the only West Indian there, but that did not hold us back. We therefore got up very late today, and have done little other than clear up and put the furniture back in place. As you can imagine, we are not particularly hungry today after all the rich food.

A Two-Year Contract

I've signed another two-year contract here, which does not necessarily mean I want to stay another two years. However, jobs don't grow on trees – particularly if I want to come back to the U.K. for a while. The Zimbabwe possibility remains open. I am not particularly optimistic about an early move but my boss is. Nicole is not very keen on the idea of making such a move – particularly before the performance of the *St. Matthew Passion* next Easter. Incidentally, I am planning to sing in the *Passion* for a change, and have been to the first few rehearsals. We now have a break for the run-up to the annual *Messiah* - a bit of a pot-boiler, I'm afraid, but it helps to finance other performances.

Family Illness

I don't think we told you that Nicole's Uncle Hector died recently. He was the father of Suzy, Anick, Yves and Gilou. He had an artificial valve in his heart for over twenty years, which is pretty unusual, and remained fairly active despite being barred from all heavy work. He still kept the shop going, and was well into his seventies. He was quite well when we visited, although complaining a bit of various troubles. Then suddenly a lot of odd things happened – he went deaf and blind more or less overnight, then recovered, but shortly afterwards died while having his afternoon nap. We shall miss him. Despite being in worse health than anyone else around him, he was the liveliest bit of that rather elderly household. Lots of love, David

The Woodstock House

...the other issue that has affected our housing plans is whether I should plan to stay with the Foundation. Recently a possible job came into the offing, which would have suited me. An organisation called the Food Studies Group, based at Queen Elizabeth House, Oxford, doing a mixture of research and commercial consultancy, was considering an expansion, and there was a possibility of them offering me a job as research co-ordinator. This was not exactly in the bag, as they are obliged to advertise jobs, and given the job market they were bound to get a good field; but the Director said he was very keen to bring me in. Sadly, this prospect has now receded. The group has a rather precarious financial base, and the discovery that it had somehow failed to bring £30,000 of last year's expenditure to account has, at least temporarily, halted recruiting. In fact, if they do not find at least one new and lucrative contract, they could even disappear altogether; but they have been through so many crises already that they don't really expect that to happen.

Return to the U.K.

Although this would be rather a gamble, I am still hoping that the prospect will open up again. I would like to re-establish in the U.K. even at the cost of reducing my salary by more than half, and I would like to get back into some research – and Oxford is a fairly ideal place. I am therefore rather hesitant about disposing of the Woodstock house at present, in order to buy an alternative home base which has no likelihood of an adjacent job.

Life Goes On

Otherwise, we are in good form and very busy. Tomorrow we start three nights of *The Messiah*. I'm afraid it will not be as polished as I would like, but as usual it will be fun. Tonight we had a rest from rehearsals, which was just as well, as I spent the whole day visiting an Agro-forestry project, and came back with a splitting headache – quickly cured by a few Panadols and a hot bath, after which we went to a cocktail party with neighbours from the British High Commission.

Agro-forestry and Food Studies

Agro-forestry projects tend to be rather disappointing to look at, except in hot high-rainfall areas with excellent management. One seems to spend one's time looking for goat-chewed dead or ailing tree seedlings in a sea of weedy crops that tower over them. Discussion of measuring biomass or fodder production often seems rather academic. In fact my own garden is a better demonstration of agro-forestry than the *shamba* I saw today.

Incidentally, in case you are puzzled or intrigued by "food studies", they do not involve some sort of gourmet activity, but attempt to develop national food planning systems and determine food production, trade, storage etc. policies.

Orchids

I have an exotic greenish-yellow cymbidium with twenty-three huge flowers on a stem a yard long, and a local "leopard" orchid that I collected from the Coast about a year ago with about thirty yellow flowers spotted with very dark brown.
Lots of love, David and Nicole

Letter from Nicole   Nairobi, 03/12/1984

A Good Birthday

Thank you very much for your birthday greetings. I was on my own on the day as David had to attend a conference at Nyeri, 22km from Nairobi, but I had a nice birthday all the same. Both boys remembered my birthday; my colleagues at work gave me a beautiful bunch of flowers and a colleague and her husband invited me in the evening, to have a meal at the

Hotel Inter-Continental for the opening of the week of French *cuisine*. It was a good meal and a very enjoyable evening.

"The Messiah"

We have had a busy time with rehearsals and three performances of the *Messiah*. David managed to take part in the first performance, then he left for a three-week trip. The performances were all very good and the conductor, who works at the teachers' training college, brought in some new soloists, her music pupils from the college. They all had very beautiful voices and it was an opportunity for them to perform in public. Of course they were Kenyan girls.

A Busy Itinerary

David left on Saturday, first to Malawi for a conference. He will then go to Zimbabwe for a week, and the last week will be divided between Botswana and Swaziland. While he is in Southern Africa he might just as well fit in as many trips as he can. While he is away I shall be able to get on with writing Christmas cards and preparing for Christmas. It will be very sad to have Christmas without Bernard, and we shall think of him on the farm. We shall spend Christmas at Lake Baringo, where our Belgian friends work on a semi-arid land project, growing euphorbia. It is very hot there. David and Dominic will be able to wind surf.

A "Bad Patch" for Dominic

Dominic has had a bit of a bad patch recently. He wrote saying that he is fed up with boarding school and he is longing for a family life. We phoned him, and the Boarding House Master, who wrote to me today after having spoken to Dominic. It is a bit difficult to move him to Kenya at this stage of his school life, but we shall talk to him during the holiday and if he is really unhappy at school I shall have to consider going to live in Thame for a few months. Of course this would involve giving up my job and leaving David alone, but I would feel guilty if Dominic failed his exams because I was not there to help him.
Love, Nicole

Letter from Nicole to Sheila and Ron

Nairobi, 06/12/1984

Back Stage Crew

It is one of the rare evenings I shall spend at home in the next few days, therefore I am trying to write as many letters and Christmas cards as possible. Life has been very hectic; I thought I was going to have a quiet time while David was away but I have been enrolled to help with one of the pantomimes, as back stage crew.

The Green City in the Sun

The rain has finally arrived and it has been raining more or less non-stop since October. Nairobi is once again *"the green city in the sun"* when it shines. The garden is beautiful and there are masses of roses. David has had trouble with baboons eating all the vegetables.

I am sure you hear often about Bernard from Mummy and Daddy. He seems to be happy and enjoying life. Dominic misses Bernard very much. It will be strange not to have Bernard with us at Christmas.
Have a very happy Christmas, Love, Nicole

Letter from Nicole to parents-in-law

Nairobi, 09/12/1984

Thank you for your letter. I do not find the time too long while David is not here, as there is a lot going on at the moment. Last night I went to a cocktail party; today I first went to an orchid meeting on behalf of David and then to a lunch party. I did not want to get involved in any of the pantomimes partly because I wanted to sing in *"The Messiah"* and also the pantomimes run for about three weeks up to Christmas, and I like to be at home when the children are here. All the same I have been asked to help behind stage for *"Cinderella"*. I am helping to dress the ladies and help with their changes of costume. I do not have to be there every evening and I get a free ticket.

Night Calls

I have not heard from David but he said he would only phone me during his stay in Zimbabwe. He should have arrived in Harare today, so I expect a call any time this week. As he is never very sure of the difference of time he often rings in the middle of the night when I am fast asleep. At least he is sure to find me home.

Illness of a brother-in-law

We were sorry to hear about David Pearce's illness. Bernard had mentioned it in his letter. As you said, Margaret is going through a very bad time and it is very sad as their children are still small. One should thank God every day for being healthy as illness arrives without any warning. One can only pray that the treatment works and that he will be with his family for some time to come.

The Boys

Thank you for having Bernard from time to time. I am sure he appreciates it and I am certain that one of the things that gets Dominic down is to know that Bernard is able to visit you often. We have heard from Mr. Pritchard, the boarding house master, who said Dominic is allowed to work in a certain teacher's flat whenever he likes.

I wish you a very happy Christmas. Love, Nicole

Letter from Nicole to parents-in-law   Nairobi, 16/12/1984

Christmas

Just a short note to wish you a happy Christmas. Our Christmas at Baringo will be a half English, half Belgian Christmas. I suppose we shall have a *"reveillon"* during the night of 24th to 25th and also a Christmas supper on 25th; it is too hot in Baringo to have a cooked meal at lunchtime.

I heard from David from Malawi, and he also phoned me last Sunday. His trip in Malawi was rather restful which is a good thing as the Zimbabwe and Botswana trips will involve a lot of work, especially in Botswana where he is staying only two days and he will have to do a lot and see many people in those two days. He will be back on Thursday at 23.30 hrs. Dominic will be arriving in the morning of that day.

I phoned Dominic today to make sure that he had his air ticket. He said that he had phoned you yesterday, as well as Bernard. I am thinking a lot of Bernard; he will be working on Christmas and Boxing Day. I was thinking that for the first time in his life he will not find a stocking at the bottom of his bed on Xmas Day. I have just finished a jersey for him today and a friend who is going to U.K. on Wednesday will take it and post it for me. It will be nice for him to have a parcel from us.

Happy Christmas and love, Nicole

Letter to parents   Harare, 18/12/1984

Praise for Malawi

I enjoyed my week in Malawi. It is extremely relaxing to spend a week at a conference in which one has no duties except to participate. In fact I wrote a short paper, but did so under false pretences since – along with other victims – I was never intended to present it.

Malawi itself is attractive, and astonishingly secure and friendly compared with the other countries I am used to. I do not approve of Dr. Hastings Banda's habit of bumping off his opponents, or the cringing behaviour he demands of everyone, up to the most senior Ministers, but the streets are certainly safer there than those of Kenya (or Tanzania, Zimbabwe, Zambia, Uganda etc). Even in friendly Botswana, there were places where tourists get mugged.

Orchid Spotting

I went out for two long walks in the hills around Blantyre, and did some orchid spotting. There is a very wide variety of terrestrial orchids in Central Africa, and I suppose I saw about six different varieties, including one which appeared to be parasitic or saprophytic – rather rare for African orchids. There were also many tree orchids – mostly of rather humble mein. I would very much like to walk on some of the higher forested areas, such as Mount Mulanje or the Nyika plateau. For my second walk I had the very pleasant company of a middle-aged Irish lady, the Assistant Director of the Irish Management Institute, who turned out to be a very doughty walker. I am so unused to finding people who actually like walking for hours through bog and briar that I am always surprised when I do come across them.

Circular Christmas letter to all friends

Getting Restless

It is 1985 and we are still in Nairobi. This is the longest time I have been in one job since I wrote my thesis, but we feel impermanent. We shall get a new Nairobi Ford Foundation Representative in a few months, which may well mean changes in our programmes, but in any case I feel the urge to get up and do something different.

An Amazing Country

We have no problems with Kenya; it offers us an unbeatable range of climates and landscapes. For example, this year we spent Christmas with one lot of friends at Lake Baringo where the climate is reliably warm, dry and sunny. We swam and wind-surfed in its murky but quite wholesome water without spotting any crocodiles (which are said not to eat people at Baringo) and went to look at hippos and herons in the marshy areas. Then for New Year we went with another group of friends to a forest house at 8,000 feet on Mount Kenya, paddled in icy streams, and collected pine cones and branches to make a good blaze on the living room fire in the evening. Nicole and I, arriving last, got the best sleeping place in front of the fire while everyone else went off to cold bedrooms. A few hundred feet further up, we would have had frost at night, and further still, snow – although at that level the atmosphere would have been too thin for comfort. Even in Nairobi the boys are surprised to find themselves puffing as they walk up the garden. Within a comfortable range, however, you can choose your climate: perpetual summer, spring or winter, just like a children's book.

Burgeoning Population

A lot of Europeans here believe that time is limited for the Kenya they like, simply because of population growth. With population doubling every eighteen years, the spaces are disappearing fast, and so are trees and forests. Our New Year spot was a good example. No-one used to live at 8,000 feet but when the Forest Department put in an experimental plantation, they opened access for squatters. After the main work force left, these expanded their herds and fields. Officially, they do not exist, but the forest guards are probably only too pleased to make money out of them. So far the incursion looks very minor, and the resulting village-in-a-forest is really rather attractive. Where the bamboo forest has been cut, there is good grazing, and potatoes and maize can be grown. In fact one has to ask whether there is really any good reason for not allowing settlement in some of these fairly flat upland pastures. Ecologically it is far less damaging than the farming that is done on steep slopes in many other areas, and it would probably produce far more livelihoods than maintaining these areas for a handful of tourists like us. Of course, wildlife would be affected, but presumably people come before elephants.

Food and Culture

There are, however, other pleasures in Kenya besides open spaces. We live very comfortably on ex-pat. salaries. We can normally buy bread, cheese, oil (when there is not a drought), good bacon, and good (cheap) meat, and other essentials (the drought is another story, and I'll come on to that). And there is a good cultural and social life. Nicole is now the secretary of the Music Society, and I still play in the orchestra. The high point of the musical calendar this year was the *Messiah* – an annual event, but this one was especially good, and very nearly complete. I took part in only one performance, as I had a non-postponable trip to make before Christmas, but I was unexpectedly promoted to "first desk" because our first cellist slipped a disc the day before the performance. Her loss was my gain, although perhaps not the audience's. I had to sight-read some new bits of music and had a few awkward moments. Our next big date is the *St. Matthew's Passion* at Easter. I hope to sing in that for a change.

The Ravages of Drought

1984 was Kenya's turn to experience drought. After three poor rainy seasons (much of Kenya has two rains per year) the longer rains failed almost completely. As a result there has been much hardship, but things could have been much worse. Graziers and pastoralists in the semi-arid areas probably suffered most. In many places they lost over half their stock, and herds will take about five years to be rebuilt. However, there was no real shortage of cereals on the market, thanks to quick action both by the donors and the Kenyan authorities. There were also relief works and distribution of food in the worst-hit areas, but I suspect these were really pretty unimportant, and that most people made do by falling back on savings or other sources of income, and on relatives with wage incomes. A good short rainy season from September has greatly improved the situation, although Nairobi is still dependant on imported yellow maize meal. This is very unpopular. It is more nutritious than the popular white maize, but it really is harder to cook, and people complain of stomach aches – probably because half-cooked maize meal continues its cooking (and expansion) inside them.

War and Hunger in Ethiopia

Kenya's drought bears no comparison to Ethiopia's, although from a geographer's point of view it is all part of the same drought. There are several reasons for this. In the first place, much of Ethiopia is permanently nearer to starvation than Kenya. There are just too many people with tiny holdings in the Ethiopian highlands (this is what I am afraid of for Kenya). In addition communications are far worse in Ethiopia (there are hardly any roads) and many peasants are cut off from markets, seeds, fertiliser etc. This has always made it easy to ignore famine in Ethiopia. The situation is made worse by all the local wars. As one weary Ethiopian said to me *"these days we seem to have more liberation fronts than provinces"*. This makes it very hard to import food, let alone to transport it internally (although interestingly some Ethiopian food relief maize has been planted by smallholders in areas of central Kenya which were short of maize seed, so the market does work, somehow).

Turning a Blind Eye

On top of this, the Ethiopian government ignored the drought until it had finished its very expensive celebrations of the tenth anniversary of the revolution. There was no excuse for this as Ethiopia has the most sophisticated drought warning system in the region as well as a reasonably effective government relief agency. But the donor countries were no better. They ignored the drought even longer, until western newspapers and TV channels started to publicise it. Please note that the drought in Ethiopia will not be over until about June/ July – and only then if the rains are good. In the meantime, the Ethiopian government is continuing what I consider to be a foolhardy policy of resettling people while the drought is still in progress.

News of the Boys

This was our first Christmas without two boys at home for fifteen years. Bernard has got the A-levels he needs for Harper Adams Agricultural College, and is doing his obligatory practical work on a large mixed farm near Oakham, fifteen miles from David's parents. Winter on a midlands farm is enough to dispel any romantic illusions one might have about farming, but that's surely the intention. He seems to be sticking it out very well, although he does not pretend to enjoy all of it.

Dominic is still at Lord William's School in Thame. He spent Christmas with us – preparing to plunge into mock O-levels as soon as he returned. He used to be a keen rugby player, but as seems to be generally the case in my family at this age, the rest of his age group has temporarily become much bigger and heavier than him, so he has transferred his aggressive instincts to hockey – although I think for all of us except Nicole the sport of the moment is wind-surfing on warm waters. We bought one board and rented another in Guadeloupe this summer, and became quite proficient.

Thank you to everyone who has sent us their news. We do enjoy hearing of friends and relatives. Happy 1985!

David and Nicole Jones

Additional News for Parents

Lake Baringo

We are busy as usual. We spent this weekend at Lake Baringo, leaving Friday evening to get a full relaxed day. Sensibly, we started home today before 4pm, and therefore made it home before it was completely dark. We should make the most of our friends at Baringo. Their project may well be closed down in March.

Eccentric Lifestyle

Yesterday we spent much of the day at a tented camp on an island (tents are the only real concession to roughing it; they have private bathrooms, and a very comfortable common area with bars, swimming pool etc). I did a little wind-surfing in the afternoon, but the wind was squally, and I spent a lot of my time in the water. Then we went to afternoon tea with one of the camp's shareholders, who lives under a tree on an adjacent island. He used to be a Kenyan white farmer, but was involuntarily bought out by the Kenyatta clan. He then married a French wife, and inherited a farm near Dieppe, but that didn't work out (he says he couldn't buy enough land to make an efficient unit) so he brought his wife out here to live in the middle of a lake under a tree. Surprise! She didn't like that, so now he's on his own, more or less.

Lucky Escape from Bad-Tempered Hippo

Today I did a silly thing, but got away with it. We had planned to go to a tourist lodge further up Lake Baringo, but a good wind sprang up, so I sailed up (unbeknown to the others). The only problem was that the area around the lodge is made up of reed-beds that are infested with hippo. I sailed to and fro a couple of times, then made an entry up a channel that was mid-way between two hippos. Unfortunately it turned out to be a cul-de-sac, and a hippo seemed to have followed me in, so there was nothing for it but to force my way through the reeds as best I could, poling, pulling on the reeds, and sloshing through the mud and tangle, being encouraged by snorting and grunting unpleasantly close behind me. A local woman was bitten almost in two there recently by hippo, so I had reason to hurry (for added flavour, there had also been crocodile there recently, to eat the remains of three hippo that had killed each other in a fight, but I didn't see them. I was told they were not very big!)

Buying a French Farmhouse

We are in the process of trying to buy a farmhouse with four to six rooms plus attic plus separate pigeon tower with three more rooms, and eight acres of land, in the Dordogne. No sanitation of any sort. I have for some time thought it would be nice to have a place in one of the warmer bits of France. This is by no means the warmest bit, but it is comfortable for a tropicalised person like me. Honestly, I don't know exactly what we are going to do with it, and for the time being it is more suitable for young relatives who don't mind roughing it and enjoy mixing concrete than for those who like comfort. Of course we haven't even seen the place! And there are many possible slips, not to mention snags. Our agent seems genuinely to

have slipped in when the predatory neighbours were not looking, but she has to keep on telling lies (that she has concluded a sale) to hold them off. We shall see.
Lots of love, David and Nicole

Letter to Sheila and Ron Nairobi, 06/01/1985

Christmas

Thank you for the thermometer. It will be very useful for the greenhouse – not that I can do very much when the temperature goes miles outside the right range for my plants, but it's reassuring to know that usually we are within a tolerable range. Nicole has asked me to thank you for the Capricorn book. Actually she's a Sagittarius but I doubt if it really makes much difference.

Crocs and Hippos

We've had a pleasant, though all too short Christmas and New Year break with Dominic, although we missed Bernard's presence. We spent Christmas at Lake Baringo, which is warm and dry, and has a huge mud-coloured (but quite liquid) lake for swimming and wind-surfing. There are crocodiles and hippo, but we have never yet seen any of the former, and for some reason they don't seem to eat people at Baringo. We have seen plenty of huge hippo, but generally they prefer marshy areas, and places where they can easily climb out to graze at night. The friends' house where we stay is at a place where the water is deep, and there is a steep bank of huge boulders and small cliffs, so the hippo didn't trouble us (hippo don't eat people, but they are bad-tempered, and sometimes bite a boat or a person in two, just to indicate their displeasure).

I then went back to work for two days before we went off to Mount Kenya to celebrate New Year in a rather dilapidated forest house at 8,000 feet, with bamboo forests and upland meadows around us, and plenty of pleasant mountain streams.

Successful Smuggling!

Dominic goes back tomorrow evening, and almost immediately has to do his mock O-levels, so he has done a fair amount of revision here. He has also done a successful small piece of smuggling; he brought his stereo radio/cassette player here in his bag, and sold it at a price which will allow him to buy something rather superior when he gets back.

The Go-Between

Bernard is not really positively enjoying his farm work, but takes a sensible stoical attitude to it. The people he works for are pleasant, but grumpy – more probably with each other than with Bernard, but he sometimes gets caught in the middle – as when the wife asks Bernard to ask her husband why he hasn't fed the heifers yet.

Living it up at the Races

We have just celebrated the end of Dominic's stay with an afternoon at the races. I'm afraid we are most unsuccessful punters. I backed only one winner – a rank outsider – but he didn't make up for my losers. Dominic had the galling experience of seeing his choice in the last race beaten at the post. Of course I know it's all a waste of money, but the ambience of a Nairobi race meeting is quite picturesque – such a range of people and dress for a start, from the very elegant (of all races) to what appear to be the beggars off the streets of Nairobi (and that's in the stands; I don't know what the public enclosure can be like).
Love to you all, David and Nicole

Letter to Margaret and David, Nairobi, 06/01/1985

NOTE - Since sister Margaret met and married her husband in Zaire (formerly the Belgian Congo) around the time of the Simba uprising, they would be particularly interested in

David's mention of acquaintances from Zaire. Margaret worked there as a physiotherapist, David as a dentist, under the auspices of the Baptist Missionary Society.

Happy 1985! I am sorry you seem to be having such a bad patch. At least you are better looked after than you would be in most other places, if that's any consolation.

We had a pleasant Christmas at Lake Baringo, which is a delightful place although the water always looks rather muddy. At least it's reliably warm, and the hippo keep away from our place, and the crocodiles have not eaten anyone in recent years, so we do our swimming and wind-surfing with a fair amount of confidence, although I admit I am always a bit wary. It's nice water to swim in. The top metre or so is pleasantly tepid, but below that it stays icy cold – presumably because the turbidity of the water prevents sunlight from penetrating. Our party included a Belgian family from a sugar estate in Zaire quite near to Matadi – the sister and brother-in-law of our host's wife.

Pine Plantation with Elephants

For New Year we chose a completely different climate – a forest house at 8,000 feet on Mount Kenya, on the boundary between the forest (natural and man-made) and the bamboo forest. The forest station had been established about thirty years back as an experiment in creating pine plantations at that height, and the experiment looked pretty successful, despite a lot of elephant damage, but there had been no new plantings since, and the station was on a care and maintenance basis (i.e. no maintenance and very little care). We rented the former forest officer's house for a very modest sum, and camped out in it – about twelve of us I suppose. The house was filthy, but luckily we were the last party to arrive, and the fore-runners had been making it habitable for three days.

Cheeky Squatters and Guards

We explored the environs, destroyed two very large (buffalo-sized) spring snares set by the forest guard or the squatters (very comfortable squatters); surprised the assistant forest guard destroying a bit more bamboo forest for his cattle and picnicked by an icy stream. There was lots of evidence of animals, but we saw nothing except colobus monkeys, and I forgot to bring a plastic sack to collect elephant dung for my roses; but we picked up lots of pine branches and fir cones to make a good blaze on the living room fire in the evening, and generally had a lazy, pleasant time. It is one of the incomparable advantages that Kenya shares with a few other tropical countries that one can choose one's climate anywhere from very hot summer to very cold spring, and drive there in a few hours any time of the year.

The Dreaded Exams!

Since I started this letter, we have sent Dominic back to school, and presume he has now arrived safely and started his mock O-levels. I don't envy him. I still wake up from time to time in the middle of a nightmare about exams, always aware that I haven't revised enough. Our love to you and the family, David and Nicole

Letter to Parents   **Nairobi, 06/01/1985**

Christmas Books

Thanks for *"Parlez-vous Franglais?"* and A.J.P. Taylor's book. We all had a good laugh over the former. I think *"Parlez-vous.."* is good value because the dialogues are funny even when translated into real English (or French, but it is basically English humour). I am well into A.J.P. Taylor. Really, I knew very little about him – so little that I tended to confuse him with Hugh Trevor-Roper (a much less sympathetic character) but I'm finding it very interesting.

We celebrated Dominic's last Sunday here by going to the races. I'm afraid we are not successful punters, but the atmosphere is very amusing.
Lots of love, David

Dominic's Departure

It seems astonishing that it is only one week since Dominic went back to school. We seem to have left the holidays far behind already. As always, Dominic was a little chagrined to leave us. I know he finds school life tiresome and likes to have some privacy and at least optional quiet, and he felt this particularly last term with Bernard absent. I hope Dominic remembered to post our letter to you when he arrived in England. He had a whole batch to hand-carry.

A Successful Biltong Box

We are having dry, breezy weather. I expect you would find it warm, but I find it rather chilly much of the time. However, it is dry and warm enough for me to make biltong – wind-dried raw meat in the South African style. I have a very swish biltong box, designed and built by me out of bits of packing cases, and protected from flies by mosquito netting. People who see it hanging on the verandah normally assume it is a cage for some sort of live animal, whereas it is really designed to exclude livestock. Last weekend I re-furbished it with Dominic and Elind (my Kikuyu "ward" – I pay his school fees, as his parents are both dead – his mother hanged herself eighteen months ago after years of mental illness). We replaced rotten mosquito wire, eaten away by fumes from the meat, and I improved the carrying capacity of the box. I then bought six kilos of silverside, cut it into long strips, marinaded it in wine, vinegar, salt, sugar and spices, and hung it up to dry in the box. We are already able to eat the thinner pieces of meat, but the thicker ones need a couple more days to dry out completely. Unless you have eaten biltong (perhaps I once brought some home?) it's hard to describe the texture and taste. It's probably not the ideal food for people with dentures. However, my biltong is in demand. One of Nicole's friends will buy some for her daughters, who are crazy about it, and I expect my American colleague, Craig, will also want a share; funny, because when he first arrived, he wouldn't touch it!

A Language Problem!

The friend of Nicole told us a funny/ sad story about her daughters' biltong. Her *ayah* (children's maid) always gives the girls a Christmas present, and asked Oriane (eight years) what she wanted. Oriane said biltong. Now biltong is not generally known in Kenya, and the Kikuyus can't pronounce "l's" anyway, and I'm sure the *ayah* was a little bit puzzled by the request. Anyway, she worked it out to her own satisfaction, and Oriane was more than a little surprised to receive a jar of "blue-tone" – a skin lightener used by Africans. Fortunately her mother was there, quickly fathomed the situation, and told Oriane *"remercie-la et fait semblance d'etre tres heureuse"*.

Orchid Envy!

Today I went to an orchid society meeting. I have nothing significant in flower, and was very jealous of the blooms on the table, although I notice that some of the best ones are usually recently purchased from overseas dealers. Our host today was the German wife of a very well-to-do Italian – probably one of the prisoners of war from Ethiopia who settled down here and flourished. Her husband used to be a contractor and owned a brick and tile factory until he sold out several years back, so naturally Ingeborg had a very smartly set up brick and glass orchid house. But it is unfair to attribute her success just to this, because she is clearly a very skilled and conscientious grower.

Baboons Win the Day

We have just taken our minute maize crop: about twelve cobs for us, and rather more for the baboons, who also wrecked the crop shortly after planting.
Lots of love, David and Nicole

Birthday Greetings (Our mother was now aged 71)

Happy Birthday Mummy! Gosh, you really are getting a big girl! And I hope Daddy's feeling better, and is up and about again. I'm afraid you must be having rather a miserable winter. If it's any comfort, it's rather cold and wet here – unseasonably so, as the short rains are meant to have finished a month ago, and it's very early for the next lot of rains. In fact, the weather is very changeable. This morning I went to an orchid meeting, and the sun was so hot that people kept on shifting their chairs to try and get a place in the shade of the awning, but it started to rain again in the late afternoon, and there is still a general feeling of drizzle.

House Buying and Selling

We have heard nothing of our progress in house-buying for almost two weeks. If there is nothing in the post on Monday we shall make another expensive telephone call to our friends near Bordeaux. Considering the doubts with which we started this venture, we are now very anxious in case it falls through. The Woodstock house is now having an expensive little improvement done to it. I have arranged for a local builder whom I know to finish waterproofing the cellar, to put in a proper tile floor, lights, power points and a radiator so that it can be used as a "recreation room". The inverted commas are there because I believe it will really make a pleasant additional living room, but I am sure that the borough surveyor would object on a number of spurious health grounds. It's funny to think that in nominal terms this will cost well over half the original value of the house. As for the Monsegur house, that will cost getting on for ten times the original nominal cost of the Woodstock house, but still seems cheap. On the other hand, my weekly salary is now worth about as many pounds as my first annual salary from the Oxford Institute of Economics and Statistics. I realise, however, that this is a very temporary situation, and would be very happy if I found something suitable in Britain for nearly half what I am earning at present.

A Change for Bernard

Bernard says that he will leave the Cavenaghs at the end of this month. Apparently he told them he wanted to leave as soon as possible some time ago, when he was feeling rather low, and not surprisingly they took him at his word and arranged for a replacement. Now he would really like to stay on for the lambing. Too bad! But he has to learn to reflect before he speaks. On a personal plane he does not seem to have made contact with the Cavenaghs, which is a pity. I can't say that I found Mr. C. very personable, but I felt that Mrs. C., despite a blunt way with words, was at least of kindly intent. Anyway, it will be very nice to have him here for Easter. We intend to go to the Coast, and a friend has said she will lend us her wind-surfer.

Time to Rear Cattle?

Our milk supplier has offered to sell us a bull calf (slaughtered) for 700 shillings, so we consulted with some close ex-Botswana friends who have greater agricultural expertise than ourselves to see if this was good value for money. We are still not sure if it is, but have hatched a plan to build a calf-house in their garden and raise our own veal. Iain, who works in the Ministry of Agriculture, says he can get day old calves for 50 shillings, so after that it becomes a question of the economics of feeding with milk substitute. I like the idea of a new farming venture. At the moment we have only my rabbits, which provide us with about one every ten days, plus sales to friends.
Lots of love, David and Nicole

Preparing to Leave Kenya

Since Dominic is going back tonight he can hand-carry this letter. I think these departures always make me morose for about twenty-four hours, although this time at least Bernard will still be with us a bit longer. It's odd to think that Dominic will not come back "home" to Kenya again. I still have not got to grips with the reality of leaving, although I try to do it by telling other people. We still haven't told the servants. From one point of view it is often considered prudent not to announce a departure too far ahead, because word gets around that there's likely to be more money in the house than normal – even if the servants don't decide they now have nothing to lose by tipping off some robbers for a few shillings. Whatever their faults, however, I don't think ours are up to tricks like that, and I must make the sombre announcement very soon now. There will be all sorts of other things to deal with too: where will we dispose of the dogs? What should we sell and how do we organise it?

Buying Furniture

Conversely, what should we buy? Last week at Mombassa I ordered a carved bed head to go with various bits of a Swahili bed I have, but there's still a lot of work to be done assembling all the pieces (in fact it has cost me a great deal more to assemble the parts than it did to buy one complete bed at an auction sale – a bit wobbly and also cobbled together from bits, but OK for Monsegur).

Proud Owners of a French Farmhouse

We seem to be making good progress with the Monsegur house purchase. I have transmitted all the funds, including an incredible 18% for various transaction costs, and we have signed a procuration at the French Embassy to allow our friends the Boudats to complete the purchase on our behalf. Bernard intends to stay at the house for a few weeks before we arrive in August. Lots of love, David, Nicole and family

Letter from Nicole to parents-in-law

Nairobi, 06/05/1985

Dominic's News.....

. We heard from Dominic last week. He seems fine, and informed us that he will stay at Lord William's to do the sixth form. It is a relief as it is one less thing to organise when I come back. When he heard that we were leaving Kenya he said that he wanted to live at home, which is understandable. We said that we would like it very much if he could live at home, but perhaps he should think about it and realise that he would have to re-adapt to a new school and make new friends. We also told him that, being in England, we shall be able to come and see him at weekends and take him out more often.

....and Bernard's

It has been very nice to have Bernard here for six weeks. He has made himself very useful and without being asked helped in the house during weekends when the houseboy is off. After two driving lessons he applied to take his driving test and to our surprise passed first time. We thought he would have to take the test again in U.K. but it turns out that the Kenyan driving test is now recognised in U.K. The British High Commission told him that all he has to do is go to a Post Office in England, present his Kenyan driving licence and on payment of £10 he will be given a U.K. driving licence. We do not know how well he can drive as he is not allowed to use our car, which is Ford Foundation property; only David and I are allowed to use it.

To Washington, U.S.A.

I suppose that David phoned you this morning while he was in transit at Heathrow on his way to Washington. I shall go to meet him in Washington on Friday 10th May and I shall spend a week there. On the way back (18th May) I shall stop in England for twenty-four hours, can I come and stay with you? I shall pick up Dominic from school and drive to Leicester. I shall take Dominic back to school on 19th May and then drive to Heathrow to catch the plane for Nairobi. Because of work and family commitments, I have never been able to benefit from the various trips offered to me by the Ford Foundation, so I decided to take up the opportunity of a trip to Washington; otherwise I would not benefit from it any more.

I hope that Daddy is feeling better. I am afraid the wet weather does not make things better. We have had a good rainy season and it still goes on raining, although it is May.

Looking forward to seeing you soon, Nicole

Snorkelling in Guadeloupe (1980)

Ascent of Mount Kenya (1982)

There are no more surviving letters until 1986. !985 was a sad year for us all as our kind and gentle Father died in May; then sister Margaret's husband David Pearce - a patient loving father and husband - died in July, leaving her with four children all still at school.

I visited our father on the day he died, with some of my family, and we had a lovely day in the garden. We said farewell to him in the early evening, and were shocked on arriving home in Suffolk to be told by phone that he had died a short while after we left, of a heart attack. Dominic was staying with my parents at that time and was very sensible and helpful.

I took leave from my teaching job and returned to Leicester the following day to be with my mother and help her prepare for the funeral. The following day brother David arrived. Brother Michael, then living in Stafford, is seldom able to leave his wife Susan for long, because their middle child is sadly disabled and needs twenty-four hour care. Sister Margaret was caring for her terminally ill husband at this time. So David and I did what we could, and enjoyed the time despite the sad circumstances. We drove to various Offices, sorting out the business side of things, and went together to the Chapel of Rest to say farewell. We also visited the huge fish market, which due to the influx of immigrants to Leicester, now has a vast selection of produce from distant parts, most species being familiar to David.

I remember David brought our mother and me early morning cups of tea in bed, wearing a natty pair of underpants, and I thought "why wasn't I given long slender sun-tanned limbs and beautiful golden hair, like my brother?!"

After forty-nine years of marriage, our mother was naturally very upset and lonely. Soon after, she moved to a bungalow. I think quite a lot of David's letters were consigned to the bin during this (and a subsequent) house move.

During 1985, David commenced work at Crown Agents (formerly "Crown Agents to the Colonies"), based in London. This new post also would involve a great deal of travel. He and Nicole sold the Woodstock house, and bought a house in Sutton, Surrey.

CHAPTER FIVE
LETTERS 1986–1996

Letters for the next few years are thin on the ground – probably because our Father's death and our Mother's subsequent house move caused "sorting out" sessions in which many items were discarded. Thus there are no surviving letters giving David's impressions of countries first visited during this period, such as Thailand, Indonesia and Mauritius.

I have my own good memories of these years, and of my own family's first sojourn at Bordepaille (near Monsegur). The farmhouse was dilapidated, with very primitive basic facilities, but was great fun to explore; house and outbuildings revealed much about the lives and work of former occupants. There was a stone-built stable, fodder trough and stalls separated by an oak partition with a row of carefully-hewn oval spaces for long necks to reach through; a ramshackle tobacco-drying barn; a stone outhouse where cider-making equipment survived under the rubble, with one wall displaying a beautifully carved tall chimney surround in pale stone, relic of a time when the building was a home; and a romantic, crumbling pigeonnier tower.

The main house sat on rough grass on high land, overlooking a lower area of neglected grass (not by any stretch of imagination a lawn!) where grew a huge walnut tree. Cherry trees bordered the extensive grounds and crickets chirped incessantly in the heat. We loved it; so did David but true to character he immediately set about thorough restoration labours.

Bordepaille, near Bordeaux 1986
House among the sunflowers

Soaking up sunshine

Letter from Nicole to Margaret   **Sutton, Surrey, 28/01/1986**

Settling in at Sutton

Things are progressing very slowly in our house. Being out all day we can only do so much in the evening. Therefore our weekends are fully occupied, but we want to do as much as we can in the shortest time otherwise the house will still be in a mess in a year's time and this state of affairs makes me very depressed. Anyway David has laid cork tiles in the bathroom and with Dominic's help has started to do the same in the sitting room. We had a carpet fitted last week in the dining room. The four-poster bed that my father has sent me has been put together but we have not got a base and mattress yet; we have given our double bed to Bernard.

Surplus Carpets

We have come to the conclusion that we have too many carpets and do not have any use for them, as all the rooms are carpeted, although it is not first class carpeting. We have three carpets to give or throw away: a stair carpet, a square blue carpet (with a hole which can be hidden under a piece of furniture), and what is left of the fitted carpet that we used in the dining room (colour mustard). The fitted carpet especially is very good hand-woven wool. If you are interested let me know as soon as possible as I have also offered them to Tom and David Wright. It will be a matter of first come first served.

David is off to Indonesia next week.

Love, Nicole

Letter to all friends at Christmas   Sutton, 12/1986

Getting Organised

This letter is under new management. Nicole has told me this year it should go out in the year, and not several months into 1987. I am less sure that this is a good idea. One hardly has time to read all the letters that arrive in the Christmas rush. I think we are much more likely to brighten your day with a letter that comes in one of the year's slack seasons.

Getting Settled In

We are now well settled in Sutton, and normally have at least one spare room for visitors and plenty of floor for any overspill. I still have to put up a few bookshelves in order to get rid of the last of the cardboard boxes, but I have not had access to so many of my books for nine years (we took a limited selection to Botswana on the grounds that it was to be a short stay).

We are pleased with our house. Its only major blemish is that some former owner has "improved" the façade. The Society for the Preservation of Ancient Buildings which I joined recently, takes the view that subsequent alterations should be respected as part of the "patina of time" but if I had abundant funds I would not mind faking a return to the rather elegant early Victorian frontage of the adjacent houses. Nevertheless, I think we made a very fortunate choice. Hardly anyone at Crown Agents can get to work as easily as I can. Even my younger staff are forced to live up to forty miles away because of house prices (a great nuisance, but not one I can do much about).

Gardening Addict

I am, as usual, starting to spend too much time gardening. We are fortunate in having an unusually large garden for our area. Half of it was a builder's yard, and half exceedingly weedy lawn. Bernard has devoted a lot of time to the lawn, and we have dug up enough of the builder's yard to find that we have two feet of good black soil over chalk. Digging the builder's yard is very hard going, because it is full of buried treasure: brick ends and pieces of iron. My main gardening tool is still a pickaxe. We have already had some good vegetable crops and even some flowers. At first I was a bit at sea, as my reference material was made up of titles like *"Gardening in South Africa"*, *"Gardening in East Africa"*, and even *"Le Potager Tropical"*.

This is not a disguised request for books, as I have now made up the gap; but like the rest of the Childs and Jones families, I am always pleased to see visitors bearing cuttings of the more interesting plants from their own gardens. I am particularly on the lookout for cottage garden and foliage plants. Does anyone have an Acanthus Mollis? Even better, anyone with a Gunnera?

A Closer Family

One of the best things about being home (I write this on the shore of Lake Malawi!) is seeing more of the boys. Bernard cannot come often in term-time, but has long holidays. Dominic is still at Lord William's School in Thame and comes home about every other weekend. Both boys are flourishing. Bernard enjoys Harper Adams College, and is sharing a house out of College for the first half of this college year before doing a work placement.

Dominic is Head of Boarding House, and is in his second A-Level year and aiming at a career in graphic design.

Wider Family News

Also on the family front, my mother is well settled into her new bungalow, less than a mile from her old house, and is surprised to find that, having seen this purely as a "sensible" move, she really enjoys her new house and garden. My brother Michael has moved to a new job in Yorkshire. From a career point of view it is a very good move; from the perspective of housing and family it has been a bit of a nightmare. His very comfortable modern house in Stafford has been on the market for months. My sister Sheila's daughter, Anne, has been the first of that generation to get married.

On Nicole's side, the news has been less cheerful. Her father had a stroke which has affected his left side. He seems to be making a good recovery however, and has never been a better correspondent.

Enjoying the French House

We spent another month this year at the house in Bordepaille, which is slowly becoming habitable. The lavatory now actually flushes! The house shows some signs of fulfilling its intended role as a place which can be used by family and friends.

Sheila and Ron and (most of) family were there to greet us with Dominic and his friend Alastair. Keith Rowe and Julia Castle came with Bernard and me (Nicole had to come a week later) and Tony, Janet and Sean Byrne were with us most of the time as well as Patrick Childs.

As a frustrated countryman (my family is full of them, slowly leaking away from town life) I would like to live at Bordepaille eventually. It should be possible to combine this with free-lance consultancy for both the Anglophone and Francophone markets. But first I have to make something worthwhile of my job with Crown Agents.

Bordepaille, August 1986 – gathering of family and friends (David back right)

Crown Agents

My job at Crown Agents is interesting and extremely challenging. At times I feel that the main challenge is the Crown Agents management, who are always complaining that we are not profitable enough. Up to now we are just keeping our heads above water in a very competitive business. I would like a few more years to see if we can become really profitable. We are now better staffed than ever before. One advantage (for me) of the present depressed job market is that I can recruit young graduates with relevant degrees for the same salary Crown Agents normally pays for a generalist with A-Levels and a few years of experience. Within this field I have really been able to pick and choose, so that I now have a well-motivated and lively team. We just need rather more paying work.

New Work for Nicole

Nicole now works full-time at Horton mental hospital. It is not the ideal job for her, but it is convenient and she has some pleasant colleagues. After a year's evening classes, she has passed a translators' examination, but now she is taking a break from that and has joined a choir.

On the Move

I have little time for outside activities because of my travels. This year I have been all over East and Central Africa, made several visits to West Africa, including two months in Chad, and visited Thailand and Indonesia. I have also become a committee member of the Tropical Agriculture Association, completing my transition to pseudo-agriculturalist. I'm off to Chad, Congo and Cameroon before Christmas.

Merry Christmas and a Happy New Year, love Nicole and David

Letter to Sheila and Ron   Sutton, 01/01/1987

Christmas

Many thanks for the jigsaw (not yet done but perhaps this evening), and the book on France. It's the right time of year to think about summer and warmer places.

We had a family Christmas, starting with Christmas stockings and ending with pheasants. Both my stocking and Nicole's had compact discs. We've just bought ourselves a new hi-fi, tape and deck etc, plus a compact disc player, which really does sound very good, but it will take a long time to build up a substantial record collection – by which time something cheaper will probably have appeared on the scene.

Visits and Visitors

Last weekend we went to see Uncle Ted and Auntie Kath, along with Brian and his two boys. Ted and Kath are very pleased to have visitors. They look remarkably well.

Last night we had two other families (ex-Kenya) for dinner. They slept around the house and left this morning. Bernard went off to a New Year Party in Oxfordshire, and is not back yet.

Gardening and Rambling

The weather remains very mild, but my garden is more or less at a standstill at the moment. I do a little digging from time to time. There's lots to be done, including turning up several more vegetable beds in the former builder's yard.

Today we went for a long wet walk on the bottom of Box Hill among the old chalk pits, and when we returned I dug out my sweet pea trench for next year – then went to sleep after lunch. I hope to see you soon.

Love, David

March 1987, Surrey, Reception at family wedding

Letter to Sheila and Ron

Family Wedding

Thanks for your letter. We're pleased to hear of Tom's wedding. Croydon is very near to us – about fifteen minutes by car – so although we don't know exactly where the Registry Office is, it can't be far away. Any of you (or all of you if you don't mind sleeping in rows on the floor) is welcome to stay at our house before and after the event. And please don't think we shall be offended if we are not invited. We know there are rather a lot of Jones / Wright relatives, and really Friday is not a particularly easy day for either Nicole or I to attend anything.

A Visit to Wisley

I would not describe the weather here as "really warm", but we have had some bright sunny days that have made me think about things like gardening. Today Nicole and I went to the Royal Horticultural Society gardens at Wisley. I particularly enjoyed the warm houses and the orchid house, but the hillside rock gardens and the heather gardens were also most attractive.

Our garden is slowly taking shape, but there are some major works needed before I am really happy with it, including undoing quite a lot of work done by the last owner.

Mother's Visit

We have told Mummy that we would be happy to collect her from Leicester and transport her back. She is keeping her options open, probably because she doesn't want to give us any trouble, but we would love to have her to stay for a few days, and it really would not be much trouble to fetch her, so do encourage her to stay with us unless you have some other plan. Lots of love, David and Nicole

Letter to mother

French Visitors

This letter will have to be brief, because my study has been lent to the daughter of some friends who are visiting us, and they have just come back from a day out in the Oxford area. The husband is the grandson of Mme Armand who used to let us stay at her flat near Marseilles, and who had been one of M. Fortuné's occasional hosts when he was at boarding school in Marseilles. Mme Armand has been dead for a good few years, and her son who was at school with M. Fortuné is now retired, but the contact with the family still goes on.

A Visit to Chad

I am preparing for my trip to Chad at the end of the week, although I am conscious of being very poorly prepared. I still have to buy computer software which is essential for our work, and I have not yet started to take anti-malarial drugs. I suspect that I have a partial immunity to malaria anyway, having spent so long in dodgy areas, so I can get away with a little carelessness, but I shall start popping pills tomorrow morning, when I get my prescription.

Bernard's Progress

Bernard has gone to York to start 6-9 months of work experience, at the immense salary of £5,000 a year. That's actually pretty good for this sort of assignment, but it's still fairly hard to live on. However, he is a frugal fellow so I expect he will get by all right. He drove up in his little car, still with its old worn-out carburettor, because the backyard garage across the road has suddenly disappeared. I expect they were moonlighting, or filling in while they looked for jobs, but it's bad luck for Bernard, because they were handy, friendly, and fairly cheap.

English Colds!

Nicole and I have had vile colds for the last few days. We have both been shivery and had slight temperatures, and I feel as if I have been punched in the tummy. I am very much better today, but Nicole is still feeling rather sorry for herself, and spent most of the day in bed.

Driving Lesson for Dominic

It was such a pleasant day that I went out for a walk with Dominic, profiting from the occasion to give him a long driving practice both ways. He's much more confident and less nerve-wracking now, and I even feel able to take my eyes off the road from time to time to look at the countryside. We went south, towards Pat and John's, and admired cowslips, primroses, wood anemones, daffodils and the first bluebells.

Au Revoir to the Garden

I have been preparing my garden for two months without me. It is really looking quite healthy, although I feel there should be more flowers. I think the solution for this time of the year is polyanthus and hyacinths, but both can look a bit straggly later on in the year. We took our guests to Hampton Court gardens on Saturday, and admired some very beautiful formal gardens there, but most of the colour was from bulbs, polyanthus and flowering bushes – particularly the magnolias which do very well in this region.

Festival Hall Concert

On Friday we went to an excellent performance of Bach's *St. Matthew Passion* at the Festival Hall. We really enjoyed it much more than the *St. John Passion* which we heard about a month earlier – partly I think because the performance was better, but partly because it is a much grander piece of music. There is an hour's break in the middle of the performance. We bought a light meal at the Festival Hall, but *habitués* had their cool boxes and set up tablecloths in the various foyers where they settled down for picnic lunches with bottles of wine.

Lots of love, David and Nicole

Letter to Mother   Sheraton Hotel, Dhaka, 13/09/1987

Attempting to reach Bhutan

I am sitting in Bagdogra (?) airport somewhere in North East India. This was not on my official itinerary, but we are in the monsoon season and the weather around Paro airport in Bhutan is too bad for us to land. We may have another try in an hour's time, failing which we shall either sleep here, or (God forbid) be taken back to Dacca. Not that I mind Dacca (now Dhaka), but I would like to visit Bhutan, and I would like to finish my trip and go home again. People over-rate this travel business. It's one thing to get to know a place and its people, and appreciate its natural history and artefacts, and a totally different thing to spend half one's time in airports and aeroplanes and the rest in hotels and capital cities.

This morning I rose early, since in theory my plane was at 10am and in theory one has to check in two hours before the flight. I think, however, that it was as hard getting out of Paro this morning as it is getting back in this afternoon, so I spent about six hours waiting for the flight.

Dhaka Town

Dhaka is not a beautiful town, but it is less grim than I had feared. It doesn't compare with Calcutta for people and beggars. Above all it is a city of rickshaws – cycle rickshaws with a little two-person cab at the back, capable at a pinch of carrying a small family or several sacks of grain and their owner, perched on top.

Bangladesh Floods

The flooding this year in Bangladesh is terrible. From the air the country appears to be mostly water, with boats trafficking between groups of houses on islands of higher ground. This is the other end of a very wet monsoon season in Bhutan and Nepal. I wonder if the Ganges is "trainable". It would certainly help Bangladesh if they could "construct" a lot more land by poldering parts of the Bay of Bengal.

Indian Racial Groups

The people up here have strong Asiatic traces. Many look like Ghurkas; and the further one rises into the foothills of the Himalayas, the more oriental they become, although they never look like the Cantonese Chinese that we are used to. The Bangladeshis are quite different – small darkish Indians, but again quite different from the people around Delhi (where colour is a good clue to caste) or Madras, where they are very dark. In Nepal I was introduced to a very genial upper-crust Nepali who when in his cups (quite frequent from my observation) sings an Indian Army song which goes: *"I love a lassie, a big black Madrassi...."* etc. When I met him he was still too sober to remember most of the words.

West Bengal Tea Plantations

The action moves on. I am now at Sinclairs Hotel in Siliguri. I'm surprised you have never heard of Siliguri! If you have a large enough map of India you will find it somewhere near the top of West Bengal, a mere stone's throw from Darjeeling. The tea estates we have passed are not a patch on what I have seen in Kenya, but no doubt we are still in a marginal area. I hope so, otherwise you can forget Indian tea.

Rumour has it that we shall get to Bhutan tomorrow morning, with any luck.

Lots of love from distant parts, David

Christmas letter to all friends   Sutton, December 1987

An Uneventful Year

1987 has gone very fast – probably because we have not had any big projects. We have not bought or sold houses nor have we changed jobs even once between the two of us.

News of the Boys

The main changes have been in the boys' activities. Bernard is still at Harper Adams, but has had a nine-month "sandwich" job with the Humberclyde agricultural finance company in York, which he has (in general) enjoyed. Dominic has finished school and is spending a year with us while he does a foundation course at Epsom School of Art. It is very pleasant to have him at home after so many years in which he was just a holiday visitor. He is working very hard, and doing weekend work as a waiter to supplement his finances. Every two weeks he brings home a rather bewildering project. A recent one involved the creation of a large wire and plaster sculpture which looked most impressive suspended from the garage roof. We were wondering how we could possibly transport it intact to Epsom, when it solved our problem by crashing to the ground and self-destructing. Fortunately a photographic record had been kept.

Difficulties at Crown Agents

My (David's) work has been very difficult this year, and I have often been on the verge of resigning in order to do freelance work. There is a great deal of competition in our field, including some large firms that are also having a very hard time. Fee rates have stayed constant for several years. In this market my unit is very small, yet thanks to Crown Agents, we have overheads that are as high as those of the larger firms. If we sold only our own staff time we would cover our salaries but not our overheads, so we really have to work as a management unit, selling bought-in skills on a margin. This is fine if one has enough contracts. As we approach the end of the year, however, things are looking a bit brighter, despite the fall of the dollar which is wreaking havoc with fees. All the same, I do not see myself doing this for more than another three years.

Consultancy Work

I have done one very interesting consulting assignment myself this year: a return visit to Chad. This time I had only two other people with me. Together we dismembered the accounts of the state cotton company and put them back together as a forecast over several years.

Fine Experiences in Bhutan

I have also made the usual business-getting/ trouble-shooting (more the latter than the former) trips including one to Bhutan, which I have long wanted to visit. I was there for only five days, but it really lived up to its reputation. Fortuitously I went first to Khatmandu in Nepal, which was sordid and touristy by comparison.

All of Bhutan is mountainous. The lowlands are mixed forest of oak, beech and conifers, rising through pure pine forest to the fairly barren upland pastures used for yaks. The capital, Thimpu, is at 9,000 feet. Traditional housing is attractive and solid, of rammed earth walls with a lot of quite decorative timber work. Travelling is not for the faint-hearted. The plane flies in down a winding valley, with pine forests on both sides. The roads are mostly single track and wind along the sides of steep valleys with a precipice on one side, and all the truck drivers have Indian driving habits.

Buddhist Monks

There are many Buddhist religious buildings, from small retreats perched on very rocky ledges to very substantial *"Tsongs"*, similar in style to the Tibetan monasteries. I visited a *"Tsong"* just outside Thimpu which also serves as home to several government ministries, and a working office for the King. A group of monks was having chanting practice assisted by a choirmaster with a whip (for the high notes perhaps).

A New View of Life

Nicole is still working in a mental hospital. This has stopped her from saying that our home is like a mad-house. The first hospital she worked at has been emptied and closed (to become a prison). It was a huge Victorian building of some architectural merit which, at its peak, held 3,000 patients and produced most of its own food. The present one is of similar size within almost equally easy driving distance.

Too Busy to Visit France

We have not seen Bordepaille at all this year, except for Bernard who spent a week there collecting furniture that we had consigned from Guadeloupe to Bordeaux. Our summer holiday – without Bernard for the first time – was in Guadeloupe with Nicole's parents. Her father had a minor stroke recently and is still recovering his mobility. He finds fading eyesight and diminished mobility very frustrating. Nicole's mother is well, but finds the management of a large house increasingly wearing. My (David's) mother is very happy with her move to a bungalow which offers fairly good scope for her gardening skills, and is as busy as ever.

Still Gardening

Gardening seems to be in our blood. I spend a lot of my weekends digging and pottering, and have deep-dug much of the builder's yard part of our garden with a pickaxe. Around this time of year I embarrass my family by wandering the streets with a wheelbarrow and spade, collecting fallen leaves for my compost heap. Most passers-by assume that I am trying to keep the neighbourhood clean. Why disabuse them?
Happy Christmas, Love, Nicole and David.

Letter to Sheila and Ron   Sutton, 01/01/1988

Old Woodworking Tools

I was quite taken aback by the size of your present, and was relieved to discover that it included a refund of my woodworking tool money. It still seems like a present, as I had forgotten that you owed me anything back. Thank you very much for all of it, and for the boys' presents. I have cleaned and smartened up the old brace and bit drill, which really now looks rather smart, with the worm-holes filled and a thin coat of linseed oil and French polish.

Succulent Goose

We had a fairly moderate family Christmas with the boys, and a good walk after lunch to shake down the goose. I really think the best part of a goose is the skin, if it is prepared carefully. We basted ours with honey and soy-sauce, and the skin seemed to disappear faster than the meat.

Last night we saw in the New Year with some friends from Kenya, who also served a goose. It's obviously the in-bird this year, until some wretched breeder manages to find a way of making it taste exactly the same as intensively reared chickens and turkeys.

Getting Away from the Office

I'm off to Malawi next week to do some work, and will be very pleased to get away from the office for a while – back in February.
Lots of love, David and Nicole

Letter from Nicole to Sheila and Ron   Sutton, 27/12/1988

Car Trouble

It is a beautiful day and we would like to go for a walk, but we are car-less. While we were driving to a suitable place for a walk yesterday, the fan belt gave up and because of the Bank Holiday and because the fan belt is an unusual one we have not been able to replace it. It has been very inconvenient, as we missed a good concert at the Barbican last night. We are going out tonight but shall go by train.

Christmas – and a New Life in Washington

Apart from that we had a pleasant Christmas. I invited a colleague of mine who is French and whose husband is from Mauritius to share our Christmas lunch. I ordered a goose at a local butcher's and it was excellent.

Thank you for your present which will be useful as David needs such things as towels for his flat in Washington. David is leaving for Washington tomorrow, travelling with Pan Am.
Have a Happy New Year, Love to you all, Nicole and David

Christmas letter to all friends   Sutton, 12/1988

Farewell Crown Agents…

I am on the move again! I have to admit that it feels good to shake the dust of Crown Agents from my feet. That was not a very successful episode, although I learnt a lot and it enabled me to re-establish some roots in Britain.

In November I joined the World Bank in Washington on contract for a year to work on agricultural structural adjustment in Senegal. I hope I will stay for more than a year; however that depends on how things work out, and whether the Bank can overcome its scruples about adding to the excessive number of Brits already on its payroll.

…and "Transmanche" for Nicole

N.icole has also changed jobs during the year, and is working at Transmanche Link, the consortium which is building the Channel Tunnel. This is five minutes walk from our home in Sutton, so she is staying put for the present, and I shall just have to depend on frequent trips home. In fact after only three weeks away, I am writing this in Sutton, taking advantage of the Thanksgiving long weekend to stop off *en route* for Senegal. I should be back home again for Christmas.

Ministry of Overseas Development

It has been a good year for me in other respects as I have done two interesting project evaluation missions for the Ministry of Overseas Development. The first was in Malawi, where I led a team to look at a long-running fisheries programme, and the second in Mauritius where we evaluated an irrigation project. Both were new subject areas for me, and I greatly enjoyed the research and writing up of the reports. I have really slated the Mauritius project, and I shall be interested to see how (if at all) ODA reacts. I rather expect that my painstakingly-prepared report will disappear with very few traces, which will be a pity as I do not think aid donors should give aid that makes the recipient poorer, even when the recipient government insists that this is what it wants.

Welcome Lodgers

Apart from work, another reason why Nicole is quite happy to stay here at the moment is that she has two lodgers – Bernard and Dominic. Bernard has finished at Harper Adams, and started what looked like an interesting job with a small public relations firm. Unfortunately the firm transformed itself into something quite different, and he found himself selling rather expensive illuminated signs from shop to shop, without even the promised company car. It soon became clear that this was unlikely to be either fun or a sound business proposition, so he is now marking time with temporary clerical work while he looks for something better.

Dominic is at Kingston Polytechnic where he has started a B.A. course in furniture and product design that he is finding both enjoyable and very time-consuming. He did not intend to work from home but digs are hard to find in Kingston, and home is not all that uncomfortable as an alternative.

World Bank

My first weeks in Washington have centred around finding my feet at work, and finding somewhere to live where I do not have to spend much of my time and energy commuting or housekeeping.

The Bank is quite an exciting place – about 3,000 rather high-quality professional staff of all nationalities. Of course there is a strong in-house philosophy which can be self-congratulatory and conformist, which could be uncomfortable at times for a free-thinker like me. However I have an agreeable group of immediate colleagues, and a lot of old friends on the Bank staff. Also, once again, I seem to have been allocated one of the better countries, although it is an economic mess.

A Fine New Flat

I have settled my housing problem by taking a lease on a large, light, two-room flat in a very well-managed condominium about eighteen minutes walk from the Bank. For those who know Washington, I am on the edge of Georgetown near Dupont Circle, overlooking Rock Creek Park. I hope to have a put-you-up sofa soon, although my rooms (leased unfurnished) are presently somewhat austere. Short-stay visitors will be welcome.

Homeless Folk, and a Multi-Polar World

I like Washington, at least on the Georgetown side. I am still surprised at the relatively low standard of living of many people, including the very large numbers of beggars and homeless. I suspect these problems will get worse under the Bush administration, which I believe will face severe economic problems. In my sweeping way, I see this as part of fairly fundamental changes that are taking place in the World order in which the two post-war superpowers will be increasingly preoccupied by internal political and economic disorder, and in which their power will be greatly diminished. If I am right, this will affect us all, and should worry us. The bi-polar world looked dangerous, but turned out to be quite stable. Now that we are congratulating ourselves on democratisation in the Soviet Union and decreasing world tension we should certainly spare some time for the dangers of a multi-polar world.

A Poor Cultural Model

On a lighter, but still serious note, the one thing I really cannot stand in the U.S.A. is the poor quality of television. At least this saves me the expense of buying or renting a set, but I am appalled to think that this is the model our misguided government is intent on copying. The only place I have come across worse TV is the Philippines!

House at Bordepaille

We had a good family holiday again in Bordepaille, which now has a fully functioning bathroom (with hot water), a good temporary kitchen, lots of British standard power points, and electric lights upstairs as well as down. My last, somewhat controversial, step before leaving this year was to buy a really large second-hand window (2.8 metres high) to be installed in our absence in our huge back room. This will give a lot more light, and will take care of a very shaky piece of wall by largely replacing it with window. I hope it works. But our next big job should be even bigger – retiling the roof, putting in Velux windows and replacing the worst of the timbers. I would like to work on this in September 1989 if I can organise it, and would welcome news of volunteers. I am quite happy to pay for the services of able-bodied youth.

Our love and good wishes to all our friends and relatives, Nicole and David

NOTE - Ron and I visited Bordepaille many times. We explored the area, gazing in consternation at homes perched high on (and in) cliffsides (Castelmoron? Would anyone dare to bring up small children in such a home?) We visited castles and fortresses (Duras was a favourite) and unspoilt medieval towns, such as Monpazier, with its arcaded market square. We wandered around Bordepaille, meeting neighbours, admiring lizards and praying mantis, and keeping a wary eye open for snakes in the dry grass. David collected wild vine leaves and demonstrated the baking of seasoned mince wrapped in small leaf parcels. He was usually busy on restoration and Ron was able to lend muscle power.

Christmas letter to all friends   Sutton, 12/1989

A New Role

The Joneses are on the move again. I (David) have been working in Washington for the World Bank for over a year, and my initial one-year contract has been extended to three years – transforming me from "consultant" to "staff". Meanwhile, Nicole has stayed in Sutton, enjoying her job with Transmanche Link (Channel Tunnel) and having a real home after so many years on the move. In the New Year she will join me in Washington.

Senegal, Gambia and Mauritania

I am still working mainly on "agricultural sectorial adjustment" in Senegal – trying to "clean up" a sector which has been immobilised by political compromises, inefficient public sector organisations, and heavy debts. It is hard going because the problems all make political sense as well as economic nonsense, but I think we are making some headway. I am lucky to have two old friends, Bill Duggan and Lynn Ellsworth, in Dakar, and benefit shamelessly from their hospitality. I also work on Gambia, and expect to extend my range to Mauritania – three countries that share common borders and little else (if one excludes mutual hostility). Despite some frustration, it is fun being back in the game as a real actor.

Staunchly European

Although I find Washington a comfortable and pleasant place to live, life there confirms and reinforces my feeling of Europeanness. There is no risk that I will be assimilated. Moreover, this has been the wrong year to be out of Europe. It has been hard to grasp the full significance of what has been happening, but often in discussion before or after business meetings, at the Bank, or at social occasions, the Europeans present tended to form little groups apart to discuss what was going on in our part of the world, with a sense of frustration at not being involved. It has gone much further and much faster than I guessed it would, and apart from the tragedy in China which I bet is temporary (i.e. ten years) most of it has been better than one could have hoped: but it is also still very unstable and quite risky. These are very exciting times.

Bordepaille

This summer again we went to Bordepaille without, for the first time, either of our sons. Of course, we missed them, but they are grown up and still very close to us and we could not ask more than that. We did, however, have a very welcome stream of guests for longer or shorter periods. The house slowly gets more liveable. For me it is a very important possession – a point of reference that I think about a lot when I am travelling.

Bernard and Dominic

As for the boys, Bernard is now a trainee processing and marketing manager working on a series of large farms and our summer holiday fell in a peak period for him. Up to now he has been in East Anglia living rent-free in a caravan, but he has just moved to Leicester for a spell with a large nurseryman. I am a little jealous, as I have always secretly cherished the idea of working with ornamental plants.

I was also a little jealous of Dominic, who went off on a two-month trip to Brazil and Bolivia by local bus and boat. Like any overprotective parents we were a little on edge, and were very relieved when he arrived back without even having been robbed. He is enjoying his B.A. course in product design at Kingston Poly, and has moved into a flat in Kingston with a number of other students.

Silver Wedding

Also on the home front, Nicole and I celebrated our first twenty-five years of marriage in August. How surprising! And how fortunate we have been.
With love and best wishes, Nicole and David

NOTE – I created a picture in pastels, using photographs for accuracy, of the Bordepaille house, with sunflowers in the foreground and romantic pigeonnier tower rising into the blue skies. This was put into an old picture frame and given to David and Nicole as a celebratory gift for their anniversary. It wasn't a masterpiece but it's the thought that counts!

Letter to Sheila and Ron
Sapu Guest House, Gambia
01/04/1990

A Moment of Cynicism!

I hadn't realised this was All Fools' Day. Nobody tried anything on me except for the usual pack of lies which aid agencies encourage their clients to recite to them about the ways in which dismal projects are supposed to correspond to the donor's initial image: regular meetings of extension staff; meetings with contact farmers every fortnight on the same day; time-tables laid down in advance so that on any day we will know where to find the extension agent or the district supervisor. Unfortunately my superiors really think that it all happens, and many of those who are meant to carry out the programmes come to mistake the image for the reality, so that my position as a rather objective observer is not entirely comfortable.

Gambia

I rather enjoy Gambia. It is such a scruffy little country that one really feels in touch with its basic realities – poor people, mud huts, poor sandy soils, a film of dust over everything, terrible roads etc. I was warned by friends to bring my food with me, although in reality I think I could have found all I wanted at the local market at much the same price as the supermarket (so-called) in Banjul, where there is a sparse and odd selection of such things as corned beef, tinned tuna, Tesco baked beans from divided-up packs of four, and so on. I wouldn't be at all surprised if someone actually had gone shopping at Tesco's in England and shipped a consignment back to fill his store here.

Seeking Realities

Today I have been out to interview farmers and extension workers. I think this is a rather unusual activity for a World Bank supervision mission, but I don't know any other way of finding out what is happening. Interviewing farmers is more fun than interviewing extension workers, because the latter keep on trotting out the silly stories and are very nervous that I will trip them up (which I do, gently, because they are not to blame) and report adversely on them (which I do not do). The farmers generally think it is all rather amazing, and seem content to sit for long periods and be asked foolish questions.

A Soggy Frugal Meal

What a nuisance! Suddenly there's water all over the place. I'm eating rather a good meal that I have just cooked myself: local rice (best quality) with a relish of tinned tuna, tomatoes (local), okra (local), beans (Tesco) and one hot pepper (local) to give it pep, accompanied by *eau de source naturelle* (Senegal). Unfortunately the *eau de source* comes in peculiarly fragile bottles. Two out of six emptied themselves *en route* and the one I have just opened has just sprung a leak, so I have transferred the remains to another bottle which also has a hole in it, in this case above the water line. While I was out prospecting for hot peppers I found a ripe pawpaw on the ground outside the fence, so that is cooling down in the refrigerator. Life is tough in Africa!

Widespread Family

Nicole is in Guadeloupe, where her father has just had a prostate operation. Dominic is in Paris, Bernard is in Leicester. I am nowhere. How we are dispersed!
Lots of love, David

Postcard to Sheila and Ron   The Gambia, 19/05/1990

An Enforced Stopover

It was very pleasant spending the weekend at Wickham Skeith – almost a month ago, I suppose. It doesn't seem that long.

I'm in transit from Dakar to Mauritania, but have to stop over here because relations between the two countries are so bad that there are no direct flights. With luck I shall continue tomorrow, although this place is crawling with African Heads of State, which is disruptive. I was most relieved to find that I still had a room at the hotel.
Lots of love, David

Postcard from Dominic to   Basse Terre, Guadeloupe,
Sheila and Ron   31/08/1990

Meeting "Cousins"

Hello – I'm doing the rounds of my Guadeloupean family. It's quite funny, actually – each time I go out I end up meeting someone who is my cousin. My "cousins" ages tend to range from two years old to eighty-five.

Apart from that, I am going for walks in the countryside and visiting sights and museums in an effort to get to know the islands better.
Lots of love, Dominic

Account by Marjorie Jones (our mother) of her holiday with David and Nicole in Washington, U.S.A., November 1990. She was accompanied by her sister Pat and sister-in-law Phyllis.

Unpredictable Weather

Pat, Phyllis and I set off on our travels on the morning of Monday, October 1st. We all carried rather heavy luggage, which included woollen suits, scarves, jumpers and even gloves, as we had been advised to prepare for cold as well as warm weather. These warm clothes proved to be entirely unnecessary, as the weather during our time in the U.S. was wonderful. Every day was warm and sunny, with temperatures up in the eighties, and it was very muggy most of the time, but fortunately there was often a pleasant breeze. We wished that we had packed more light cotton garments.

Queues and Boredom

Pat and Phyllis were driven to Heathrow by Patrick. I had a somewhat worrying start as the taxi I had ordered to take me to the coach station in Leicester arrived half an hour late; I thought I should miss the coach, but arrived just before it left, rather flustered. We all arrived at Heathrow at about the same time, and began a journey which I think can well be described as "Queues, boredom, food and drink!" We had first to join a very long and slow-moving queue to get our luggage weighed and checked in. Here, by a slight misunderstanding of the way the queues were formed, which was slightly untidy, we managed to queue-jump for the first and only time. Usually we were gifted at bringing up the tail end.

The Flight

On the plane, we were packed in like sardines in the economy section – there were 396 of us. We had very little leg-room, and because of the height of the seat backs we were not able to see our fellow travellers, or the TV screen. We were constantly plied with food and drinks, and this helped to pass the long hours of the journey. There were several periods of turbulence, when we had to fasten our seat belts, but it was mostly an easy journey, with very smooth take-off and landing. The lady who sat next to Pat was a secretary at the World Bank, and knew David slightly. She was happy to chat to us. We arrived at Dulles airport, Washington, just before 9pm, and were very pleased to find David and Nicole waiting for us. With their help we collected our luggage and were off quickly for the forty mile journey to their house in Alexandria.

Life in Alexandria

We had a very welcome cup of tea and were glad to get to bed at eleven o'clock. I think we all slept well.

Up Tuesday at about 7.45am. David had left for work, but Nicole had the morning off and took us to the bank in Alexandria to change some of our travellers' cheques into dollars, and buy postcards. We began to get a vague idea of where we were, and liked the look of Alexandria. Back "home" we sat in the tiny garden under the large catalpa tree, and Nicole went off to work. In the afternoon we went into Alexandria again and walked in the sunshine beside the Potomac River. We also went into the historic Christ Church, a few hundred yards from David's home, and were shown the Washington family pew, which was still square (as all the other pews had been originally) so that the family could bring their own heating stove into the church and sit round it during the service. Across the aisle was the family pew where the Lee family had worshipped. We saw Robert Lee's ancient family home, and were surprised to see some large and ugly commercial buildings very close to the lovely riverside.

Washington

Wednesday – another wonderful day, sunny and hot. We visited Washington by Metro, and began to master the system of buying advance tickets from machines and popping them into slots to open the gates for entry to the stations. We learned quite a lot about the city and walked many miles. We passed the White House, which was under repair and was covered in scaffolding and plastic sheets. The queue to go into the house was dreadfully long and very slow moving, so we contented ourselves with a glance at the exterior and passed on. Finally we discovered the Mall, and the Smithsonian Centre, and went into the National Air and Space Museum. Here we had a much needed self-service lunch in the cafeteria, before inspecting planes, rockets, etc. We went inside the body part of a rocket and saw a revolving trash seat (? the loo?) and a shower arrangement as used by astronauts. Most things in this museum were beyond our understanding.

Friendly Americans

People everywhere were most kind and helpful to us, and wanted to chat. As we sat resting on a circle of seats round a fountain, I noticed the fruits from the black walnut tree above us. These are inedible, hard and heavy, and the size and shape of a tennis ball. As we examined one of them an excited man came over to us, gesticulating and banging his hat, and it took us some minutes to realise that he wanted us to move to another seat, away from the tree, in case one of the nuts should hurt our heads!

During the day we saw the Capitol building, the Vietnam Veterans Memorial, the Jefferson Memorial, the Washington Memorial (which is a very tall tower and can be seen from many miles away), the Supreme Court and the Smithsonian Museums – not bad going, and we are beginning to know our way around. More walking then along the Mall, where we found the Metro station which was to become so familiar during our stay. There was no station building – just two escalators, one up and one down, in a cement-lined tunnel in the grass. We were "home" by 4.45pm, utterly exhausted, and I felt it must be bed time! We made a cup of tea and all had an hour on our beds. We were all so tired, but had enjoyed the day.

November 1990 – entertaining relatives in north-eastern U.S.A.

"Pregnant Penguins" at Niagara Falls! Nicole, Marjorie, Phyllis and Pat

The Pentagon

Thursday – We started by finding the Post Office, buying stamps, and posting our cards. Next, to the bank, which refused to accept Pat's Access card, so she did not get any money. Then we caught a bus to the Pentagon, where we had a very interesting tour, led by a pleasant and humorous black soldier. There are 23,000 people working there, half of them civilians. It is the control centre of the Army, Navy, Marines, Air Force and Rescue Services, and is a wonderful building, like a city, with seventeen and a half miles of corridors. It was designed over a weekend and built in sixteen months at the beginning of the Second World War – basically built from silt dredged out of the bottom of the neighbouring Potomac River. We toured corridors lined with photos of all the ex-presidents, pictures of battle scenes, war heroes, state leaders, lovely state flags and so on.

More Museums

We next caught the Metro from the Pentagon station to the Smithsonian stop in the Mall, where we had lunch, then spent the afternoon looking at the exhibits in the Natural Sciences Museum – a wonderful African elephant and a host of birds and other animals large and small, also minerals and jewellery, dinosaurs, the history of U.S.A. Indians, and much more. Home, weary, to cook the evening meal of risotto from what we found in the store cupboards, since we had not been able to find any helpful shops!

Preparing for a Journey

Friday – domestic morning. We rigged up a Heath Robinson clothes line and washed our "smalls", then went to Alexandria to look around, get travellers' cheques changed at the bank, and look hopefully in the shops for summer clothes. I was really looking for a skirt, but bought a colourful jacket instead! Phyllis splashed out on a very much reduced denim jacket. We admired the market square, with its lovely pool and fountains, then went "home" for a late lunch and to pack up ready for this evening's start to a four-day trip with David and Nicole.

A Long Drive

We set off at about 6.30pm when they returned from work, and travelled about one hundred miles to Hagerstown and the Travel Lodge where we had booked for the night. We had two chalets, very quaint "Old English" *décor*, hot water, baths and showers and TV sets. There were mock oak beams across the ceilings, and the oddest painted doors, windows and plants (all paint, nothing more) on the walls. It was roomy and comfortable and we were surprised to find that our terms had been doubly reduced, because we were both pensioners, and foreigners. We visited MacDonalds for supper, which was a bit basic but satisfying, then retired for the night.

The West Virginia Fall

Saturday – We had a lovely day. All three of us woke very early, bathed in disappearing water (the plugs were not very efficient) and went along to Reception with David and Nicole. There we found we could have good hot coffee *ad lib*. We drove off through West Virginia, mile after mile of country roads, past the Appalachian hills and woodlands, and our first sight of the wonderful autumn colour everywhere. We had a short walk and a picnic in the woods at lunchtime, then pressed on to Jamestown, which is in New York State, where we had booked our night's rest. We had three chalets this time and were very comfortable. I greatly appreciated my good bed, as the previous night I had a truckle bed with next to no mattress, on which I managed to cut my leg quite nastily. We found a breakfast spot, not the MacDonalds this time, and were ready for another day.

Niagara, and Pregnant Penguins!

Sunday – another perfect day. We drove again through banks of most wonderful colour, and also passed many vineyards in this district. We stopped at an extremely attractive roadside market and bought grapes (which had a very odd smell, described by David as "foxy"), apples, and jars of maple syrup to take home as presents.

We set off again in the direction of Niagara Falls, through the frontier town of Buffalo. The colour everywhere is quite breathtaking. The TV weather report this morning said that this week is the peak period of the most brilliant colours in living memory. How lucky we are. We crossed the Peace Bridge into Canada, had our passports stamped, and drove to Niagara and the Falls. They are quite wonderful! We queued for a trip right into the mist under the Falls in the *"Maid of the Mist"*. We all had to wear heavy, hooded blue waterproofs, and with our belongings stowed in front of us under the macs we made a truly comical sight: men and women just like a crowd of pregnant penguins! It was a most enjoyable trip.

Comfort and Do-nuts!

"Home" by a wonderful scenic route to the "Ecocentre Motel". Very comfortable, I had a large double room with all mod-cons to myself. We went out to an excellent supper of soup, salad, half a barbecued chicken, and tea, and so to bath and bed at 10.30pm. We are meeting a wonderful mixture of nationalities everywhere, and have such friendly greetings wherever we go.

Monday – a good start, with coffee and a lovely mixture of warm so-called "do-nuts" on the house – four varieties of these, some chocolate coated, and all delicious. We spent the morning at the Corning Glass Centre Museum, which was a fascinating place. Nicole bought twelve good wine glasses. We all enjoyed the visit. After this we reached the Pennsylvanian Grand Canyon, by a lovely road with tree-covered hills on both sides, and the wonderful autumn colours everywhere. We collected food (called hot roast beef, but it was actually the usual enormous sandwiches with beef and mushrooms and lots more as the filling) from a country store in the woods, and carried it to a quaint wooded spot for a picnic.

Amish Country

Drove through Nippernose valley by the Susquehanna river towards our night stop, the "Dutch Maid" at Ephrata, Lancaster City. During our afternoon drive we came to some really fertile and well kept farming country, quite unlike what we had been through before, and we saw a young Amish lad working a field with implements drawn by two small carthorses.

Mennonites

Went out to a very excellent evening meal of fish, with self-serve salad and ice creams to finish. There was a Mennonite family there enjoying a birthday party, the children helping themselves very happily to all the good things.

Tuesday – a very comfortable night but we were surprised in this Mennonite establishment to find an envelope for "tips" in the room. Last night at their hotel there had been a notice to say that tips would be appreciated. Obviously the Mennonites are not averse to making good money.

No provisions or coffee provided today, so we breakfasted at a nearby restaurant.

Amish Experience

We then spent the morning among the Amish folk – most interesting. They had an auction sale of the contents of a large house; a large number of them were gathered in a tent for the sale. About forty of their one-horse carts were garaged outside, and there were mules and horses in a nearby field.

We went into a craft centre and saw wonderfully pretty quilts and oddments. The lady in charge said that each quilt was made in about two and a half months, usually by a mother and daughter working together. The boys leave school early to work on the farms with the men, and the girls are taught to cook and sew and keep house. All the men wear dark old-fashioned suits (with no buttons as these are considered to be showy) and either black felt hats or straw hats. The women and girls wear long black or dark dresses and aprons, black shoes and stockings and white or black bonnets, covering hair all pulled back and in a bun. The little girls wear the same – very quaint and plain, but they all looked content and the women had lovely skins. The men are not allowed to have moustaches, as they are thought to have a military connection, and these people are very convinced pacifists. It was a most interesting time.

Wild Life in the Woods

We crossed the state line into Maryland, and bought a picnic meal which we ate in a wood. Here we saw a little jumping shrew enjoying life among the wet leaves, and we also found a lovely little box-turtle which came out of its shell and let us examine it. This was at Camp Wome-to!

"Home" then via Baltimore on Chesapeak Bay – we crossed the Francis Scot Kay Bridge, a toll bridge one and a half miles long. We then went to Annapolis over River Severn, saw the

American Naval College there, and walked for half an hour round the quay.

We drove home along country roads, and saw tobacco hanging to dry in sheds. Home in the early evening after a really wonderful trip of 1,040 miles, and beauty all the way.

Relaxed Sightseeing and Shopping

Wednesday – Nicole had a day off work and the four of us went to a vast supermarket and did a lot of shopping, then we looked at the art and pottery workshops in the old torpedo factory. We lunched on drinks and sandwiches by the fountain in the town hall square, and then Nicole drove us to see "Mount Vernon", George Washington's old family home, an old farmhouse in a lovely position beside the Potomac River. It was very hot, with a thunderstorm in the evening.

Thursday – We took the Metro to Washington and visited the museum gift shops to buy trays etc. for presents. Pat collected some special printing ink to take back to her local museum, and we all went up in the lift to the top of the Washington Monument. We lunched again in the American History Museum. Went home fairly early, and had a delightful visitor, Cindy, to dinner – a post-graduate student working for her finals with David.

More Washington Sights

Friday – We took the Metro to Washington, visited Chinatown en route, and admired a very colourful "Peace Bridge". Had lunch with Nicole in Phillips Collection Gallery. Here we had proper china plates for a change, but an odd lunch of enormous portions of brie or paté and the most horrible little slices of dry stale French bread. We did not complain! We bought a pretty necklace as a thank you to Nicole, looked around the gallery, and enjoyed especially a lovely picture by Renoir.

We bought tickets for blue Tourmobile buses and saw the tower we climbed yesterday beautifully reflected in water. We then visited the Arlington Cemetery and saw thousands of war graves, the changing of the guard, and the John Kennedy grave with a perpetual fire burning. Home late and very weary to enjoy a good meal before bed.

Crabs and Cathedrals

Saturday – Clothes shopping first at "Second Choice" across the road. Off next to the fishmarket with David. This was a lively sight! We bought no end of fish including half a bushel of live crabs – dozens of them. Next we visited the Cathedral, which is only recently finished but is modelled on the really old cathedrals. I thought it looked rather like a copy of Canterbury Cathedral. There are lots of good stained-glass windows, and even gargoyles on the exterior. Off again for quite a long drive to Columbus Street, after we had replaced the wandering crabs in their bag with their friends. We have in the boot crabs, shrimps, clams, squid and scallops, and it was pretty niffy. At home David started at once to cook the crabs. I tried to help but the first one I picked up got firmly and painfully attached to me by one claw, and had to be prised off. Retired hurt! I think we shall be eating crabs for the rest of our stay (twelve dollars for two dozen crabs, or fifteen dollars for our vast, shaken-down half bushel, about fifty!) – we await the first meal.

Friends from Oxford

Went out to a very elegant evening dinner with Nicole's old friends from Oxford, Ruth and Andy Johnson. A very smart house, warm welcome and lovely food. He is an army major, but seems to work at the Embassy, looking after British servicemen.

Church, and a Friend from Tanzania

Sunday – Nicole went to the Roman Catholic Church and we three went to Christ Church just down the road, the one with the Washington family pew. A very large congregation and a pleasant service. The sermon largely about tithing for church work. In the afternoon we had a longish drive for a tea-time visit to Pu Chin Waide, another old friend from Tanzania whose husband is an economist. An interesting house by a lake, with a pottery workshop and a mixed bag of friends and relatives. We had a most excellent chocolate-covered carrot cake – must try to make one.

Now we are to sup on David's fish soup, containing the large variety of fish we bought at the fish market yesterday. Another day of sunshine and hot weather.

Gardens, and Bizarre Art

Monday – perfect weather again. I started with Pat at the Botanical Gardens in Washington, where there were large, lovely and scented orchids among many other interesting growing things. I stayed there while Pat made a tiring and rather frustrating visit to the Capitol. She climbed many steps in the hot sunshine, but was not allowed into the centre as she had no passport with her. We then went to the Museum of American Modern Art and Sculpture, which we found puzzling and extraordinary. Then to a sit-down lunch in the Palm Court at the Space and Science Museum (we are eating our spare American cash)! Here we had vast plates of food, and ate enormous sundaes, far too big but it was fun. Phyllis meanwhile had been shopping and joined us for a late lunch. After lunch we returned to the Modern Art Museum and saw a video about the exhibits, hoping to improve our appreciation, but it did no good – the sculptures still mostly looked quite ghastly. A few Henry Moore sculptures we did enjoy. We then went home by Metro, tired and happy.

A Pleasant Last Day

Tuesday – our last day. We spent the whole day very happily in Alexandria. Did a little shopping, wandered down to the Potomac for a last look, and investigated busy little shops in tiny old side streets. We had a very successful lunch in a tiny sea-food restaurant – a whole lobster each with salad and vegetables, rolls and butter, good coffee, and such friendly service. Went home fairly early, to pumpkin soup and toast, and finished packing. At 6pm we set off with David and Nicole for Dulles Airport. We passed easily through the luggage check etc. and were off at about 8.30 for our six-hour night flight. All went well, and the customs officers at Heathrow did not even glance at us. Patrick met us, and saw me to my coach before taking the others on to Surbiton. I had an easy ride home, but felt very sleepy. So ended a really wonderful holiday.

General Comments

We found the American people very welcoming and kind and anxious to get to know us. The streets are much cleaner than ours. Many of the people are very overweight. The food is very odd. Sandwiches are not like the ones we know, but consist of a small loaf, cut across, and filled with about one-inch depth of meat or fish and salad greens. No butter, but usually a slice of cheese of the Kraft type under the meat. These we found very difficult to eat in a mannerly way!

There was an extraordinary variety of religious sects. I made a list of twenty different names, but there were many more.

The houses, apart from the cities we saw, were all of Colonial type slatted wood, painted in light colours. Most had "decks", a kind of un-roofed verandah, where the people sit and have barbecue meals, in preference to using the garden as we do.

Crops, Plants, and Pumpkins

Gardens are generally just grass and bushes – very few flowers. In general, where we were the fields are small and the soil not very fertile. The most usual crops are maize, sorghum and soya beans, and in the valley bottoms lots and lots of pumpkins. We saw pumpkins everywhere – growing in the fields, arranged in piles or rows or patterns, for sale, decorating windows, on house doorsteps. It was a bumper year for them. There were vineyards in some places, and tobacco.

The farms owned by the Amish people were quite different. They seem to own very good ground, to farm it very well, and to grow most things. I imagine that all their mules and horses are a great help, and they do believe in land and hard work.

The most plentiful wild flowers in October were michaelmas daisies – large deep mauve ones and tiny white ones everywhere. There were also patches of cosmos. Poison ivy was plentiful too, some of it a lovely crimson colour, but apparently very undesirable and able to kill off trees and other growth. We also found witch hazel in flower in the woods.

I am very glad our mother spent this holiday with David. She loved his company and usually saw him only for brief visits, en route to somewhere else. David knew she missed him badly and I am sure this motivated his faithful, regular correspondence with her over the years.

Christmas Letter to all Friends

431 N. Columbus Street,
Alexandria, USA

10/11/1990

Into the Computer Age

The time for our annual letter has come round again. And at last we are automated. I have been talking about buying a home computer for about the last four years, and in the meantime they have got cheaper and better so for once my indecision paid off.

At Home in Alexandria

We are a lot more settled than we were a year ago, although my view that this would never really feel like home for us is unchanged. Nicole has been here almost a year, and we have rented a small 120 year old house in Alexandria – not in the most chic part of town, although I think that would be rather like going back to Woodstock, with tourists all over the place in summer. Alexandria, for those who do not know it, is across the river from Washington, and was a port before Washington was established. It is one of the oldest cities in the U.S. Last week our road was resurfaced, which involved scraping the top off with some huge machine, and there underneath was the original road surface of large round water-smoothed stones. I think we chose well. We are out of the violent city of Washington, without being miles out in the leafy 'burbs. The leafy 'burbs are attractive, but impersonal, and generally involve driving miles through rush-hour traffic every day, and accommodating oneself to car pools. We have a reasonable community life around us, and an easy Metro ride in to work. We happen to have landed in one of a few fairly tranquil racially-mixed city areas in this part of the world. In some ways this is because we are in the mid-point area. "Old town" Alexandria is almost exclusively white, and a couple of blocks from us one is in an almost exclusively black area.

On-Going African Work

I (David) am still working on Senegalese agriculture, with excursions into Gambia and Mauritania. This is an interesting but frustrating region. I enjoy being there, but I wish we were more often at common purposes with our opposite numbers. They are very cultured and charming, but they basically want us to shell out "adjustment" money so that they can go on doing exactly what they did before. Since the purpose of adjustment lending is to help them to stop doing what they did before – in terms of public policies – so that they do not need adjustment loans any more, this attitude on their part is inconvenient.

Working with Other Donors

I also continue to try and maintain agreement with an ever-growing number of other donors, who also have rather different views of the problems from our own: France (two agencies), EEC, USAID and German (GTZ). We fortunately fended off the Japanese. Happily, I get on well on a personal level with the people responsible in the other agencies, even though we fight officially. In fact our meetings in Brussels, Paris, Dakar and Washington have the sense of a sort of class reunion. We must, however, conclude a loan in the not too distant future, or our seriousness will be seriously called into question.

Nicole as Linguist

Nicole has found a job with a medical consultancy firm based in Washington that works in Francophone areas – West Africa as well as Haiti. She has had the new experience of having to use Creole in her job, telephoning Haiti and having to pass on messages to domestic servants who speak no French. Other than that, she is learning the vicissitudes of consultancy: that you spend a lot of time not succeeding in getting jobs. In fact, she is not finding the pace overwhelmingly demanding.

Bernard and Dominic

Bernard is in Boston, England, working with a grain broker for the time being. His training comes to an end in a few months, and he has decided that he enjoys trading, but I am not sure that he is coming on to the job market at the best possible time. He visited here with his girl friend Stella in early summer, but unfortunately I didn't see him, as I was in Africa.

Dominic is in his final year of his 3-D design B.A. at Kingston Polytechnic, and is enjoying it very much. He spent about four months on an EEC-funded exchange at the *Ecole National de la Creation Industrielle* in Paris, which was clearly important in making him think about what he was doing in a different way, although he is still a very anglo-saxon pragmatist (although he may not approve of my saying that). Whatever the disadvantages of our way of life for our sons, it has certainly left them more cosmopolitan and adaptable than the average. Not perhaps more than I was at their age, but I had to work at it, whereas for them it comes fairly naturally.

Bordepaille

We went to Bordepaille again this summer and did more work. Bernard couldn't come, but we were very pleased to see Dominic, in between other trips. This summer he managed to fit in France – but that's home – Italy, the U.S.A. and Guadeloupe. We have had the roof refurbished and insulated, so it is now thoroughly waterproof and much cleaner. It was just as well we had the insulation, as this summer in southern France was exceptionally hot, and there were days when we really did not want to venture outside except morning or evening. We have decided to spend a little serious money converting one lot of our out-buildings into a *"gîte"* and have entrusted an architect with the task (and heard nothing more so far, but I telephoned him the other day, and he promised me he is about to start).

Celebration in the Ariege

One fun side-trip this summer was a visit to Jean-Marc and Anne Segers, my Belgian friends from my Chad consultancy, who have bought a big old farmhouse in the Ariege, and gave a great party to celebrate the engagement of their son Yves. It was good to see them again, not too far from Bordepaille.

Three Enterprising Ladies

The big feature of this autumn was a visit by my mother, her sister Pat, and their sister-in-law Phyllis. They spent two weeks here, and were very enterprising, seeing lots of things that Nicole and I have not yet found time to see, and chatting to all sorts of people that they met in the Metro or on park benches. I was afraid I was going to have to go away to my donor club during their visit, but that was postponed, and we really enjoyed having them. Come again! We took a very memorable long weekend off with them to see the fall colours, driving up to Niagara Falls, over to the Canadian side (best view), a boat ride to the foot of the Falls, and a really beautiful drive back through Eastern Pennsylvania, ending up in the Amish country. By chance, we found an estate auction at an Amish house. We didn't buy anything, but it was very interesting, real and unreal. They are clearly practical and business-like people in their strange way.

World Politics

What I said in the last two letters about the dangers of the ending of the bi-polar world seems as true today. I am dismayed by the disorderly disintegration of the Soviet Union, afraid that the process will unleash a lot of nasty little-minded nationalisms (anti-Semitic, anti-Islamic, anti-Christian), and possibly a nasty big reaction from the old communist forces, including the army. I also fear that we are heading for a war in the Middle East, that will be no clear surgical operation, and may have results that are far from President Bush's mind. I do not approve of Hussein at all, and I have long felt that if the big powers wanted to make responsible use of their power, they should do it to prevent nuclear proliferation and the spread of chemical and biological weapons. However, they did not do this, and they are still not doing it. Instead they are fumbling into a war, without knowing what they expect out of it. I wish us all peace in 1991, but I am not optimistic about the chances.

Nicole and David

Letter to Sheila and Ron

Alexandria, USA
31/12/1990

A Touch of Pride!

Happy New Year, and thank you for the tea towel and oven gloves. They are certain of grateful use. I also enjoyed your Christmas letter, with its interesting references to your brother in America. I'm ashamed to admit that I always like reading about myself.

Seasonable Snow

We have had a pleasant quiet Christmas, very happy to have Dominic with us for ten days. The weather has been very variable: a bright clear Christmas day, rather like the best of October or March, followed two days later by a couple of inches of snow, which thawed quickly leaving only the odd pile of mucky slush where the snow ploughs left their loads, and again, bright mild weather. I'm afraid we have failed to take advantage of it today, as we got up late, and then went shopping to take advantage of the New Year sales.

Bernard and Stella went to the Cotswolds together for Christmas. They seem to have enjoyed themselves, and do not say anything about snow drifts, so I suppose that the snow has either disappeared, or they have come to regard it as normal.

At Work on Boxing Day

I was at work from the 26th – admittedly not doing very much, but someone had to mind the shop, and I am happy to save my leave for the summer. It's quite pleasant being in the Bank at these semi-holiday times, when those who do come in feel tremendously virtuous, and have time to chat a bit between such undemanding jobs as clearing the back-log of their in-trays.

Old Friends

On Saturday we went to Wilmington, Delaware, 140 miles north of here, to spend a day and a night with Penny and Bob Sullivan. Penny's an old friend of ours from Woodstock – American – and Bob works at Du Pont chemicals, which is based in Delaware. It's an easy drive up on highways which start very close to our house and end very close to theirs.

Back on the Treadmill

Real life starts again in 24 hours. Dominic flies home tomorrow night, and will probably bring this letter with him. We end our New Year break on Wednesday. I expect to be back in Senegal in about three weeks, but have not yet fixed a date. I am having a hard time with the policy project that I am preparing there, and may have to put it on ice, but not before we have had another try.

Bordepaille

The house in Bordepaille seems particularly far away at this time of year, and it is hard to get used to the idea that we ought to start planning for the summer. Our architect has so far not produced any plans for the conversion of the *pigeonnier* and barns behind the house, and I am getting a bit fed up with him. So far I have been very polite, and have given him only one telephone and one written reminder. I shall soon start being very much more pressing.

Suffolk Swimming Pool

Your swimming pool plans sound fun, but is Ron really digging a hole by hand? That sounds like unnecessarily hard work. A JCB – even a small tractor-mounted one – digs so much faster, and without putting the same strain on the back, and they are not hard to hire (or even borrow) for modest jobs. I think it's better to save human energies for the things which really are expensive if other people have to do them, like building the walls around the pool, and tiling or finishing them. The other thing that sometimes comes as a surprise is the discovery that having a pool is quite hard work, as daily attention is needed. Still, it is very pleasant to have a pool in hot weather. Friends of ours, whom we visited last summer in the foothills of the Pyrenees, had given the pool priority over fixing the house, and the investment was much appreciated.

Lots of love, David and Nicole

Letter to all friends   Alexandria, USA

02/12/1991

Moving to Senegal

Last year we were feeling more settled. This year we are preparing to leave for a three-year posting in Dakar. I decided I either had to give Senegal up as a bad job, or prepare for a long haul, and I opted for the long haul. It's not a good career move, but I might achieve something, and I'm not very interested in trying to climb up inside the Bank (the jobs seem to get worse as one rises). It is also a way for me to revert to being a general economist – which would create new opportunities – rather than an odd sort of agriculturalist (although agriculture remains dear to my heart). We are not sure when we are going, which is unsettling. Our lease here expires at the end of January.

Senegalese Fantasy World

I'm not sure why working with Senegal is so difficult. I think it is the Francophone equivalent of Ghana – a middle-income African country, which thought it could remain an extension of left-wing Europe, and concentrate on redistributing rather than generating wealth. Like Ghana, it has now ceased to be middle-income, but unlike Ghana, it has not yet woken up to the fact. The French were so proud of their cultural success (Dakar and St. Louis were part of France before Nice or Strasbourg) that they have gone on paying for it. Worse, they have charmed us, USAID and the EEC into doing the same. The result is that the Government lives in a fantasy world where someone else always pays the bill at the end of the month (quite literally). Until this changes, I think there will be little willingness to put the house in order. There are, however, signs that it is changing.

Pros and Cons of New Location

Despite the depressing economy, Nicole and I look forward to living in a Franco-phoney atmosphere for a while. Dakar is not only very French; it is also quite close to France. The downside is increased distance from Guadeloupe. This is a real loss, as Nicole's father died in the spring, and from Washington she can fairly easily visit her mother – although surprisingly there are now no direct flights, and she has to go via Puerto Rico.

News of the Family

We are all in good shape. Bernard has joined a big flower wholesaler based in Bedford, and manages contracts with supermarkets. He has just become engaged to his Stella Brown. They are too busy taking courses and examinations this year to get married, but the date has been set – in 1993. Dominic finished his degree in industrial design at Kingston Polytechnic and is now doing a degree in architecture at Central London Polytechnic. He and his friends couldn't find acceptable affordable lodgings in central London, so they have taken over our house in Sutton, and commute.

World Travel

We still do a lot of travelling. I travel mainly to Senegal, and manage to return via Leicester several times a year to see my mother. My frequent-flyer bonus miles come in very handy, and have taken Nicole to Guadeloupe and to the U.K. for family visits. In September we went to San Francisco for a long weekend with Suyin Yu, whom we know from Kenya, and her husband Jim – just before the big Oaklands fire. We really enjoyed this taste of the West Coast. California has a very different "feel" from the East Coast; more freewheeling somehow, and a lot more Asian. I expect it will recover as quickly from the fire as from the earthquake. When we got lost on the freeways, people explained that they were even more confusing than usual, because whole sections had been destroyed in the earthquake. That, however, was the only visible reminder of the earthquake.

Napa Valley Wines versus Bordeaux Wines

The differences between wine-growing in the Napa Valley and in Bordeaux were striking. In California almost all grapes are still picked by hand, using cheap Latino labour, whereas in Bordeaux they are all mechanically harvested, and growers have forgotten how to organise labour gangs. Also, the French control their industry more. In the Napa Valley, for instance, all vineyards have irrigation, which is forbidden in France. It doesn't stop the Californians from making good wine. I suspect it is really easier to produce good wine with a dry climate, which reduces disease, and some supplemental irrigation to get the right degree of development in the grape, than to rely on highly variable rainfall. The Valley was full of wine-tasting tourists (the U.S.A. is much laxer on alcohol and driving than the U.K. or France) but in the hills the roads were deserted. The landscape reminded me of Southern Africa. If we were permanent U.S. residents (perish the thought!) I reckon we would aim for that part of the world.

Bordepaille

We visited France again this summer, and worked on the house at Bordepaille. Dominic arrived before us, and spent a month stripping old plaster from walls. Nicole's mother joined us there for the first time, and put up well with our rustic existence. It's much less rustic than it was, but I have decided that it is time for a dramatic improvement in home comforts, and before next year we should have two professionally finished upstairs bedrooms, a new oak staircase, and banisters along the balcony. I hope my carpenter really understands that my vision is the seventeenth century, not twentieth-century off-the-shelf joinery. We are also converting the pigeon-tower and adjacent buildings into a *"gîte rurale"*, which is exciting.

Indoor Waterfalls

Our most dramatic building activity this year was to hire bulldozers and JCBs to move 500 cubic metres of earth away from the house to improve drainage and give the new *gîte* a view and a terrace. The work took on a new urgency when we had a downpour, and large amounts of water poured in through the walls of the house. We had always wondered about the damp patches! The east side of the house looks dramatically different, but bed-rock turns out to be at exactly the same level as our floors. I think I have put an end to indoor waterfalls, but I am still going to have to slice through some rock with a pneumatic drill before I am really satisfied about the drainage.

A Disastrous Frost

This year's wine harvest in our area was truly dreadful. I happened to telephone a builder in April about some work, and he commented that everything was white with frost. It took a few days for people to realise how bad the damage was. All new growth on the vines was killed. They recovered slowly, and by September there were some grapes but they were at vastly different stages of development. It was unusually humid, so there was a lot of disease; finally it rained heavily at harvest time, splitting and rotting the fruit. As a rule of thumb, I suggest avoiding 1991 Bordeaux.

A Dangerous World

Over the last year, the world is not a better or safer place. I have just flipped back to what I said last year about the dangers of ending the bi-polar world; sadly the situation is little changed. The Iraq question is not settled. I believe the U.S. held back from eliminating Saddam Hussein for fear of encouraging Iranian expansion. This was both a moral and a tactical mistake. The signs are that the Iranian revolution, nasty as it was, has run out of steam anyway. The U.S. is showing more concern about nuclear proliferation, but has no idea what to do about it. The Soviet Union is still disintegrating, and the East European situation is far from having been stabilised.

Morally Bankrupt

I am appalled by Yugoslavia. A friend who works on the ex-communist countries observed recently that their real problem was not that they were bankrupt, but that they were morally bankrupt; a whole generation thought that vindictiveness, theft and lies were the normal way of conducting public affairs. This seems to sum up Yugoslavia. I honestly think that the EEC, or NATO, or both should intervene. We may not be able to stop Serbs and Croats from killing each other on the ground, but I think we could stop the Federal navy from shelling Dubrovnik, control Yugoslav airspace, and even largely prevent the use of tanks and heavy artillery. Why? For humanitarian reasons, and because we should not accept the re-drawing of boundaries by force in Europe. We probably don't have these options in the U.S.S.R. but we should be willing to pay a very heavy financial price to try and avoid economic breakdown there.

The Way Forward for Europe

I am unimpressed by British small-mindedness on Europe. We do have some values that are worth defending, and encouraging other countries to adopt, and a federal EEC is still the best place to do it. This has very little to do with silly regulations, like outlawing round cheeses, but does involve common legal principles, democratic structures and defence cooperation. Much obviously should go on being managed nationally. Inevitably, if the EEC means anything at all, national parliaments have to lose some powers, and they should do so to accountable bodies, not to an independent EEC bureaucracy. The British parliament has, in any case, been unable to handle the whole workload of government for years, and has been looking for solutions, so it is hard to see what all the fuss is about.

Again, we wish you peace in 1992. Please visit us, wherever we are. We are always happy to see friends and relatives.

Nicole and David

Letter to Sheila and Ron

Banque Mondiale, Dakar,
Senegal, 07/03/1992

Practical Gifts

Thank you very much for the tea and teacloth. It was an unexpected pleasure to find gifts in Christmas paper waiting for me in Leicester. Actually, the tea was rather an inspired idea, either for Senegal or the U.S.A., as it is quite hard to get the sort of tea we are used to in either of those places, and my own taste runs these days to the East African teas, which have much more flavour than the Indian ones (some people unkindly say that they are "coarse", but this coarseness gets them a better price at the London auctions than all except the very best Indian teas, which are pale and flavourless rather than "refined"). Did you conspire with Margaret to make this a tea Christmas? Our presents from her, also waiting for us in Leicester, were a teapot stand and a net cover with shells around the edges, to stop the flies from sharing our food. The cover will certainly come in useful in fly-ridden Senegal. Actually, because of the dry climate Dakar is less bothered by flies than some other places I have been, but they still have an unpleasant tendency to drown themselves in open jugs of milk, or to participate in the feast when there is any food uncovered on the table.

Waiting Around in Senegal

As you can see, I am now in Senegal. I travelled easily, with a relaxing 48-hour break in Leicester along with Dominic, who had come to meet me at Heathrow. I arrived in good form only to have to wait about an hour for my suitcase to materialise; then my promised World Bank car and driver failed to materialise. Someone I met on the flight had proposed to wait for me outside with his car, in case of such an event, but had also given up by the time I got out.

A Hair-Raising Ride

Fortunately I always keep enough local currency with me for such emergencies, and in my softened-up state I allowed myself to be shepherded by taxi touts to what must be absolutely the worst-looking taxi that I have ever allowed myself to be driven in. Most of the interior fabric and all the door handles had disappeared, and the doors kept on flying open, but to my surprise we made it into town without even a minor breakdown, and without having to put the brakes to any sort of serious test, which I suspect was just as well.

The taxis here are a very mixed bunch – mostly second hand cars imported from Europe, and patched up *ad infinitum* as they disintegrate. The owners employ a series of drivers on a revenue-sharing basis in order to keep them on the road as much as possible. The night watches, however, scrape the bottom of the barrel in terms of both vehicles and drivers, because police supervision (minimal at the best of times) is about zero then. Despite this, I usually find that the drivers themselves are quite pleasant and correct, but it is somewhat disconcerting occasionally to find that one has a driver who is unfamiliar with his car, and with the physical layout of Dakar, and with the French language.

A New Home.....

I am staying with my friends Bill and Lynn for the time being, as our house is not quite ready for us to move in, and I have very little interest in managing a household before Nicole gets here. Also, we will have to hire a maid (maids here, not male house servants), and Nicole would certainly like to have her say in that. I went round to look at the house yesterday, and it was in pretty good condition, except that there is a water heater to install in the kitchen. It is rather sparsely furnished, and looks vast and bare without the rubbish and bits and pieces that come with occupation. We have very little of our own furniture coming, but we will have our handsome bed from Guadeloupe, which is just as well, as at present there is a huge bed with a very grubby mattress that is several sizes too small for it. The local Bank administrator is a friend of mine, and is usually pretty obliging about such things. I have started work in a leisurely sort of way, which cannot last long, but I felt that I was entitled to reflect a little on what needed to be done.

...and a New Garden

The weather here now is cool and fine – very pleasant. I slept with my windows open last night, and awoke to a good chorus of birdsong. Which reminds me; outside the front of our new house there is a dried up platycerium (a sort of epiphytic fern) fixed to the trunk of a palm tree at about waist height. I have told the guard to water it, and it appears to be returning to life. As I was peering at it yesterday, a tiny red humming bird flew out of what looked like a mouse hole, and inside was a nestful of babies, all huddled up together in a mass of grey fluff with shiny black dots for eyes.

Holidays and Family

Are you planning to come to Bordepaille this year? It would be very nice if you could. We intend to be there for the second half of August, first half of September. We are also expecting Mme Fortuné, who enjoyed her stay last year so much that she wants to come again, and Bernard and Stella will probably come for our last two weeks. I am trying to persuade Mummy to come too, but I think a condition of her coming will be that she flies, probably with Bernard and Stella, as she does not like the idea of a long car journey. We are not yet sure of

Dominic's intentions. He would really like to go travelling somewhere, but has not found the time to work to earn the necessary money. Dominic telephoned me last week, and Nicole telephoned me last night, so I am not feeling out of contact with the family.
Lots of love, David

Letter to Sheila and Ron   Dakar, 20/06/1992

Power Cuts

I was just starting to write this letter with my own fair hand, because we have had a power cut all day, when the power came back on. How nice! We shall not, after all, have a freezer full of thawed and spoiled fish and meat.

Bordepaille

What are your intentions this summer? You had spoken of coming to Bordepaille, and we would be very pleased to see you. We shall be there 22nd August to 20th September. You are, of course, also welcome to use the house when we are not there, but my old friend Chris Woods (he of the butterfly eyebrows, former Young Liberal and now an Irish historian in Dublin) will be there for about two weeks from 14th July, with his family. If you do decide to come when we are not there, I suggest you telephone Mme Fabienne Grillon because she has the keys.

If you come when we are there, you will need to bring camping gear, or at least sleeping bags, as our sleeping space will all be taken up from the arrival of Bernard, Stella, Mummy and Auntie Pat on 2nd September.

A Typical Weekend

I have had a typical weekend – hot, not much going on, but a lot of shouting and talking from the street, as we live next to a politician who has a constant stream of visitors. We got up late, and Nicole went to church while I did some reading and pottered in the garden, and did the washing up because Awa the maid has Sunday off. Then I had a caller named Yousson, who works at a nearby petrol station, and is helping me sell my predecessor's old Mercedes in the expectation of a commission on the sale, and we drove around back-street car mechanics who passed us on eventually to a Marabout – a religious leader who can probably get away without paying too much tax.

Outside my window, my guard is dozing in his chair listening to his radio.
Lots of love, David and Nicole

Letter to Sheila and Ron   Dakar, 22/07/1992
from Nicole

A Welcome in Bordepaille

We shall be very pleased to have you to welcome us in Bordepaille and after having spent the night in the airplane it will be nice to have a meal ready for us when we arrive. I had asked Mme Crivellaro to do some shopping for me but if you are there let her know that you will do it. Here is our itinerary –
August 21: leave Dakar 22.10 hours   August 22: arrive Bordeaux 5am

Dominic might be already there when you arrive, or will arrive shortly after you. He is spending five weeks in Ecuador learning Spanish. He is meant to be back around 18th August and is intending to come down to Bordepaille for a few days. We have not had a letter from him yet but he has sent a fax to Bernard to let us know that he has arrived safely and has enrolled at a school.

Dominic has mentioned to me that some of his friends might stay at the house for a few days in August. At the moment David's friend Christopher Woods and his family are staying there.

Scorching Heat in Senegal

It is already very hot here but I am told that it will be hotter in October. Fortunately there are air-conditioner units in all the rooms in the house and our car will also be air-conditioned. It has finally arrived but we reckon it will take the Customs Authorities another two weeks to process the custom documents. We have already waited four months so what is two weeks!

I am off to the swimming pool and I shall leave some room for David in case he wants to add a few lines. Love, Nicole

Letter to all Friends   Dakar, 25/10/1992

Life in Dakar

I'm happy to report that the Joneses are in pretty good shape. I'm enjoying Dakar more than I thought I would. The government is a model of *immobilisme*, which is frustrating, but it's a very easy place to live; the climate is quite pleasant; there is not a serious crime problem; there is a large expat. community, and there are many pleasant, urbane, cultured Senegalese. Nicole has not found a job, apart from a two-month fill-in at vacation time at the Canadian Embassy, but she finds this enforced leisure less onerous than she had feared. She rather enjoys getting up when she feels like it, and having time to go to the American Club for a swim.

Bernard and Dominic

Bernard is a manager with Zwetsloots, an anglicised Dutch firm based in Bedford that supplies Tesco and Sainsbury with most of their flowers. He and Stella plan to get married in June next year (nothing impulsive!). Dominic abandoned his B.A. course in architecture at Central London Poly, because he was repeating much of the work he had done in industrial design, and is feeling very pleased with himself for getting accepted to do an M.A. at the Royal College of Arts. For the time being, he shares a flat in Stockwell. To our alarm, he travelled to Ecuador this summer by way of Colombia, to improve his Spanish, but he returned undamaged.

Two New Homes!

We arrived here in March, stayed with our friends Lynn and Bill for three weeks, then were able to move into the house Nicole had found last year. We were very preoccupied with houses, as we had just bought one in Alexandria. It's a weakness of ours. It just seemed a good time to buy, with interest rates low, prices low, and a sporting chance of a healthy bout of inflation in the U.S.

The House in Alexandria

It's a spacious 60-year old (i.e. OLD) frame house, probably Sears-Roebuck mail order, in a quiet street. I never thought I would want to buy a house made out of wood, but having looked at a lot of places which said nothing to us, this one just felt right. The agent was so doubtful about it that we almost missed it off our tour, but we moved very quickly from "Well, we'd better at least give it a once-over" to negotiation. It's very light, with a huge number of sash windows, mostly gummed up with paint, and a lot of charm. It was in good structural shape, but poor decorative order. A friend of a friend, Zhe Hung, who is an engineer, but does not speak much English, moved into the house for three weeks with his bed-roll, saucepan and bag of rice. He filled all the cracks in the plaster (the middle of the house had recently been jacked up two inches!), repainted everything, and fixed all the little broken things like door handles. I helped evenings and weekends. By the time we left, we regretted that we could not move in straight away. For the time being it is let, and for the first time in our lives we are saddled with a substantial mortgage.

The House in Dakar

Our house here (rented, of course) is a very different proposition. It's in an old residential area ("old" again being a very relative term; about 40 years). It has been remodelled to look very modern, but has odd features, like our bedroom opening off the living room, because the core structure effectively resisted remodelling. We have a huge marble-floored living room/ dining room, and lots of space for visitors. Please visit. We can promise you your own bathroom.

The Dakar Garden

The garden is dull, but I have an excellent gardener, Ousmane, two days a week, and we are beginning to make it more interesting. Senegal is not a great place for gardening. The soils are poor, it is very dry and dusty, and water is expensive, so the strategy is to have areas that feel lush without using lots of water, and shrubs rather than flowers.

The Bordepaille House

My favourite house is still Bordepaille. We went there again this summer. My mother, and Nicole's, and my aunt Pat spent most of the holiday with us, and Bernard, Stella and Dominic, my sister Sheila and her husband Ron all visited for part of the time, so we had a good party. Daisy Crivellaro, who now lives much of the year just up the road (350 km) from us in Mauritania, kindly let us overflow into her house. The plasterers, commissioned a year earlier to make two upstairs rooms habitable, arrived two days before us, so we had the pleasure of their company (actually, quite good company) and the carpenter who was meant to have rebuilt the stairs came to measure up the work shortly before we left. With luck we will have new stairs by next year, but I'm not putting any money on it. In any case, we have two more very civilised bedrooms. There's one bedroom to go, and the big living/ dining room is still a workshop.

Elections in Senegal

In Senegal, the government is interested in one thing only: elections (presidential and parliamentary) in February and May next year. There is a real risk of their running out of money to pay civil servants before then, but they manage not to think about that too much. Their main concern is to avoid doing anything that might rock the boat; they do not seem to have noticed that it has a hole in the bottom. The World Bank and the IMF have told the government not to expect any budgetary help until they start to tackle their economic problems. The Bank has been blunter on this than the IMF, yet the IMF bears the brunt of the government's displeasure. In the meantime, there are interesting things to be done preparing projects for the parts of the economy that still work, and working on policy issues that may be tackled after the elections.

Maastricht

I was distressed by the narrowness of the "yes" victory on Maastricht in France. It seemed that to vote "yes" one had to believe that everything about the Treaty and the EEC and the Commission was perfect. The "noes" were a coalition of fascists, communists, xenophobes, people who just wanted to vote against Mitterand, agricultural protectionists (how can a French farmer vote "no" over the CAP?) and people with legitimate (and illegitimate) but minor grudges about the Treaty or the EEC.

U.K. Reactions

I was even more upset by what I regret I can only describe as the idiocy of British reactions, both to Maastricht and to the currency crisis. The EEC is not perfect (no institution made by man is) but it has given us prosperity that we would not have had without it (we could have had more, but it's our fault we didn't) and an economic and political independence that we would never have had on our own, or by hanging on to America's coat tails. And yet what we have is very vulnerable unless we move towards some form of central democratic structure. The currency crisis was 90% of Britain's own making, and would not have happened with a European central bank. No doubt this looks more obvious from outside than from inside, but I am horrified that we cannot read the lessons from Yugoslavia. We have something in the

EEC that is well worth defending and developing, which boils down to a conception of civilised society, tolerance and social obligations. It is little comfort that American political and economic life is in an even worse trough than that of the EEC.

Yugoslavia and Somalia

As for Yugoslavia, I think that the democratic world's reluctance to act will look, in retrospect, almost as shameful as appeasement, or ignoring the treatment of Jews in Germany before the last war. Appeasement was really more defensible, because there was a legitimate argument for buying time. Over Yugoslavia, we are just losing time, letting a small problem become a big one, for the sake of avoiding the costs of dealing with it. I would put Somalia into a different category, not because it is less horrible (it is more so), or because it leaves us with no moral obligations, but because, short of re-colonising it, it really is both out of our control and out of our legitimate sphere of influence. Frankly, I think we are in for another tough and dangerous year. On that sunny note... Happy New Year!
Love from David and Nicole

Letter to Mother
Dakar, 22/11/1992

Solo Living

I have survived one bachelor week. I don't like to make Nicole feel smug, but I really do not enjoy living on my own. I'm a sociable enough person to need company, but not a sociable enough person to find the company I need without some help. Nicole and I managed to talk to each other last night, after several abortive tries on both sides. She is over her cold, and enjoying Paris. She's going to the U.K. this week, to stay with Dominic. I hope he lives in civilised surroundings.

Meeting the Khalife

I had an interesting outing this week; I met the *Khalife Generale des Mourides* at Touba. This probably doesn't mean a lot to you, so I'll give you some background.

Senegal was islamicised mainly in the last century, at about the same time as the French were extending their control inland from the coastal towns which they had occupied for two hundred years. The Mauritanians were Muslims, as were many Malians, and Islam had extended into the Senegal River Valley which is the frontier with Maur and Malian territory, but most Senegalese were animists. There were various kingdoms, and warlords, more or less involved in slaving.

Amadou Bamba, an Islamic Marabout

Around 1860, Amadou Bamba, from the Senegal River Valley, set himself up as a marabout, or leader of an Islamic brotherhood, and started converting the Wolof interior of the country. He was treated as a prophet, and wrote a lot of Arabic religious verse, a little after the style of the Koran. Personally, he was austere and ascetic (and rather irritable). The most powerful of the remaining warlords, Fall, attached himself to Amadou Bamba, and helped with his not entirely peaceful religious conquests. I don't think he was the first marabout by any means. The Tidians, who started in Morocco, are much older. However, he was the first important African marabout in this region.

Planting Groundnuts under Marabout Orders

One of Amadou Bamba's particularities was that when a tribe or village submitted to him, he ordered them to go off and work. Under his orders, and those of subordinate Mouride marabouts, they cut down the forest and planted groundnuts, and gave him the proceeds.

The French were never quite sure what to do about Amadou Bamba. On the one hand, they approved of forests being replaced by peanut fields, but on the other, they were afraid of his power. In fact, he never resisted the French, but they exiled him to Gabon in the 1920s, when he was already an old man, and eventually let him back when he was even older.

Amadou Bamba had several wives and a lot of sons, and since his death they have continued to succeed him. So the present *Khalife Generale* is one of the remaining sons, and when he goes (and his remaining brothers, if any) they will start again with the (by now venerable) sons of the older brothers.

Present-Day Mourides

The reason I got to see him is that the Mourides are still attached to cutting down forests and planting groundnuts, and 18 months ago managed to persuade the government to agree to destruction of 45,000 hectares of classified forest and grazing reserve, and called the disciples in to cut down the trees. All the donors made a great stink, and the Bank said that if that was how the government intended to look after the environment, it was not going to get any World Bank money for anything connected with the environment. Things have been rumbling on unhappily since then. The government is unhappy to have offended the donors, but is scared stiff of the Mourides, who have the potential to deliver or refuse a huge block of votes, and to paralyse the economy. The Mourides, for instance, have a religious city in Touba, where no-one pays any taxes, and the faithful go there on pilgrimage, as if it were Mecca. Some actually believe that Amadou Bamba was the prophet Mohammed. In fact, strictly speaking, the whole set-up is highly heretical. Moreover, some of the descendants of Amadou Bamba have got immensely rich, and contracted enormous loans from the banks which they do not repay. The more modern Mourides have gone into trading, and control the informal sector here, with links to Paris, Rome, New York…

Forest versus Groundnuts

I made the trip with a distinguished Ivorian environmentalist and ex-minister to see what was really happening. We had a large official entourage, and spent two days on the trip. In fact, a lot of trees in the so-called forest are still standing, but the grazing reserve will be destroyed, to the detriment of the non-Mouride herders who simply got kicked out, and the sandy soils are going to degrade rapidly and blow all over the place. There's an official development plan, involving planted tree belts, but since the basic land parcels within the narrow tree belts are each 5km by 6km (about ten square miles), the trees are not going to do much good. The official promoter, who is the *Khalife's* son (for whom it is a personal business venture) came and greeted us very graciously, and we were all very polite and diplomatic; but we cannot pretend there is no problem.

A Little Old Man in a Dirty Boubou

The meeting with the *Khalife Generale* was quite unexpected, and was not at all as I would have imagined. We went past all the grand buildings, and were shown into a very modest, scruffy and rather dirty house. The KGM was sitting on a slightly raised area, a little old man in a dirty *boubou*, with his Koran on a stand beside him. We showed our respects in more or less extravagant ways, depending on whether we were Mourides, other Muslims, or neither, and had a very diplomatic conversation in which he mumbled almost inaudibly in Wolof, and was translated to us; after which he said a prayer and dismissed us (he didn't tell us to go and plant peanuts). The son was much more urbane, and took us to a modern guesthouse, where we were served a great deal of barbecued sheep and other food (I'm rather partial to barbecued sheep).

Magic Charms

Incidentally, some of the minor marabouts make money by selling *"gri-gris"* or magic charms. This is even more heretical. I had a taxi driver the other day, who chatted to me about his friend who was a taxi driver in New York, and had a wonderful *gri-gri* that turned bullets to water. It must be very reassuring in New York; he could do a good business in Washington too. Personally, he had not seen the need to invest in anything so extravagant in Dakar, and had made do with a *gri-gri* to protect him against knives.

Swimming and Airplanes

I have been swimming a couple of times this weekend; only 30 lengths. I feel that it does me good (except that the chlorine really irritates my eyes), but it's such a bore grinding up and down the pool like that. I can also buy a hamburger there, which saves me the bother of getting lunch, and say hello to a few people. Today and yesterday I met our friends the Lombardos there. I was chatting to them when an aeroplane passed overhead, and I glanced up. Lesley Lombardo surprised me by saying "Airbus 300". Then later in the conversation she gave me the name of an American transport plane. I asked her how she knew these things, and she revealed that she had been involved in military procurement in Washington for the French (she's the English half of the family) and knew of Andy Johnson, who was involved in military procurement (as well as the financial aspects of dental bills and home leave). We have heard from the Johnsons, by the way, and they are quite enjoying life in Hong Kong.

I had a very good dinner with the Swiss *chargé*, M. Lardi and his wife, on Friday. They were on the trip Dominic took with us, and asked after him.
Lots of love, David

Letter to Mother   Dakar, 06/12/1992

Welcome to Nicole

Well, thank goodness I am almost through my period of looking after myself! Nicole is meant to arrive in two and a half hours. I hope she has had a good flight and that she arrives on time.

In truth, the work of looking after myself was not all that arduous. It turned out that I had quite a lot of meals away from home for one reason or another, and for the rest of the time, Awa kept me pretty well (if slightly monotonously) fed. Mostly it has been fish and rice, but cooked in several different ways, with a large (too large) avocado salad to start. Avocados are in season, and very good, but it is hard to eat a whole one at one sitting. I even entertained. We had some people from Washington, and I invited my working group of Senegalese economists to dinner with them. We served skewered fillet of beef, cooked on the barbecue.

Christmas is Coming!

Things are beginning to slow down for the Christmas and New Year period. We hope to go away with Bill and Lynn, but all of us are working, and our preparations so far are restricted to talking about it. I have just been to the American Club with them for a hamburger snack dinner and a game of darts (Bill won). This was my second visit of the day, as I also had lunch there (Sunday being Awa's day off), combined with my healthy exercise swim. I had hoped that the swimming would become more effortless, and I think it did at first, but I seem now to have reached a plateau.

The Garden

I also had to spend some time supervising work in the garden. Today, we have moved a tiny mandarin tree which I grafted a few months ago. I hope we are doing the right thing. It's cool these days, and the citrus trees are completely static (not dormant, of course, being evergreen). I am getting a nice lot of fruit for juice from two of the mature trees. We also made a wire trellis on the wall outside the kitchen for an epidendrum-type plant which would like to climb, but whose efforts to cling seem to be defeated by the paint on the wall. And we have taken the first very timid steps towards the establishment of my orchid house: a shallow foundation trench. Lynn is amused that I should do all this for six very sorry-looking plants, but the point is that I cannot get any more until I have somewhere more suited to their likes and dislikes.

Grass Roots Politics

My gardener, Ousemane, was very talkative today on the political problems of the country. Evidently, he is a supporter of the best-known opposition presidential candidate, and he thinks the government is going to use fraud (again) to stay in power. He may well be right, although I would have about as much difficulty voting for his candidate as for the incumbent. He also had a lot to say on the links between the political situation in Dakar, ethnic divisions in the population, and the smouldering separatist war in the south of the country. He belongs to one of the substantial minority groups, the *peuhls*, identified in this country with nomadic herders, but in his area, nearer to the Guinea frontier, often consisting of sedenterised cultivators. In politics, the ethnic divide seems to be more important than the religious one. The majority group, the Wolof, are almost entirely Muslim, whereas the people of the south are a mixture of Muslims, Christians and animists (often animist as well as one of the other religions).

Belief in Supernatural Charms
I was a little disappointed that Ousemane (a Muslim) believes all the stories of charms that turn bullets into water. He also believes that the Casemance rebels have the power to turn themselves into mosquitoes or snakes when under attack, and to slip away in this guise (or if a snake, bite those attacking them).

Petite Côte Conference
I spent a couple of days this week at a conference on the Petite Côte, 90km south of here. I could have stayed overnight and relaxed a bit, but I needed to be at work in the intervening day, so drove there and back each day. It was not a very impressive conference, despite being organised by a large and prestigious international research institute based in Washington.

Intervention in a Troubled World
I am surprised to hear that the Americans have decided to get involved in Somalia. I shall be glad if they manage to stop the fighting, but I'm afraid I am not convinced of their altruistic purposes. I expect that they want to establish a compliant government and a naval base. I wish they would also get involved in Yugoslavia, although really that should be an EEC/ WEU responsibility. I am appalled by the reports of what is happening there. An African friend said the other day *"I'm quite comforted by what is going on in Yugoslavia; they are so much worse with each other than we Africans are."* And, although I am not comforted at all, it is true. In Africa, only Somalia currently comes close to Yugoslavia. Liberia is probably much less deadly. Elsewhere, people occasionally go mad for a few days, and commit horrible atrocities against their neighbours, but they do not go on and on for months on end, systematically massacring people and driving them from their homes. I am ashamed how little we are doing. Like it or not, Britain and the other civilised European countries should offer refuge (at least on a transitory basis) to the unfortunate Muslims of Yugoslavia, if we will not stir ourselves to protect them.
Love, David

Letter from Nicole to Sheila and Ron   Dakar, 06/01/1993

Christmas at Cape Verde
After two weeks of festivities all is now back to normal and everybody went back to work on Monday.

Dominic arrived on 19th December, and on 22nd we flew to one of the Cape Verde islands which are former Portuguese colonies off the coast of Senegal. We spent four days on Santiago Island and two days on a smaller island, Fogo. Most of the Cape Verde islands are mountainous and very dry; it hardly ever rains – every twenty years or so! The Cape Verdians manage to grow some maize, beans, bananas, vegetables and even grapes from which they make an awful wine. Despite our lack of Portuguese we managed to make ourselves understood with the dictionary and Dominic's help. He speaks a little Spanish and it seems that Portuguese-speaking people understand Spanish, and vice versa. Knowing French also helped.

New Year

We celebrated the New Year with our French friends at their beach cottage, and spent last weekend at a National Park where we were hoping to see a lot of birds but hardly saw any. Now Dominic is spending a few days in Mauritania with our Bordepaille neighbours, Daisy and Jackie Crivellaro.

We do not have freezing temperatures as there have been in Europe, but the weather has been on the cool side since the beginning of the year. It even rained on Monday, which is very unusual for the time of year.

Thank you for the bag which will be very useful for carrying my knitting and embroidery. We phoned Bernard last week and he said he was going to visit you with Stella at the week-end. Love, Nicole

PS from David – Thanks very much for my tree. I doubt very much if Owen has been able to plant it, but I like the idea.
Lots of love, David

(NOTE - The tree was a chestnut which I grew from a conker, and gave to Margaret's son-in-law Owen who travelled to Bordepaille to plant some fruit trees for David.)

Letter to Mother   Bordepaille, 17/06/1993

A Scandinavian Cruise

We were interested to receive your postcard and Auntie Phyllis's on the same day. I hope the remainder of your trip was fun, and that the land of the midnight sun was not too chilly for comfort.

(NOTE – Once again, our Mother went on holiday with Pat and Phyllis, this time cruising up the Norwegian coast and right into the Arctic Circle.)

Progress at Bordepaille

We have been having rather poor weather for once, with a lot of grey skies and intermittent rain, which is doubtless re-charging the groundwater. I have been very busy working in my new bathroom, which is coming along well, but is still not functional. Yesterday I put the bath in place and checked that I could run water into it and out again without leaks. I have managed to find two more sets of old brass taps – wash basin and bidet – to match the bath/shower set we have had lying around for a few years, and spent the time necessary to make them work properly. They have all been waving around in the air at the top of copper pipes. Now I have to put in the various fixtures they are meant to supply.

Visitors at Bordepaille

We enjoyed a visit by Jimmy Wright and his girl-friend Maryam, at the end of their long stay in France – Maryam is very pretty and seems very pleasant. Jimmy looks less than his 28 years. Nicole doesn't think he feeds himself properly! However they appear determined to get enough sleep. We didn't hear or see either of them until mid-day. I must say it was pleasant having some young people here – I miss ours and am happy to have surrogates.

Peter and Dawn (parents of Stella, Bernard's fiancée) seem to be enjoying themselves despite the dubious weather. Nicole has been very industrious on their behalf, taking them around the place to do some sight-seeing, all in places I know well, so I have been free to get on with my work.

The French Garden

The garden is at a different stage from that of earlier years. The wild cherries in the hedgerows had a lot of fruit on them, and the birds have been having a field day – including a couple of hoopoes. I have heard the cuckoo a couple of times – first time for about ten years.

Under the lime tree by the house we found a couple of clumps of tall white lilies –
Madonna, I think – very strongly scented and attractive, despite the attentions of snails and
the lily beetle. I found a purple orchid in the meadow in front of the house, and hate to think
what we must have covered over in the earth-moving. I have also found a very odd orchid in
the waste land in front of my carpenter's workshop. I think it is one of the many varieties that
mimics an insect. The labellum (central lower petal) is about one and three quarter inches
long, and brownish purple, and a couple of smaller sepals hang down as legs, so a not-too-
observant dragon fly might conceivably be fooled – despite the absence of anything
resembling wings. The colours are far from spectacular – yellowish browns and brown-purple,
with odd touches of purple. M. Gervais was mildly intrigued when I showed them to him and
said I was welcome to dig them up. I might try and transplant a single plant with a good
volume of earth around it. If you can give any help in identification I would be grateful.

A Magnificent Staircase
I forgot to mention that my staircase is magnificently finished. M. Gervais is very proud of
his work.
Lots of love, David and Nicole

Letter from Nicole to Margaret   Dakar, 11/08/1993

A Quiet Time in Dakar
I am enclosing a photo of Bernard and Stella's wedding with this letter. I have been back
from my holiday for exactly a month. Dakar is like Paris during the summer; there is nobody
around (I mean ex-patriates, as the Senegalese are still there in vast numbers). The ex-patriate
community starts its exodus at the beginning of July and does not come back until 25th
September when the French school re-opens. Life is very quiet and apart from going to the
swimming pool and to the beach at the weekend (for those who own a beach house) there is
not much to do.

Plenty of Translation Work
All the same I have not been idle. The NGO for which I do translating has bombarded me
with work. I have just finished a translation, and I am now working on revising the French
translation of their Organisation Manual. The translation was done initially by someone from
Haiti and is not very good at all. I more or less have to start all over again.

Beach House Life
For the last month we have been fortunate to have the use of a beach house which belongs
to some French friends who are away at the moment. It is very basic (just two huts) but there
is a kitchen with refrigerator and a gas cooker, an outside toilet and a shower. There is no
running water, but the toilet and shower are connected to a water tank. Two ladies from the
village bring about ten large basins of water to fill it at the weekend. We have been enjoying
our temporary ownership but I am afraid it is now over as our friends are coming back. We
have a standing invitation, but we cannot impose on them every weekend.

An Appalling Road Accident
On our way to the beach house last Saturday we nearly got involved in a car crash.
Fortunately David was quick enough to get off the road. We were driving along when
suddenly we saw a *"car rapide"* (they are buses but they are called by this name because they
are driven very fast and not maintained or insured) coming in the opposite direction but
straight on us. David drove quickly off to the side of the road which was fortunately free of
trees etc. The bus swerved on our side, crossed the road, turned over and then stood up again
facing in the opposite direction. We did not think at first that there were people injured, but
when we went near we realised that a lot of people were hurt. Most of them had head injuries
and broken ribs and some were complaining of back pain and could not move. With the help

of some soldiers, who arrived from I know not where, and of passing cars, one of which had a doctor on board, we organised the transport of the injured to Dakar. There was no telephone nearby and there was no need to wait for the police or ambulance who would never come. We went back to Dakar taking in our car a young lady who could not move and was in great pain. We delivered her to the hospital and we hope she is improving. We were very lucky and every time I think of what could have happened to us, I shiver. We drove once more the 70km back to the coast and had a pleasant weekend.

News of Bernard and Stella, and Dominic

Bernard and Stella are well and trying to buy a house. They do not have much money, but if they don't buy now they might regret it, although house prices are not going up much according to the Financial Times. The flat is expensive and they will pay less in mortgage payments than they now pay in rent. Dominic is off to Guadeloupe next week. His plans for working in Japan did not materialise.

The rain is plentiful this year and everything is so green that we have the feeling of being in some other country. David joins me in sending his love to you and to those of your family who are with you.
With love, Nicole

Letter to Margaret, Sheila and Michael   Dakar, 02/10/1993

A Special Birthday

Nicole, who is much more thoughtful than I am about such things, reminds me that Mummy has an 80th birthday next February. Do you think this would be an occasion she would be happy to celebrate, and if so, how? We could have a family get-together and a meal, if you thought that she would like this. For myself, I like the idea, and we have a trip in the bag that we could use to get there. The best place, from Mummy's point of view, would probably be Leicester, since most of her friends are there, although I see a slight snag using Stoneygate church hall, as Mummy would probably feel awkward not inviting the whole church. Can you please discuss among yourselves, and then talk to Mummy, and let me know what you have decided. If you decide that it would be best to order a meal at a local hotel, we would be happy to come up with half the cost, as we currently have fewer family responsibilities than the rest of you.

News from Home

We have enjoyed getting letters fairly recently from Sheila and Margaret. Everyone seems to be in reasonable shape. Bernard has just told us that the company he works for has been taken over by a much larger one that may be more interested in the company name than in its employees, and is waiting anxiously for Monday to find out if he still has a job. Dominic, poor mite, has had a summer without a real holiday; just a couple of weeks in Guadeloupe, thanks to Grandmère Fortuné and ten days in Italy with the college. We saw such alarming television coverage of floods in Italy that we telephoned him in a hurry to make sure that he was back in one piece – which he was. We are now feeling as if we had not had a summer holiday, as it is now so long ago. Of course, Nicole has had one trip back since then, using up the last of Dominic's educational travel entitlements.

Feeling the Heat in Senegal

It's still very hot here, but we are probably getting to the end of the worst of the summer. It's just as well, as we keep on getting power cuts, and these have burnt out our largest air-conditioner. The Government is in deep financial trouble, and has brought in an austerity budget with salary cuts for public employees. We have already had one twenty-four hour general strike in which the power supply was not cut, but we are being threatened with a seventy-two hour strike in which the main union involved has its political base in the power company. The World Bank is very much in the news, as many people suppose (quite incorrectly) that the Government is following instructions from us and the International Monetary Fund. As for the Government, their attitude is *"since we are doing things that are tough, you should give us some money to keep our heads above water, even though you don't think what we are doing is going to work"*.

Speaking the Truth

I am often the acting Representative of the Bank, and so I get telephoned by journalists trying to get me to make imprudent statements. Actually, I made one on the promise that I would not be identified, and the journalist kept his promise in such a way that everyone knew it was me. My friends in the other donor agencies were delighted, as they had not dared to say such things, but the Government people were quite upset. I also received a delegation of the opposition leaders. The Government didn't like that either, but couldn't see any good reason to refuse to receive elected members of the National Assembly, and I did it all very correctly. The truth is, I quite like this sort of stuff, even though I never really intended to spend so much of my life working on Africa, and I think I have worked on this continent long enough to be entitled to tell the truth about its self-made problems. And one of the nice things is that a fair number of the Africans I work with now are very bright people who are as tough on these issues as I am.

Electronic Possibilities

Incidentally, I now employ a very good Senegalese statistician (former chess champion of the Paris universities) who is a delightful young man, and whose real aim is to set up a software company here. If Jimmy or Thomas had stuff they wanted to sub-contract, I'm sure he would be only too pleased to do some moonlighting. We are contactable (somehow) on Internet (we use the VTERM link through the World Bank in Washington which is accessible through major electronic mail networks; they'll probably know what I'm talking about).

Nicole's Career

Nicole is now working part-time at the U.K. Embassy here, which she is very pleased about, although she goes on doing part-time work translating for American NGO.

House Hunting in France

We are interested in Sheila's French house-hunting. Yes, it would be nice to have another family house in France. But have no illusions; every house has at least a roof to keep in expensive or labour-intensive repair, not to mention doors and windows that go rotten eventually. Otherwise it just falls to bits. The roof is by far the most important thing structurally in a traditional building, since it is usually extremely heavy and not very waterproof, but everything else, including walls, depends on its upkeep. I'm glad you realise the importance of access. There are lots of very charming bits of rural France that are very inaccessible, and you waste half your holiday getting there. In fact, we have more or less given up going by car to Bordepaille.

Bordepaille becomes Le Puy

I should mention that, strictly speaking, Bordepaille exists no more. The commune has been completely absorbed by Le Puy, which is iniquitous, as Bordepaille is bigger than Le Puy, and is simply not on the *"puy"* (the rocky outcrop). The only sound reason that I can think of is economy on the size of the nameplate at the entrance to the village. Anyway, go on addressing any correspondence to Bordepaille, Monsegur, 33580. I will.
Our love to you all, David and Nicole

Letter to Sheila   Senegal, 19/12/1993

80th Birthday Celebration

I'm glad you were able to persuade Mummy that a birthday party was a good idea. I hope she sticks to this new persuasion. Anyway, I enclose a cheque for £200 towards the cost. I'm glad it is you doing the planning, not me.

The costs sound OK, and I am not surprised by the wine price, but have you tried asking the hotel if you can supply the wine (and take away what was not drunk – the wine, not the guests, of course; with the guests you normally have to take away the ones that are drunk). They might ask you to pay "corkage", but that can hardly exceed £1 per bottle. But don't bother unless you a) have time and b) can be sure of getting decent wine cheaper (why not see what Stephen says?)

February 1994, Leicester – Celebrating Mother's 80th Birthday

Sheila's French House – and How to Pay!

I'm pleased you have now found a house you like. The important thing is whether it really is what you like. If you are going to start wishing in a year or two that it had a super view, wait until you have found one that has.

I move money about very simply by giving written instructions to my bank(s). The cost of moving money in Europe is scandalously high, and will probably amount to about 4% on top of the cost of the house. It's actually cheaper to do from a U.S. account than from a U.K. account.

You could ask your bank to put French Francs in my French account, and I would write a cheque for you, but it is probably simpler to ask your bank to provide you with a French Franc "bankers' cheque" with which you can directly pay the seller's *notaire*. In the long run, I would advise that you open an account at your nearest French bank, which is likely to be Credit Agricole in a rural area. I have been quite happy with my contact with Credit Agricole, but I have been astonished a couple of times by things that the local branch has felt able to do without me telling them to: once Nicole ran out of shopping money, and they simply debited my account and gave her some (it is not a joint account).

You may be a little shocked by the amount you have to pay to the *notaire* and the government to complete your transfer. It can run to 10-15% of the price. Have you bargained over the price? It's worth it, as there are not many buyers around at the moment. You might ask the seller to pay the legal fees.

Successful Negotiations

I've just come back from ten days in Washington, partly to attend a training workshop on negotiation. This was interesting, but had more to do with complex negotiations with many parties and many aims, where one side's gains would not necessarily be the other side's loss, and where you would probably want to go on having a reasonable relationship with the other side. We had some exercises. A couple of us, including myself, successfully skinned the opposite party alive in our simulation, and were surprised to find that this was not regarded as very nice behaviour. However, buying a house is not like this. It is quite clear from the outset that you want to pay the lowest price you can, and never want to see the seller again once the transaction is over.

A Favour

I want to ask you a favour. A member of our staff here, Augustine Mourret, needs to learn English. She goes to classes but is unsatisfied with her progress – which truly is not very visible as she is rather a shy person, particularly when it comes to striking up a conversation in a language she doesn't speak. She would like to spend some time in an English-speaking household during her annual leave, which she would probably take late spring or summer (despite the name she is Senegalese and doesn't fancy what she has heard of the U.K. in winter). She is local staff, hence not very well paid, and would be willing to work her way (unofficially) by helping with housework etc. She is a very charming person whom I would highly recommend as a guest. Could you put her up, or do you have friends with children who might? Age about 32 – seems younger.

Dominic is here for Christmas, as well as Mme Fortuné. Nice to have a family here!
Lots of love, David

Letter to all friends   Senegal, 07/01/1994

A Busy Life

Nicole and I are still in Senegal, probably for another fifteen months. Nicole now works part-time with the British Embassy, and free-lances as translator for an international NGO (non-governmental organisation, for those gnot in the gnow), as well as continuing some of her "accompanying spouse" things like singing and needlework, so she's very busy.

Standing in for the Chief

I'm set to spend an indefinite period as acting Chief of Mission as my boss, Elkyn Chaparro, is going back to Washington earlier than intended, and the Bank has not yet decided whether or when to replace him.

Financial Doldrums

Life is hectic, although our programme here is in the doldrums. We have doubts about the Government's economic policies, and that makes it hard for us to do much lending for projects – not because we want to make policy, but because we have to stop the money we lend from being wasted, and our only criterion is our own best judgement. The Government badly wants some more lending. It is extremely short of cash, and can't pay its contributions to the running costs of existing projects, which is bringing them to a halt. The financial situation got so bad that public service salaries had to be cut by 15% - and it is still hard to meet the wage bill.

Political Discontent

This situation is not wholly unconnected with the fact that from about June 1992 through May 1993 the Government concentrated only on winning parliamentary and presidential elections, but the size of the problem did not become clear (at least to the Government) until the elections were over. The opposition won a lot of parliamentary seats, including a clean sweep of the capital, Dakar, but they lost overall, and continue to dispute the results. Political and economic discontent has led to several partial "general" strikes, and quite a lot of demonstrations. Another new feature, which is more disruptive to our daily life, is frequent power cuts. Fortunately we now have a handsome stand-by generator which kicks in after a few minutes of sitting in the dark, but the power fluctuations still play havoc with our electrical equipment. Our water supply now also seems to be getting a bit dodgy. Normal post takes ages to reach us, and frequently gets lost on the way, but mail sent via the World Bank in Washington takes a fairly reliable ten days to two weeks from the U.K.

Compensations

Still, life is not too hard. Senegal lacks the charm of (pre-crisis) Kenya, but there is a lot of social life, we swim a lot at the American (!) Club and at the Petite Côte, and my orchid house has produced a few very nice blooms. Nicole's mother valiantly came all the way from Guadeloupe for a month with us at Christmas, and Dominic favoured us with ten days of his presence.

Surrey, June 1993 – Wedding of Stella and Bernard.
Left: Marjorie, David, Margaret, Phyllis   Right: Nicole, Bernard, Stella, David, Dominic

Family Wedding

The big family event this year was Bernard and Stella's marriage in June. They had good weather and an enjoyable day (at least it was for Nicole and me), with a good turnout of immediate family. Bernard found a new job, close to Sutton so as to avoid commuting, and he and Stella were about to find a house, when his employer announced that he had sold out to a larger firm, which wanted the business but not the staff. Great trauma at this time! But to everybody's surprise, including Bernard's, he found a new job before he was formally finished with the old. He now markets pot plants to supermarkets, whereas previously he marketed cut flowers.

End of Student Life

Dominic is in the final year of his industrial design M.A. at the Royal College of Arts, and is eager to put education behind him and do some work. I hope the job market is kind to him. One project design he was involved in has been constructed: a children's playground in Japan.

Bordepaille – Work in Progress

We went to Bordepaille again this summer. The house is steadily becoming more habitable. I have decided to hurry things up by having some of the more substantial remaining pieces of work done in our absence. I hope that by the time we get there next year the third upstairs bedroom (Dominic's) will have been completed, and the biggest downstairs floor, but I daren't count on it; the local craftsmen over-commit themselves hugely, and it takes dozens of telephone calls and interventions by our local friends to get them onto the site and keep them there. I hoped rising unemployment and deepening economic depression would benefit us, if no-one else, by making it easier to get work done, but it seems to have made no difference at all. We plan to celebrate our 30th wedding anniversary there this summer (22nd August) and would be pleased to see any recipients of this letter.

My sister Sheila is also buying a house right in the middle of France. Originally, she was looking for four walls and a roof in good condition, but she seems to be ending up with something much more substantial.

World Problems

1993 has been a rather bad year for the world as a whole, and particularly for Europe. I am ashamed that the European Union was so feeble over former Yugoslavia. I'm afraid we may in time pay a heavy price for not intervening. I like to think we have values that it is worth some sacrifice to maintain, if only around the borders of the E.U., and I fear that by refusing to accept this cost, we have strengthened some of the most unpleasant politicians to have emerged for a long time in Europe.

We are in a very dangerous period. I always feared it was wishful thinking to suppose that the end of the Soviet Union would usher in a long era of peace, prosperity and democracy. If Russia sorts itself out economically and politically, it will probably re-emerge (as it always has) as a power which always has to be regarded as a threat to smaller surrounding nations; if it does not sort itself out, there could be civil war with nuclear weapons. The first alternative is preferable to the second, but in either case, the notion that all the risks are over, and that we can demilitarise without any risk, is stupid. And that's just Russia; then there's China, getting more prosperous at a quite astonishing rate, heavily armed, politically unstable, and totally un-democratic. Somehow we have to get back on track towards greater international control of nuclear weapons and the environment – the two things that pose the greatest risk of destroying the world – but this is not populist politics.

A World in Transition

Meanwhile the change in the world economic order that we talked so much about in the 1970s has happened, though not exactly as we expected. Europe and the U.S.A. are adapting painfully, unwilling to recognise that they may be left behind as a sort of Latin America to Asia's U.S.A. Average incomes are already higher in Hong Kong than in the U.K. – and mostly we just do not realise it is happening. This failure to see what is in front of our faces is very odd!

A Soft Spot for Africa

The only apparently unchanging feature is that Africa remains the basket case. I am more and more convinced that Africa's problems are more self-mutilation than economic aggression, and that the most helpful thing outsiders like myself can do is to say so quite bluntly. However, I still have a very soft spot for Africa, and hope that it can get to grips with its problems – and even that I can help it to do so.

Best wishes to you all for 1994, David and Nicole

NOTE - Ron and I were guests at the 30th Anniversary party at Bordepaille that summer. The day was scorching hot, and multi-national guests, many of them French speaking, milled about consuming wine and spit-roasted lamb. Never one to do things by halves, David roasted two fat lambs, and the wine was limitless. Fortunately there was plenty of wonderful

French bread to soak up the alcohol and fat! We finally crawled into our tent feeling rather more than replete. It was a clear warm night, ideal for star-gazing; an exuberant party which we will always remember.

Letter to Mother
Dakar, 04/04/1994

Sine Saloum Estuary

I had a hard week, ending with meetings with the Minister of Finance on Saturday morning at an hour when we were supposed to be on our way south for a long Easter weekend with friends. He let me go at about 11.30am, and I was able to change out of my suit and tie into tee-shirt and slacks and make a getaway. We had aimed to share someone else's car, but of course the others had all gone on ahead.

Our objective was Sine Saloum, a very extensive estuary system serving a largely prehistoric river system. Its watershed has been cut off by other rivers, and the rainfall in what is left has declined, so there is very little flow apart from the ebb and flow of the tides. I like this area; it is more interesting than the Petite Côte, because there is a variety of natural features, like mangrove swamps and a network of inland channels, and islands made of oyster shells and cockle shells piled up over thousands of years by people. These islands usually have old baobab trees on them, which is a sign of old human settlement.

Missing Ferry Boat

The hotel was on the southern side of the estuary, and there used to be a car ferry linking it to our side, but it sank last year and has not been replaced, so now one has to drive to the nearest small town, Fatick, and telephone ahead for a *pirogue*. Surprisingly in Senegal it is fairly easy to find a telephone in small towns and even large villages. There are some phone boxes, which as often as not do not function, but owning a public telephone has become a recognised business, and all over the place there are "telecentres" with one or two telephone booths and fax machines for sending written messages.

Fawlty Towers at Forty Degrees C

What really took us by surprise in Fatick was not finding a telecentre, but getting out of our air-conditioned car and almost being struck down by the heat. We had slept without an air-conditioner the night before, because Dakar was still quite comfortably cool, but inland the country is already heating up, and will go on doing so until the rains in July – or August, or September, *in'ch Allah!* We had day-time temperatures over 40'C (the lower 100's Fahrenheit) throughout the weekend.

We had a very pleasant break, despite a Fawlty Towers atmosphere. The hotel used to belong to a wealthy Bordeaux business man, who also owned the Bordeaux football team, but is now in prison for fraud. The new owner was new to Senegal (though not to Africa) and, I think, new to the hotel business, and had taken the place over in December after it had been closed for at least a year. His friends had told him that the tourist season ended in March, so he had reduced the staff and used up most of the food, and was planning for a maximum of fifty guests, instead of which he found himself with a hundred and twenty-five because his Senegalese manager had seen the possibility of boosting the cash-flow and had refused no-one. In fact I think we were all local residents. He was also in dispute with the electricity company, and was trying to depend on his own generators, which kept on breaking down. Last night we ate in the dark, and were just debating whether to take our beds outside and sleep by the swimming pool (we had little cabins that were designed for air-conditioning, and it was much cooler out than in) when the power came on again. I suspect he got desperate and made an illegal connection to the power grid, because I went to have a look this morning, and there were naked wires all over the place.

Quantity not Quality

He almost ran out of food, and was serving whatever he could find in the vicinity. The kitchen staff was of the "quantity not quality" school. We had lamb stew with tennis-ball-sized lumps of lamb that appeared to have been chopped up with an axe – which they probably were. One of our party was a tough police advisor who went and told the proprietor that he was serving canteen food, after which it improved somewhat. In fact today we had a very tasty lunch of wild pig, except that half our company had been so scared by stories of all the nasty diseases wild pigs could carry that they refused to eat it (in fact it had been refrigerated for a month, which kills most things, and simmered for five hours, which kills everything else).

A Good Time Had By All

A variety of entertainment was available. I went on a fishing expedition in a *pirogue*, which is not usually my cup of tea, but all of us including me caught a lot of fish – two huge bags full, which we gave away to our boatman. We had a rather hilarious group cart-ride through the village and the salt-flats, being mobbed by hundreds of children asking for sweets (white people give away sweets). They had a number of local horses, and I went for an hour's ride on a fairly amenable horse, with a groom to give me some advice. In the end I developed enough confidence to do a bit of trotting without falling off. Sitting on a horse that is simply walking is really rather boring. The horses here are not very big, so there isn't a long way to fall. Nicole and a few of the others went to Easter mass in the local church (it's an area with a mixed Catholic and Muslim population). The priest honoured their presence with a little homily in French. I'm sure the collection was much better than usual.

Vanishing Footwear

Today Nicole went on a boat ride, while I went wind-surfing, which I have done before, but for which I am quite out of practice. I managed a few good runs, falling off only on some of the corners, which are the tricky part. On one of my falls I was surprised to land in very deep sticky mud, and lost one of my plastic sandals. I spent several minutes searching for it with my toes, but I think it was under at least a foot of mud, so I abandoned it. I also almost abandoned one of my fingernails. I never seem to manage to wind-surf without a few little incidents. By my standards, this was a fairly good day.

We are back home now, of course, and after all this tourist luxury, we will enjoy the comfort of our bed and our reliable electricity supply.

Lots of love, David

P.S. from Nicole – "Adventure Trips"

I like going on these adventure trips, but sometimes I wonder why I leave a comfortable house in order to endure the heat, mosquitoes etc. But they are nice memories and the people we go with are pleasant.

I hope your arm is gathering strength.

Lots of love, Nicole

(NOTE - Our Mother broke her arm during a shopping trip.)

Letter to mother   **Dakar, 15/05/1994**

Misfortunes

Mme Fortuné had to go into hospital in a rush last week and had an operation last week; a cyst, and an unspecified lump, removed. She is home and feeling all right now, but as usual in Guadeloupe it is difficult to get information, reassuring or otherwise. The doctor who did the operation left immediately afterwards for several weeks in France. Nicole will be going out there for three weeks.

The other sad event of the week was the death of Robert, husband of Suzy, Nicole's cousin. He had been having chemotherapy for colon cancer for the past year. He managed to stay reasonably active until a week or two before his death. I spoke to him three weeks ago on the telephone, and he had just come back from a short goodbye visit to Guadeloupe. We were fond of Robert. He was a very gentle and considerate person. I arrived in Paris the day of his funeral, but Suzy had decided only to invite her children to the farewell.

Ten Days in Washington – Orchid Propagation

I enjoyed my stay in Washington, which I extended by a week, as I found that the time I had originally set aside (4-5 working days) was insufficient. The first weekend I was there I hired a car, and went to visit an orchid nursery on the other side of Baltimore. It was a very interesting place, run by a retired medical researcher who had worked with human tissue culture, and was applying this to orchid propagation. There is nothing novel about this; it is the normal modern way to propagate orchids, but I had never seen it done. He grew hundreds of tiny plants on agar-agar jelly in bottles rather like square pint milk bottles, then transferred them to large test-tubes for despatch through the post. I bought two tubes, and was given a third which was supposed not to have worked well enough to be put on sale, as well as a number of larger plant bits. I have planted them all. Three days later, out of about ten plantlets, only one still looks as if it might be alive. I think I should have left them longer in the flask, as many had not developed roots, but it might not have been any more successful since most had not made contact with the nutrient jelly.

House in the Hills

The weekend after, I went "to the mountains" with our former next-but-one neighbours, the Conovers. They have a little house in the hills of West Virginia where they go to relax and soak in their outdoors hot tub. We duly relaxed and soaked in the hot tub. It was very pleasant, even though it rained all the first day. I was surprised to find that they relax so consistently that they had never walked to the top of the small wooded hill on which their house was built – just a little higher than the upper limit of their property. I made the pilgrimage and looked over the top into the next valley.

To The Gambia

Tomorrow afternoon I am off again for three days in The Gambia. This is for a big get-together between the Bank and the Gambians, and should not be too exacting. I should get back before Nicole goes off, unless she finds an earlier flight.

Bovine Tragedy

I'm sorry about Ron's cow. Surely they should have done a caesarian? I thought it was very standard these days, but maybe it simply wasn't worth the extra cost. I wonder if Ron will be able to resist buying another cow. Ron's leg operation sounds gruelling: I hope it was worthwhile.

Buying and Selling

Margaret must be keeping her fingers permanently crossed over the sale of her house. There are so many slips in this business. Bernard says he is more or less at the end of the process of their purchase, and that they expect to move in about a month after completion, because of the work that needs to be done. Our latest tenants in Sutton have moved out. They were very reliable in terms of paying the rent. It's not a great investment, but it more than covers its costs, and we will try and re-let it for the time being and hope that house prices go up a bit more before we think of selling.

A Tardy Project

Dominic is very on edge about his project. He started it so late that he may well have to defer his examination. Apparently he can do this, but it is a nuisance, since it may mean he cannot join us in the summer. I feel fairly sympathetic, as I found it extraordinarily difficult starting to set pen to paper for my thesis, and was possessed by a great deal of self-doubt.

You do get a lot of fun out of your little pond. I keep on thinking of building one here, but of course I can't just buy a plastic liner, and it means first assembling all the materials, then setting aside a couple of week-ends for the job.

Lots of love, David and Nicole

Letter to mother   Dakar, 05/06/1994

A Bad Back

I am trying, not very successfully, to minimise the time I spend sitting at a keyboard. I spent most of last Monday and Tuesday on my back, and my friendly (but I fear not very competent) doctor says I should stay there for ten days, but that's absolutely impossible. It's incredibly boring. You can't even read comfortably on your back.

I started having a very nasty back pain last Sunday evening which just got worse and worse and did not go away when I told it to. In the end I gave up and went to bed. I thought I must have a pinched sciatic nerve, but it's just lumbago. I get joint inflammation when I'm tired and under stress, and this time it was in my back. I also have "Land Rover back", or "parachutist's back" – vertebrae knocked out of line. In my case it's probably a mixture of Land Rover, falling off the trapeze, and heavy-footed running. Anyway, the only cure is to take pills to reduce the inflammation and take it easy until it goes away. After the first 24 hours it got a lot more bearable, and I can now do complicated things like tying my shoelaces with hardly a second thought. I realise that I was under a lot of stress. The last straw was a couple of disagreeable telephone calls on Friday afternoon, presaging an even more disagreeable meeting with the Minister of Finance. This was on my mind right through the weekend. As it happened, we eventually met yesterday, and he couldn't have been more cordial, so I could have saved myself the worry.

A New Boubou

One of the consequences of this indisposition is that I have acquired a second *boubou* – a long nightshirt-like garment which is traditional dress here, and which I put on when I am pretending to relax on my back or when I get home from work. I telephoned Nicole's friend Claude, and asked her to get one made to the same dimensions as the one I already had. I had it by that afternoon. It really is much more comfortable in this climate than shirts and trousers, and of course when my back was really painful it was a lot easier to put on. The guards and the gardener were very taken by my Senegalisation when they first saw me like this, but they are now perfectly used to it. I do also have a *"grand boubou"*, but that is a much less practical garment. You are meant to wear baggy trousers (crotch somewhere around your knees, identical front and back), then a *petit boubou* like a short nightshirt, then the *grand boubou* itself, which goes down to the ground and is as wide as it is long, with a lot of machine embroidery. Mine is white, and was made to fit a Senegalese friend who turns out to be an inch taller than me, so I keep on tripping over it.

Orchids from Guadeloupe

I talked to Nicole a couple of days ago, and to Mme Fortuné who sounded very fit and spry. She seems to have recovered very well, and Nicole is enjoying the change – though finding it much hotter than she remembered. She has promised to bring me back an orchid. My orchids are doing quite well, but the only one flowering is the one which I received in flower from Jean Monneret. I expect Nicole back on the 11th.

Lots of love, and sorry to be so preoccupied with my ills. David

Letter to Mother   Dakar, 16/06/1994

Fluctuating Correspondence

I'm afraid I have not been keeping up with my letters to you. Nor have you with your letters to me. Who has the better excuse? Anyway I like getting letters, so I had better write some. I even quite like writing them.

Reception at the Embassy

We have had another week of cocktails and receptions, including the French 14th July, which is the biggest one of all. Several thousand people are invited, but there are definite classes of invitation. The ordinary French citizens have to go to the Embassy to collect an invitation, and can queue up to get through the gates from 7pm. It is believed that somewhere around a million Senegalese are really entitled to French passports, but not all of them have them, and most of those that do keep quiet about it. But there are thousands of "real" French people here as well. Diplomatic people and French officials are invited at 6pm, but mostly they have to enter on foot. Heads of missions are allowed to drive in, in their official cars, and (whereas everyone else goes straight through to the grounds and joins the food fight) they are ushered into a large room where the food and drink are relatively easy to get to. This year we were in this last category (last year too, as Elkyn was away).

Stand to Attention!

The advantages of this discrimination were mitigated by the fact that the room was very crowded and stiflingly hot, so when I thought we had done the statutory amount of socialising we went out to the gardens (where it is only crowded around the food and drink), only to be halted on the terrace by the Senegalese military band playing the Marseillaise and the Senegalese national anthem; five minutes standing to attention, more or less.

Of all the countries I have worked in, Senegal is the one whose national anthem is the least familiar to me. I hear it only about twice a year, and I would have no idea what it was if it were not being played by a full military band with everyone else around me standing to attention, just to give me a hint. It's not much of a tune either; several odd changes of key signature and tempo, but nothing catchy about it. By contrast, the Tanzanian national anthem is a really good tune (it is actually the pan-African national anthem, so it happens also to have the same tune as the Zambian national anthem and the new South African national anthem). As for Botswana, I can even sing most of the first verse of their national anthem (in Setswana). The Kenyan national anthem (which may have been changed by now, as President Moi hated it) is like a plaintive bugle-call, a bit reminiscent of the Last Post, and both pleasant and easily recognisable.

Nervous Farmers

The weather is getting hot, and we have had the first rains. We could do with some more, or at least the farmers could. It's been raining quite well in the south for the last month, but in the drier north the farmers planted their seeds about two weeks ago, and they will lose the planting if there is a long break in the rains. This is particularly disastrous for the groundnut crop, as groundnuts have very heavy seeding rates; one has to plant about one-ninth of the volume that one expects to harvest, whereas with most cereal crops the seeding rate is less than half a percent of the expected crop. So a failed groundnut planting is likely to leave the farmers with nothing to plant when the rains start again.

Dreaming of Bordepaille

We are, of course, also getting towards holiday time, not only for us but for everyone else, and one of the consequences of this is a very welcome easing off of the Washington-dictated work load. I actually have time to think about some of the longer-term things we should be working on. My mind is turning more and more towards Bordepaille. Chris Woods should be there now with his family. I'm afraid he will have found a bit of a mess in the big room, as the carpenter has finished his bit of the floor, making a criss-cross latticework of oak planks on the raised part, but the tiler has not yet filled in the gaps with tiles. All the same, it's a lot more advanced than last time he was there, and there are now three upstairs bedrooms.

We are due to arrive in Birmingham on 12th August, and will hire a car there and come to Leicester to see you. We will leave again very early in the morning of the 15th. Sure you don't want to come with us and enjoy the sunshine and nice soothing red wine? Dominic says he will be in Bordepaille from 4th August, and will have the car waiting for us at the airport. Bernard and Stella come later.

I think Bernard and Stella are in their house by now. They have really waited until it was comfortable to move in (I expect a caustic comment from Nicole on that, as my tendency has always been to move in as soon as possible, to avoid having to pay for two lots of accommodation, and in order to use my spare time to do the repairs).

I hope you have not been too uncomfortable during the really hot weather, and that the warmth has made your fingers and right arm feel better. My back isn't giving me any trouble at the moment – risky thing to say!

Lots of love, David and Nicole

Letter to Mother   Dakar, 19/06/1994

Tamkharit Feast Day

Today it's Nicole's turn to come back from a nice weekend at the beach as an invalid. Same beach, same friends, but she has stomach trouble not back trouble. I expect she'll feel better tomorrow. Anyway, she can take it easy, as tomorrow has been declared a public holiday to celebrate the feast of Tamkharit, which falls a certain time after Tabaski. One of our party had a list of the things you are meant to do at Tamkharit. It includes washing really well (not just the little wash of feet, hands, face and rinse out your mouth that one is meant to do before all five daily prayers), give alms, put your hand on the head of an orphan, feed your family well, and fast the day after. Well I reckon we should be fasting the day after, because we ate very well today, although I have to attend a conference in a big hotel tomorrow (the holiday was declared too late to cancel it) so fasting may be difficult.

A Chatty Friend

We were bidding farewell this weekend to two friends who are leaving Dakar and going on to another post in Benin. The husband is a *pied noir* (born in North Africa) and talks all the while, and the wife hardly talks at all, but they are both very nice even though Christian is a little tiring as company. It is almost impossible to read in his presence. Nicole told me today that their eighteen-year-old daughter died of anorexia four years ago, and that this had a great affect on them both. Thank goodness sons seldom suffer from this strange and difficult affliction. You would have thought it was almost impossible for an otherwise normal person to starve himself or (usually) herself to death, but it is surprisingly common. I knew of a fatal case in Botswana (an ex-patriate wife who helped the process on by compensating with gin what she missed in solid food).

An Orgy of Food

No-one was suffering from anorexia yesterday. We started with assorted *hors d'oeuvres* (to be avoided, because these are virtually meals, not nibbles), then a nice big lump of *foie gras*, then a good plate of smoked salmon, lumpfish roe (I don't think it was real caviar), sour cream and *blinis* (little pancakes), and finally to fill the remaining gap, two barbecued lambs. In the end I more or less took charge of the barbecuing, as our friends spent a great deal of time discussing the finer points, but when push came to shove they turned out to be remarkably incompetent over the practical details: lighting the fire, getting the carcases close enough to cook but far enough not to burn, and finally dismembering them fast enough to serve hot. Fortunately we had two Senegalese to turn the spit, and they were a lot more practical than the majority of the party. They were also well recompensed with a very good share of the meat, as people did not seem to be extraordinarily hungry by the time it arrived on the table – but it was very tasty. I did all the carving; I don't know why this always falls to me, but I was elected an honorary *pied noir* in consequence.

News of Relatives

I received your letter. I knew Phyllis's son Robert had been unwell, but not that he had cancer. What appallingly bad luck! But I gather from our telephone conversation that Auntie Kath is still with us, and I am full of admiration for Uncle Stan's enterprise. Where does he find them? *(NOTE - Elderly Stan Jones had married for the third time!)*

A Fortunate Conference Location

With luck I shall spend next weekend in Bordeaux, representing the Bank at a meeting of the Bordeaux Chamber of Commerce on Africa, and I intend to hire a car and spend Saturday night at the Crivellaro's house. I'm not going to go to the trouble of getting out all our bedding for just one night. Daisy tells me that neither Gervais nor Gettoni (carpenter and plasterer) has yet started work on their jobs for this year, but that the combined Grillon and Crivellaro families are pursuing both of them vigorously. On Monday she will spring on them the fact that *"M. Jones arrivera ce weekend"*. Lots of love, David and Nicole

Letter from Nicole to Sheila and Ron   Dakar, 15/09/1994

A Good Holiday

We had a lovely time in the Pyrenees and stayed at the Grillon's beautiful house. The Pyrenees are a beautiful region, worth visiting, and the walks are endless.

We came back on Sunday and we are finding it difficult to adapt as it is very hot and humid. We both started work on Monday.

Daisy (neighbour at Bordepaille) was pleased to receive your card and very complimentary of your French. Last week she packed the things which are on the way to Mauritania. She herself is leaving on 28th September.

David did not manage to do much work, but he tiled the bathroom floor as well as around the bath.
Love, Nicole

Letter to Mother   Dakar, 23/10/1994

Family News

I gather from a letter received last week from Margaret that Auntie Kath died. I hope she just sunk away quietly. I didn't really know her very well, but she always seemed both very nice and very sensible. I fear that Uncle Ted will greatly feel the loss. We have sent him a little note.

Margaret seems to be very happy with her new house in Devon; but I hope Timmy finds a job there. It's a part of England that is full of retired people of reasonable means, so there ought to be gardening jobs there if anywhere.

Lazy Weekend Among Friends

We have spent a lazy weekend. Our friends George and Claude having left, we no longer have free access to the beach house they rented on the Petite Côte, so we have taken to spending our Sunday lunchtime at the swimming pool of one of the hotels here, with a variable group of friends. The hotel has kindly given most of us complimentary passes in the hope of attracting the custom of our institutions. I can't say that I have actively steered any business their way, but a number of Bank people are in the habit of staying there because it is the best-situated in-town hotel, overlooking the sea, with pleasant gardens and an Olympic-sized swimming pool (50 metres). Anyway, they get their money back all right from the club sandwiches and drinks we consume on the premises. Nicole and I go there quite a lot at lunchtime on weekdays. I do half a kilometre and feel very virtuous about it. It's a sociable place, much patronised by the Lebanese community.

Health Troubles for Expectant Grandparents

Nicole's leg is still not completely better (I think I told you she had paraphlebitis, for which I find she takes a medicine which is an extract of the herb rue). We should spend about five days in Britain at the beginning of December, on our way to a meeting in Kenya, and we hope we can get her looked at by a specialist, to seek the source of the problem. The other (and original) reason for this side trip is, of course, to try and see the grandchild. It's meant to arrive on 23rd November, so we cannot be absolutely sure that it will be there by 3rd December. Hope so for Stella's sake.

A Tedious Conference and Dinner on an Island

In principle I was meant to spend most of last week at a conference in Dakar, but two colleagues came from other resident missions, and I was very pleased to leave most of it to them. It was a "regional tripartite conference" of governments, trades unions and employers' federations on the effects of the big January 1994 devaluation in ex-French Africa (which all has the same money) – but since it is really too early to know what has happened, and since dialogue between these three parties is pretty stilted at the best of times, it was pretty boring. I was lucky having my office on hand. My colleagues really had no excuse to do anything else, but they went away saying how much nicer Dakar was than where they lived. This reaction was very much influenced by a dinner we had the day before they went, on the Isle de Goree, the oldest settlement here. It's a former slave trade despatch point – but very charming despite its history, and requiring a pleasant twenty-minute ferry journey to get there. The night was balmy, and the food was at least fairly good.

More Orchids

Yesterday afternoon I popped over to have a look at the orchids of our friend Jean – a much more serious orchidist than me. When I got there he said *"you must have smelled that there was something here for you"* and gave me two very interesting plants that another mutual friend had brought back from the Comorro Islands. Very exciting! Now it's more than ever important that I find some way of bringing my plants into the U.S.A. when we return there – which in principle is March or April next year. I have two plants in flower at the moment, and another two about to flower, so I'm doing pretty well by my standards.
Lots of love, David and Nicole

Letter to Mother   Guadeloupe, 07/01/1995

A Caribbean Break

Welcome to 1995! Only five years to go before the end of the millennium.
Nicole and I have spent a very pleasant and relaxing week in Guadeloupe. I haven't been here since 1987, although Nicole has visited a number of times in the interim and both the boys have been here. I put Nicole on her plane this afternoon, and I shall leave tomorrow via Washington where I shall spend most of a week. It will also involve my touching down in Porto Rico for the first time. I have just been reading a short popular history of the Caribbean by Alec Waugh (brother of the more famous Evelyn Waugh) and he makes Porto Rico under the Spanish sound a most peculiarly backward place – but of course the Spanish were thrown out by the Americans around 1902 so I expect things have changed (according to Waugh, practically the only agricultural implement was the machete, and the whole population lived in hovels).

Hurricane Hugo, and Large Families

Guadeloupe is much more built-over than last time I was here – partly the result of hurricane Hugo, which led to a lot of French and EEC subsidies for rebuilding, and partly the result of the reproductive energies of the Guadeloupeens. The rest of France is at about replacement level in terms of family size, but in Guadeloupe they go on having 6-7 children, often in rather amorphous families. It's not so much a matter of single-parent families as of multi-parent families.

A Prolific Black Sheep!

Mind you, the Fortunés, St. Clements and Noels are largely excluded from this process. With the one notable exception of "tonton Guy", the black sheep of the family who produced something like thirteen children, mostly by a lady to whom he was not married, there is a remarkable lack of succession, and most of what there is, is not in Guadeloupe. There is only one three-year-old, Leo, tardily-produced offspring of Nicole's cousin Gilou and his American wife Carmen – nice, attractive little boy .

NOTE – I remember an amusing anecdote about "Tonton Guy's" family. His wife was asked why she agreed to care for (some of) these "extra" children from time to time. She replied with disarming simplicity – "They are the children of my husband!"

Age Takes its Toll

The house in Basse Terre is now inhabited by Mme Fortuné's three sisters – a sad stewpot of frail hypochondria – plus Anick who must have a hard time, but somehow keeps in good spirits. Mme Fortuné is by far the sprightliest of the four sisters and does well to stay independent, and although the big house in Ste Anne is a lot of work and worry for her, I think it keeps her in much better physical and mental shape than if she were to join her sisters at Basse Terre.

Visits, Beaches and Orchids.

We have had a fairly active week, starting with *reveillon* in Denys' new house, then back to Ste Anne, then a night in Basse Terre and a visit to Ste Claude up on the mountainside, then a visit to one of the most active orchidists here – a white Guadeloupeen, M. French – and back again to Ste Anne, with some beaches and swims scattered through the programme. I have collected some orchids, both from other collectors and from the wild, which will further complicate my return to the U.S. (probably in about six month's time).

Water-Powered Rum Distillery

We visited a small rum distillery. It is quite a well-known brand in Guadeloupe, but was remarkably primitive. The small sugar-cane mill was still worked by water, with a big iron water-wheel. There appeared to be about ten or twelve permanent employees working in a rather leisurely fashion, wrapping bottles up in cellophane by hand, or cutting up hot peppers and onions for the piment plant (nothing to do with the rum), and a rather beautiful garden with a stream running through it to feed the water-mill and a crayfish farm. It seemed a rather idyllic existence, and I think I shall look out for a small distillery to which I can retire! Unfortunately there are not very many, and they seldom come onto the market.
Lots of love, David

Letter to Mother   La Saumone, Senegal, 29/01/1995

Beach House

No, we have not moved: the address is our friends' beach house where we are spending the weekend. The sea is calm and rather chilly, the sky overcast, the temperature very agreeable. We did go swimming yesterday afternoon, but I think that today we will wait until the sea has warmed up a bit. Nicole is cooking lunch – a steak and kidney pudding which smells very good although it is too soon after breakfast to feel really hungry. I expect that when she has finished this stage of cooking we will take a long walk down the beach to work up an appetite. I have just been in to give a hand with the pastry and eat a few lumps of meat.

Sleeping on a Slope

We brought with us a visiting World Bank friend – a Scottish lady long established in Washington – and gave up our usual bed to her, so we slept in the tent. I can't say that I slept quite as well as in my bed. I did not take the trouble to level our sleeping area before pitching the tent, and although it was quite smooth, it had a strange slope. Also some of the Lebanese neighbours were having a noisy party a few hundred yards away until the small hours of the morning. But I expect in total I was awake for only about twenty minutes in the course of the night, so I can't really complain. I think Nicole slept very well (she'll probably say the opposite: that she was awake for hours while I was asleep and snoring loudly. I have to say that she was not snoring!).

A Move from Leicester to Devon

I wouldn't worry about selling your house. All houses do eventually sell, and if they seem to be hanging fire you put down the price. Estate agents know the market and by and large they have the same interests as you – but perhaps they are a little less worried than you about selling fast, because you bear the cost of financing two houses whereas they get paid according to the price they obtain – but they are also interested in getting them sold in order to keep their income coming in. So, generally, take their advice not mine!

Good News from Dominic

Just got a letter from Dominic; fairly up-beat. He now hopes to finish all the work in March and to present in May. He's working part-time, teaching a foundation course, which he enjoys and which is good for morale. Bernard, Stella and Alistair seem to be in good form too.
Lots of love, David and Nicole

Letter to sister Margaret   Dakar, 05/02/1995

A Surprising Gift

Thanks for the wooden platter of extra-large sugared almonds. We are keeping them for just the right set of visitors: the ones whose teeth look as if they need just a small shock to finally fall apart (no, I'm not being serious). In fact the plate and its contents will probably part company, as Nicole thinks that the stones will do nicely for Japanese flower arrangements. But how did you polish them? Has one of your family invested in a stone polisher?

Difficult Gardening

It was very nice to get your letter. You seem to have had an active Christmas. I really do very little gardening at present, apart from my orchids. The latter are really a very different sort of activity, as I don't even have to go outside to look after them, and I have altogether given up the use of both earth and organic supports (not counting charcoal) as far too liable to harbour insects and encourage rot. This is not a great country for gardening. We water everything, but few things grow really well, and rather a lot of things start growing and then mysteriously die. I think the water is partly to blame (lots of chlorine and traces of salt), and the unpromising soil and dry dusty climate finish the job. The only thing that does really well in our garden is oranges, and a tough climbing plant that our gardener calls "the Algerians" but which to our surprise really is called "Algerias". My orchids suffer a bit from the water, but generally do reasonably well all things considered. I usually have one or two in flower or coming up to flower. I hope I do not have to dispose of them all when we leave, but it seems all too likely.

A Rough Swim

We spent the day at the beach with an old friend – the godmother of Patrick Regaud at Bordepaille, who has worked here for thirty years and finally retired here. It was a pleasant day, quite warm, but I was the only one who went swimming as her little beach house is on a beach that catches the full force of the waves, and they were really crashing in today. It was quite tricky getting into the water, and even trickier getting out again. In fact I think one could get quite badly banged around if one did not judge it right between waves. Lots of love, David and Nicole

Letter to Mother   Dakar, 12/02/1995

HAPPY BIRTHDAY! I didn't mean to put that in capitals, but they look right, so I shall leave them.

Under the Weather

The weather here is cool, dry and dusty, which takes its toll on the lungs and throat. Nicole has been struck down with a very nasty bout of tonsillitis and has been in bed for the last week, but is beginning to feel better, though tired. I've kept well, although I still have a slightly sore arm which I am beginning to fear is nothing more than rheumatism – i.e. perfectly banal, but likely to come back if it ever has the grace to go away, and I am tired.

An Intricate History

It follows that we have not been doing a great deal in the way of outings, although we did go to the beach last Sunday, to the house of the Regauds' old friend Mickeye – a doughty lady, who has lived here all her working life, and finally retired here. Her husband retired from her life about thirty years ago to live with another lady, and to ensure that Mickeye would not have rights to his (reportedly) considerable wealth he put most of it in the name of the new lady, who has recently got tired of him and kicked him out. Now Mickeye's nightmare is that he will try and claim a share of her very small (indeed almost imperceptible) fortune. She also has a son, who is the apple of her eye, and who has done very well for himself in the French diplomatic service, but he has acquired a wife who apparently decided to cut her out of her family's life, and the son goes along with this – very distressing!

Important Visitors

I have just been to the airport to meet the vice-president and chief economist of the Bank, who is visiting Dakar for two and a half days. He seems a nice enough chap, but you can imagine that this sort of high-level visit takes an enormous amount of organising. In his luggage, as it were, he also brings my Washington colleague who is economist for the Senegal programme. As soon as they go, I shall go off to Washington myself for about twelve days. My trip has two purposes: to help my French volunteer buy us some computer software and hardware, and to do some "fishing" for interesting new posts. The fishing grounds are looking pretty barren at the moment, as the Bank is "downsizing", and despite protestations that this would not lead to redundancies, the first of these are beginning to appear. Consequently morale is very low in the institution. African programmes are more or less spared the worst of the downsizing, because the Bank is increasingly concentrated on Africa, but the geographical department I belong to also has low morale, because its new director doesn't command much loyalty.

Grandson Alistair

Bernard and Stella report that Alistair is putting on weight fast, and behaving rather considerately towards his parents. Lucky them! Long may it last.

November 1994, Bernard with son Alistair

1996 – Dominic, Stella, Bernard with Alistair, David

233

Carnival in Cape Verde

While I am in Washington, Nicole goes away on a spree with a bunch of French friends, to enjoy the Carnival in Cape Verde, and visit several of the islands. I'd like to go too, but I don't think I can give myself another week's holiday.

It's time I went out again (7.30pm) to preside over a restaurant dinner with our vice-presidential guest. Ah me!

Lots of love, David

Letter to all friends   Dakar, 14/03/1995

Late Again!

By the time I get this finished, I guess it will be the latest Christmas letter I have ever written. My feeble excuse is that I have had a lot to do.

Devaluation

Our stay in Senegal is nearly at an end. In March we shall have been here three years, a normal World Bank tour, and I am planning for a mid-year return. But we have had an exciting year. In January 1994 the African Franc zone countries bowed to the inevitable – much too late – and devalued by 50%. We had been working for this, but it was the French who pulled the plug. The governments were not well prepared, and we had some chaotic days helping them decide what to do immediately afterwards, by way of temporarily freezing some prices, cutting import duties, modifying the budget, and so on. The Bank had done some preparatory work, which was then absorbed into similar IMF work. Then we set aside our normally tedious loan procedures to make a very quick recovery loan.

The devaluation came as an enormous shock to many people, including businessmen whom we thought had anticipated it, but the overall effect has been good, at least in Senegal. There have been no disasters, businesses have generally welcomed the change (winners have outnumbered losers) and government has accepted that it has to make reforms. The rest of the year was taken up with rather frustrating, seemingly interminable debate with the government, within the government, and between the government and the interest-groups on the nature of these reforms. This held up our lending activity, but the log-jam has now broken.

Expanding the Office

During all this time I have been acting Resident Representative here, and it has been wearing but fun. We have a good, mostly Senegalese, resident mission – the largest in our Sahel region – and although the World Bank was cutting back on Washington staff and closing small resident missions we have been allowed to expand. We ran out of space, so we rented two apartments adjoining our offices and had them entirely rebuilt. For several months I was able to enjoy one of my favourite activities – building – as part of my legitimate work. I did not actually wield a trowel, but I struck the first sledge-hammer blow to break through the massive concrete wall between the old and the new areas. We now have the best office suite in the region.

A 50th Anniversary

Another nerve-wracking activity was the organisation of an "open doors" event to celebrate the World Bank's 50th anniversary. We hired the Chamber of Commerce, put up stands, and held public events with media coverage. It could have been a disaster. My staff (despite huge qualities) have an "it-will-all-come-right-on-the-night" approach to forward planning, but to my surprise it did come right. People kept on saying *"I suppose all the World Bank resident missions are doing this"*. In fact I think we were the only one in the world.

Meanwhile, back at the ranch, the World Bank was embarking on deep budget cuts and reorganisations, probably more drastic than those of 1986-7, with the difference that then there appeared to be a grand plan, whereas this time the decisions seem to emerge piecemeal. I am sure that surgery was needed, but the way the knife is being wielded is not doing a great deal for morale or (in the short term) for efficiency.

Family Celebrations

On the family front, there were three big events: my mother's 80th birthday in February, with a big family gathering; Nicole's and my 30th wedding anniversary in August, with a big family and friends party in Bordepaille (and a two-sheep barbecue); and the biggest event of all was the birth of Bernard and Stella's son, Alistair Adam, in November. He's growing fast (very fast) and is the first real red-head in our immediate family. Bernard's doing well with selling flowers to supermarkets, and Dominic is still finishing his M.A. at the Royal College of Art, with a project on doors (yes doors; quite a lot of them).

Various Islands

We gave ourselves an unusual luxury this year, and spent New Year in Guadeloupe. I hadn't been for about seven years, and never in wintertime; very pleasant, although it was a surprise to find the sea rather chilly. Nicole has just been off to the Cape Verde carnival in Mindelo, while I was on a working trip to Washington. We know and like Cape Verde (completely different from Senegal, physically and culturally). Apparently the carnival was a lot of fun, and it also gave her the chance to visit the most spectacular island, Sao Antao. I made up partially for this by my first visit to Guinea-Bissau – strange, and very undeveloped country.

Social Life

Nicole is extremely busy with her half-time work at the British Embassy, the diplomatic wives association, sewing group (quilting is the great passion; extremely laborious when done well), and singing. Most weekends we go to friends' beach houses at the coast, and several evenings a week there are social activities. Although she will never admit it, I am sure she will miss Dakar – at least some aspects of it anyway, although it is a filthy city, and one gets tired of *"la main tendue"* (the outstretched palm). As for my hobbies, I have got very slack on ordinary gardening, but my orchid collection now numbers about fifty plants, and from time to time one of them actually does me the honour of flowering. I hope I shall be able to take a lot of them back to the U.S. with me.

Progress at Bordepaille

The house in Bordepaille is becoming more and more habitable, with three proper bedrooms upstairs (i.e. with walls and doors) and two functioning bathrooms, one *en-suite* to our bedroom. My original plan was to take advantage of a difference in floor levels to make a sunken bath, but fortunately I tried it out before it was finished, and found it was quite difficult to get in and out of, and extraordinarily hard to clean (the only practical way to clean a sunken bathtub is to get into it). So I compromised and we have only a half-sunken bathtub. The big room downstairs (14 metres long), which used to be a barn, now has a very handsome terracotta tiled floor. We are still waiting for our incredibly slow and un-cooperative local joiner to put in a double door to the great outside (East end), and I still have to build a fireplace. Nicole insists that the next big priority is the kitchen. I had not noticed this, but I have to concede that she is probably right.

World in a Muddle

As for the world, it is a bit of a mess. Illusions that the transition to democracy and liberal economics in Eastern Europe and the former Soviet Union would be straightforward have (fortunately) been dispelled, and my unfashionable pessimism on this subject in earlier letters (since Christmas 1991) has been pretty well on the mark. Russia remains a danger to itself, to the other republics of the FSU, and to the rest of Europe in that order. Internal disorder, like the Chechnya war (which I'm sure is not over) will probably preoccupy it for some years, but not make it nicer to live with. However, we still have not drawn the obvious conclusions from this new realism. The political and military feebleness of the European Union as a structure to defend liberal and humanitarian values within and around its borders remains extremely worrying, as does the short-sightedness and narrow-mindedness of most of my compatriots over foreign policy in general and Europe in particular. The general British view seems to be that Europe does not need to be a political entity because this is expensive and involves giving up sovereignty to foreigners, and because we can always depend on the U.S.A. to defend "liberal" Europe. I find this very stupid. The U.S.A. will always do, more or less, what is in its own interest – an interest presently perceived in a pretty short-sighted way.

The New China

Another thing that we tend to forget all about until it happens is that 1995 – 1997 (at least) promise to be a period of uncertainty and instability in China. Nicole and I are going to be watching this area of the world with some quite immediate interest over the next month or two, as Dominic has decided to go to Hong Kong with his portfolio while waiting for his exams. I think Dominic's trip to Hong Kong has at least as much to do with Hele's being there as with job search. Hele couldn't stand mainland China (or rather mainland Chinese) and dumped her scholarship, and is now teaching in the New Territories.

We'll probably be in France this August. What about you?
Love, David and Nicole

Letter to Family   Dakar, 02/04/1995

Jones, Johnson, or Johnes?

I have had a very busy week, with a variety of openings and public events at which I had to speak, and several meetings with ministers, and I am feeling a bit tired out. Monday night I leave for a week in the States, which should be fairly restful. I unwittingly caused a certain amount of amusement this week, when the radio news quoted me as M. Mark Johnson, the World Bank representative. Mark Johnson is actually the U.S. ambassador, but the name Jones causes a certain amount of confusion among Francophones, who usually spell it Johnes. Luckily Mark Johnson is not a hypersensitive type (and is out of town at the moment; his interim was most amused).

The Vital Siesta

Another rather exhausting aspect of the week was an excessive number of evening dos of various sorts; enjoyable enough one by one, but each usually means another late night, and these days I work Saturday mornings as well, so I only get Sundays to catch up on sleep. However, I have really instituted my siesta. I lock my office door, and after eating my salad I spend 20-30 minutes on the carpet, with my appointments diary under my head (it has a nice comfortable padded cover, and is almost two inches thick). It is now well understood that I am not to be interrupted during this period.

Off to Hong Kong

We wished Dominic a safe journey to Hong Kong the other night. I suppose he is there by now. I'm not sure if Nicole has an address for him. We are naturally a little anxious for him, but he's a seasoned traveller, and I suppose that Hele is around to take care of him. He says he has finished his doors except for two handles, which he did not need for his portfolio as one can only photograph one side of a door at a time.

Curious Behaviour of the Church of England!

Nicole brings home a strange variety of English newspapers from the office, with slightly stale news. Over the last few weeks I have been engrossed in the strange scandals of British life. It seems to me that the Church of England should be getting worried about charges that it practices a strange form of sexual discrimination: they really should appoint some non-homosexual bishops.

News of Family

I'm impressed by reports of young Alistair's growth. Bernard must be feeding him some sort of fertiliser. I fully expect to find him running around and talking next time I see him.

Bernard, what is the situation on the house in Alfred Road? I thought the tenants had given notice, but I have nothing written on this. Please can you check, and if this is the case, please ask Pollard Machin to re-market. I have decided not to sell it right now.

Now I have to get dressed for a reception at the British Embassy for a group called Jamaica Jazz, I think. That could be quite pleasant. Tomorrow we will go to the Petite Côte, and I have to do my packing in the evening.

Lots of love, David

PS from Nicole

The jazz concert at the British Embassy was excellent, but short. If it had not been for the fact that we had to get up early today in order to go to the beach I would have convinced David to go to the jazz club where the group was playing from 11pm. The group consists of players of Jamaican origin, but from England. It was meant to be a concert, but the music was so catchy that everybody was dancing in their seats and I was pleased when the Ambassador's wife got up and started to dance.

We spent the day at the beach but only the men were brave enough to swim, as the water was not only cold but full of small white pieces of algae. It also had a funny yellow colour. As usual we ate and drank well and everybody had a siesta afterwards.

The next two weeks will be very busy as my choir is giving several performances of *"The Pirates of Penzance"*. David is getting fed up with hearing the music all the time, but playing the tape helps me remember the words.

Lots of love, Nicole

Letter to Mother   Dakar, 23/04/1995

A Frustrating Journey

Last weekend (Easter) we went as far as we could go from Dakar without leaving Senegal. This was Kedougou, in the bottom right-hand corner of Senegal. We had intended to make it a four-day weekend, which would have been a bit more relaxed, but my planned return from Washington on Thursday was messed up by fog at New York, as a result of which my flight from Washington flew around for a while, and took off for Philadelphia. All we saw of Philadelphia was an airport lounge, but by the time I actually did make it into Kennedy, it was well past the departure time of my flight to Dakar, and I made a forlorn telephone call from a hotel in New York to Nicole to tell her to expect me when she saw me. By coincidence I was travelling with a young Senegalese minister whom I knew slightly, so we stuck together and tried to sort things out – not always an easy companion, as he kept on losing his temper with the (admittedly fairly incompetent) people around us. Anyway, we discovered the next day that we had not missed our flight at all, as it also had been unable to land, and took off around mid-day Thursday. So we could have gone off to Kedougou on Friday after all.

Enduring the Heat

We set off at 7.30am on Saturday morning, and I drove all 700km with just a short stop for lunch and various stops for refuelling. The road was generally good, and the trip was without incident, except that the fan on the air-conditioner broke down after the first 200km, and after that we just had to drive with the windows open and suffer the same heat as the Senegalese. And it was HOT. We had to go through Kaolak, which is often one of the hottest cities in the world, but as we went further south from there it got still hotter. We were very happy when we rolled into our *campement*, and found a *rondavel* with a rather feeble air-conditioner.

Forests and Fires

The journey was very interesting, as it took us through a gradual change of landscape and vegetation, from the very degraded and almost treeless landscape around Dakar and Kaolak, to the much more heavily vegetated savannah woodland in the south east. Mind you, there was depressing evidence of the damage done by the charcoal burners, and even in the relatively uncut area of Senegal Oriental there was a tremendous amount of fire damage, with fires still burning all around us.

I had not realised how widespread certain trees were in Africa. I saw a lot of trees that are common in Northern Botswana and Zimbabwe, including a very good timber tree (*Pterocarpus angolensis* to you). I shudder at the thought of this fine cabinetry wood being reduced to charcoal.

A Primitive Animist Tribe

On Sunday we hired an ancient Land Rover plus guide/ driver, and he took us for a walk to some villages in the hills. These belonged to a rather primitive animist tribe who had gone up there to get away from the islamicised tribes in the plains. It was much more picture-book Africa than most of Senegal, complete with rather attractive and scantily-clad young ladies with decorative straws pushed through the pierced septums of their noses. We were received in a very friendly fashion (we were armed with packets of cigarettes and bags of sweets), except by the adolescent boys preparing for initiation. The latter were not hostile, but part of their preparation consisted of spending the whole day marching rapidly non-stop around the village area with their arms stretched out in a "V" diagonally to the ground, in complete silence. It was interesting, but again very hot (around 100 degrees Fahrenheit) which made climbing the hills hard work.

A Welcome Dip

Then we went off to a famous waterfall – one of rather few in Senegal – where a small cascade comes down a corner in a rock-face that must be around 500 feet high. We were preparing to bathe in the small pool at the bottom, when a series of rocks fell down into it (probably thrown by monkeys) so we contented ourselves with a shower under a protective overhang.

We returned all in one piece, despite a sudden flat tyre at speed. We couldn't find out what had caused the tyre to burst, but it was so hot that we could not touch it, so that may have borne much of the responsibility.

Springtime in Washington

My previous weekend had been quite different. Washington was going through its sudden and short-lived Spring. All the cherry trees and magnolias were magnificently in bloom, but being torn apart fast by the wind and the warm weather. I spent Saturday putting up a rabbit/ ground hog fence around Pu-Chin's vegetable garden. On Sunday I went with Senegal friends to a lake cottage in Virginia, basked in the sun, and boated on the lake in a rubber dinghy with two totally undisciplined Italo-French-American teenagers and their father in such strong winds that we had great difficulty returning to shore (a little more co-ordination would have helped).

Cosmopolitan Social Life

We have had a lot of dinners out this week, and it was our turn to entertain last night – mixture of French, English, Malian and Senegalese, which does not always work, but it went very well. All very tiring, however, and I have another UN/ TV "do" this afternoon. Nicole has gone out to church and to vote, and I guess she is standing in a queue, as she is much later than usual. No news from Dominic for the last ten days; hope things are going smoothly for him in Hong Kong.

Lots of love, David

Letter to Mother   Dakar, 07/05/1995

A Vision of the Future

It was a relief to us anxious parents to know that Dominic had safely returned from Hong Kong. He insists it is perfectly safe compared with Latin America, and is a vision of the future.

He describes a sort of vertical city, with shops and factories half-way up skyscrapers, and motorways passing by the windows of the 15th floor. At first he stayed in a dismal dormitory with a lot of chain-smoking migrant workers (mainly British), but then someone from Kingston Poly took pity on him and put him up in his apartment. From a work-finding point of view it was disappointing, as most Hong Kong businesses are in too much of a hurry to employ designers, but he did get one nibble to follow up. And I was sorry but not surprised to hear that he and Hele had broken up. He does not seem too broken-hearted.

Contact with a Classmate

I think I told you that I had rediscovered one of my school friends, through his son who is the BBC stringer here. "Friend" is perhaps too strong a word for Richard Winter, although we got on well, and were both slight oddities, but whereas I was always an awkward type – a nail sticking out and just asking to be hammered flat – he was very earnest (and clever) and became school captain. He sent me a letter, in response to one from me, in which he said he remembered me for two things: my insistence on doing my own thing, and my saying to him *"you must be very proud to be Jewish"*, which he said was a sort of flash of discovery for him.

As an adult he seems to have been more or less of a conformist. He split with a first wife after a short marriage (the African factor, perhaps, as he was in Malawi at the time), then had a daughter with someone else, then married again. He is a professor of education at the Anglia Polytechnic University, and seems to be quite an eminent chappie. There's a good chance of his dropping by to see us in France this summer.

Other Schoolmates

It makes me wonder what happened to the rest of my sixth form colleagues. I would guess they are a pretty academic bunch. The only other one I am at all in contact with (Sigee) is a research fellow at Manchester University. He told me that he sometimes ran across Bailey (amiable fat boy, who wrote "unions" when he meant "onions", and said he couldn't see why it should not be spelled that way) who is in the same field (biochemistry). Tim Flowers was last heard of at a U.S. university, teaching and researching plant physiology. Richard Winter was on the other side: an English and French literature specialist before he became an educationalist.

Leaving Senegal

So much for nostalgia. We are starting to think seriously about packing up and selling things. I think we have a buyer for the car, the television/ video, the food mixer, the garden tables and chairs, the cool boxes.... But I am very preoccupied about my orchids. There does not seem to be a legal way of getting them into the U.S., which is a shame, as I have some really interesting plants, including some that I collected myself, and one which I have always coveted (*Angraecum eburnaeum*, found rarely in coastal Kenya, but this one is from the Comorres).

An Inflammatory Summit Meeting

The big event last week was the African-African-American summit in Dakar; huge disorder, leaving a trail of angry and dissatisfied people behind it, not least angry of whom was the French ambassador when the U.S. Commerce Secretary, Ron Brown (who used to do public relations lobbying for the Duvalier family) declared that they were going to release Africa from the clutches of the European countries that had been responsible for slavery and underdevelopment. I managed to restrict my involvement to a single cocktail. We did, however, have a visit from my former director, Katherine Marshall, on behalf of the Bank, and I had to put a lot of energy into important tasks like finding her a hotel room, and finding out when she was expected to make her speech. Fortunately, she is quite a nice and informal person.

Senegal Civil Service

I also gave a speech to the school of public administration on the future of the civil service in Senegal, which was quite interesting, although I find the Senegalese concept of a "round table" rather odd. It is usually anything but round in either the literal sense, or the figurative one of facilitating free and equal discussion. I found myself on a podium with about five bigwigs, each of whom made a long speech (including me) before the unfortunate students were allowed to speak. But when they were unchained, they made speeches too – so long that only a handful of them got the chance to speak at all.

Reformed University

Yesterday I went to the University with two of my colleagues to meet with the economic faculty. The University has really been tamed – largely as a result of processes started by the World Bank. After years of strikes and political pandering, the army cleared the place out, and reforms were pushed through, introducing firmer hierarchical control, and sending down students who failed their exams. Six months later the students are at last concentrating on working, not on demonstrating. The army is still there. In the quadrangle of the Economics faculty there were two soldiers, perfectly at home, sitting on a bench with their weapons in the hedge behind them (very easy to steal), chatting up a girl student. I get on well with a number of the university people. The dean (an old Marxist who opposed me in a TV debate) embraced me warmly when I arrived. Fortunately the rest of the faculty felt no need to embrace me, although I now put up with this without embarrassment from African and Arab colleagues.

French Presidential Election

Today Nicole voted early in the second round of the French presidential elections. I tried to persuade her to vote for the socialist, because I wanted Chirac to win as narrowly as possible, but she wasn't having any.

Tabaski Holiday

Then we went to the beach house of the Regauds' old friend Mickeye; retired gym teacher from the French *lycée* who was recruited locally and has too small a pension to retire in France, but is not too bothered because she prefers to live here. I swam a couple of times, and slept or read the rest of the time, except when we were eating. On the way we bought three animal head masks. I doubt if they are old, but they are not touristy rubbish. Street prices are low this week as everyone needs money to celebrate Tabaski. Rams for sale all over the place, and being transported in all directions on top of buses and taxis!
Lots of love, David

Letter to Mother   Dakar, 27/05/1995

Packing Up

My thoughts are increasingly dominated by the impending return, although there's a great deal still to do – in fact hardly anything yet done. The packers have come to look at the stuff to be packed, but we haven't yet fixed a date to get out of the house. I have spent a certain amount of time and effort getting export certification for my orchids, which is a necessary preliminary to getting them into the U.S. In the end I used my contacts in the Ministry of Agriculture here, and they duly stamped a form which I had adapted from a European Community export certificate, and a letter saying that all my plants came from the personal collection of a friend (who has import certificates), and a phytosanitary certificate saying that all the plants had been meticulously inspected and found to be pest-free – all this without anyone setting eyes on my plants. Let's hope the Americans believe it, and that I manage to get an import authorisation before I actually leave Senegal.

Carpentry Work for Bordepaille

My other special task has been some last minute carpentry work – done not by me, but by a Senegalese carpenter. I have had made a rather smart little corner wardrobe, to fit over the pipes in the corner of the entry-hall in Bordepaille, and I was so pleased with it that I asked the same man to make up the missing parts of a four-poster bed that I have in Bordepaille;

then in a spurt of energy I have drawn a whole series of kitchen units, also for Bordepaille. I went over these plans with the carpenter this morning. He's not cheap by Senegalese standards, but very cheap by U.K. or French standards, and should be able to supply me solid wood units at a lower price than the stuff made of chipboard and printed veneer in France. It's a pleasure working with someone who is eager to get the work, and is bright enough to see exactly what I want – and make suggestions for improving it – without a great deal of effort on my part. Mind you, I provide fairly meticulous technical drawings. It took me a day off (religious holiday) and several evenings to do them. It's one of the most useful things I learned at school.

Encounter with a Bus

To my great annoyance, I scratched the car today against a *"transport en commun"* – a communal bus. It was my fault – at least technically. There are a lot of VIPs in town, and I got diverted all over the place on my way into work this morning. At one stage I got stuck behind this *transport en commun*, which had simply stopped in the middle of the road to put down passengers. I was fed up and tried to squeeze by, and presto! Nasty scraping noise. I didn't do much damage to the *car rapide*, and paid the driver off on the spot, with the equivalent of £15; but it will certainly cost me a lot more to take out the scratches and little dents, and it is doubly annoying because I have a buyer for the car.

I'm going out to dinner in a few minutes. Think I had better go and have a shower. It's beginning to get hot and sticky.
Lots of love, David

Card to Sheila and Ron from Nicole   Bordepaille, 27/08/1995

Work at Bordepaille

We have had a violent storm last week and since then it is not so hot. David is trying to finish the second bathroom but doing several jobs at the same time. Dominic is with us, and is installing the plumbing for the kitchen. I might have a proper kitchen in a year or two!
Love to you all, Nicole and David

Letter to Mother   Alexandria, USA, 19/11/1995

Dominic's Career Takes Off

Dominic is being offered a definite assignment with the design firm in Ohio that interviewed him in the summer. This will be a great encouragement to him. He called me ten days ago, while I was in Mali, to discuss his options, because the offer came just as he and his friend Chris were apparently getting takers from an approach they were making to a plastics firm to develop a line of products from their materials. He was quite excited about the possibility of doing this freelance work, but they would have earned very little, and with Fitch he will be earning a reasonable salary, and learning something about working, which I think is very important even if his real aim is to work freelance. We are, of course, delighted that he will be nearer to us for a while, although it is a mistake to think of Columbus, Ohio, as "near"; it is in fact all of ten hours' drive from here.

Life in Mali

I quite enjoyed Mali. It is much poorer and at the same time less pretentious than Senegal, and one is less aggressively pursued by beggars and street traders. I had a very busy trip, starting off with a team of my own of seven people, who gradually whittled down to three, and at the same time there was a massive presence of other Bank people who were there for a programme review. This was a nuisance to me, because I found I was obliged to waste most of the first week attending the review, even though this was not the real purpose of my visit, so we had to work like crazy in the second week.

At Home in Alexandria

Back at home, things are now more or less in order. We have moved back into our bedroom, which is a good thing, as it is now quite chilly, and the basement has no heating. We are still waiting for Bobby to install a second radiator in our bedroom, but its temperature is tolerable. Also, our new bathroom is now functioning and looking rather smart, although it is too bad that Bobby did not protect the bathtub while doing his long tiling and re-tiling job, as repeatedly walking around in it with shoes on, crunching in rather abrasive bits of tile and tile cement has not done its surface any good. We still lack various fittings, like towel rails and a shower curtain – as a result of which Nicole usually goes off to the guest bathroom to use the newly installed shower cubicle there.

Unhappy Orchids

The weather is cool but fine. I think there has been a touch of frost, as I notice that some of the most cold-sensitive plants in the garden have scorched leaves, but our chrysanthemums are still flowering. My orchids are a bit of a problem. They are in our sun room, and to keep the humidity up we have a humidifier going. This produces so much condensation on the windows that puddles of water form on the floor, which is beginning to suffer as a result; despite all this, my plants still look pretty unhappy.

Donkeys in Devon

Your donkey shed sounds as slow as our bathroom. I am interested to hear how you actually get on with your new asinine friends (I suppose that is the right word; I have never heard it used except in a derogatory sense, but if you have bovine, ovine, caprine and equine you must surely have either asine or asinine).

Redundancy for Michael

Thanks for the family news. Too bad about Michael's job. But I am really a little jealous. I suppose he will get a reasonable retirement package, having been with local government for so long. But then what will he do? Look for another job, or freelance, or switch to buying and selling silver? He's very capable, so he should be all right.

I must go and pay some bills. They do tend to pile up when I am on trips.
Lots of love, David

Letter to Mother   Alexandria, 03/12/1995

Homeless Donkeys

We await with interest the next news on the donkeys. What I find hard to understand is that there are these hordes of aged donkeys in England looking for foster homes. I have only ever seen donkeys at the beach, and then only a few of them, something like thirty-five years ago, and I cannot believe that these donkeys have left hordes of progeny. Perhaps you can ask your donkey home where they all come from. Is this all a cunning plot to increase the donkey population of the U.K.?

"Thanksgiving" in New Hampshire

We had a very pleasant Thanksgiving weekend last week, spending five days in New Hampshire with Penny (friend from Woodstock days) and her husband Bob. I think of New Hampshire as real backwoods country, and there certainly is some of this, but Penny and Bob live in a sort of yuppie housing estate of imitation colonial-period houses (complete, of course, with double garage and remote-controlled doors), and this sort of housing seems to make up a very large part of New Hampshire. There are, however, some very old towns, a bit like Alexandria: Exeter and Portsmouth for example. We bought Maine lobsters off the boat for the last evening meal there (not very meaty lobsters, but I made a terrific sauce, including flaming whisky). I also stuffed and carved the Thanksgiving turkey.

Teething Troubles with Television

We returned on Monday, and have since had a busy week. We are still really in the process of settling back in, and yesterday we went out and bought ourselves a huge television set and a video. Do we really need these? I'm really not quite sure we do, although it is nice to be able to watch "telly" from time to time, and to have the wherewithal to watch videos. However, we are still not able to watch anything, as television now mainly comes by cable, so we have no aerial. We do have a cable, but every time we reconnect it a large lorry comes down the road and rips it off the side of the house. Next time we will ask the repair men to fix it on higher up (not "better" because if they did that the house might be pulled down as well as the cable). Then when I came to install the TV I found that the plug I had to use was an old-fashioned one without an earth, so I spent much of the morning putting this right. I was rather pleased with myself, as I did this quite fast and very cheaply, even though it involved pushing another cable through the wall, and I don't think I have ever come out of the do-it-yourself warehouse with less to pay (3 dollars 40c). Then I put up towel rails and things in the bathroom, so that is now almost fully functional, although we still have a hole in the wall where the radiators are meant to be.

Crickets and Jumping Spiders

The weather here is cold but brilliant, and the trees still have a surprising number of leaves left on them. One can measure the advancing seasons by the livestock in the house. When we first arrived here, the house – and particularly the basement – was full of crickets. They came in all sizes, looked hideous, made a horrible mess when squashed (some sort of advanced evolutionary protection?) and chirped away in odd corners of the house. Now we have another sort of beastie that is possibly another sort of cricket, but is more like a giant jumping spider. They are quite innocuous, and I usually let them be, but I notice that they are getting increasingly lethargic and decrepit. Many of them now have only one large jumping leg (don't know what they have done with the other) so that when startled they go up in the air sideways and land on their backs; than there is a great scrabbling about until they get right way up again.

News from the Boys

We have had both boys on the phone today. Bernard, Stella and Alistair seem to be on good form, with an offer on their house which seems firm, but nothing that they like yet in Bedford. Alistair is now walking and has totally given up crawling. Dominic is doing some free-lance work for which he is being paid (pleasant change), and is negotiating with the firm here to try and get a better deal, although at the end of the day he will take whatever they stick at. We look forward to seeing him at Christmas.

Lots of love, David

P.S. from Nicole
A Cultural Week

Thank you for your birthday wishes and the cheque. On the evening of my birthday we went to the theatre to see a play by an American author, Albee (author of *"Who's afraid of Virginia Wolf?"*). It was about old age, and slightly depressing, but there were some funny parts. It was quite a cultural week, as on Thursday we went to a concert by courtesy of our friends Teresa and John Conover (ex Columbus Street neighbours). They have a subscription for concerts at the Kennedy Centre and as they were in New York that day, they offered us the tickets. It was a Beethoven evening and very enjoyable. We appreciate having the Kennedy Centre so near. I have bought tickets to go and listen to the *"Messiah"* on 15th December.

A Tidy Neighbourhood

Today everybody in our street was busy either sweeping the leaves or decorating the outside of their houses for Christmas. There are some quite elaborate Christmas decorations. I have not decorated the house but I swept the leaves into the gutter. Every other week, from November to

the end of December, the City Council picks up the dead leaves left by house owners in the gutter outside the houses. It is a bit untidy for a day or two, but it is a good service.
Love, Nicole

Letter from Nicole to all friends

Putting the House in Order

After three years in Senegal we are now back in the U.S.A. We left Dakar last July and came straight here in order to get settled, to accustom ourselves to living once again in the States and to put the house in order before going on holiday in August.

As you all know it was a very hot summer and in Washington the heat was unbearable. We knew that the air-conditioning in the house was not very efficient (having bought the house just before leaving for Senegal we had never lived in it), but we found out that it was useless, so one of our first priorities was to have central air-conditioning installed before next summer. Before we left for our holiday in France we had also arranged for a builder friend of ours to start doing some alterations in the house (extending the main bedroom and bathroom and building a new bathroom). He had promised us that the work would be finished on our return in September, but in fact he only finished last week. In the meantime our sea freight was delivered at the beginning of October, but because of the building work we did not have access to the first floor and had to store everything in the basement. Until three weeks ago we were also sleeping in the basement where fortunately there is a bedroom and bathroom. Now that the building work is finished I can tidy the house and I certainly feel more settled.

Welcome to Alistair

As most of you know, the big event of our life last year was the birth of our grandson, Alistair (Bernard's and Stella's son) last November. He is a very cheerful red-haired one-year-old now and I was able to see a lot of him this year. I even spent three weeks in September looking after him during the day while his maternal grandparents, who look after him twice a week, were on holiday.

Family News

The other important event this year is that Dominic obtained his M.A. in Industrial Design from the Royal College of Art. Last week he was offered a job with a firm in Columbus (Ohio). It is strange to think that for the first time in years we shall be living on the same continent. Bernard and Stella have lived in North Cheam, Surrey, for the last two years, but Bernard was made redundant in September, and was fortunately offered a job by his former employer in Bedford. To their regret they will have to move to Bedfordshire. They have been very fortunate up to now, living near Stella's parents who look after Alistair twice a week, while a child-minder looks after him on the other two days. Stella does not work on Fridays so she is able to stay with him.

A Lady of Leisure!

For the first time in my life I am not working and I am not in a hurry to look for employment. I have plenty to do at home for the time being. Now that I am not working I am also able to join in the various activities organised by the World Bank Spouses' Association.

As usual the autumn in Washington has been beautiful and not too cold. Until the beginning of November it was still warm and it is only in the last few days that the trees have lost all their leaves. I am pleased to be back here, although I miss all the friends I made in Dakar and sometimes I wish I had a maid again, but it is nice to be back in civilisation. David finds the change more difficult as it is not easy to suddenly become an ordinary employee of the Bank after having been a Resident Representative and a very important person in Senegal. He will continue to travel and is just back from a trip to Mali. David joins me in wishing you a Merry Christmas and a very Happy New Year.
Love, Nicole and David

Budget in the Offing

Another Christmas has gone by and life is quieter for a few days until next weekend when everybody will be busy getting ready for New Year celebrations. In D.C. life is still at a standstill for the federal workers who are at home waiting for the politicians to come to a decision regarding the budget. Some of the museums and places of interest have reopened, thanks to private funding. What a good thing there are some wealthy people around!

Festive Season

Thank you all very much for your presents. The drying up cloth is very colourful and makes me feel nostalgic as it reminds me of France and the holidays. I know that David is enjoying the book. Once again Dominic acted as Father Christmas and brought with him all the presents (even his own which I had already bought in September when I was in England).

We were just the three of us for Christmas, but there was just as much cooking as if we had been ten. For the last few years we have had a goose for Christmas. Having had turkey for Thanksgiving a month ago, we did not want another turkey meal.

Peace on the Home Front

We have now settled well in our house in Alexandria. The building work was finally finished a month ago. Just before Christmas I had the dining room, sitting room, the TV room and the staircase decorated. The rest of the house needs decorating but we shall have to do it ourselves. Dominic has hung up most of the paintings, African masks and ornaments on the walls and I feel more at home with all my possessions around me.

Sunny Weather

It has been very cold and windy all through the week and we have had a few snowflakes on several occasions, but the weather is dry and sunny which makes all the difference. One of the good things in the Washington area is that we enjoy sunny weather during the winter.

We spent Thanksgiving in New Hampshire at a friend's whom we knew in Woodstock. At that time her husband was English, but since then she has divorced, returned to the States and remarried. New Hampshire is a very beautiful part of the country and one has the impression of being in England as so many of the towns have English names.

Blizzard of the Century
14/01/1996

Since starting this letter we have had the blizzard of the century and life is slowly coming back to normal after a week of hibernation. The snow is still piled high on the sides of the roads and it makes walking and parking cars very difficult.

Dominic has heard from the U.S. firm and is starting work on 1st February. Unfortunately he will not have time to come to Alexandria before going to Columbus, but I expect that we shall drive to Columbus to see him when the weather is better.

We hope to see you in France this year and we are also very pleased to welcome friends and relatives in Alexandria. Washington, D.C. and Virginia are worth a visit.

P.S. from David

Yes, I did enjoy the *"Fenland Christmas"*. Astonishing how cold those 1890's winters must have been to make skating a quite predictable winter sport. I also enjoyed the butcher's reminiscence of the winter fatstock – *"great walking masses of blubber!"* Mind you, like yourself I have an unfashionable and unhealthy liking for fat, but seem to get away with it healthwise – maybe through a prudent and purely medicinal dosage of red wine and a lot of garlic.
Lots of love, David

Office Closed

Last week was very odd. As I predicted in my last letter, everything was closed Monday, and we had some additional snow – three or four inches of it, so that my path-clearing had to be done again. I was able to do some quite useful work at home, uninterrupted, and I also spent a lot of the day in my electronic office (i.e. on my computer, plugged into the telephone) sending messages back and forth. In fact, that was a bit irritating, as my division chief had just come back after six weeks away leaving me in charge, and she started going through her several hundred accumulated messages and asking me what I had done about each item. Now I am a fairly conscientious administrator, and I deal with stuff as it comes in, but we get deluged with all sorts of silly little requests for information and that sort of thing, and a month later I really don't have the first idea what half these *"What did you do about this?"* messages are all about.

Tuesday, I consulted my computer first thing and saw another "office closed" message, but I would have liked to go in, so I called the office security to see if the heat was on. They told me it was pretty chilly, so I spent another day at home. There was, however, well over a foot of snow on the ground still, and our road had still not been cleared, so we did not venture out except for a very pleasant walk in the afternoon, which showed that not just our road, but most of the nearby main roads were also snow-covered.

Trudging Through the Snow

Wednesday, same story, but by this time I had had enough, and I put on my Wellington boots and trudged off to the Metro with a rucksack on my back and a thermos of hot coffee. I found a heated but very empty office, and to my surprise most of the main roads around the Bank and the White House were still covered with snow. Perhaps I should not have been surprised. Washington D.C. has a dismally poor administration, badly run (the mayor actually served a prison term a couple of years ago for drug use) and is strapped for cash. The original idea was that the District of Columbia would be a prosperous little island carved out of corners of two states, but now it is mainly inhabited by poor black people, and the wealthy who are attracted to the capital live outside its borders.

Shopping Frenzy

Wednesday evening Nicole and I decided that we should really go shopping to replenish our stocks. Our road was still hard packed snow, and the car stopped moving as soon as we hit this, but a friendly Canadian neighbour brought his snow-skills to help us get the car out. When we reached Safeways, we found that the whole of the rest of the world had come to the same decision as us. I have never before seen an American supermarket with empty shelves, and parking was very difficult, but we came back with enough food for at least another week.

Snowbound Again

Thursday, it was "everyone back to work" if you can make it (what is called "liberal leave policy"). The situation on the ground had not, however, changed very much, except that large numbers of people were suddenly trying to get in and out of the city. The result on roads and Metro was chaotic. Only a third of the metro trains had been dug out of the snow, but there were 20% more passengers than usual.

Thursday night/ Friday morning down came the snow again. I think we got another six inches. The seat of the children's swing that our predecessors left in the garden was finally submerged. My computer said that the office was closed, but I decided to go in all the same. The roads were almost deserted, but as I reached the station I met people coming the other way, who told me that all the above-ground metro stations had just been closed – so I went back home again (this is a ten-minute walk in good weather; a lot more in snow).

Martin Luther King Day

Over the weekend, the weather has warmed up, and everything has become very wet, but it takes a long time for two feet of snow to melt, and of course it is now piled up all over the place in filthy heaps. We went for a long and very pleasant walk yesterday afternoon, but it was wet underfoot. And today is Martin Luther King Day and a public holiday. I have been taking it in a relaxed way; up late, a little bit of office work in the morning, then out to the do-it-yourself store and an afternoon and evening spent making up a bath shower curtain rail out of plumbing materials.

I'm off to Mali for three weeks at the end of this week, so there may be a pause in my correspondence.

Lots of love from both of us, David and Nicole

Letter to Mother-in-law from Nicole   Alexandria, 31/01/1996

Cheap Travel by Concorde

David has been in Mali for a week and a half and will be back on 10th February. As usual he left just when the weather was getting very cold again. This time he travelled by Concorde to Paris. Two weeks ago it was Concorde's 20th anniversary and a seat in Club class cost the same as a seat in Club class on an ordinary plane.

I am back from an errand in the Old Town and although I was intending to combine this with a walk to the river, it was so cold that I came back home straight away. The thermometer on the porch is showing 3' Celsius, but it feels as if it is minus 10' as the wind is very cold. Snow was forecast for today, but did not arrive. In the early hours of the morning the temperature went down. Apparently there will be another storm tomorrow night, therefore I will go to Safeway tomorrow morning to replenish my larder in case we cannot go out for two or three days.

Visitors Seeking Employment

I have had visitors staying with me for a week and they left this morning at 6am. Their next destination was Panama where they are going to visit friends from Senegal. The husband will only stay a week in Panama and will be passing through Washington on his way back to Paris next Tuesday, and the wife will do the same on 24th February. Daniel, the husband, has not had a permanent job since he left Dakar where he worked with UNESCO. He does consultancies for the World Bank from time to time and the aim of his trip here was to see people to try to get more work and present himself as a potential candidate for a permanent post, in case there was one. He has had a lot of promises, but nothing certain. He also took the opportunity to finalise his last mission in Cameroon and get paid for a day's work. He is a very pleasant, sensible and quiet man. Aleth, the wife, is very pessimistic – even worse than me! We tried to visit the Vermeer Exhibition at the National Museum on Saturday, but the queue was about two kilometres long when we arrived at 10am and Museum staff announced that they were not accepting any more visitors for the exhibition on that day. The Vermeer paintings are on loan to the National Museum by the Dutch government for three months and the exhibition has been very popular. I was sorry for Aleth and Daniel, but as for myself I am going to see the exhibition with the World Bank Spouses Association on 9th February. I did not mind not having to stand in a queue all day as it was raining cats and dogs.

Computer Skills

All last week I attended a computer training course and I enjoyed it. I now feel more familiar with the programme which everybody has been using in the last three years, but having been in Senegal I was still using Word Perfect 5.1 and I did not know my way around Word 6.0. There are still things which I cannot do and do not understand. Every so often, the World Bank organises a computer training course for spouses to help those who want to go to work. The teacher was very good and I would not mind taking an advanced course with her. Not being used to work any more I was worn out by the end of the week.

Good Neighbours

A week ago I invited for coffee the neighbour across the road and her son, Johnny, who is three months older than Alistair. He started walking just before Christmas. Her husband had helped us to push the car when we were stuck in the snow and she works as a research assistant at the Bank on a part-time basis.

I believe Dominic has not left the U.K. yet and I hope his visa and work permit will not take too long to come. It is as well that he did not leave when he was intending as the whole of the region west of Virginia has been affected by the snow once again. I shall phone him to ask him to ring you before he leaves.

Love to Margaret and thank her for her letter.

Love, Nicole

NOTE – Our mother's new Devon home was a restored clay-lump barn, converted into two dwellings. Sister Margaret lived in the larger, right-hand section, and a communicating door allowed indoor access between the two.

Letter to Mother   Alexandria, 17/03/1996

Donkeys and Family

I'm glad the donkeys have at last arrived, and that you like them. I hope they do not wear you out. I remember my mornings mucking out after several hundred cows, and I found that very hard work. We were interested in your other news too. We had not heard about cousin Tim Childs' new baby. Nor have we recently heard anything about Robert. I hope that in his case no news is good news.

We have been having some beautiful days: bright sunshine, blue sky without a cloud and temperatures in the 50s, but it rained last night, and today it was chilly. We are still some way behind the weather you were having when I visited you, but I am sure that in no time at all we shall be enjoying – if that is the word – hot and sticky weather, and be grateful for our new air-conditioning system.

A Strange Smell in the Cupboard!

Over the last week we have been more concerned about our central heating than about air-conditioning. I had been surprised to see paint peeling on a cupboard next to the chimney in the living room, and when I touched the wood I found it was quite damp. I started to investigate a number of different hypotheses, starting with melting snow, but Nicole pointed out that there was also a strange smell in the cupboard, and eventually I put two and two together and realised that our central heating boiler flue was leaking into the room. This may well account for Nicole feeling unwell from time to time over the past few weeks, as there is no doubt that we were getting some pretty noxious fumes. Anyway, we called in the chimney doctors (one of whom gave an estimate of $4,000 and the other $2,000 – you can guess which we took) and they spent a couple of days opening up the chimney, removing a very well-packed grey-squirrel nest, and inserting a steel liner. We should now have a very healthy chimney. Apparently the squirrel problem is a very common one here, and we now have a sort of cage on top of both our chimneys; as for the leaky flue, that too is common in old houses, because modern boilers send much less smoke and heat up the chimney than the old ones, but what does go up is full of moisture and corrosive acids.

Excitement in Guadeloupe

Great concern in Guadeloupe: Anick, who had been the mainstay of a house full of fragile and hypochondriac old ladies (her mother and two aunts) has announced that at forty-eight she is moving out to live with an old boyfriend who has come back into her life after a twenty year absence. Mme Fortuné felt the need to go and spend a few days with the newly orphaned aunts to comfort them. Of course, it is a bit of a problem. The aunts, who range from seventy-five to eighty-five, have never really left home, and do not have Mme Fortuné's robust morale, and they are not really capable of looking after themselves. Someone will have to be found to come in and look after them, day and night. However I reckon they can afford that, and I am glad Anick is enjoying herself a bit.

Micro-Finance

I have had a rather pleasant week attending a training course on micro-finance – i.e. finance for micro entrepreneurs – given by USAID, with an eclectic mix of participants. My immediate neighbours are a very lively – even extrovert – Japanese girl with a U.S. MBA, who works at the Inter-American Development Bank, and a very pleasant Albanian man from a USAID project, who patently does not understand very much of what is going on. When we have to work things out he sits there looking over my shoulder and trying to read what I am writing down. It is like being back in class, and my first reaction is to want to hide my work, but in fact I usually take some time to try and explain it to him. It's also interesting, because in agriculture one spends a lot of time agonising over whether peasant farmers can support normal interest rates, whereas here I find people arguing that poor traders etc. can afford to pay interest rates around 40% - on the very reasonable grounds that that is what it costs to service small loans, and that well-run credit schemes at such interest rates find it hard to keep up with the demand.

Preparing for Guinea-Bissau

I have had a very busy weekend doing things around the house before I go on a trip to Guinea-Bissau next weekend. I have finished putting up a long wall of shelves in the basement for all our books. They look pretty good if you don't look too closely. I have also put up a roll-down window blind in the bathroom, as Nicole feels self-conscious taking a shower in full view of any neighbours who happen to be looking out of their windows at the time, and I have completed a rather curious two-sided shower curtain rail, which I constructed myself out of plumbing materials – soldered polished copper pipe with brass bends. In retrospect there are things I could have done better, but at least it is up and much solider than anything I could have bought in a shop.

Absent Visa

No news yet of Dominic's visa. We are getting quite worried about it, but I think the truth is that the firm that is hiring him (we hope) is just very disorganised. This is not too reassuring, and is very tough for him, but he seems to be managing OK. He has just been best man at the wedding of an old friend from school, who was marrying a girl-friend from Croatia. Bernard is quite up-beat about work, but he doesn't mention any progress on the sale of the flat.

Nicole is curious to know whether you received our birthday present (a book). Your silence on the subject suggests that it has gone astray, which would be a pity.

Lots of love, David and Nicole

Letter to Mother
Alexandria, 28/04/1996

Pottering in the Garden

The weather has been brilliant this weekend – not ever so warm, but a clear sky and bright sunshine. Yesterday I pottered in the garden. We really ought to do some quite radical things to it, including bringing in some more soil to change the slope so that rain does not gather in a small lake at the far end, but for the time being I am contenting myself with making it look respectable. Last weekend I managed to get our motor mower going for the first time since our return from Senegal, and for a time it poured out a lot of filthy smoke, but once it had cleaned out its insides it worked OK, and made the lawn look a little more respectable (a mixture of tufts, bare patches, wild onions that stink when cut, violets and dandelions – but cut short no-one can tell the difference).

Squirrel Vandals

This weekend I finished planting out the seedlings I have grown (apart from some delphiniums, that still look too fragile, and the three black hollyhocks that were all I raised from a packet of seeds). I also planted a variety of plants and seedlings that we have bought, like all Americans, from our nearest hardware supermarket. All my beds are covered with about six inches of leaf mulch, which is a little difficult for tender seedlings to root into, so I make a hole for each one and fill it with a few handfuls of potting soil. The biggest menace in this system is the grey squirrels, who are very numerous and either think they have hidden something under the mulch or are presently in the course of hiding something. They have no malicious intent insofar as my plants are concerned. They just do not notice them. Anyway, I have a mixture of candytuft, achillea, larkspur, dill and parsley, and some very etiolated sunflower plants (all my own growing) along with pansies, petunias, impatiens and azaleas (all from the shop), not to mention several roses, three different types of bleeding heart, several rather sickly-looking tree peonies, a herbaceous peony found growing on the lawn, and other bits and pieces.

Native Azaleas, Dogwoods and Wisteria

This is azalea season here. One forgets what an ideal climate and soil it is for them. Ours are almost all new little plants bought for $3-4 each, but many of the houses in our road have big bushes three or four feet high and absolutely covered with flowers. It is also dogwood time. These are not the rather insignificant plants grown in the U.K. for their coloured stems in winter, but small trees that are covered with four-petalled (really, sepalled) large flowers – very spectacular! They grow wild in the woods. Unfortunately a new disease is slowly moving across the U.S. and wiping them out. Gardeners will be able to replace them with the hardier Asian dogwoods, that are very similar, but they will slowly disappear from the woodlands for a century or so.

We also bought a small wisteria for the front of the house, and found it very hard to plant, as the foundation slab goes out a long way. I have another very small wisteria plant at the back that I collected as a self-rooted layer from a wild plant on a vacant lot in Old Town before going to Senegal. It has not got very far, because our tenants' or agents' idea of gardening maintenance was to cut everything down. Wisterias grow wild here, and at this time of year one sometimes sees very beautiful ones climbing up roadside trees.

Springtime in the Appalachians

Today, the fine weather continued, and we went out for a long drive to the Skyline National Park in the Appalachians, about a hundred miles away. Spring and Fall are the really beautiful seasons here, and we timed this trip very well. Along the roads the trees are just beginning to come into leaf, and on the edges of the woods there are cherries, dogwoods and *Cercis Canadensis* (almost the same as the European "Judas Tree") which is covered with tiny red flowers all along its branches (not just at the tips). It was very noticeable that as we got into the Appalachians, and started to gain altitude, the season changed back from late spring to late winter. At 3,000 feet the trees are still almost all in winter dormancy, with the exceptions of the ones I have named. These are getting past their peak on the plains, but are now at their best in the mountains. There was also a pretty white-flowered tree in the under-storey of the woods – I don't know what. We went for a long walk down to a mountain stream. In a month or two these paths will be in deep shade, but now they are in full light, and the spring flowers that depend on this are just at their best. There are lots of little anemones; violets, of course (including yellow ones); and just as I was trying to explain to Nicole what Trilliums (May flower, Lent lilies) look like, we came across some other walkers photographing a clump of them. They are very attractive pink or white flowers, with three large petals surmounting three radially-spaced leaves on a long stem. We also found a little star-like yellow flower – maybe a wild tulip.

Wild Mushrooms

My own favourite *trouvaille* was a good bunch of Morel mushrooms (*Morchellus esculentus*, or maybe even *crassipes*, which is more unusual and said to be tastier). It was only a little frustrating that Nicole said she had seen a lot of them a mile or two back, but had not even realised they were mushrooms. I cooked ours tonight with a very tasty cream sauce, and we are still alive.

Skyline is said to be the home of the greatest concentration of bears east of the Rocky Mountains, but the only animal we saw was something about the size and shape of a beaver, but without the big flat tail.

Dominic's New Employment

We spoke to Dominic yesterday. He has a new address, sharing with a colleague, Greg Hewish, in Columbus, Ohio. He says he is really enjoying the work and the people he works with. We plan to go and see him next weekend, leaving Friday night and getting back first thing Monday morning.

I hope the donkeys are still giving satisfaction.

Lots of love, David and Nicole

Letter to mother   Alexandria, 23/06/1996

An Auction

We have had a pleasant weekend here doing very little. This morning we decided to go to the auction at Manasses, about 40 minutes drive from here. We arrived in good time for the viewing, but the lots to be sold were so uninteresting that we went through them twice, and headed back home. It would probably have been good strategy to stay, as we noticed other people with the same reaction as ourselves, and they probably ended up with only a handful of buyers, and very low prices. But then, what would we have bought? Nicole is looking for a presentable chest of drawers, and some more farm-style chairs. The latter certainly exist; but pleasant chests of drawers – by which I mean cherry, oak or mahogany, real wood (or good veneer on wood) and a minimum of about 120 years old are rather hard to find at a reasonable price. It is a pity we sold off one of our bow-fronted ones years ago in the course of one of our moves (not great quality, but nice looking). Another acceptable variant here is painted pine. There is quite a lot of old painted furniture about, originally the poor man's option, and quite pleasant. We do have a nice solid Victorian chest in the house in Sutton, but that's no use to us now. Anyway, there was none of this at the sale this morning except, frustratingly, among the items that had been sold and were awaiting collection.

A Day in the Garden

It was a pleasant day, not too hot, and we were able to have both our lunch and our dinner on the deck, and cook the lunch on the barbecue, plus a potato, yoghurt and dill salad, with all the herbs from the garden – very tasty. It is amazing how few of our neighbours seem to spend any time in their gardens. They spend money, getting the lawn manicured, and buying in plants, but all this seems to be for the sake of keeping up appearances. Both sets of our immediate neighbours are young and childless. Those on the left have two Dalmatians, which is fine except that they make the smelliest messes imaginable, usually just next to our garden, and the wind is generally in our direction. I don't know what they must feed them on. I find this a little nauseating, but they are pleasant and well-meaning people so I keep quiet about it. They have a much bigger garden than ours, and last year they put a lot of work into it, but since the arrival of the dogs they have rather given up at the back, and devote their gardening attentions to a smart little patch at the front. The neighbours on the right are (relatively speaking) keen gardeners, and they have a mother-in-law who keeps a garden centre and gives them plants and mulch. Their real aim is a garden that looks after itself. In any case, they are very slow at getting things done. They had a party two weeks ago, and the cool box is still on the lawn, half full of water, because of all the rain we have had recently (we have had some pretty dramatic thunderstorms, accompanied by radio warnings to keep inside and keep away from the windows).

Aches and Pains

I'm sorry Susan is having more kidney trouble. Let's hope this does not necessitate another big operation. I prefer the idea of blasting the things away with sound waves, but I did not realise one had to keep going back for repeat sessions. So far as I am aware, I do not suffer from this problem – just a variety of inflammatory aches and pains in my back and elsewhere. Fortunately, I have no difficulty sleeping flat on my back on a fairly hard mattress.

Talking of backache reminds me that I saw a substantial article the other day about the Cooperative Wholesale Society farms at Stoughton. I expect it was the Financial Times. The CWS is apparently one of the largest landowners in the country, and they were celebrating some anniversary by showing off a new super-modern cow unit more or less where I learned to be a farmer's boy. The muck-shovelling was all automatic and computer-controlled. This would have done me out of my most substantial job, which even at that age caused me quite a lot of discomfort.

E-Mail versus Traditional Letters

Dominic is about to have his 3-month review, but has been told unofficially that he is OK. He has an internet address, which is very handy for sending quick letters. Really, Mummy, it's time you or Margaret got a computer and an internet address. Of course I am sure you will not, and you probably prefer getting your letters on paper, in envelopes with stamps on them. So do I, actually, but it is rather convenient to be able to type a letter like this and zap it off in the knowledge that it will arrive virtually instantaneously (it then sits there in an electronic mailbox until the owner of the box decides to open it and have a look).
Lots of love, David and Nicole

Letter to mother   Alexandria, 30/06/1996

Hot and Sticky!

My downstairs office is very nice to have, and very convenient, except that there is no movement of air so it gets very hot. And when I open the windows, all sorts of bugs fly in. However, I am comfortable compared with my situation this morning. I decided it was time to insulate under the "sun room", which is an add-on at the front of the house on what used to be an open verandah. We noticed last winter that there were a lot of cold draughts coming up through the floor, even though the space underneath is fully enclosed with access only through a 15-inch square hole in the wall of the boiler room/ workshop. I had picked up a bundle of glass fibre insulating mats for a few dollars at a yard sale with this in mind, and they were taking up a lot of space and getting wet under the deck at the back. When Nicole was out at church, I put on my protective gloves and a dust mask and threw everything through the hole in the wall, plus a light on a cable, and wriggled through after them. We still had not reached the maximum heat of the day, but it was like being in an oven down there. There was not enough room to stand up, and the floor was earth plus all the rubbish builders had thrown in over the years. Then I had to fasten the glass fibre mats up above my head, with all the bits of itchy fibre falling down into my face. Fortunately, I had bought myself a heavy-duty stapler, which made the job much easier, but I was terribly pleased to get the job finished and be able to get out, drenched from head to toe. I hope the results will be noticeable.

Wooden Frame Houses

It is interesting to be able to see how the house has been added to. I am not terribly keen on wooden house construction, but it certainly lends itself to piecemeal changes and additions. I had guessed that our sun room was not original – any more than the one at the back which is now incorporated into our bedroom at the first floor level – but down there I could see that the old verandah deck was still in place, and that a new floor had been built on top of it by laying another set of joists on it. A house of the same age as ours whose back garden nearly abuts onto ours is going through a lightning transformation of this type. It was dressed up as red brick, but this was just "siding" nailed on over the old lapped boards, and a lot of it has been ripped off to put on a new two-storey addition. The frame has gone up in the past week. Now they have to do the finish, which is the most substantial piece of the work, and I expect they will cover it all with plastic vinyl siding, made to look like wood; cheap and nasty, but quite effective.

A Glove Box Courtesy of Dominic

I did another satisfying little job this weekend, which was to make a glove box for the back of our coat cupboard door. I have been meaning to do this for ages, and although it is just a simple box to put things in, I think I have done it rather nicely. Of course, this is very much Dominic's "door" idea, but without any pretensions to design.

An Old Acquaintance

I telephoned Richard Winter (from City Boys) on the spur of the moment, to tell him when we would be in France. It was a bit strange to talk to someone whom I had not met for over thirty years, and fall into a conversation about philosophy, as if we had only spoken the week before. Unfortunately, he cannot visit us in France, as he and his wife will be there earlier for a short stay, and have to hurry back for a bedridden mother-in-law. Perhaps we can manage to call on them on the way to see you or on the way back. I shall have to explore the possibilities. You may remember, I re-established contact through his son, who was stringing (technical term for a part-time reporter paid on a results basis) for some newspapers and the BBC in Dakar.

Modern Water Sports

This afternoon we decided we needed to get some fresh air, despite the heat, and after looking at the maps we went to a small state park about 35 miles away, on the banks of the Potomac as it widens out before entering the Bay. The park is the site of a 200-year-old plantation-house, which one can visit, but we decided to save that pleasure. In fact Gunston Hall is so smartly kept up that it might have been only five years old, but no doubt the interior is more revealing. We had a very pleasant walk through woods on raised causeways over muddy creeks, where we could admire all the insect life – and they no doubt could admire us. There were lots of butterflies, including some fairly magnificent swallow-tailed jobs. All is not well, however, as pollution in the river has killed a lot of the underwater vegetation and the more violent movement of the water that results is eroding the banks rather fast. We were also able to see people enjoying the water by roaring around in motor boats and on water bikes. This I find worse than pointless. I love water, but I love it for calm, and for the gentle sound it makes. I feel it should be used in an almost silent way. Rowing, or kayaking or sail is fine, and demands a certain art, whereas any dumb fool can get in a motor boat and roar around making a lot of noise and sending up spray.

A Welcome Survivor

The garden is feeling the heat. Several of my plants, including most of the larkspur I planted, have succumbed suddenly to fungal diseases. I shall learn not to plant them again, or at least, not in peat, since the plants in soil seem to be surviving better. After years of saying we need to plant a Lagerstroemia ("Pride of India" – which will not mean anything to you since it is a sub-tropical plant that just survives here, but not in the U.K.). Having been deterred by the

253

absolutely exorbitant price asked at the smart garden centre, we find that the shoots from a dead stump that we have been trying to kill with weedkiller are Lagerstroemia, trying to recover. In fact we have two plants. Our herbs are mostly doing well; almost too well. Tonight to Nicole's annoyance I picked a large bunch of parsley to chop up and put in the freezer for the winter. I have coriander and basil on the way, and dill, fennel, chives, chinese leeks (a more garlicky form of chives), thyme and mint as well. And on a non-herb note, I have discovered to my surprise that it is very easy to take cuttings of bleeding heart. To think that I paid $6 a plant!

Storms

I forgot to mention that we had a tremendous storm last Monday that blew lots of trees down in Alexandria (worse here than in Washington), and put the power out of action for 24 hours – very hot and uncomfortable without air-conditioning.
Lots of love, David

Letter from Nicole to Sheila and Ron   Bordepaille, 11/08/1996

A Visit to the Creuse

Thank you very much for looking after us. It was interesting to visit another region of France which is so different from the Aquitaine. I enclose the newspaper article on the Creuse. We came back via Limoges which was shorter in terms of kilometres, but about the same in terms of hours. It was a more scenic route and the autoroute from Gueret to Limoges is worth taking.

Our friend Teresa, from Alexandria, arrived three days ago and has undertaken to paint the landing.
Best wishes to Linda, Love Nicole

Letter to Margaret and mother   Alexandria, 18/08/1996
from Nicole

No Peace on Holiday!

I cannot say that the holidays have been very restful this year. David has undertaken to install the kitchen elements and I have not had a kitchen for most of the time. Our friends from Alexandria are here and they have been very helpful. Without them David would not have been able to attach the cabinets to the walls.

The weather has been excellent for the last ten days and it is getting hotter and hotter. I am including the photos taken during our stay in Devon. Would you be kind enough to send a photo of the teashop to Vivian. We shall write to Ted and send him a copy. I leave some space for David to carry on.
Love, Nicole

Letter from David to Mother

Crooked Cabinets

Sorry not to have written more. In fact there has been quite a lot of visible progress in the house, but the kitchen is still not fully installed. There is a lot to do, as my carpenter made only cupboard fronts, and some of the measurements were out, and on top of that some of the things have warped a bit in the last year, so there is quite a lot of work to be done, fitting crooked cabinets into a crooked room. Fortunately our visitors enjoy doing this sort of thing. John is very resistant to suggestions that he should go and sight-see.

Sheila's House in the Creuse

I found Sheila's house rather a joke. Compared with that this is a three-star hotel. They start off with only one more or less liveable room and all the rest is rough farm building. Of course it could be made into a most delightful large house, but Sheila is very insistent on doing things her own way – without proper building tools or even a spirit level. No doubt she will get more skilled as she goes along, but I fear that by the time she reaches the top of her rustic stone staircase she will want to rebuild the bottom, and by that time it will be very hard to do, because the cement is perfectly good even if the stones are crooked. Never mind!

I think I was able to be quite useful on the plumbing front, as I was able to get the lavatory, sink and washbasin connected up, and help Ron to buy the necessary materials to do this.

A Strange Boarding House

I should say that we thoroughly enjoyed our visit. Nicole preferred not to camp, so we found a strange sort of boarding house. It too was some sort of a family project, built by three generations under the impulsion – I guess – of the grandparents, who had by now died or got too old to continue. The middle generation were themselves rather elderly and appeared to have run out of energy, and the young were not in evidence. The house itself had been built from scratch, and was very large, and made out of excellent materials – lots of oak – but was of uninspired design and not quite finished. Still, we slept comfortably in a bed, and had running water, and were able to devote all our energies to building and socialising.

Meeting Sheila's Houseguests

Jane (David W's on-off girl friend) was there with him, as was her father, who turned out to be a very interesting man – in his early seventies and retired from the International Atomic Energy authority, but still pursuing a variety of interests, such as training people in developing countries in how to maintain scientific equipment. He lives in Budapest much of the time, because he enjoys it and finds that his money goes a long way. We also met Sheila's very nice neighbours, including a very delightful old bee-keeper.

I'm impressed that you should have won prizes at the vegetable and flower show. How surprising to find that Margaret's asparagus peas were good for something – even if not for eating. Lots of love, David

August 1996 – David sorts out a plumbing problem at Sheila's fermette in the Creuse

Letter to Sheila and Ron,
from Nicole
                                          Alexandria, 10/09/1996

Hurricane Fran

Although it is the middle of September, it is still summer here and very hot and humid. We have to keep the air-conditioning on day and night. Some leaves are just starting to turn red. Last week we had very severe rain for three days, because of hurricane Fran, and serious flooding followed. Part of Old Town Alexandria was flooded and the road which goes from Alexandria to Washington, D.C. and runs along the river was closed yesterday. Last Saturday night, Hortense (which was only a tropical storm then, but since has become a hurricane) went over to Guadeloupe but did not cause too much damage.

News of Dominic, and Stephen Wright (at Lake Placid, New York State)

Two weeks ago, we had a long weekend because of Labour Day, and drove to Columbus, Ohio, to visit Dominic. He is now well settled and is enjoying life. He likes his job and his bosses are pleased with the way he is working. He has a small flat, which is rather bare at the moment, and of course a car.

How is Stephen enjoying his new job? Send him our address and tell him that he is very welcome to come and stay with us.

I am sending you the negatives of the photos we took during our stay with you, as I am sure you will want to have reprints done for David, Jane, her father, and Linda. .

On our return from the Creuse, David started working earnestly on the kitchen with the help of our American friends, Teresa and John. They made quite a lot of progress. I have finished painting our bathroom and Teresa painted part of the kitchen, the landing walls and the other bathroom.

I hope that going back to school was not too hard for Sheila, anyway you can look forward to your next holiday in France in November.
Love, Nicole

(Continued by David)

I was very earnest, but we did not quite finish the job. Most of the cabinets are up, the sink reinstalled, and the wall-mounted gas heater replaced by connecting up to the "cumulus" in the nearest bathroom. I am keeping the heater and the old sink-base for eventual re-use in my workshop, which I foresightedly connected up for water and drainage when Ron helped me lay the concrete floor. However, we still have to tile the kitchen work-tops, put up one last cabinet, put handles and catches on everything that opens and shuts and do other bits of finish. And I have decided that my long-term plan now includes turning our present front door into the kitchen into a window, replacing the other front door with something smarter, and following your long-ago advice to put a window in the north side of the downstairs big room to make a view through from front to back.

The Visit to Creuse

We did enjoy our stay at your house, although I am rather struck by how much you have to do to it. I enjoyed your neighbours too – particularly the old beekeeper. It is a very different France from our bit.

Evening meal in the garden, Pradelette, Creuse

I will not bore you by reiterating my advice on masonry skills, except to say that I am pretty unhappy about some of my earlier work that is, unfortunately, hard to undo now. In fact, quite a lot of effort has gone into removing mortar that was the wrong colour, etc. And without mentioning the word s****s, I think it is well worth while reading up whatever you can get hold of about relevant building techniques between holidays. Apart from anything else, it's a wonderful excuse for creative daydreaming. I enjoyed reading the books produced by the Society for the Preservation of Ancient Buildings (SPAB) – founded by William Morris and remaining in his spirit. They also organise healthy weekends on such subjects as "how to make and apply traditional limewash", which I never quite got around to.

Gigantic Pumpkins

My garden here is not at all a competition exhibit, but my pride right now is in my pumpkin plants. I wanted to have home grown pumpkins for Thanksgiving, and presently I am on the way to having three of a variety whose sole selling point was its enormous size. Mine are not yet as big as an ox, but two of them are already about sixteen inches in diameter, and still growing fast. The plants took advantage of my absence to quit the narrow flower beds and invade the lawn. Every day or two I rearrange them and point the leading tendrils back whence they came – and still they come… I feel like the character in *"The Day of the Triffids"*, who was so proud of his plants until they ate him.

Sir Hans Singer

I went to a seminar given by Otti's father-in-law the other day. I don't think he recognised me, although we used to know each other quite well. He's Sir Hans now. I disagree with much of what he has to say, but he is remarkably sprightly and alert for his age. Lots of love, David

NOTE – It was lovely to see David and Nicole at our Creuse farmhouse. This was the last time we ever saw David. He was quite right about my granite stairs. I created two unusual sets of stairs to the first floor, using unshaped granite and a lot of optimism. For myself, I was thrilled and amazed that they were so solid and resembled stairs at all, and small details like keeping risers all equal and steps all horizontal escaped me. The real hero was Ron, who kindly and patiently added solid wood banisters and rail, so folk had at least a fighting chance of arriving safely at the top. To date, no one has come to grief and the stairs are certainly rustic.

Typically, on the day he arrived with us, my brother would not sit down to a meal until he had solved a plumbing problem. I will never forget that last time together.

Letter to mother   Alexandria, 06/10/1996

Off to Chad

We're off again. I am going to be Resident Representative in Chad from the New Year. Career-wise this is a good move, as I have recently been promoted to fill a vacant higher grade in recognition of the work I was doing in a structure which has in the meantime disappeared in our latest reorganisation. I am thus working at a salary which is higher than normal for the job I am doing. Moreover, all HQ staff are now working on the basis of "task contracts" which provide an overall dollar budget for the task in question and take into account the real dollar cost of the people who are working on it. My promotion, welcome as it was, meant that I was a rather expensive resource so budget-conscious managers were likely to look for someone younger and of a lower grade. Moreover, because of budget cuts, most staff do not have contracts for all of their time. I spoke to one yesterday who said she was billing a lot of her time to "educational reading", but was not sure how long she would be allowed to do that.

Dreaming of Retirement

Although I shall not mention this in the Bank, I am also thinking of Chad as a good pre-retirement move. Three years in Chad (the normal tour) will bring me up to fifty-seven, which is five years from normal retirement. If I then feel that I can afford retirement, I may well go.

Of course, I earn more abroad – partly because I will get paid various supplements (which the Bank is thinking of reducing) and partly because the normal bills are paid by the Bank, and we can let the house here. Nicole says that so far as she is concerned, the only good reason for going is to finish the house in France, which I think is fair enough. I also aim to finish paying off this house (my only debt, now of quite manageable size).

No Rest Cure

Chad is not paradise, and will not be a rest-cure, but the general consensus is that the people are pleasant (despite their fighting tendencies) and that the government is more competent and serious than many. I went there a number of times around 1986-1987 as a consultant, to work on the cotton sector. It is an artificial country, like most in Africa. The North is desert or semi-desert, with muslim nomadic tribes, and the South is savannah country with settled agriculturalists, many of whom are Christian or animist. The southerners dominated the country at independence – the common story of settled and Christianised people getting the education – and the northerners have effectively taken over through a number of periods of civil war, and then had a few more bouts among themselves. The present government has been in power for about four or five years. It appears to offer a good prospect of greater stability, and some of the ministers, whom I have met, are clearly very capable people. Also, they have discovered petrol, so there is an interesting problem of how to manage the money that will start to flow in. At present, it is one of the poorest countries in Africa and their capacity to manage a sudden flow of funds is very low. I have to strengthen a very neglected Resident Mission (the last Resident Representative fell out with the Government and was withdrawn over a year ago).

N'djamena

I know roughly where we will live – on the outskirts of N'djamena (formerly Fort Lamy) on a high bank overlooking the River Chari – one of Central Africa's big rivers. The French *Caisse Francaise* representative had a house in the same area. Apparently we have some sort of a swimming pool, which is nice, but I have no idea what shape the house is in. It is a landlocked country, so there will be no Sundays spent at the beach. I recall that one sometimes saw hippo in the river about there. I wonder if they are still there, or if they have been despatched by a non-so stray bullet in the meantime. Although there are not an enormous number of flights in and out, flying time to Paris is only about four and a half hours. Nicole is counting on getting a lot of trips.

Party for a Vanishing Division

We had a party at our house yesterday, for the staff of the Division that was abolished in July. It was a very pleasant occasion. We did it on a "pot-luck" basis, which means that everyone brings something to eat and drink. The result was masses of food – about twice as much as we could eat. My former division chief, Silvia, came along. She has been having an eventful and somewhat stressed time recently. She was seconded to a senior advisory job at the Inter-American Development Bank – also based in Washington – in July (a good move that enabled her to escape the chaos of being reorganised), and shortly before that she had married Magdi, a senior person from another part of the Bank. He is an Egyptian Copt, whereas she is Uruguayan. Both had been married before, and Magdi has daughters in their twenties. When I got back from holiday, I heard that Magdi had had a stroke (which gave pause for thought, as he is two years younger than me). He was said to be doing well. I telephoned Silvia to cheer her up, and she was understandably rather weepy. Her seventy-eight-year-old father had also just been hospitalised for major heart surgery, and she was about to go off on a combined work mission and sick visit.

Elderly Expectant Parents

Silvia arrived yesterday with a certain amount of drama, having telephoned from the car to say that they had a flat tyre on the freeway, and that Magdi was out there with cars whizzing by him, trying to change it. We were worried for them, and a few of us were about to set off to look for them, when they finally turned up, and Silvia revealed that she was four and a half months pregnant. She's forty-five, but she has had all the tests, and everything seems OK. Magdi was very proud of himself for having changed the tyre – saw it as a "confidence building" achievement. However, it is hard to see him as a prospective young father. Fortunately his speech is not at all affected, but he still walks awkwardly with a special stick.

Pumpkin Harvest

It is getting very autumnal, which as you know is a very pleasant season here. Nicole and I have just been out for a walk to the River and back through Old Town, with lots of people out enjoying the brilliant sunshine. Yesterday I gathered my three ripe pumpkins – there are still two unripe ones – and put the two biggest ones on display on the front steps (traditional here at this period). They are still not the usual deep red-orange, but they are monsters. I weighed them in on the bathroom scales, and each of them is about 65lb (four and a half stone).

You say that your letters must be dull because you do not do anything, but I do not find them dull at all. I think you write very entertaining letters, which are not simply lists of events.

We have just had Bernard on the telephone. All is well there.

I hope the de-loused donkeys are well.

Lots of love, David

P.S. from Nicole

I might knock on your door for a bed from time to time, as I cannot see me living in Chad for months and months without getting away.

Love, Nicole

CHAPTER SIX
N'DJAMENA, CHAD

Letter to Mother   **Bamako, Mali, 10/11/1996**

Bamako Compared with N'Djamena

I don't know when I shall send you this letter, but I have complete leisure this afternoon – absolutely nothing else to do – so I have gone into the Resident Mission to look for a newspaper (no luck) and kill some time.

I arrived in Bamako last night. What a busy and prosperous place it looks after N'Djamena! And yet this too is meant to be one of the poorest countries in the world.

It is really quite difficult to give an idea of what N'Djamena is like, because I doubt if you have ever seen anywhere remotely like it – maybe during your visit to Zaire, but there is no Sahel in Zaire, and I think you were in the tropical part. It is a little like something out of the Wild West; dusty dirt streets and battered buildings, and lots of people, sheep and goats with very little traffic sense. Many of the men wear long *boubous* and a sort of turban of very thin cotton, which they may or may not loop under their chins, and which they wrap around their faces in sandstorms. The women are mostly wrapped up in many folds of thin cloth, which they mostly wear over their heads, and play with all the time, as they are always falling off the hair, which should be kept covered. Very few are really veiled as in the Middle East. Clothing of children is very varied, and may consist of nothing but a dirty tee-shirt for the little ones. There is a lot of rubbish in the streets, and for quite a lot of the people it is their toilet and bathroom as well as their home.

The People – and Soldiers with Time on their Hands

The people are of very varied physical types. South of N'Djamena they are generally of typical African Bantu type – like the Nigerians or the Zairois. North of N'Djamena they are much more Arabic in appearance, and some of them are described as "black Arabs". There are also people of Touareg type – much lighter skinned, with straight hair – and Peuhls (or Fulani) who are a culture rather than a homogenous ethnic group, but include many light-skinned and recognisably Nilotic people. The Goran are usually very lanky with a fuzz of hair, thin noses, and very black. They are a warrior people, and most of the ones in N'Djamena are soldiers. People are wary of them, as they are very fierce and fearless, and they often understand neither French nor Chadian Arabic, so when they start waving a gun at you it is hard to explain to them satisfactorily what you want. There are lots of soldiers, without much to do. They do not get paid regularly, so they cause a lot of trouble. A lot of them are due to be demobilised soon. The President, a professional soldier from the North, wants a smaller and more professional army. It remains to be seen whether demobilised ex-soldiers will be more or less trouble than under-employed and underpaid soldiers.

Smuggling Across River Chari

N'Djamena is on the banks of the big river Chari, which is very large at the moment, because although the rains are definitely over for the year, a lot of water is still coming down from Central Africa. On the opposite side of the river is a strange almost disconnected part of Cameroon, which is also very wild. There is a lot of small-scale smuggling across the river – sugar in particular, as it is very expensive here compared with Cameroon. In the dry season people can wade across, but at present they have to come in *pirogues*. One of the more convenient crossing-points, with good access to the water, is right next door to the house we will inherit. Usually there are people there trading sugar, and frequently the customs men come and try and grab them, sometimes firing a few rounds in any old direction to make their point. Two days before I left, I was waiting to meet a minister in an office with a good view over one of the few tarred thoroughfares, when a truck full of customs men came rushing by with horn blaring. A minute later hundreds of people started to run in the direction it had gone. Apparently it hit another truck head-on and there were lots of serious injuries.

Random Collection of Buildings

The buildings are pretty nondescript. The main shopping boulevard, *Avenue Charles de Gaulle* (no less!) was in the front line of battle for some time in the early 1980's, and when I came here in 1985 much of it was in ruins. Now it is about three-quarters patched up, much of it with quite pleasant arcades, under which traders set out little stalls. There is a gaping hole at the city centre end where there used to be a French colonial supermarket, "SCORE" (originally *Societe des Comptoirs Ouest Africains*, SCOA). In 1985 one could still see that it had been a rather remarkable building, covered with murals in ceramic tiles. Apparently the owner of the site was starting to redevelop it when he got assassinated, so it has stayed like that. Almost opposite it, however, there is the smartest and newest building in N'Djamena – the Central Bank (part of a regional central bank), and nestling in the corner of that concession is a nondescript trio of colonial buildings, which we aim to turn into our new Resident Mission.

Converting Colonial Buildings into a Resident Mission

If all goes well, I shall start my tenure with an intense bout of building activity. We will take a five-year lease, and advance the owner enough money to completely remodel the buildings to our standards, under the supervision of a local architect. The architect, Mr. Loubah, is a southerner with an impressively scarified face – basically fine parallel scars starting at the forehead, missing the eyes and continuing on down the cheeks. I'm fairly used to such adornment now, and setting aside the scars, he is a businesslike and well-trained guy who has spent a number of years training and working in Dakar, so – up to now – we get on well. I still have to get my money agreed by HQ and sign a lease, then we can move.

Search for a Better House

If possible, we will also move house. I like being on the river bank, but the house is not a very good one, the lot is too small for entertaining plus gardening, and the presence of the smugglers and customs men next door is a disadvantage. However, I am rapidly finding that good houses are few and far between. Normally, one has to do the same thing as for the Resident Mission: sign a five-year lease, and advance funds for rebuilding. Unfortunately, most of the houses are on rather small plots, so it is difficult to get the combination of entertaining space and garden space that I want; but we have six months to look.

Optimism About Chad

I realise I am not giving you a very tempting picture of N'Djamena, but there is an up-side, which is that quite a lot of the people we work with are intelligent and serious, and are keen to get the country back on track. It is true that there is also a highly predatory bunch, and that sometimes people somehow combine both sets of characteristics; but a lot of my colleagues see Chad as one of the all-too-rare countries where it is possible to get things done.

Danger in the Dark

It is getting dark. I am in a rather crummy little hotel, run mainly as a snack bar and bar by some very Africanised Italians, because the usual place where I stay is booked up (I forgot to re-book when I changed the date of my visit). But at least it is better than the mosquito-ridden dump where I slept last night, and is in walking distance of the Resident Mission. All the same, I do not make a practice of walking here after dark – a bit imprudent. So I shall sign off. Lots of love, David

HAPPY CHRISTMAS! ALL THE BEST FOR 1997!

On the Move Again

We are on the move again. We had almost finished unpacking the stuff we brought back from Senegal, the stuff we had left in storage when we went there, and the stuff that was still in storage from the previous move from the U.K., when I accepted the job of Resident Representative in N'Djamena, Chad.

Why would I do such a thing? N'Djamena is not the Paris of Africa; it is hardly even the East Grinstead of Africa. The fact is that I started hankering after the hands-on activity that comes with a field-posting, added to which, the atmosphere in Washington headquarters is pretty unsettled. Budgets go on being cut, and the "contracting" system, introduced in the latest reorganisation, has created an atmosphere of insecurity where people scurry around trying to collect enough contracts to justify their existence.

Challenge

Anyway, Chad is an interesting country – if you like a challenge. It is at the meeting point of North, Central, East and West Africa (neighbours include Nigeria, Libya, Sudan and the Central African Republic), and has had recurrent war and civil war since the 1960s. The North is in the Sahara and the South is almost tropical. It is one of the poorest places in the world, with terrible communications – both inside the country and with the outside world. Nicole has just made her first trip to N'Djamena and was a bit shocked by the lack of tar roads, the lack of shops, and the battered appearance of the city, but she is a good soldier. Incidentally, there is no lack of soldiers or weapons. They are all over the place. Another doubtful plus is that Chad now has oil; not oceans of the stuff, but enough to justify a 1,000km pipeline to the sea, and the first revenues start to come in about a year.

Looking Forward Hopefully

My colleagues are surprisingly enthusiastic about working in Chad, because they like the people, and they feel it is a place where it is fairly easy to get things done. Government tends to do what it says it will. It is not completely unknown territory for me, as I did several consultancies there in the mid-1980s before joining the World Bank. It was my introduction to the Sahel and to West Africa. I expect to start working there in January (Nicole probably in February). My first task will be the conversion of three small colonial villas into a smart new office. Our landlord has to do this, but to our plans and with our money, so I shall have both the fun and the headaches that go with supervising construction. I am a builder by nature, and I enjoy this sort of work. I spent a lot of my last visit adapting lease documents from Kiev and an architect's contract from Brussels to fit this case!

A Former Foreign Legion Outpost

I had the good luck to get in a quick trip to Faya (or *Faya-Largeau*, but the Chadians don't think much of naming cities after French soldiers). This is an oasis and former Foreign Legion outpost 1,000km from N'Djamena. It is a surprising place, because it is in a depression with ground water only a few feet below the surface. There is also a deep aquifer under natural pressure, so boreholes gush water (tasting of iron) which is used for very inefficient irrigation of date palms. The town is of *banco* (adobe), and quite attractive. It was occupied for years by the Libyans, but they were driven out in 1990 in a little-publicised war. The French immobilised the Libyan air force, while the Chadians used mobile unconventional tactics to rout the slow-moving and heavily-armed ground forces, leaving masses of broken military material behind. We almost spent the night in the Foreign Legion fort (looked after by one solitary French officer), as the military aircraft went back without us. It was summoned back, very grumpily. The crew tried to punish us with a most original take-off that first glued us to our seats, then left us momentarily weightless. Luckily we all had strong stomachs.

Family News

The family is well. Bernard and Stella have moved to Bedfordshire to be near to Bernard's work, and have exchanged their small apartment for a house in Great Barford. It seems incredible that Alistair is two years old and talking. Dominic works for a design company in Columbus, Ohio, and greatly enjoys it. He does not live in luxury (and was surprised to find that a car was a necessity), but finds the wide variety of work very stimulating. My brother Michael has beaten me to retirement (local government downsizing), and is devoting his energies to renovating a house in the North Yorkshire countryside – so I will soon be the only member of the Leicester Joneses to live in a city. My mother now lives in Devon, next to my sister Margaret, where she gardens a lot and looks after hens and two retired donkeys. The latter need much more work than the donkeys I see looking after themselves in Africa, and leading an idle life of plenty, which makes them fat.

French Holiday

We spent a very happy summer month at the house in Bordepaille. The very big room downstairs is now quite grand, with a new French window and the stonework of the walls all properly pointed. The only blot is the space where the big new fireplace should be (I want it English-manor-house size; I have taken dimensions from my sister Sheila's 450-year-old house in Suffolk). We now have to brace ourselves financially to put in central heating and finishing touches like new floors. The job in Chad should help. Our friends from Alexandria (Virginia), Teresa and John Conover, visited us this year and (despite our protests) laboured hard, fitting kitchen cabinets that I had had made in Senegal. Bordepaille is our house in the country. It gives me constant satisfaction, even though we are there only one month a year, and we have many friends in the local community. We briefly visited Sheila and Ron's house in the Creuse – lots of potential; but masses of work to be done. I'm glad we started the really rough part of our house when we were ten years younger.

Political Pondering

I don't think 1996 was a bad year overall. The dirty war in ex-Yugoslavia is over, even though it left a crop of unsolved problems. I am more sure than ever that, at least in Europe, we cannot afford the luxury of saying it is not our problem. Most of the horrors could have been avoided if "the West" had shown more foresight and political courage. It could easily have escalated to surrounding countries. Now, Zaire is starting to come apart. That is a very different matter: anarchy, rather than civil war. If the breakdown gets worse, I do not think the West can do very much, other than provide humanitarian aid. Eastern Europe and the former Soviet Union seem to have bottomed out. I am not surprised that people in the FSU feel cynical about the supposed advantages of capitalism. However I think their real problem was not that they moved from socialism to capitalism, but that the state fell apart. The American presidential election was boring, and the results suggest disengagement and complacency. America feels it is doing well enough not to risk change (just look at stock prices), despite disturbing evidence of social decay.

Powerful China

I think the big surprise parcel of the next few years is going to be China. For now, Russia has too many domestic problems to make problems outside its borders, but while Russia has been getting economically weaker, China has been getting stronger. This is both hopeful and dangerous. I cannot feel bad about millions of very poor people getting richer, but China (unlike the U.S.A.) could sacrifice soldiers without worrying about domestic political consequences. Moreover, China has been humiliated in the past, and has old scores to settle. The absorption of Hong Kong may well prove difficult, and provide an interlude, but it seems certain that pressure on Taiwan will increase, as well as pressure for a clearer sphere of regional influence. And there is always a risk of domestic political breakdown, because China is run by a tiny minority. I do not want to be alarmist, but anything could happen. Let's hope. Affectionate greetings, David and Nicole

A Foot of Snow

You talk of your "arctic" weather. It's been pretty cold here, and yesterday afternoon the television and radio news started to threaten snow; first 4 inches, then 10-12, and later 12-18 inches. We laughed a bit, as they seem better at scare-mongering than at forecasting, but by the time our guests – John and Teresa Conover – left us at about eleven o'clock, it had started to snow, and by this morning it was deep on the ground. It went on falling until lunchtime, by when we did indeed have over a foot of snow, and more is expected tonight. We'll see, but already there's enough of the stuff on the ground to bring Washington to a complete standstill. I expect all the schools will be closed tomorrow, and probably the World Bank as well. I shall not complain, as I have some work to do here if that happens, and I can "talk to" quite a lot of my colleagues from home on the electronic mail system.

Shifting Snow

We have spent much of the day indoors, but at mid-day Nicole and I went out to do a bit of snow-clearing. First I cleared a path along the sidewalk in front of our house, which was very public-spirited of me, but rather pointless, since none of our neighbours did the same. Then I cleared a path for us to get the car out, which is slightly more useful, although I have no intention of driving anywhere unless I really have to. The road itself has not been snow-ploughed, but there is a path of compressed snow wide enough for one car. The snow was quite light and powdery, but moving a foot of it was hard work, and created a little problem of where to put it. I got very nice and warm after about an hour of this – even my fingers.

Creating a Work Bench

My other weekend job – apart from putting up pictures and things, which is still not completely done – is making my new work bench. I think I told you that I was converting the rather rotten old wash-basin stand from our old bathroom into a general-purpose work bench. I think Nicole has to be given credit for the idea. The result is rather smart, as it has little drawers and a cupboard, so I can reduce the clutter in my work room. In fact this is the boiler room, and it has pipes everywhere, rather like the engine room of a ship, but rather to my surprise I find that I can make quite a satisfactory little work space there (though not as good as the future workshop in France). I went out yesterday, before the snow, and bought myself a woodwork vice and a metalwork vice for my bench, without both of which life is really not complete.

Good News for Dominic

Dominic telephoned us two days ago to say that his employment has been made permanent. They offered him another $2,000, which is enough for a few hot meals. He is meant to start on 1st February. It's going to be quite a rush for him. I'm sure he is very relieved. He was beginning to think that he had offended them by asking for more, and that they had decided they did not want him after all. I'm interested to know how he finds this work experience. He may well find it very tedious, as he is used to doing everything himself. His idea is that he should not spend the rest of his life as a salary-man, but I think the experience of working in a commercial and well-established design firm for a year or two should stand him in good stead if he wants to work on his own in the future.

Mme Fortuné

Nicole's mother has been unwell. It seems she has intestinal polyps, and will have to have an operation. I hope they have been found at an early enough stage, although one of the few advantages of age is that although all sorts of little nastinesses develop, they do not develop fast. Lots of love, David and Nicole

A Busy Schedule

I'm sorry to have been a poor correspondent over the last few weeks. I wish I could say that it was because I had been getting ready for the move, but in fact I do not feel ready at all, and there is a lot to do before next weekend. I leave on Friday evening (17th) but will return at the end of the month for two weeks of training, and leave again around 15th February.

Two Islands of Guadeloupe

We very much enjoyed our stay in Guadeloupe. Ste Anne has got a lot busier and more touristy over the years. Neither M. nor Mme Fortuné is from that part of Guadeloupe. As you probably know, there are effectively two islands just about joined together at a point (there is a river-like channel between them). One island is volcanic and forested, with mountains in the middle and streams running down to the sea; the other is a low plateau of coral rock, much flatter and drier (no rivers). To complicate matters, the mountainous one is called Basse Terre and the flat one is called Grande Terre (the *"basse"* in Basse Terre means that it is downwind, and has nothing to do with altitude). The Fortunés come from Basse Terre, but when M. Fortuné decided to build a new house, he guessed right that Grande Terre would be the more attractive for tourism, as it has better beaches.

When we first started visiting, twenty years ago, the beaches of Ste Anne were almost empty. Now there is hardly room to sit down in the tourist season. Most of the tourists seem to be staying in *gîtes* (lodgings in people's houses) so it is not very high- class tourism.

A House Built on Clay

The house in Ste Anne, which was Mme Fortuné's pride and joy, has developed quite a lot of problems over the last twenty-three years. It is built in black clay soil, which moves, so there are a lot of cracks. It would have been wise (in retrospect) to build up the area where the house stands with a foot or so of crushed rock, and then pay a lot of attention to foundations. Also, the salt in the air gets into the reinforced concrete and attacks the reinforcing rods, which expand and crack the concrete. The steel railings on the verandah are starting to rot away for the same reason, and so on. I do not think there is anything structurally dangerous, but Mme Fortuné finds it a preoccupation, and Denys (who is now the legal owner) is busy and doesn't have time to see to the repairs that are needed.

Three Aged Sisters

Of course, this is nothing to Mme Fortuné's problems with her sisters. She is very lucky that Anick and her boyfriend are there to look after them most of the time. All three of the sisters are now pretty well helpless in different ways and to different degrees. I just spoke to Nicole, who is returning tonight. Guichette, the oldest, is physically fit and has the best morale, but forgets and loses everything. Gilberte, the youngest, is also reasonably fit, but is unable to look after herself because of her manic depression. Yvana, Anick's mother, is almost totally helpless, mentally and physically.

Dominic Gets Back to Work

Dominic came back at the same time as myself, and we said goodbye in Miami airport. He has sent me a brief electronic mail to say that he got home all right, that it was very cold in Columbus, and that he was very busy. It's cold here too. There are about two inches of snow on the ground.

Death in Niger

We had one very sad piece of news this week. The wife of a couple we know quite well from a French aid organisation was killed by car thieves in Niamey, Niger, last weekend. They have two children, and her husband (with whom I have worked in Senegal) has had a series of back operations, and was often transported by Christine, lying on his back in the back of the car. One got the impression that it was really Christine who was the lynch-pin of the family. I cannot imagine how they will manage.

Lots of love, David

P.S. from Nicole

I came back from Guadeloupe last night and I am trying to get back to normal life. For the last three weeks I have had an easy time; my mother planned the meals and all I had to do was take her around in the car and go to the beach. She has received your card and was very touched. Do not be offended if she does not reply soon as she has a lot to do and now spends most of her time with her sisters.

Love, Nicole

Letter from Nicole   Alexandria, 23/01/1997

Plans for Chad Living

First of all I must thank Margaret for the pretty tea towel which will be very useful as I am in the process of renewing my tea towels and trying to replace them with attractive ones made of linen.

David has now been in Chad for nearly a week and is settling in quite happily. He is living in the house left by his predecessor, but when I get to Chad we shall have to start to look for something else, or have alterations made to the house. He has hired a temporary cook/ housekeeper who seems to be quite competent and who can read and write. Until I arrive I do not know whether I shall keep him on a permanent basis; it all depends on whether he is able to plan and prepare a dinner party. I will have to test him and try him on some fancy menus. David is already quite busy as there is a high-level mission arriving from Washington this weekend, and this usually involves lots of meetings with officials of the country, and long working hours.

Organising the Move

David is coming back in a week's time to attend a Resident Representatives' training seminar, then he has another seminar after that, and we shall leave for good on 14th February. We shall travel via England and will spend the weekend with Bernard and Stella. We are flying to Chad on 18th February. We are being packed on 10-12 February. The removal company has sent me a few boxes, which has enabled me to start packing clothes, linen and the not-so-delicate items. The packers will take care of china, pictures and fragile items because if anything is broken it will be their responsibility.

The estate agent put this house up for renting last week and up to now there has been one couple interested, but they wanted the house for the beginning of February. This weekend we might get more enquiries, as people usually go and visit houses for sale and rent at the weekend.

Snow, and a New President

After two weeks of bitterly cold weather, it has been mild for the last two days. We had a snow fall two weeks ago and until yesterday there was still snow on the ground. We had a card from Stephen Wright and he complains about the lack of sun in New York State. By the way, the snowfalls were very heavy in this part of the States. One of the good things in Washington is that we have very sunny winters.

I watched the inauguration festivities on TV last Monday. Nowhere in the world is there so much pageantry for the election or the re-election of a President or Prime Minister. The United States always does things on a bigger scale. When watching the festivities and hearing the comments of the various speakers on TV one could not help noticing the variety of races in this country and also the nationalism of North Americans, even if they do not agree with the views of the President. They are all so proud to be American.

Love to you both and to Margaret's family. The photo is for Mummy. Nicole

A Welcome Letter

I was very surprised to find a letter from you when I got here. It must have arrived quite fast too, because it is dated the 6th and I arrived the 19th. Maybe the Chad post is better than the Senegalese post. I am generally telling people to send mail to Chad Resident Mission, Care of World Bank, U.S.A., which is sure to arrive, but has to take about two weeks. Mind you, I have received nothing since I arrived (apart from a few late New Year/ Christmas wishes; the French give themselves until the end of January). It says something for our way of life and for Nicole's superior qualities as a correspondent/ contact maker, that more than nine out of ten of our cards is postmarked somewhere other than the U.K. Over the years we have given up collecting stamps for various charities and children, but we would be a good source.

Harmattan Winds

I am meant to be in the U.S. today, but am still here, feeling sorry for myself. For the last two days we have had bad harmattan winds bringing dust down from the nearby Sahara and reducing visibility. My plane was meant to leave after midnight last night, but it over-flew on the way out to Donala. The revised plan was to pick passengers up on the return leg, so I hung about until 2.30am, when 'they' announced that it had again over-flown – this time quite unnecessarily as the wind had dropped and landing conditions were good. I shall write a stiff letter to Air France (sometimes it produces a small cheque or some other token). This night I can see the stars, so with luck there will be no problem (except that again I leave in the small hours). Fortunately my new red *laissez-passer* gets me into the V.I.P. lounge here, which is quite comfortable (a flexible interpretation of V.I.P.s).

A Very Poor Country

I have been very busy and have had an interesting field trip – seven hours' drive starting at 4am, followed by a long day's work – in fact by two long days' work – and a plane trip back. It is a very poor country. We visited a number of awful schools. The worst had two hundred and thirty filthy tiny tots squatting on a mud floor in rags, supervised by a man with a whip, and occasionally erupting into surges of fighting. I called it the *poulailler* (chicken coop) and the name has stuck. Of course nothing was being learned. I was able to find one child who recognised the letter 'a', but nothing beyond that. My 'k' was taken for a '3'. I did better with my picture of a dog. Dogs here, by the way, really do have curly tails.

The Rules of the Sewing Club!

Interestingly, the best school by far was an old one built by missionaries, now long-departed, in a half-Christian village. We even found one well-dressed woman with the rules and regulations of the sewing club. These included, if an officer of the club is involved in sin, a large meeting will be called to discuss the matter and suspend her. Incidentally, my temporary servant René – a very serious man with eight children – seems to have brought an extremely battered Bible to study in his spare moments (of which there are many when I am on my own and spending the whole day at work). I think the language is Sarr. I can recognise few words except for proper names and "Allah", although strangely I see the word "LOGOS" for "Word" (*"In the beginning was the Word..."*).

Recruiting Bahai Colleagues

I am collecting a lot of job applications, as I need to do some recruiting, and I got a very impressive C.V. from a general services officer at the U.S. embassy – as usual, a Deep Southerner with a lot of tribal scars. My admin. officer Youssouf (despite the name a protestant with a U.S. education) said *"Of course he's a Bahai – the whole of the U.S. Embassy General Services is run by Bahais under Mr. Linklater"*. I had expected to find some problems between North and South and between Arab and Christian, but not to find an enclave of Bahais. You may not know the Bahais; my old friend Marius Szanto came from a Bahai family.

It is a syncretic religion started in the Middle East in the 19th century, predominantly an offshoot of Islam, but very tolerant and much hated by Islamic fundamentalists who regard them as apostate and therefore worthy of death. The Iranian revolution scattered a lot of Bahais (many were killed) and created new communities. They are generally very tolerant people, accepting many prophets but giving precedence to none. They are (despite some rather odd mystical beliefs) modern, pro-education and hard-working, which means they are a very prosperous community when left alone.

Scrap Metal Implements
Work has been started on my Resident Mission. I signed the lease last week (taking a slight risk as I did not have written approval) and I went down today with my architect Mr. Loubah (another one with tram-lines all over his face – you get used to it) - to see the unwanted bits of the old structure being hacked to pieces with primitive instruments made of bits of scrap metal embedded in club-like handles and wound around with bits of tin-can.

Family News
I am very impressed by Sheila's M.A. She has really plugged away at it. I had no idea. Also, I spoke to Mick around Christmas. I know he is very happy to get a call from the family. The house sounds fun but hard work. I reckon that a certain type of person (of whom I am one) needs to get at least one house out of his or her system in a lifetime. Usually that is enough, because it is very hard work and takes much longer than expected.

Hope the donkeys are well; lots of spare ones here if you need some more.
Lots of love, David

Letter to Mother   09/02/1997, Alexandria

A Pleasant Training Session
I'll write you a very quick letter before I disconnect the computer for the packers. I have been back from Chad for a week, spent up to Friday at a very swish conference centre about forty miles from here in semi-rural Virginia. We were a group of about twelve new Resident Representatives or deputy Res. Reps. learning about the pitfalls of the job. They were a nice and varied bunch, many already with field experience, and the whole thing was both pleasant and useful.

Corruption in Azerbaijan
There was one particularly nice guy from the Azerbaijan mission – a Turk, so he more or less spoke the local language, but he was somewhat shocked by the place he had been pretty well parachuted into. Azerbaijan sounds to be as corrupt as the worst of Africa, to the extent that there is virtually no sense of opprobrium attached to corruption. His solution in setting up a new office had been to hire only people too young to have had any previous significant work experience. However, even this was not absolutely plain sailing, as school examination results were also purchased on a standard fee basis – so much for a pass, so much more for a distinction etc. Fortunately, he has a tremendous sense of humour to carry him through.

Non-Stick Stickers
We are well into the final stages of packing, sticking red and green stickers to everything to show whether it is to be transported or stored – although unfortunately we have easy-to-remove stickers that are so easy to remove that they usually fall off on their own after a few hours. We shall sleep here today and tomorrow, then go to a hotel for the rest of the week, with Nicole coming in daily to watch the packers. Yesterday we found a buyer for the car, and today I think we found tenants for the house.

Taking Walks
We have snow on the ground, but temperatures well above freezing, so it is melting fast. This afternoon Nicole and I went out for a walk down to the river and back through town, but

the weather suddenly turned colder again as we were on our way back.

I forgot to mention that one of the main pleasures of my training was that – not having to take any time to get to work – I was able to go for a country walk in the grounds every morning before breakfast, before anyone else was out (not very early – about 7am). Every day I saw dozens of white-tail deer, some of which waited until I was within a few yards of them before bolting away. Not to be outdone, Nicole saw a raccoon sauntering down our street the other day.

That's the last letter you get from this computer for a while. I hope you are keeping well. Lots of love, David and Nicole

Letter to Mother   N'Djamena, 22/02/1997

Dust and a Sore Throat

Nicole is in bed with a sore throat while I finish our first weekend together in N'Djamena. It is probably a combination of the flights plus two days of bad dust – hardly sandstorms, but a brownish sky and high winds for most of the night bringing in a fine covering of dust that is imperceptible at first, then a faint bloom, and finally disaggregates into untidy little ripples and clots like curdled milk.

A Last Weekend with Bernard and Family

We spent a very pleasant weekend with Bernard, Stella and Alistair, staying just down the road from them in a half-timbered pub – much messed about over the years, but parts of it certainly 400-500 years old. We thought we were going to be cold, but they must have turned on the heating in our room when we arrived.

Alistair is a very lively little boy, developing very much as originally promised. He is good-humoured most of the time, sociable, very fond of his food, with a growing and eclectic vocabulary which is beginning to coagulate into sentences. He loves to be read to, although one is not sure to what extent he follows complicated story lines. That is to say, he is beyond the simple identification of objects, but the full extent of an adventure of *Thomas the Tank Engine* probably escapes him. On the other hand emotions (*"Thomas is sad"*) clearly have a lot of meaning. *Tom Kitten* is just about able to hold attention.

Khmer Treasures and the Forbidden City - in Paris

We then spent three days in Paris, not that I really wanted to, but it was a choice of no days or three days because of flights. I had some contact-making to do, but it left time for me to see the exhibition of Khmer treasures (Angkor Wat etc. in Cambodia – very interesting stuff – mainly sculpture and some bronzes – from the 7th through 15th Centuries, and also an exhibit on the Forbidden City in Beijing (Peking). We stayed in a Japanese hotel; choice of the World Bank's travel agency. They chose on the basis of bed/ night rate but the hotel compensated on extras. A breakfast consisting of coffee, rolls, and not-very-good orange juice cost the equivalent of £13. We spent one night with Suzy in her new home – an exciting acquisition after years of living in flats. It is sixty years old, nicely built, and plenty for one person. We also had a meal with her son, Bruno, his wife, and daughter (a little younger than Alistair) in their tiny Paris flat.

The New Mission in Chad

I have had two short days of work so far, and am rather horrified by the varied back-log that awaits me. However, the new office is progressing well. Walls are being knocked down and others are being built up. The new building will be a strange amalgam of materials and ages. The oldest sections were built in 1941 by the father of the present contractor, of local burnt brick, with walls of an impressive thickness, but limited foundations. The latest additions will have foundations going down ten feet, entirely passing the clay, which makes bad foundations (expands and contracts with the rain) and reaching a bed of compacted river sand. We spent some time on the site this evening with the architect and an HQ guy who arrived this afternoon, to design the electronics cabling aspects of the office – all the special wiring we now need for computers and telecommunications.

A Worrying Site for a House

The house is inhabitable, even though none of our freight has yet arrived – not even the special air freight that was meant to get here before us. However the site is not good. There is a constant traffic of contraband passing in front of and beside the house, and from time to time the customs men raid them and shots get fired. It's small-scale stuff – big cardboard boxes of sugar, soap, cooking oil. I saw two ladies come across in a *pirogue*, and was surprised that they seemed to have no merchandise, but when they disembarked and hurried away I could see that they were both a very strange shape – probably carrying large loads on their backs under their wraps. It is very entertaining, but I do not want to get caught in any cross-fire.

Unhappy Orchids

My orchids are in very poor shape. The constant dry wind is very bad for them, and has finished some of them off very fast. I have taken most of the remainder indoors, but as in Senegal, I have no appropriate place for them and need to think something up. I'm wondering about building in mud bricks this time!
Lots of love, David

Letter to Mother N'Djamena, 08/03/1997

Flying Through Dust Clouds

We spent Tuesday through Thursday last week on safari in the south of the country – not that one talks of being on safari here, it's an East African concept, although it might well be understood, as the Arabic for "to travel" is "safari". We took Air Chad down to Sarh with a visiting colleague and a couple from the International Monetary Fund who had been turned out of an alternative journey with his team because the petroleum company Exxon (Esso) refused to carry a non-official wife. As it happens, we had the best deal; they were meant to fly to another southern town, Moundou, but there was so much sand in the air that the pilot couldn't see to land the plane, and after three attempts they gave up and went to Lake Tchad instead for a day. I was afraid the same thing might happen in our case, as we also overflew Moundou, but when we reached Sarh and started to descend the dust-cloud below slowly started to yield details that turned out to be roads and houses. Even so, we missed the airport completely at the first try!

A Sugar Factory

This was, of course, work – familiarisation *avec le terrain* – and we did two very full days of visits and meetings. We stayed at the sugar factory, which was one of our policy targets, and were made very comfortable despite our somewhat hostile intentions. Nicole had her first visit to a sugar factory (by no means my first) and found it both interesting and an awful place to work. We are still in the cool season (all is relative) but a sugar factory is basically a very large corrugated iron structure full of boilers, kettles, furnaces and other heat-producing equipment, and everything is sticky.

We also had a tour of the estate, which was more of a novelty for me because it used centre-pivot irrigation – i.e. a long perforated arm which moved slowly in a circle. In this case it was a very large circle: each centre pivot watered 130 hectares (about 280 acres). The arm was supported on a series of powered wheels, each "walking" a circular track, and controlled in a way that was remarkable for its simple ingenuity: the arm was not rigid, but hinged at each pair of wheels. The speed was set by the wheels furthest from the centre of the circle, and when the next hinge started to bend, this powered that set of wheels to catch up. The same system worked at the next hinge, and so on.

Cane Burning

We were also treated to a spectacular display of cane-burning. Each parcel of cane is set on fire before harvesting to make it easier to cut, and to drive out snakes. This sounds perverse, but is quite rational. Sugar cane is, as you know, a giant grass (about ten foot high) and it is covered with abrasive cutting leaves just like pampas grass. It has slightly more sugar if cut unburnt, but demands much more labour, and the job is really unpleasant.

For the burning, a group of incendiaries is equipped with long bundles of grass (again, really long grass, about seven foot) which they light and at a signal they run around the edge of the parcel setting light to the dried leaves at the bottom of the canes. These catch fire very quickly, and the flames rush through the parcel (of 32 hectares, a quarter of a pivot) creating a huge sheet of flames and a tower of black smoke. The heat is intense, even from several hundred yards away, and a lot of birds suddenly appear – presumably from nests in the canes. Within about twenty minutes it is all over, and all that is left is a mass of blackened canes that do not look as if they could possibly produce white sugar.

Schools and Hospitals

The rest of the time we spent visiting schools and hospitals (stench of urine!), and being shown around Sarh itself – a town that has seen better times. The schools were a bit of an eye-opener to Nicole. We started out with a rather smart one, built with World Bank funds, but we went on to others that were community-built. In fact "community supported" would be more accurate, as there was very little building. In the centre of Sarh we visited the *"Ecole du Centre Culturel"*, which I had expected to be some sort of showpiece, but it was built entirely of grass mats, and the children sat on little piles of broken bricks or broken car batteries. The communities also pay many of the teachers. In the first "smart" school the community teachers were paid between £7 and £10 per month (less than a tenth of what we pay our cook, but he is better educated than most of the teachers!)

Poor Quality of Education

The most depressing thing about the schools is not their physical condition, but the poor quality and near-uselessness of the education they dispense. These children, most of whom will never really need to speak French, have to learn to read in a language they do not speak. Most of them drop out before they can do much more than copy phrases they do not understand into their exercise books. I am now fairly at ease going into a classroom and testing a few children at random in as friendly a way as possible (they also see very few white people) on their reading skills, or for the very little ones, on their recognition of letters of the alphabet.

A Few Excellent Scholars

The encouraging, or half-encouraging, thing is that in most classes one finds at least one child who has really learned something and can read with comprehension and without stumbling, or do simple arithmetic. The odd thing about this is that these children are so head-and-shoulders beyond the rest that it is hard to see how they could have made the breakthrough, but some do. The *Prefet* of Sarh, who was on a nostalgia trip, took us to see his old primary school, and we found a group of teenage boys using the classroom after hours as a convenient quiet place to practise quite advanced maths (which means I don't think I could now do it) in preparation for their baccalaureat.

Keeping Girls at School

We also organised a meeting of the parents' association in one school. The parents came in their best clothes (mixture of traditional and western, generally very used) and crowded the benches (this was the smart school) while we sat in a row at the front and asked questions. We had a minister with us, who did not speak the local language any more than we did, so it was hard to get a relaxed dialogue going. We spent a lot of effort trying to get their views of girls' education (far lower enrolment than boys and much faster drop-out). There were a number of explanations given. One was that girls did not want to go to school. One man told us that he had whipped his daughter all the way to school, but even when she got there she refused to stay, and when his wife saw the whip marks she was mad with him. Another reason is that somewhere between ages eleven and fourteen most girls in this region go through initiation rites involving clitoral excision ("genital mutilation"). They have to be taken out of school for this, and seldom go back, as this is usually the prelude to being married. Others said that if they went to school as teenagers they usually got pregnant anyway.

I think there was only one woman in our meeting – a cheerful talkative gap-toothed lady, who had never been to school herself but had sent her eight children there. She was a widow (which is probably why she was allowed to attend) and clearly a person of character.

Ancien Combattant, and Chefs de Terre

As we drove to our meeting, we passed an old man on a horse going the same way, wearing a sort of gold-braided hat, and half-way through the meeting he came in with two other very old men in Arab dress (red fez-type hats), and everyone started to make room for them in the front row. They were the spiritual/ traditional leadership. The two men in Arab dress were the *Chefs de Terre* – the traditional land judges. They said nothing, but carried tremendous authority in their silence. After them, there was a further succession of very old men who had to be found good places, and from time to time someone had to be sent outside to shout at the children.

The old man in the braided cap was very properly dressed in European style in a black suit with a (grubby) white shirt and a necktie. He introduced himself afterwards as an *Ancien Combattant*, who had crossed the desert with General Leclerc's army to Tripoli and on into the liberation of Italy.

I think that's enough letter for this week, except that we survived a very long dirt road trip back and are in good health and spirits. Hope you are ditto.
Lots of love, David

Letter to Mother

N'Djamena, 16/03/1997

A Shaky Current

I have just hooked up my computer, but I am keeping my fingers crossed, as I have a very improvised system for converting the current to 110 volts, which has a safety device (to prevent overload) but this is meant to work through an earth (the third pin on the plug) and every time I try to rig up an earth connection, all the lights go out. What this means is that I am now working without a real safety system to protect against the very variable electric current in Chad. In fact the lights keep on going dim and then bright as I write.

Soldiers with Kalashnikovs

I have had a busy week, with missions from Washington, and ending up with a meeting with the President and most of the cabinet. I was not the main speaker at this meeting, but my presence is part of the protocol. We had to tell them some hard things, and when I came out of the meeting and had to walk past a line of soldiers with kalashnikovs it did occur to me to hope that they were not going to be pointed at us. The week was hard also because I was recovering from a very nasty cold and sore throat – more or less what Nicole had ten days earlier. We have had a pretty relaxed weekend, and I hope that the coming weekend will be easier than the last two.

Useless Cheque Book

Another source of business is the fact that I am sending most of my small staff on training, and we are consequently even more short-staffed than usual. I was very fed up with my administrator, as he went off to Washington without telling me he had not finalised the change of signatures for the Resident Mission cheque book (as he was supposed to have done), and I did not find out until I started signing cheques and having them rejected. I can hardly believe that he could be so irresponsible, and he is going to have quite a talking-to when he gets back. He left in a great rush, as his flight was put forward from mid-day to 9am, but it is not as if he was then out of contact with me, as all he had to do was sit down at a computer and send me an electronic message.

No Luck Finding a New House

We continue to prospect sporadically for alternative housing, but the field does not seem very rich, and I think we shall have to stay where we are – if we can negotiate an extension of lease at a reasonable rent from our landlord. Most of the houses we see in N'Djamena are rather old and run down, and on rather small plots. Yesterday we went to see one that was on the river bank, like ours, but although it was very modern and convenient, the builders had contrived to make the worst possible use of a very special site. Two houses had been put on a plot that was big enough for one (they were meant for the managers of the next door enterprise), the garden was small, and the whole thing was enclosed by high walls, so that one might just as well have been in Slough as on the banks of the river Chari (give or take some differences of climate).

An Exciting River

At our house, the security is probably poor, but at least when we want some entertainment we can go out and look at the river. There is constant traffic to and fro just by our house, much of it smuggling, but some of it just ordinary ferry activity. I am very tempted to go and take a ride, but I'm afraid I might be arrested as an illegal entrant to Cameroon on reaching the other side. Opposite us there is another town, built of mud brick (like much of N'Djamena), and one large tree that rises up over the houses so that at first sight it looks like a small pyramidal hill. The river level is still falling fast, and new sandbanks appear all the time, then grow grass, and get peopled with goats and sheep. At the beginning of the week, I was delighted to see three hippos in the river just by our house. I had told Nicole to expect them, and she was very sceptical. They have gone away again, but we now know they exist. Also, today for the first time, a really big wooden boat chugged by for the first time, carrying a lot of people and smaller boats. Our guard said it was on its way to Lake Tchad, to bring back soda and vegetables – a two-day trip. That would be a very adventurous trip, but more in Dominic's department these days than my own.

Dried Up Orchids

My orchids continue to suffer from the climate. The ones in the house look somewhat happier than those in the garden. The basic problem is simply that the humidity is very low indeed (about 30-40% relative humidity), and they cannot cope with the water loss that this involves. As soon as we are settled on where we are going to live, I shall have to build something for them.

We have not yet called your friends, but we shall do so – maybe this week.

Lots of love, David

P.S. from Nicole

Life is very unsettled and there do not seem to be a lot of activities for expatriate wives. I have spent the week unpacking the essentials, but before I open more boxes I wait until we know whether we are going to move house. I do not mind staying where we are as I do not think I could go through another removal in such a short time. It is very hot, but the air conditioning works well.

Love, Nicole

Letter to Mother

N'Djamena, 22/03/1997

Uncongenial Climate

This week I am feeling a lot better and Nicole is feeling a lot worse. She went to the doctor yesterday and he diagnosed her as having a whole lot of "itis": pharyngitis, laryngitis and sinusitis. She is taking a whole lot of stuff for them and sleeping a lot. I think she is feeling a whole lot better today than she was yesterday.

Let's hope this is part of getting used to the climate, not its permanent effect. It is very hot and dry now, and remains dusty although we have not had any of the really nasty dust storms in the last week. Our thermometer gets up to 45′C mid-day (113′F) and goes down to about 28′C at night (82′F). However, it is so dry that (in my view anyway) this is not nearly as uncomfortable as it sounds, except that it does dry out your nasal passages. It dries everything else too. You realise this, for instance, when you handle a sheet of paper. It feels and sounds quite different from usual. Or last night we had a glass of medicinal Guadeloupean rum with a twist of lime in it. This morning when I did the washing up, not only were the glasses quite dry at the bottom, but the twist of lime had dried out too.

Essential Freezer
The kitchen is like an oven. This is more the fault of the refrigerator and the freezer than of the real oven. I think the big chest freezer is on its last legs, and as a result has to keep working all the time, and pumps out heat like a radiator. We will need to get it fixed, as it is a very necessary convenience. Apart from the things you would expect to find in a freezer, we use it for things that might get weevils, like flour and beans, and our stock of brown sugar from the sugar factory that would otherwise quickly be full of ants.

Procuring Staff
My duties have not been too onerous this week, except for the fact that my administrator is still away, so I spend a lot of time dealing with the cash box and signing cheques. I think I am well on the way to recruiting two more senior staff, and I have also done a first round of interviews for a secretary (Nicole did that for me) and a new assistant administrator. We have been very scientific so far. We tested the secretaries in English and French typing, spelling, and composition of a letter (the latter only in French). We got a good spread of marks, but the best were quite good. For the administrators I gave them the transaction slips for the petty cash box and the print-out of the previous two months, and asked them to tell me various things about our expenditure, including how much I should have in the cash box. Again, the three best were pretty good. For both jobs, I intend to do a second round, but my first impression is that I can recruit an assistant administrator who is considerably better than the existing guy, which could make for some sparks.

Good Progress on the Mission
Our new building is going along fairly well now. The quality is less sure than in Dakar, which is a little worrying, as one has to keep a good eye on things, but the walls are mostly up and the new roof is going on. We have kept one small swimming pool to serve as an underground water storage tank. This is a sensible precaution here. We have a large tank at the house too, with a pump. Unfortunately it was driving Nicole crazy, as every time we turned on a tap there were successive explosions of air, which splashed water all over the place. I am rather proud that I eventually diagnosed the problem as a leaky pipe downstream of the pump, so we drained the tank and sent our odd-job man in to have a look. The water is all right now, except that it tasted very odd for the first few days. I suppose that is not surprising, considering that Alexis was paddling around in it for most of the morning, although for some reason there was a strong flavour of soot. We boil and filter all our water, so we would not have come to any harm, but for a few days we have kept to expensive bottled water.

Pitfalls of Renovation
Did I mention that I had a letter from Michael? He seems to be enjoying his building work still, but is surprised to find that it takes so much longer than it was meant to, and that unexpected problems keep on cropping up. I could have told him all about both these aspects of doing up old houses. The only easy way to do up an old house is to leave it in the hands of a builder and look the other way. The builder will only do what he has to do, and will hide

away again all the problems that an owner-builder would feel obliged to tackle; and 90% of the time nothing nasty happens until (one way or another) the owner has moved on.

Déjà vu (Again!)

Last week there was a regional conference on agricultural research going on here. I went to attend the closing, and had the strange feeling that I had walked out of the same event about ten years earlier, and gone back in to find exactly the same debates as before with a different cast of people. There were people from the Overseas Development Institute, who knew people (or knew of them) that I had worked with, and a very nice forceful lady from the Overseas Development Administration where I also worked. There was also a guy from the Bank, on detachment from a French research organisation, who hailed from the little commune of Ste Claude in Guadeloupe. This is, in a sort of way, the home of the Fortuné clan. We had him and the ODA lady over for drinks, and when I was delivering him back he introduced me to another French research guy, stationed in Dakar, who was also from Ste Claude. Small world! Lots of love, David

P.S. from Nicole – It is a tough place and climate!

The last personal letters David wrote were to his sons, Bernard and Dominic. The two last letters Bernard received both include pictures – photos or drawings – no doubt included to involve Alistair, David's precious first grandchild (the only grandchild he was ever to meet). The following excerpts are from the last two letters written to Bernard and family.

Letters to Bernard and Family   N'Djamena, 23/03/1997

This (picture) is a Merganser, a fish-eating duck. I very much doubt that it is anything like the curious duck that I have just been looking at through our binoculars – curious, because its tail seemed unusually long, and it sat at a strange upright angle rather more like a goose. Others to be seen included a lot of white storks, and a black and white kingfisher (picture of stork below)….

The final letter, written just three days before David's untimely death, is quite revealing of the way of life imposed by the job and location, and of Nicole's great loyalty in continuing to follow where David led throughout his career.

N'Djamena, 27/03/1997

(first part of letter written by Nicole)

I interviewed a cook this afternoon. He has worked mainly at the U.S. Embassy here, in Cameroon, and in *Côte d'Ivoire*, and his references are very good… it is said that he can cater for a dinner party of up to thirty people, and is also able to cater for a cocktail party and provide small eats. He looks very smart and capable, but will he be able to get on with the present cook, René? This man says he can work late, while René has to leave early. David is never home before 5pm (he starts work at 7am and does not stop for lunch) and I feel bad to keep René so late; he starts work at 6am. If René wants to stay, I have warned him that he will have to take second place and be responsible for the housework. Of course he will help the cook and I will give him the opportunity to do some cooking.

Walking in Circles

This morning I went for a walk with three other ladies. It is not a very exciting walk as we do the same circuit five times, but it is within the compound of the veterinary school, there are trees and birds and one is not bothered by beggars or others.

David has gone to a cocktail party to which I was not invited. I think it was only for men. *Grosses bises de Maman*, Nicole

Letter continues, hand-written by David
(including some comic drawings of unlikely candidates applying to work as his secretary)

Mummy is scandalised that I came back and told her that after all, wives were invited. She would have been very welcome to go in my place. The cocktail parties are all held at one or other of three hotels (this the least tacky, but that's not saying much); there are always speeches and the food is always poor – and one meets the same people although it is true that this time there was slightly more variety because of a scattering of wives.
Lots of love, Daddy

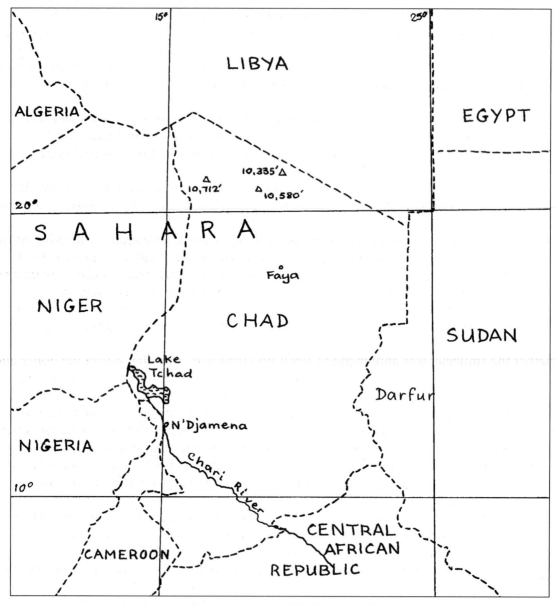

Map showing location of Chad, central Africa

CHAPTER SEVEN
30th MARCH 1997 AND AFTER

It was Easter Sunday, March 30th, when around noon the happiness of our family gathering for Easter, (in Wickham Skeith, Suffolk) was shattered. We had returned from Church, and were cooking a turkey for ourselves, our younger daughters Elisabeth and Juliet, our oldest son David and his partner Jane, and our third son Jim, when the dreadful news came. My sister Margaret had received the call from Bernard, who had received the shattering news direct from Chad. Margaret had the unenviable task of phoning other members of the family.

David Brian Jones, our lovely brother, had taken a Sunday walk into the streets of Chad. Nicole was busy in the house, and David, ever curious about street life in Third World countries, wandered into the bustling thoroughfare to see what was going on that Easter morning.

Nicole, in the house by the river bank, heard a loud noise in the street. A few minutes later the watchman knocked on the door to tell her that David had been hit by a speeding car, and killed instantly.

It could have been worse – at least David died quickly, without long-drawn out suffering or hideous disablement. But he wasn't ready to die; he loved life and wanted to go on living it.

The tragedy was accidental – although it fully justified David's reservations about living near the ferry crossing, where small-time smuggling was rife and customs men frequently contributed to cross-fire and traffic accidents in their attempt to keep some semblance of law and order in a poverty-riven environment. David was hit head-on by a smuggler trying to evade the police and the customs officers.

Whether the smuggler was apprehended, what his crime was, and what action the police and customs men took, has remained unclear. Only one thing really mattered to Nicole and the family – David was dead, and nothing would bring him back.

On that day, my husband Ron and I had planned to set off for Prague, with our son Jim who was engaged to a Czech girl, Martina. Our van was loaded up with furniture for their new home, and we were excited by the prospect. But as the terrible news struck home, I realised I could not go. After a doleful meal, we left the family in charge and set off towards the ferry, but with a detour to drop me off on the outskirts of London, where I would catch a train to Devon and stay with my devastated mother.

This was normally an idyllic place to visit: our mother and Margaret shared a large garden and orchard, also two fields housing Golden Guernsey goats, chickens, and contented donkeys; but today it seemed a desolate destination.

My journey was difficult, since British Rail save up all repairs for weekends and the first leg of the "train" journey was by bus, followed by numerous bewildering changes on the underground, with information hard to come by and lost travellers on every platform, all vying for news of connections and diversions. I sat dumb, tears running down my face, but thanks to "British phlegm" no-one appeared to notice. I was strangely comforted by the presence of many black travelling companions. These were the race for whom my brother had worked for so many years, the race who surrounded him in death.

In Chad, Nicole was tended by many sympathetic folk, both black and white. She must have been in a daze as things took their stumbling course in a country where poverty, war and an exhausting climate made life such an endurance test. The authorities in Chad were contrite and did all they could to help her. I am sure this accident to an expatriate who was working to improve conditions for Chadians was an embarrassment to them.

Three days after the accident Nicole was flown to England in the President's private plane, accompanied by the coffin, a doctor and a minister of state. She went first to Bedford where Bernard and family lived, and David's body was handed over to the authorities to await the Inquest. The Coroner's Certificate gave the cause of death as *"Severe Brain Injury and Fracture of the Skull"*. The body was taken to a Chapel of Rest, and thanks to the devotion and skill of persons unknown to us, I am told the injuries were not distressingly evident and David appeared genuinely at peace.

Nicole and her sons composed a fitting newspaper announcement of death –

> **"JONES, David Brian, 30th March 1997,**
> **aged 54. A tragic accident in Chad.**
> **A loving husband to Nicole, cherished**
> **father to Bernard and Dominic, and**
> **a dear son to Marjorie. Thank you for**
> **the love, joy and energy you shared**
> **with all your family and friends….."**

Nicole travelled on to Devon, while Bernard took charge of funeral arrangements in Bedford. We grieved together; but nothing anyone said or did could alter the facts. The days and nights before the funeral passed in a daze. Nicole, her sons, our brother Michael, Margaret and I somehow cobbled together a funeral programme. In recognition of David's enjoyment of his cello, Elgar's *Cello Concerto* was among the music chosen for the farewell gathering at Bedford Crematorium. I spent my time trying to comfort my mother and Nicole, and preparing a hand-out for those attending the funeral, containing short passages from David's most recent letters. My intention was to give people some idea of why David had been in Chad, and what his aims had been. The funeral would take place on 9th April.

The Funeral

I was full of admiration for Dominic and Michael for their moving tributes, which they spoke clearly and with courage –

Dominic Jones spoke first –

Thank you everyone for coming here today. I would like to thank you also on behalf of my mother and my brother for the support that you have given us.

David, whom we are here to remember, was a husband, father, son, an architect, gardener, cook, musician, dancer (not a very good one but he always tried), a lover of Africa, a linguist, plumber, scholar, explorer… and the list goes on as he so enjoyed life and cherished what could be gained and given in it.

I feel lucky (as any child should) to have had my parents as parents. I sometimes feel a victim of parent-worship. However during the last week I have felt reassured that I was not the only one to have admired my father for his energy, goodness and knowledge.

He was a doer. As a child he told us that he had been inspired by the stories of missionaries accomplishing things for other people in far-flung places. As such, though his life was cut short in time, I feel content in my mind that it was long in the achievement, richness and experience that he had wished.

The passing of any active life can only be an untimely one, especially for those of us who are left behind and have to learn to cope without that person. My father would not have been who he was without the people who were around him from childhood to his death last week in Chad. For being a part of this I thank all of you. Because of this I know that though he is no longer here in body, there are many parts of him here in the relationships that he shared with all of you, something that I again am very grateful for, and hope you shall be able to share in by being here today, and meeting people from many different spheres of his life.

I would ask you that if you will mourn the loss of my father, also rejoice in the memories of him and the things that made him so enduring to us. With that thought I would like to read a short poem that I had sent to me for this time.

"If I die, survive me with such sheer force
that you waken the furies of the pallid and the cold,
from south to south lift your indelible eyes,
from sun to sun dream through your singing mouth.
I don't want your laughter or your steps to waver,
I don't want your heritage of joy to die.
Don't call upon my person. I am absent.
Live in my absence as if in a house.
Absence is a house so vast
that inside you will pass through its walls
and hang pictures in the air.
Absence is a house so transparent
that I, lifeless, will see you, living,
and if you suffer, my love, I will die again."
Pablo Neruda

Next came Michael –

Welcome, and thanks to you all for coming to share in the sad occasion of the committal of our brother and friend David's body, following such a tragic accident in Chad. It says a lot for the esteem in which he was held that so many of us have gathered from all quarters, and that there were so many offers from family and friends to speak for him today – too many for the time available – but thank you for all your kind thoughts. I would like to spend a couple of minutes to recall some of my memories of his youth. Growing up in David's footsteps, following two years behind him through the same schools, and many of the same clubs – scouts, life-saving, orchestra – I saw much of the development of his character into the man we loved and respected.

One characteristic that particularly stays with me was his courage to be different; to plot his own course rather than follow the crowd. With his excellent diction, he was prominent in the grammar school's amateur dramatic society, landing good parts in several of the annual productions at a local theatre. With it being an all boys' school, the female roles were always a problem, and they usually had to resort to borrowing budding actresses from the local girls' schools. However, when David was fifteen and "Romeo and Juliet" was planned for the annual event, David agreed to play the female lead. Whilst most adolescent boys would have shied away from the prospect, for fear of ridicule from their peers, David had the courage to take it on, and did it so well as to earn widespread respect rather than derision.

Another example that springs to mind occurred a few years later when David was first setting up in a flat in Oxford on moving out from Hertford College. He needed transport to go around looking at furniture that had been advertised, so I gave him a lift on the back of my motorbike. I had no spare biking gear and he was wearing just a tweed sports jacket. Although it was a fine day, he was soon getting decidedly chilly from the wind blowing into the front of his jacket. So what did he do? He asked me to stop while he turned his jacket from back to front and got me to do the buttons up down the back! At first glance, you couldn't tell whether he was coming or going, and as you can imagine, we got a few funny looks, but it did the trick. Perhaps a trivial example, but it illustrates both his flair for original thought and his self-confidence to follow through, no matter how it might look.

Of course David is well known for his love of travel, which was obvious from his early teens. Come the school holidays, he would pack his rucksack and set off on his own, first to thumb his way around this country, and in later years to explore much of Europe. As a student, he also found much appeal in the social aims of the Bahai religion. Their objectives for the elimination of all forms of prejudice, of equality, and universal education, struck a chord with his own beliefs, and the career that he took up with the Overseas Development Agency, Ford Foundation, and World Bank allowed him to further both these ideals and his love of travel. The choice of the Chadian Children's Fund, which promotes education, is therefore a particularly apt choice for charitable contributions in his memory.

His globe-trotting lifestyle did mean that in recent years, we saw much less of him than we would have liked. However he was always an excellent correspondent, and Sheila and family have compiled extracts from his many letters to give an insight into his later life, copies of which will be available at the reception to be held at the hotel afterwards.

I'd now like to welcome George ("Jorje"), a friend of David's from Senegal, to share in French his recollections of David.

There were many visitors from overseas at the funeral, and because David had worked in many countries where French was the official language of government, many of these visitors were French speakers, as was Nicole's family. So it was appropriate that the last tribute was in French. I have never seen a transcript of this speech so cannot include it here.

At the reception that followed, my mother got into conversation with a gigantic African in stunningly bright national dress. He spoke to her of the unusually high esteem in which David was held by those who worked alongside him. This esteem resulted from David's easy approachability and his down to earth practical attitude. For example, if the job in hand were vaccinating a herd of cows against disease, David would not stand aloof, watching, like the majority of white officials. He would be right in there, helping herd the cows, getting his hands dirty and actually sharing the work. And he was always ready to converse with the poorest of the poor, listening to their stories as one human being to another.

This encounter greatly heartened our mother. Because the funeral was thousands of miles distant from the countries where David had worked, and was inevitably held at short notice, many were unable to attend; so it was good to meet a handful of those who knew him in his African work.

In the weeks following David's death, dozens of messages of condolence arrived – for Nicole, for my mother, and for me as well. Many wonderful thoughts and prayers came our way. Here I will mention just a representative few. My mother received, from our cousin Patrick who had visited David and Nicole during their Nairobi years, this message –

I am not sure that I can write to a parent at such a time of grief and shock, but I would just like to say one thing. As well as all his other good and kind qualities, which were many, I always admired David's special inner self-confidence. It was a warming example to more cautious people such as myself.....

My lifelong friend Otti, who was our neighbour as children in Morland Avenue, wrote to me thus –

I can't tell you how sorry I am to hear your bad news. David was a wonderful man, warm, open minded and adventurous. He will be sadly missed.

Death makes a hideous hole in people's lives and it remains an uphill battle to fill it, particularly when it is so untimely. I will be thinking of you all over the next bleak weeks. Please give my condolences to Nicole and the boys whom I found very charming and attractive when I met them about six years ago. It must be a terrible shock and blow to them all. I can only say that time does heal to some extent...

From one of our own grandchildren, Jessica, then aged eight, we received an extremely touching letter adorned with a hundred kisses. It began –

I am sorry Grannie's brother died. I wish I was at the funeral so I could've seen your family. I read the letter from the funeral and I thought it was very interesting. I don't like the idea of the schools in Chad and I'm glad that I don't live there. I got a globe for my birthday and I found Chad on it....

280

For Nicole, those first weeks were desperately hard. On top of the shock, grief and loss she had so many decisions to make. She was suddenly left in charge of a house in London, a house in Alexandria, U.S.A. and a house in south-west France (the first two being let out), while many personal possessions and some treasured furniture were in far-away Chad. Her mother Suzette Fortuné, who had been very fond of David, needed comfort too, but was thousands of miles distant, in Guadeloupe, as was Denys, Nicole's brother. Some of the people she needed most urgently to contact over business and pensions, were in Washington, U.S.A.; others were in Great Britain, and still others, in Chad. Somehow she managed. Dominic accompanied her to Chad.

Three weeks after David's death, Nicole sent our mother this update –

I have been back in Alexandria since Sunday afternoon. I was not sorry to leave Chad, although a little sad to leave all the nice people I met in the last two weeks and who have been very good to me. Had I met them when I arrived two months ago, I am sure things would have been different. Everybody was also very nice to Dominic and it was a great help having him there with me for a few days. I was able to finish the packing very quickly. During his spare time Dominic did quite a few drawings and I was surprised to notice how well he draws....

Since I have arrived I have been spending my time seeing all sorts of people explaining to me about benefits and taxes in the U.S. and U.K. and my mind is full of foreign terms, which I do not understand. It just happened that yesterday a British financial expert from the Fry Group in London gave a seminar on tax and investment to British expatriates from the Bank, and tomorrow I will have a private meeting with this man.... Today I spent again most of the day at the Bank talking to the Human Resources man who gave me all the information on the benefits I will receive and went with me to the Federal Credit Union, which is the Bank of the World Bank staff, so that I could open an account. Tomorrow I shall also have a meeting with the tax person at the World Bank regarding U.S. tax. It is not easy and I am scared of doing anything wrong which might jeopardise my finances. I have also been in touch with the lawyer and fortunately David had listed all his assets and mine when we made the will, and the lawyer has a copy.

Being a retiree from the World Bank I get 90% of my medical expenses paid, even if I am in the U.K. In case of an illness requiring hospitalisation I will be able to afford a private hospital. I suppose it is a consolation.

It is very strange being here and not being in my own house. I really feel like somebody without roots at the moment. All I wish is to have somewhere as soon as possible where I can settle. Depending on what the British finance man advises me to do, I will know by tomorrow when I can go back to England. In principle, I can only stay here sixty days because of the special visa Bank's employees are given, but I can get a tourist visa afterwards. It is very good of John and Teresa to accommodate me but I would not like to impose too much on them...

Washington is very beautiful at this time of year; the dogwoods are in full bloom and the azaleas are starting to flower. It is not cold, but the rest of the week will be wet.

I still find it very hard to accept David's death. We did not always see eye to eye on everything, but we got on very well. Coming back here was not easy as everywhere I go reminds me of him....

Thank you very much for all the love and sympathy all the family gave me.... Nicole.

On 15th May she wrote again from Alexandria -

Things are taking their course, I am not very busy, and I find that time is dragging. I must fix a deadline for my return to England... I shall write to my Sutton neighbours Colin and Carol to ask them if I can use their attic flat for a few weeks. As I intend to go to France in August, it will only be for the month of July. I hope that by the beginning of September, the tenants will have left. I wanted to sell the house in Sutton and buy a flat instead, but David did not agree. What a good thing he did not, as today I would have found myself with a one-bedroom flat and I would have had to start all over again.

Two weeks ago I had a yard sale to get rid of the items I did not want to take back to England. Dominic came for the weekend and it was very nice to see him and have his help. Our friend Pu-Chin let me use her garden and her brother put his truck at my disposal, and came with me to the warehouse to collect the things I was going to sell. It was a very cold and rainy day, but fortunately Pu-Chin has a covered garage in front of her house, so we could keep the items for sale under cover. Only two customers came, but between them they took all the bulky items such as chest freezer, sofa bed, queen size bed and IKEA shelving. Of course, I sold everything at a give-away price….

I am in the process of selling the house in Alexandria. Last week I had dinner with friends whom we knew in Senegal. The wife is a financial planner and she gave me some very good advice….

(the advice was, to sell to the existing tenants without going through an estate agent, thus paying no agents'commission, and this is what Nicole did).

Two weeks ago the World Bank organised a Memorial Service for David. I did not want it to be anything religious. Instead, I asked some friends and colleagues to each write something about David. None of the pieces were the same, but all of them praised David's honesty with himself and others, his independence of character, and his sense of humour. The World Bank has made a video cassette and I'm sure you will like to see it. I have had a lot of letters from people with whom he worked. Only now do I realise how much he was appreciated and well thought of. You can have copies of all these letters, although most of them are in French.

I am grateful to John and Teresa for letting me stay with them… they have a house in the mountains in West Virginia and we go there for the weekend. I will return their kindness when they come to France this summer. Last year they helped to install the kitchen cabinets and they want to come this year to finish the work and the tiling of the work surfaces….

At our mother's request, Edward Hawkins of the World Bank sent a list of David's publications for the World Bank (see below). Mr. Hawkins also wrote about the Memorial Meeting held for David on May 7th, saying many moving tributes were paid to him by fellow staff. The last paragraph of this letter reads -

I was very pleased that I was able to join this tribute to David. It was clear from the attendance – the room was packed, with people standing at the back – that he was held in high regard by his colleagues and will be greatly missed. The tributes included two Vice Presidents for Africa and a number of his friends and colleagues. As you will hear (a tape recording was included with this letter) they spoke especially of his devotion to Africa and his desire to help in its development.

Although the many business matters Nicole had to cope with kept her occupied, she naturally missed David terribly. I received this letter from her, written on May 13th –

…..I have been thinking of you and was intending to write to you soon. Thank you for the story tapes which I am sure will be a great comfort. Since David died I have not been sleeping well at all. I go to bed and fall asleep straight away, but I wake up at about 2am and stay awake until the morning. It is at this time that I think of all the problems and how I am going to solve them…

Life without David is very lonely. I have received so many letters from people with whom he has worked all over Africa and I never realised how much he was appreciated and liked. In his field he was very much thought of and everybody liked him for his honesty, his intellect and his sense of humour…

The World Bank Spouses' Association has been very supportive. It was a good thing that I did not go back to work when we returned from Senegal, as I was able to be very active within the Spouses' Association and made a lot of friends that way….

Love to Ron and whoever is staying with you, Nicole.

My admiration for Nicole increased as I saw how courageously she coped with everything. She spent that summer in Bordepaille, accompanied by various friends and family including Dominic, her mother Suzette Fortuné, and Aunt Phyllis (David's aunt).. While in France Nicole visited friends from Sutton who had a house near Toulouse, and friends from Senegal days who had a house near Pau. Obviously the cosmopolitan life style with David had equipped her with an army of friends and acquaintances which in these sad days bore much fruit.

Her home base became the house in Sutton, but she continued organising the developments at Bordepaille which had been so dear to David's heart. Bravely, she took up again the plans she and David had made to convert the tumbledown stone barn and picturesque *pigeonnier* into a lettable *gîte*. With the support of her sons, and after *"numerous exchanges of drawings between France, the U.S.A. and England"*, the restoration commenced. Nicole enjoyed furnishing and equipping this unique gite. She says *"The result is very satisfying and the architect and various tradesmen saw to it that the renovation work was in keeping with the architectural character of the region"*. David would have been so delighted. For Nicole this provides an added interest in her busy life. There is also land of around eight acres to be cared for, but Nicole is not easily daunted and David would be proud of her. He somehow, when still a young man, found the woman best fitted to accompany him through his globe-trotting lifestyle; a letter from Nicole dated October 2003 makes this abundantly clear. She writes –

Once again I have to start thinking of Christmas early, as I am leaving for a trip to Vietnam and Cambodia. I've always wanted to visit those countries, having heard a lot about them through my paternal grandmother and my father. My grandfather was a French colonial civil servant and was posted in Indochina (where he died) for eighteen years. It means that I will not spend Christmas in Guadeloupe this year. My mother was disappointed, but I will visit her next summer instead to celebrate her 95th birthday. I've not been in England for Christmas for the last three years and I'm looking forward to spending Christmas with Bernard, Stella and the grandchildren. It would have been nice to have Dominic with us, but he has not been granted a Green Card yet and is still not allowed to leave the U.S... I had an enjoyable stay with him in Boston a year ago....

David could not have made a more appropriate choice of wife! As he himself remarked, when Nicole agreed to accompany him to the inhospitable landscape of Chad, *"Nicole is a good soldier..."*

David and Nicole, August 1996, Pradelette, France

Nicole is also a survivor and life goes on. In November 2006 she was writing *"The family is well and Alistair and Logan are growing very fast. Alistair is twelve years old this month and is beginning to act like a teenager. Logan is eight years old, has joined Alistair at Bedford School and has adjusted well to his new school. We had a family reunion in France at half-term last month. Dominic came with Megan, his girlfriend, whom we got to know better. Alistair and Logan were very happy to see Dominic who is more like a brother to them than an uncle. It's nice for them to have an uncle who is available, at least for the time being, to share their games and do interesting things with them, such as building tree houses. The weather was warm and sunny and we had a very enjoyable time."*

I believe both Alistair and Logan have inherited their grandfather's love of music, language and literature. Logan has had a poem published through his school, really enjoys singing and has already won prizes for prose reading in public competitions. Alistair has written a fantasy adventure story, which I was proud to publish (details of this are in the end pages of this book), and is learning to play the cello (his grandfather David's cello, refurbished and beautiful).

Top left and right
July 2005, Nicole and grandsons
enjoy the Bordepaille garden

Bottom
Family group - Bernard, Dominic,
Alistair, Logan and Nicole

As I write now, in June 2008, the family are preparing for Dominic's wedding to fiancée Megan Cooney in Cape Cod in October.

David's writings for the World Bank were mainly *"Departmental Working Papers"* and include the following titles –

"Outline of issues on urban financial management policy" (1983); "Substantive upgrading of municipal responsibilities: financial management implications" (1985); "Financial appraisal strategy for water supply and sanitation projects: guidance for financial intermediaries" (1986); "Financial appraisal of public infrastructure projects and implementing institutions: guidance for financial intermediaries" (1986).

One Paper had been published as an article in the *"Journal of Modern African Studies*

(U.K.)" in December 1982, under the title *"State structures in new nations: the case of primary agricultural marketing in Africa"*.

Mention was also made of David's Editorship in 1972 of the 4th Edition of the *"Oxford Economic Atlas of the World"* for Oxford University Press.

So we know a little more about his work – but we also know that dearest to his heart had been "hands on" work, meeting and getting to know the people of the many African countries he visited. After his death, I often felt glad that he did not know about the many troubles that beset Africa. I remember a long letter from him (now lost) in which he tried to explain the complex history behind the Hutu and Tutsi factions, that eventually erupted so horrifically in the troubles in Rwanda and Burundi. Since his death there have been escalating conflicts and disasters in so many countries – Uganda, Ethiopia, Sudan, Somalia, Darfur, Zimbabwe - and also in towns he knew such as Nairobi and Kisumu. I think David would have been personally distressed by these events. Yet somehow, in his working life, he managed to stay realistic but positive about the future of Africa.

David's enduring concern and love of Africa is reflected in the Memorial Fund set up by the World Bank in his memory.

THE DAVID JONES MEMORIAL FUND

This Fund took time to organise. The charity proposed at the funeral, The Chadian Children's Fund, was for some reason not viable. Donations by cheque had to be returned, pending the setting up of a new charity by the World Bank. A year after David's death, this letter was sent to Nicole from World Bank officials –

Dear Mrs. Jones,

I hope that you will accept my apologies for the time it has taken us to put together the proposal I am sending you today for the use of the David Jones Memorial Fund. My concern has been to ensure that the incoming Resident Representative be committed to what we propose and the selection process has taken longer than expected.

Knowing David's deep commitment to education and to the people of Chad, we thought that the sizeable sum which was donated would be well used in support of women's education in Chad.

We propose for the Fund to grant scholarships to fifteen girls entering lower secondary education over a period of four years. Direct costs related to school attendance are the primary reason why so few Chadian girls enter secondary school and why many drop out before completing the four-year cycle. By covering expenses for textbooks, notebooks, uniforms and shoes, the Fund would give the fifteen selected girls a much improved opportunity to complete lower secondary education. Such an education will considerably enhance their personal development and give them much broader opportunities in the future. As a result, these girls and their children will have a much better chance to lead healthier and more productive lives.

Five schools have been selected and three girls from each would be eligible for scholarship. After supporting a cohort of girls for four years, some monies will be left in the Fund, but not sufficiently to finance another cohort. With your agreement we would like to envisage a yearly drive to replenish the Fund and continue to support as many girls as our yearly collection will allow. The resident mission in N'Djamena will manage the Fund and the selection of candidates.

I hope that, in your eyes, this proposal adequately reflects David's belief in education and development in Chad, and would be grateful for your endorsement and/ or suggestions.

On behalf of all those who contributed to this effort, please accept my sincere condolences.
Serge Michailof,
Country Director for Chad, Africa Region

EPILOGUE

It is a bewildering and somewhat unreal situation when death occurs in a far off, distant place, unfamiliar to many of those left behind. Nicole, of course, was with David in Chad; but it did not seem appropriate to ask her to describe events in any detail, and in any case thankfully she did not witness the accident.

Some eighteen months after the accident, an acquaintance of the family sent them a cutting entitled *"Echoes"*, taken from a Chad newspaper. This provided curious, even sinister, information: the smuggler who had been driving the fateful car that Easter Sunday in 1997 had later been involved in another incident which almost had similarly tragic results –

"The Prime Minister and the Minister of the Interior escape an attack on their lives.
The Prime Minister Nassour Guelengdouksia Ouaidou and his Minister of the Interior, Oumarou Djibrilah, were almost crushed to death at Milezi on Sunday 13th September 1998 by a vehicle driven by the same person who had been responsible for the fatal accident leading to the death of Sir David B. Jones, Representative of the World Bank in Tchad. On the Sunday the two ministers, wishing to see for themselves the level of the flood waters threatening to inundate the town of N'Djamena, arrived in the Milezi district situated to the north of the town, with only low-level protection. The PM was only accompanied by one member of his protection squad, whilst a driver acted as body guard for the Minister of the Interior. As they walked along the riverbank, they came face to face with a Toyota car jammed full of bags of granulated sugar (the result of fraud). On being asked to present himself to the authorities, the driver quite simply started up his vehicle and ploughed it towards the ministers, whose lives were saved thanks to their legs. It was the Interior Minister's driver who stopped the deadly path by pulling on the vehicle. The driver was arrested and handed over to the police, who already know this frequent offender – a fraudster well known to the Government's Presidential office, who it is said even has armed guards for his own protection."

ÉCHOS ...

Le PM et le ministre de l'intérieur échappent à un attentat
Le premier ministre Nassour Guelengdouksia Ouaidou et son ministre de l'Intérieur, Oumarou Djibrilah ont failli être écrasés à Milézi le dimanche 13 septembre 1998 par un véhicule conduit par le même chauffeur qui avait causé l'accident mortel le 30 mars 1997 de Sir David B. Jones, représentant résident de la Banque mondiale au Tchad. Ce dimanche, Nassour Ouaïdou et Oumarou Djibrilah qui voulaient se faire une idée de la montée des eaux fluviales qui menacent d'inonder la ville de N'Djaména, se sont rendus au quartier Milézi situé au nord de la ville avec une protection «allégée». Le PM n'était accompagné que d'un seul élément de sa protection tandis qu'un chauffeur faisait office de garde du corps du ministre de l'Intérieur. En longeant à pied le fleuve, les deux ministres tombent nez à nez avec une Toyota bourrée de sacs de sucre en poudre (produit de la fraude). Invité à se présenter à ces autorités, le conducteur du car a tout simplement démarré son véhicule et foncé droit sur les ministres qui ont eu la vie sauve grâce à leurs jambes. C'est le chauffeur du ministre de l'Intérieur qui a stoppé la course meurtrière du car en tirant sur le véhicule. Le conducteur arrêté a été remis à la police judiciaire qui connaît très bien ce récidiviste, fraudeur, bien connu de la présidence de la république et· qui disposerait même des éléments armés pour sa propre protection .

It appears David's initial assessment of the town being "rather like the wild west" was pretty accurate. This man was obviously a desperado, a gang boss, with absolutely no regard for the law or for the lives of others. An unwelcome thought popped into my mind – could he have been a paid hit man?

(I also had a little chuckle at the sudden elevation of David to the knighthood! He loved recognition and would have been tickled pink to see himself referred to as "Sir David B. Jones!)

Very recently, through friends of my sister Margaret (who had herself worked on the Mission field in Africa), I received a letter from Liz Cleak, a missionary who had worked many years in Chad. She and a colleague had arranged to meet David and Nicole on Monday 31st March (the day following the accident). These are her memories of the day:-

….yes, it was a shocking accident…… I'm so sorry that it happened. Along with my colleague Pauline, I had an appointment to meet your brother David and his wife Nicole for the day following the accident. So we never did meet your brother, although we went across to meet and give condolences to Nicole when the news came to us through mutual friends.

As far as I know the accident happened very early morning, when David had gone out for a stroll along the main road just outside their house. Quite a lot of smuggling goes on across the Chari river, customs tax avoidance by bringing goods across, usually at night. From time to time the Douane (Customs) make a big push to stop the trade. I think at the time of the accident they had just been issued with new vehicles to get around better for surprise raids.

So David was killed in a high speed car chase by the customs vehicle chasing a car-load of smugglers. The vehicles came round the junction, swung too widely at too high a speed, and thus hit your brother as he returned along the mud and grass verge towards his house (there is no raised pavement alongside the road).

I would imagine they did not stop. Sorry, I can't answer your question about whether these people were prosecuted or punished for the incident. Because your brother was not only an expatriate but also the World Bank Representative, there may have been some follow-through for discipline, but I don't really know for sure. There were several accidents during such high-speed chases around that period. I would assume that the incident would have been seen by folks walking past or the guards who are generally posted at the gateways of larger European residential properties in that area.

As a generalisation, individual human life is not valued in Africa as it has come to be at present in Western society. So abuse of power and resources is pretty commonplace.

I worked in Chad from 1976-2000 with a Christian mission organisation called WEC International (this is inter-denominational). At the time of this event, my role was team leader (with the colleague I mentioned earlier) and administrator. At other times we worked out of town in a village as linguists in a local language. Presently I live in England as my mother is elderly and needs care, but I am also able to work from home with editorial work for our mission magazine.

I hope this description is of some help to you. Yours, Liz Cleak

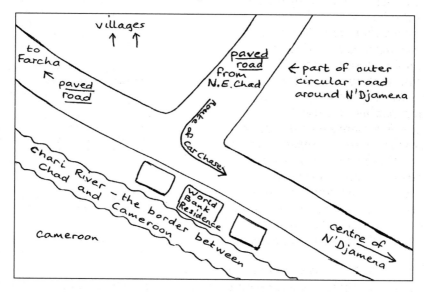

Liz Cleak kindly included this sketch map of the location, marking with arrows the route of the cars involved. After receiving her letter I was much more able to accept what had happened; it was just accident, and life anywhere involves risk.

A CHARMED LIFE

Reading these hundreds of letters while preparing this book, I have been struck not by thoughts of the misfortune that carried away David - rather, I have been impressed by realisation of the good fortune which followed him.

He might after all have been drowned in the Indian Ocean (where he capsized when yachting, a good two miles from land while based at Dar es Salaam). Or one of the tiny planes he travelled in might have crashed in the desert. Hippos or crocodiles might have seized him, snakes in the long grass might have bitten him, lions might have mauled him. He could have succumbed to hypothermia and altitude sickness on Mt. Kenya, or to heat stroke on some scorching beach, or muggers in some dark alley....

Yet none of these things happened. Instead, for over fifty years, David revelled in life in all its variety, never tiring of new experiences, endlessly inquisitive, fascinated by his fellow human beings, and secure in the love of his family. He lit up the atmosphere wherever he went, through his energy, enthusiasm and tremendous zest for life. He would not have relished being described as any kind of hero, nor as a victim of tragedy. He was simply a man who made the most of life and loved each day. He will never be forgotten.

What more could any man ask?

Sheila Wright
(Photo by Graham Sessions)

About the author

SHEILA WRIGHT M.A. (nee Jones) was born in 1939. Educated at Wyggeston School in Leicester, Bretton Hall in Yorkshire and the U.E.A. in Norwich, she taught in many village schools, first in Hertfordshire, then in Suffolk. She is married to Ron, a music teacher and band master. They have lived since 1970 in a Tudor farmhouse, and have seven children. Sheila is a Lay Reader in the Church of England. Her hobbies include music, drawing and painting, gardening, keeping poultry, escapism in the French countryside, and enjoying the company of her children and fourteen grandchildren.

Also published by KISUMU BOOKS

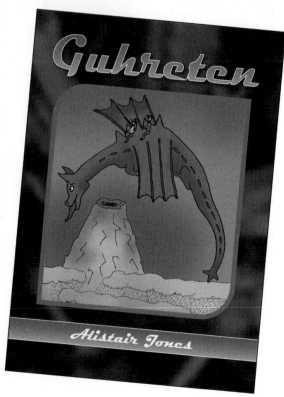

GUHRETEN
Fantasy written by Alistair Jones

Alistair is elder grandson of David Jones, and was aged twelve when he wrote his gripping tale of dragons, witches and goblins, published in March 2008. With illustrations by the author, this is a book no child will be able to put down unread.

Alistair writes "when Sam and Alex make a startling discovery on a beach in France, their lives are changed forever. Meanwhile, in the heart of a volcano, deep in a mysterious rainforest, the Queen of the Witches makes her preparations – preparations which will wipe her greatest enemy off the face of the earth…"

ISBN 978-0-9555417-1-1   32 pages, A5   Price £3.20
(£3.50 if delivered by post in the U.K.)

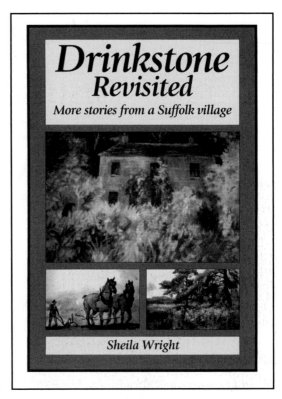

Drinkstone
School and Village
A Suffolk History
ISBN 1-902019-08-3

Drinkstone
Revisited
More Stories from a
Suffolk Village
ISBN 1-901253-30-9

Drinkstone lies nine miles south-east of Bury St. Edmunds. Sheila Wright taught at the
village school in the 1980's, until the closure of the school in July 1986. Many small
village schools in Suffolk were facing closure around this time. Sheila decided to
investigate the history of the school and the lives of its pupils and other villagers. This
research resulted in two fascinating local history books giving a vivid, nostalgic and
frequently awe-inspiring insight into country lives over two centuries. Every facet of life
is here – war and peace, joy and sorrow, sickness and health, tragedy and comedy – of
destitute cottagers, hard-working labourers and domestics, priests, tradespeople, landed
gentry and the aristocracy. The books include the reminiscences of dozens of villagers
told in their own words.

Dr. Nick Sign, Review Editor for the Suffolk Local History Council, writes –
"Sheila Wright has made excellent use of her long experience as a teacher and her
personal knowledge of the school, its pupils and their parents, to provide an in-depth
survey of education and life in this small Suffolk village over a century and a half. The
narrative is supported by many high-quality illustrations, including some very clear
maps made easier to read by the large A4 format, many well-chosen quotations from the
documents used for the research and also some very useful appendices containing
extracts from County Directories...."

The second volume came about as a result of enthusiastic response to the first. Both
books have over 200 pages and each is £10.99 (plus p. & p.)

Published by Leonie Press as one of its many titles on the experiences of British homeowners in France:

BON COURAGE, MES AMIS!

Thoughts on restoring a rural ruin

Written and illustrated by
SHEILA WRIGHT

In 1994, primary school teacher Sheila Wright suddenly had the means to buy a house in the Creuse department of France but the amount of her legacy meant that she was looking at "the bottom end of the market". She found herself falling ridiculously in love with a very old stone house which had been abandoned for years and had an alarming 20ft crack up the front.

As she looked round, the smell of damp stone and ancient dust was all-pervading. In the gloom, shadowy alcoves and battered wood frames were barely visible on the rough granite walls. Mysterious bits of string dangled from the immense beams above, and between these beams were dark, narrow boards through which light filtered where rain had rotted them away.

One wall of the room was taken up by a vast fireplace with a huge hearthstone.

Up the wide chimney, past various sinister blackened iron hooks, a patch of bright blue sky was visible. The wall separating the adjacent cellar-like room from the adjoining barn had crumbled and fallen, covering the earth floor with tons of loose granite. The jagged top was now only five feet high and over this, the neighbouring cart bay, cow shed and stable were all visible.

From these inauspicious beginnings, Sheila and her family worked hard to create a habitable holiday home full of happiness, music and peace. Along the way she developed a passion for building with stone, constructing two granite staircases herself over a five-year period. French neighbours seeing the Wrights tackle the enormous task fervently wished them "bon courage" which could perhaps be loosely translated as "Good luck - you'll need it!"

This book traces the story of the ongoing restoration in a series of chapters giving Sheila's thoughts on many other aspects of Creusoise life and her own experiences in France.

ISBN 1-901253-30-9 184pp, A5, numerous illustrations Price £8.99
For more information visit www.leoniepress.com
or contact Sheila Wright on 01449 766392